D1214979

Gramsci's Prison Letters

Gramsci's Prison Letters
Lettere dal Carcere

A SELECTION TRANSLATED AND INTRODUCED BY
HAMISH HENDERSON

ZWAN

in association with the *Edinburgh Review*

This edition first published 1988 by Zwan Publications
11-21 Northdown Street, London N1 9BN
in association with *Edinburgh Review*
48 Pleasance, Edinburgh EH8 9TJ

Distributed in the USA by Allen & Unwin Inc.
8 Winchester Place
Winchester
MA 01890, USA

Introduction copyright © Hamish Henderson 1988

Typesetting: Ransom Typesetting Services, Woburn Sands, Bucks
Printed in Great Britain by
Billing & Sons Ltd, Worcester

This selection was first published in 1974 in
issues no. 25 & 26 of the *New Edinburgh Review*,
a quarterly paperback journal of literature and
ideas that became the *Edinburgh Review* in 1984

Letter 10 was published in 'The People's Past',
ed. E. J. Cowan (Polygon, Edinburgh, 1980)

British Library Cataloguing in Publication Data

Gramsci, Antonio
  Gramsci's prison letters: a selection
  1. Gramsci, Antonio 2. Communists —
  Italy — Biography
  I. Title II. Lettere dal carcere
  Selections. English
  335.4'092'4   HX288.G7

  ISBN 1–85305–021–0

Contents

Acknowledgements

I should like to express my deep indebtedness to the following:

Amleto Micozzi, who sent me the first (1947) edition of *Lettere dal Carcere* as soon as it appeared.

Carlo Gramsci, youngest brother of Antonio, who gave me invaluable assistance, particularly as regards the Sardinian background.

Sergio Caprioglio, joint editor (with Elsa Fubini) of the definitive (1965) edition of the *Lettere*, who sent me numerous publications relating to Gramsci.

Luigi Castigliano and Tom Nairn, who provided a great deal of useful help and advice.

Marian Sugden, who made the original typescript.

Michael J. Law, who gave me much practical assistance.

Piero Sraffa, Felice Platone, Cesare Pavese, Elio Vittorini, Alfonso Vinci ('Bill' of the 2nd Partisan Division of the Valtellina) and 'Al' Aldovrandi, all of whom talked to me about Gramsci and gave much appreciated encouragement.

People in the Letters

Gramsci's Family

His father Francesco Gramsci ('Signor Ciccillo') was a native of Gaeta, a coastal town between Rome and Naples. Francesco came to Sardinia at the age of 20, and took charge of the Registrar's office in the village of Ghilarza. Two years later (1883) he married Peppina Marcias, a local girl; they had seven children, of whom Antonio was the fourth (born 22 January 1891).

The other children were:

Gennaro ('Nannaro'), born 1884, worked first at Cagliari and then at Turin, was beaten up by Fascists in 1922 and emigrated to France, leaving his daughter Edmea ('Mea') at home in Sardinia with Peppina, his mother. Fought in the Spanish Civil War against Franco. Died in Rome in 1965.

Grazia ('Grazietta'), born 1887. Helped her mother to look after Mea. Died 1962.

Emma, born 1889. Died in 1920 from malaria.

After Antonio ('Nino'), who was born 1891 at Ales. Mario, born 1893, moved to Varese. For a time secretary of the local Fascist Federation. Fought in the Abyssinian War, and later in North Africa. Died 1945.

Teresina, born 1895. Worked in the post office at Ghilarza. Married, four children. Died 1976.

Carlo, born 1897. Officer in World War I. Present at Antonio's trial, 28 May to 4 June 1928. Got a job in Milan 1931 and did much to help his imprisoned brother. Present (with Tatiana Schucht) at Antonio's funeral, 28 April 1937.

Francesco (Antonio's father) died a fortnight after his son, 16 May 1937. Antonio's mother Peppina had died in December 1932, but he was not informed of her death until much later.

Gramsci's Wife and Sister-in-law

His wife, Julia (Giulia, 'Julca') Schucht was born at Geneva 1896, fifth child of a cosmopolitan Russian family. Her father Apollo Schucht had earlier spent years in Siberian exile for anti-Tsarist activities. Julia's childhood and teenage years were spent in Italy, and she got a music diploma after studying violin at the music school attached to the Santa Cecilia Academy at Rome. Returned to Russia when aged nineteen, and taught music in the Lycée at Ivanovo Vosniesensk. Gramsci met her in 1922, through her sister Eugenie, who was a patient at the sanatorium where Gramsci had been sent for a rest cure. Julia bore Gramsci two sons, Delio (born 1924) and Giuliano, 'Julik' (born 1926). She spent close on a year in Italy (1925–6), then returned to Moscow; Gramsci never saw her again. Later she suffered a severe nervous breakdown – there was a strain of mental instability in the Schucht family – and Gramsci's attempts to get through to her make many of the later letters poignant and even agonising reading.

Tatiana ('Tania') Schucht, an elder sister of Julia. Remained in Italy when most of the family moved from it just before World War I; earned her living as a science teacher. Did not meet Gramsci till 1925, but soon became a close friend and (after Gramsci's imprisonment) was his most precious confidante and helper, virtually devoting her life to succouring him. Weak physically, but spiritually indomitable, Tania is owed a debt of gratitude by all who honour Gramsci. She moved to Milan when Gramsci was transferred there; paid frequent visits to him at Turi. With Carlo, helped to preserve Gramsci's prison notebooks after his death. Returned to the Soviet Union in 1939; died there in 1941.

Piero Sraffa

Born Turin 1898. Met Gramsci 1919 when a student at Turin; translated English Texts for *L'Ordine Nuovo*. When Gramsci was arrested, Sraffa was teaching economics at the University of Cagliari; the following year (1927) he took up a post at Cambridge. Author of a celebrated letter to the *Manchester Guardian* concerning Gramsci's fate (October 1927). Paid for the books Gramsci received from a Milan bookshop; maintained contact with Tatiana in Italy and with Gramsci's wife and children in Moscow, sending them presents. As Gramsci's health deteriorated, worked tirelessly to relieve his sufferings. Was largely instrumental in securing Gramsci's transference from Turi Prison to the clinic at Formia (December 1933). Died in Cambridge in 1983.

Giuseppe Berti

Born at Naples 1901. Secretary of the Communist Youth Federation 1921. Banished to Ustica 1926. Freed in 1930; emigrated to France and then to the US. Conducted vigorous anti-Fascist propaganda. Returned to Italy in 1945, elected deputy and then Senator. Author of various historical works.

Introduction

HAMISH HENDERSON

One of the most striking pictures in the exhibition *The Vigorous Imagination: New Scottish Art*, which opened at the Scottish National Gallery of Modern Art on 9 August 1987, was 'The Self-Taught Man' by Ken Currie. This – like another of Currie's pictures, 'Ship-Yard Poet' – shows a Clydeside worker with a book in his hand. The poet is holding his own manuscript notebook; the 'self-taught man', sitting at a table, with the dove of peace on a poster behind him and a notebook open in front of him, is holding a volume on the cover of which, plainly visible, is the name GRAMSCI.

That a Scottish working-class intellectual – a stubborn survivor in Thatcher's Britain – should be interested in Gramsci's political thought in the 1980s is readily comprehensible. Indeed, he and folk like him might well have thought the fare through to 'East-windy West-endy' Edinburgh well worth the money if they had managed to get tickets for a film called *Gramsci* – sub-titled 'Everything that concerns people' – which was premiered at Film House a week after that same exhibition opened. In this film, made by Pelicula of Glasgow, a sort of Scottish connection was quite noticeably underlined, in that the Sardinian characters who are Gramsci's mates in Turi prison speak with recognisable Scots accents.

What, one wonders, would the ordinary film-goer make of this arguably rather dubious ploy? Does the implied parallel hold water, or are we faced with mere jokey self-indulgence on the part of a young Scottish film-maker?

To the student of European history Sardinia and Scotland might not seem very plausible yoke-fellows – a much closer parallel might seem that between Sardinia and Ireland, both victims of centennial foreign domination – but a closer examination suggests that there are similarities which lend body and substance to the film-maker's contrivance.

First and foremost, both communities (? countries, ? nations) have maintained, against the odds, dourly intransigent ethnic folkways which still exhibit a marked idiosyncratic 'national' character. The island of Sardinia has had to combat, from Carthaginian and Roman times onwards, the ruthless exploitation of its natural resources by a series of foreign invaders, and consequently its heroes, through the ages, have been what Eric Hobsbawm called 'primitive rebels': outlaws, brigands and freebooters who took it upon themselves to defend a last-ditch desperado independence against the ceaseless encroachments of self-seeking profiteering central authority. In one of the letters (no. 79) printed in this selection, Gramsci mentions a couple of these celebrities, and suggests that twentieth-century Sard children would have a more natural patriotic interest in them than in the tuppence-coloured heroes and heroines of 'official' history.

If Sardinia has had its Francesco Derosas and its Giovanni Tolu, Scotland has had its Rob Roy, its Gilderoy and its James Macpherson (hero of the famous 'Rant') – undoubtedly more 'real' (and 'patriotic') for Scottish children than the somewhat cartoon-like figure of Robin Hood.

There is another trait, common to Scots and Sards, which again seems a legitimate point of contact. The Sards, who for many generations provided soldiers and policemen for the service of Piedmont (and later for the Kingdom of Italy itself) have developed a very understandable respect for education, and all the advantages it can bring: Gramsci's own scholastic career bears eloquent testimony to this, as do many of his letters home, written when he was in prison (cf. letter 61, with its comments on how his niece Mea was being brought up). It is hardly necessary to underline the well-documented Scottish reverence for education and book learning, particularly among the militant workers, who threw up a very special breed of working-class intellectual from the second half of the eighteenth century onwards. The Glasgow weavers – as the balladeer and playwright Freddy Anderson has recently written (*Scottish Trade Union Review*, no. 35, Summer 1987) – had

a great hankering for 'learning', and came to be the most educated and advanced of the working people of Scotland. Poets and scholars in various sciences arose from their ranks ... in the middle of the 19th century the banner of the vanguard of working-class struggle passed from the weavers into the hands of the iron and steel workers, the shipbuilders of Clydeside, and thus into another great period of intense struggle, which culminated in the early part of this century in the real legend, not myth, of Red Clydeside, with its famous shop stewards' committee, its brave women like Mrs Barbour of Govan and Helen Crawford Anderson, and the thousands of others who have carried on the struggle of the Calton martyrs [striking weavers who were shot down by the military at Drygate Brig on 3 September 1787].

Finally, like other *meridionali* (southerners), the Sards are credited with being a dour, laconic, stubborn, self-analytical people – cf. note to letter 192 – and the formidable sinewy toughness to which many travellers have borne witness is not the least noticeable attribute of Antonio Gramsci himself.

This great Marxist – of whom Eric Hobsbawm has written that he was 'an extraordinary philosopher, perhaps a genius, probably the most original communist thinker of the twentieth century in Western Europe' – was born at Ales, in central Sardinia, the fourth of seven children; his father Francesco (who came of a well-to-do Neapolitan family of Albanian origin: *his* father had been a colonel in the Bourbon gendarmerie) was Director of the Office of Land Registry in the small town of Ghilarza. His mother, Guiseppina Marcias, a native of the island, was the daughter of a local tax inspector; she seems to have been a quite exceptional woman – and not only because, in the midst of a largely illiterate population, she was able to read and write. In brief, this was a petty bourgeois family which considered itself a cut above the peasants who made up the bulk of the local population.

When Antonio was 18 months old a servant girl who was holding him allowed him to fall from her arms, and as a result he gradually developed a bad spinal curvature.[1] When he reached adulthood his deformity gave him the appearance of a hunch-backed dwarf: he was less than 5 ft in height.

In letter 90 he describes a childhood illness which nearly did for him, and adds that 'until round about 1914 my mother kept the little coffin and the special little shroud that they were going to bury me in'. As for school life, his first experiences of it were bitter in the extreme, because the other boys, with the cruelty of children, made merciless game of him and never admitted him to their games. Small wonder that he is remembered by the more honest of his school mates as a pitifully withdrawn little boy, the victim of constant bullying and persecution.

In 1897 an atrocious misfortune struck the Gramsci family. Francesco, father and wage earner, was suspended without pay on suspicion of 'improper conduct' of the local administration; eventually he was sentenced to nearly six years' imprisonment. In all probability the wretched man had been framed for political reasons: he had supported the losing party in the elections of 1897. Peppina, the mother, had to bring up her seven children on her own, with no other money coming in to the family but the exiguous sums she earned as a seamstress. These years must have been appalling ones for the family; little Nino learned the horrors of dire poverty when he was at his most vulnerable through illness, and the experience stayed with him for the rest of his life. When he was eleven he had to go to work in the registry office, shifting large ledgers, and letter 150 gives us a heart-piercing account of the excruciating pains he suffered through doing work which was much too heavy for him.

His first years of schooling were badly disrupted by these misfortunes, but in spite of all this he managed in 1908 to pass the examination to enter the senior *liceo* in Cagliari; while in the island capital he lodged with his elder brother Gennaro, who had found work there after returning from military service. Gennaro had become a Socialist during his time in

Piedmont, and he naturally lost no time in trying to indoctrinate Antonio, whose first political leanings were nevertheless towards Sardinian nationalism. After two years at the *liceo*, Antonio won a scholarship (for 'financially deprived students') to the University of Turin: he sat the exam at the same time as his colleague-to-be Palmiro Togliatti. At Turin, as at Cagliari, Gramsci was in miserable straits, physically and financially; his sister Teresina (in the same interview in *Gramsci Vivo* already quoted) puts on record letters home which are mainly continual pleas for comparatively small sums of money – 10, 15, 25 lire – and which, according to her, became a veritable incubus for the poverty-stricken parents themselves. Some of the prison letters describe the fearful conditions of extreme cold and malnutrition which Gramsci had to suffer as a student; during his first winter he did not even have an overcoat, and his suit was a summer suit more fitted for Cagliari than Turin. Most of the time he was an invalid, and eventually 'dropped out' of university life for the most comprehensible reasons – and also because, from mid-1915, he had moved over, as a committed Socialist, to political journalism.

If I stress the hardships of his youth, it is to make the point that, almost alone among the major Marxist thinkers of the twentieth century, Gramsci – although not of working-class origin – was subjected all through his early years to a poverty fully as corrosive as any contemporary proletarian could have had to endure, and this was compounded with health problems which would have driven most other men to the wall. Instead, he drew on the traditional fortitude and toughness of his Sard ancestors, which he himself extols in a letter to his sister Grazietta (156); in the same letter he recalls his mother's self-sacrificing heroism after the disaster which hit the family. One feels that his intransigent moral fortitude must have been largely due to his affection for her, and his memory of her unyielding tenacity.

There was, however, another element in his character which Teresina stresses in *Gramsci Vivo*: when liberated from the mockery and bullying of other school children, and when among his own brothers and sisters, he showed that behind the defences he had to put up he possessed a lively sense of *humour* (Teresina uses the English word).[2] She says repeatedly that he was 'merry, witty, ironical', and supplies several anecdotes to prove it; some of these are amusing fantasies about the supposed adventures of his younger brother Carlo. Although one must take into account Teresina's natural wish to counter the picture drawn by others of a withdrawn and melancholy child, there is plenty of independent evidence as to Gramsci's wit, and his satirical gifts. As for his storytelling capacities, also vouched for by others, we can readily recognise another well-attested Sard trait: the island storytellers are given to weaving fantastically convoluted folktales, adapting the stock of international *Märchen*, and giving them a 'local habitation and a name'. Writing to his wife Giulia on 1 June 1931 (letter 81) he gives an outline of a Sard folktale, and asks her to 'flesh it out' for his sons Delio and Giuliano. The Sards are also devoted to their very ancient ancestral types of folksong and music, and there are frequent references in Gramsci's letters to his childhood memories of the island's distinctive and attractive 'folk-life'. There can be little doubt that, along with Gramsci's ironic spirit and his heroic political commitment to the betterment of the lot of the world's lowly, it was the memory of the popular culture of his native island which helped to sustain him during the darkest days of the 'long prison Calvary' (Guiseppe Fiori's phrase). Although he never completed his university studies – and his teachers, especially Matteo Bartoli, had foreseen a brilliant future for him in the realm of glottology and linguistics – Gramsci owed much to Turin University. It was there that he sharpened his love for exactness, precision and logical reasoning; there that he brought to full bloom his contempt for woolly superficiality, so often apparent in the prison letters. And there, too, that he met men like Umberto Cosmo, the renowned Dante scholar, who appears as a 'character' in the letters, and whom Gramsci remembered with affection – cf. letter 74 – in spite of a serious rift in their relations when Gramsci reproached his mentor for a dilettante approach to the workers' movement.

To Cosmo, too, Gramsci was indebted for his first introduction to the friend who was to play an enormous part in making more bearable his prison years: this was Piero Sraffa, the economist who was teaching at Cambridge when Gramsci was sentenced to 20 years' imprisonment in 1928. (A brief biography appears under the heading 'People in the Letters'.) Sraffa, from his secure and prestigious academic base in a famed redoubt of 'bourgeois' culture, was able to exert considerable moral pressure on the Fascist authorities, and he used this privileged position to the full. At the same time he was completely trusted by Togliatti, and other Communist leaders, and was therefore an invaluable personal and epistolary go-between in the prison years. That he maintained this position *vis-à-vis* the party without wavering, even after Gramsci's death, was ingenuously made clear by Maria-Antonietta Macciocchi in a rather baffled and acerbic account of her 1973 visit to Cambridge which she included in *Pour Gramsci* (Paris, 1974).[3]

It cannot be too strongly stressed that Gramsci was the inheritor of meridional high culture, as well as meridional hardship and poverty. Among the thinkers to whom there are frequent references in his writings is the philosopher Giambattista Vico (1668–1744), author of *La Scienza Nuova*, who, born like him in the backward tail-end of Italy, was nevertheless an important forerunner in a line which includes Marx himself. Writing about Vico, Gramsci usually prefaces his reference with the epithet 'the Neapolitan', and one senses that the word immediately brought another more recent Neapolitan philosopher to his mind. As Tom Nairn has written:

Gramsci's cultural formation remained decisively marked by Southern Italian idealist humanism – the dominant school of thought among the educated classes of a still recently united Italy embodied in the personality and wide influence of the Neapolitan philosopher Benedetto Croce (1866–1952). This intellectual high culture was linked to a political liberalism which proved itself first corrupt and then, in the 1920s, ineffective against the rise of Fascism. There was to be no more penetrating critic of Italian Idealism than Gramsci himself; however, it should also be recognised that its influence furnished him with a degree of intellectual insulation, first against the determined economic Marxism of the Socialist Second International and then later against Stalinism. His own mature outlook was a sustained and quite self-conscious attempt to rethink Marxism in a kind of critical dialogue with the native philosophical and political idiom, and something can be seen from the title of the famous 1917 article with which he greeted the Bolshevik seizure of power in the Socialist Party daily *Avanti!*: 'The Revolution against Capital'.

Among the most interesting letters written by Gramsci in prison are those containing reflections on Croce's historical writings, and his 'revisionism' (of Marxism); these re-phrase in often more accessible terms the same thoughts which occur in sections of the prison notebooks. For this we must surely thank his devoted sister-in-law Tatiana, who had clearly – in the gentlest possible fashion – laid out a bait for him after reading *A History of Europe in the Nineteenth Century*. The letters in question are 125, 126, 128, 129 and 133.

The effects of the October Revolution in Russia were felt immediately throughout the world, and nowhere more than in Italy, where a few months earlier the proletariat of Turin, 'Italy's Petrograd', had risen in a fierce spontaneous insurrection. After its suppression many of the most militant workers were sent to the front by the courts, and nearly all the most important Socialist leaders were arrested. Gramsci, who had joined the PSI in 1913, quickly emerged as effective leader of a party in disarray; he took over the editorship of *Il Grido del Popolo*, the party weekly, at the end of August 1917, and was soon pointing to the Soviet model of workers' and soldiers' councils as the way forward to a proletarian revolution. (The inspirational figures in other European countries who most closely resemble him, at this point in history, are Karl Liebknecht, Rosa Luxemburg and John Maclean.) In April 1919, with Angelo Tasca, Palmiro Togliatti and Umberto Terracini, Gramsci founded a new weekly 'review of Socialist Culture' called *L'Ordine Nuovo* (The New Order): this journal soon acquired immense influence among the Torinese workers, and it was in it that Gramsci mapped out the plan of action which was to lead to the development of the shop stewards' committees (*commissioni interne*) – 'an embryonic form of worker government' – into factory councils, and eventually to the high point of Socialist militancy in September 1920, when the workers' occupation of northern Italian factories broke out in Milan, and soon spread to other industrial towns. However, the canny policies of the Liberal Prime Minister Giolitti (soubriquet: 'the old fox') ultimately prevailed; he refused to send in the troops – as some of the employers were demanding – and offered a compromise of 'industrial co-partnership' which never of course came to fruition, once the factory occupations were called off. As Gramsci was the first to recognise, this militant action could never have led to actual revolution; it was premature and uncoordinated.

Even before the occupation of the factories, Fascist squads had begun to use strong-arm tactics against Socialist centres and publishing houses, and the employers were soon pouring massive funds into Fascist organisations. The forces of reaction grew apace, and in October 1922, with Mussolini's 'March on Rome', the hopes of the Italian proletariat for a revolution on the Soviet model were obliterated.

At the PSI national congress in Livorno (January 1921), the Communist fraction at last rebelled against the supine 'centrist' leadership of the traditional ruling groups in the party, and the Partito Comunista d'Italia (predecessor of the present-day PCI) was formed. Gramsci was among its founders, but the unquestioned leader – and the dominant figure in those early days – was Amadeo Bordiga, whose 'left-sectarian' views were attacked in Lenin's famous polemical treatise *Infantile Extremism*, written in May 1920. It was one of the curiosities of the first edition of *Lettere dal Carcere* (published by Einaudi in 1947) that all references to the personal friendship that existed between Gramsci and this charismatic character were carefully excised.

In the Spring of 1922 Gramsci was sent to Moscow as representative of the PCI on the Executive Committee of the Communist Third International (Comintern), and could thus observe from a 'ringside seat' the beginnings of the power struggle which, well before Lenin's death, was already revealing itself, boding ill for the future well-being of the CPSU (Bolsheviks). However, the serious nervous illness which soon prostrated Gramsci and led, at the insistence of Zinoviev, to a lengthy stay in a sanatorium, was already in evidence before he left Italy; the defeat of the premature revolution must have been a serious blow to his morale, and undoubtedly exacerbated the crippling health problems from which he had suffered all his life. It was while he was recovering in the sanatorium that he met his future wife, Giulia (or Julka) Schucht, a member of a 'bourgeois' anti-Tsarist family which had spent prolonged periods in Italy. Julka was the one love of Gramsci's life, and she bore him two sons, one of whom (Giuliano) he never saw. Exceedingly sensitive and highly-strung, Julka seems never to have come to terms with the cruel fate which befell her husband, and eventually she suffered a severe nervous breakdown. The evidence of their gradual estrangement, becoming increasingly obvious from the first months of 1931 onwards, makes tragic reading in these letters.

Giulia's elder sister Tatiana had remained in Italy when the rest of the family returned to Russia not long before the outbreak of the First World War, and she it was who devoted the rest of her life to succouring her brother-in-law. (See 'People in the Letters'.) The precious *Quaderni del Carcere* (Prison Notebooks), which are now regarded as one of the major Marxist classics of the century, were saved for posterity by the agency of two people: one was the Bolognese cell-mate of Gramsci, Gustavo Trombetti, who tended him during the paroxysms of one of his worst illnesses, and who succeeded in secreting the notebooks in a trunk when Gramsci was moved (in November 1933) from Turi prison to Dr Cosumano's clinic at Formia; the other was Tatiana, who after Gramsci's death took charge of his effects, lodged the notebooks in the safe of the Banca Commerciale in Rome, and eventually – a year later – sent them to Moscow in a trunk (cf. P. Spriano, *Gramsci in Carcere e il Partito*, Rome 1977, Chapter VII).

Although poor Tatiana had to bear the brunt of Gramsci's black moods of desperation, induced by 'prisonitis' as well as by harsh, unendurable physical pain – at one point we even hear from him the cry '*Ho rovinato la mia existenza*' ('I have made a ruin of my life'), which (for me) tragically recalls Rimbaud's agonising words, in his last letter to his sister '*Enfin, notre vie est une misère, une misère sans fin. Pourquoi donc existons-nous?*' – she never faltered in her devotion to her brother-in-law, and was with him as much as possible right up to the early morning of 27 April 1937, when he breathed his last. 'I watched over him all the time, doing what I could, moistening his lips, trying to restore his breathing by artificial means when it seemed to want to stop; but then there was one last loud breath, and an irreversible silence. I called the doctor, who confirmed my fears. It was 4.10 a.m. on the 27th' (Tatiana's letter to Piero Sraffa in Cambridge, printed as an appendix to *Lettere dal Carcere*, 1965, pp. 917–18).[4]

We must now turn back in time for a brief account of Gramsci's life from the time he married Julka in Moscow, up to the day of his arrest in 1926. Towards the end of 1923 he was sent to Vienna, where he spent five months in charge of a Comintern 'information bureau' whose aim was to coordinate anti-Fascist action. In April 1924 he stood as a parliamentary candidate – Mussolini was still tolerating an elected parliament, although the election took place in a climate of violent strong-arm harassment throughout the peninsula – and was elected a deputy by a constituency of the Veneto. Relying on parliamentary immunity, he returned to Italy the following month, and for the rest of his time as a free agent he attempted to combat the ever-tightening grip of Fascism on the life of Italy by constructing alliances with other socialist or democratic forces. This entailed a sharp fight against the 'élitist' left sectarianism of Amadeo Bordiga, and at the Third Congress of the Party (held at Lyons in January 1926) his leadership was decisively confirmed, his policies obtaining 90 per cent of the vote.

The power struggle in Moscow was increasingly preoccupying him, and in October 1926 – only a month before his arrest – he sent a hard-hitting letter on behalf of the Political Bureau of the PCI to the Central Committee of the CPSU – care of Togliatti, who was embarrassed by it, and did his best to keep it dark, showing it only, it seems, to Bukharin and Manuilski. He attempted to justify this course of inaction in a letter to Gramsci, which the latter indignantly rebuffed. In his letter to the Central Committee Gramsci made it clear that the Italian Party leadership supported the Stalin/Bukharin majority in the Russian party, and blamed the 'Left' – Trotsky, Zinoviev and Kamenev – for the deep cleavage which had opened up, but he made no bones about his concern lest the Russian leadership tear itself apart. Indeed, he was bold and forthright enough to remind the CC of its responsibilities to the international proletariat. 'Today you are in the process of destroying your own work ... you are running the risk of compromising the directing role which the Communist Party of the Soviet Union had acquired under the impulse of Lenin ... Unity and discipline cannot be mechanical and coercive; they must be loyal, and the result of conviction, and not those of an enemy unit imprisoned or besieged – thinking all the time of how to escape, or make an unexpected counter-attack ... comrades Zinoviev, Trotsky and Kamenev have contributed powerfully to our revolutionary education; they have sometimes corrected us with a good deal of rigour and severity; they have been counted among our masters.' One does not have to read between the lines to realise that Gramsci foresaw a bureaucratic degeneration in the Soviet Party which would lead inexorably to the elimination/liquidation of the opposition, and to the absolute personal power of the victor – in a word, to Stalinist dictatorship. Maria-Antonietta Macciocchi is undoubtedly right when she comments (*Per Gramsci*, Bologna 1974, p. 125): 'Could Stalin ever have forgotten or forgiven Gramsci, the leader of the Communist Party, for this firm act of criticism, directed openly to the International, and admonishing it in such terms?'[5]

Here one confronts the appalling paradox clearly enunciated by the painter Renzo Galeotti when he remarked (in a conversation with the present writer): 'By shutting him up, and keeping him shut up, Mussolini saved him' (*Mussolini l'ha salvato*).

On 8 November 1926 Gramsci was arrested in Rome, and after six weeks in political exile on the island of Ustica, 30 miles off the north coast of Sicily, he was taken to San Vittore prison in Milan, where he remained until May 1928. Put on trial in Rome on the 28th of that month, he was sentenced to 20 years, 4 months and 5 days imprisonment, after being found guilty of conspiracy, and of agitation, provoking class war, insurrection and alteration of the Constitution and the form of the State through violence. Some of the Prosecutor's words – reputedly echoing a demand of Mussolini himself – have become famous (or rather infamous): 'We must prevent this brain from functioning for 20 years.' On 19 July he arrived at the 'Penitentiary for Physically Handicapped Prisoners' at Turi, near Bari, and there he remained for the next five years in conditions which ensured that this physically ailing man had in effect received a death sentence. The progress of his destruction is revealed in cruel detail in these prison letters.

It was not until 1929 that he received permission to write anything other than letters in his cell; on 8 February of that year he began making notes in the first of the *Quaderni del Carcere* (Prison Notebooks). When he left Turi for the clinic at Formia (19 November 1933), there were 21 of these, and we have already related how they were saved for posterity. Gramsci was prevented by illness in 1935 from writing any more, but by that time there were 2,848 tightly packed pages in no less than 33 notebooks. They undoubtedly constitute a prodigy of will, intellect and indomitable staying power. I have no space here to attempt even a bald summary of the major strands of Gramsci's thought, as they can be discerned in these amazing manuscripts. His concepts of hegemony, civil society, 'national-popular', passive revolution, organic intellectuals, historic bloc, 'integral state' and war of position – to name only a few of the principal headings – are now the common currency of Marxist discussion.[6] The reader is referred to the annotated booklist which can be found at the end of the Introduction.

The three numbers of the *New Edinburgh Review* devoted to Gramsci in 1974 included the papers read to, and discussed at, the First National Day Conference on Gramsci, held in June 1974 at Edinburgh University (two papers were also included which were not read). The following is a list of the contributions: Stephen White, 'Gramsci and Proletarian Power'; Ann Showstack, 'Gramsci's Interpretation of Italian Fascism'; Gwyn A. Williams, 'The Making and Unmaking of Antonio Gramsci'; Stephen White, 'Gramsci in Soviet Historiography'; V.G. Kiernan, 'Gramsci and the Other Continents'; C.K. Maisels, 'Gramsci between Two Internationals'.

As will be seen from this list, the emphasis at the Conference was very much on Gramsci's political thought, and his part in Italian history. However, it is his writings on cultural matters – and in particular on popular culture, folklore and linguistics – which have increasingly occupied commentators in recent years. The compendium *Selections from Cultural Writings*, edited by David Forgacs and Geoffrey Nowell-Smith, and translated by William Boelhower, provides many of the basic texts. These display, more eloquently, perhaps, than any other sections of the prison notebooks, the astounding breadth of Gramsci's reading; his omnivorous interest (recalling Rabelais and Joyce) in words and all those things of which they are symbols; his penetrating powers of analysis when dealing with the different modes of perceiving society and the world to be found in different human groups and classes; and, last but not least, his real literary gifts when dealing with subjects which stimulated and challenged his imagination.

The Open University has greatly assisted in a wider diffusion of Gramsci's ideas on popular culture. In their second level course (U203), his name makes regular appearances, and there is a useful summary of his ideas on how the cultures and ideologies of different classes are related to one another in Tony Bennett's booklet accompanying 'Popular Culture' Block 1, Unit 3. Bennett draws to a considerable extent on the writings of Stuart Hall.

Mention should also be made of the role of *Marxism Today* in applying Gramscian methods of political and cultural analysis to the concrete situation in Thatcher's Britain.

In Vol. 2 of *International Folklore Review* (1983) Moyra Byrne has an excellent article on 'Antonio Gramsci's Contribution to Italian Folklore Studies'. She begins by surveying his notions of multiple levels of culture and society within and also linking and even transcending the broad designations of subaltern and hegemonic classes. She stresses the fact that the categories of thought and behaviour which Gramsci identifies as 'common sense' and 'good sense' ('good sense' being already more self-aware and therefore on a somewhat higher level than 'common sense') are found at all levels of culture and society. She then goes on to examine the apparent paradox which seems inherent in Gramsci's view of folklore: on the one hand he elevates folklore to the status of a world-view which demands serious study, and on the other hand he defines it as an incoherent heap of detritus which must be swept away by the class-conscious broom of a future working-class hegemonic culture.

It is this fruitful thought-provoking dialectical confrontation which has incited several warring factions in Italy and elsewhere into controversy; these have, over the years, tried to make sense of and synthesise the seemingly ambivalent and contradictory Gramscian views of folk-culture.

At this point, I hope I may be allowed a personal reminiscence. When Alan Lomax arrived in Britain in 1950, at the start of an ambitious marathon of recordings for the Columbia World Albums of Folk and Primitive Music, I was working on the translation of Gramsci's prison letters which forms the basis of this new edition. He contacted me, and I interrupted the work to discuss Scottish and Italian folk-culture with him. On the table lay *Letteratura e Vita Nationale*, which had just been sent to me from Italy, and I took the opportunity of introducing Lomax to the name of Gramsci, saying he was undoubtedly a major philosopher. Being a practical American, Lomax asked: 'What has he got to say to us?', and I told him, 'Quite a lot about folklore.' Also, to be practical, I gave him the name and address of Roberto Leydi, whom I had met in Milan a few months earlier.

In 1981 Moyra Byrne interviewed Leydi, who paid tribute to Gramsci's influence on Italian folklorists, and he explained to her his own role in the Italian folksong revival. He told her: 'I couldn't identify with the Italy of Victor Emmanuel, the history of wars, the battle of Solferino, generals, and so on – and yet each of us has the *need* for patriotism of some sort.' He then went on to discuss a phenomenon which, many years earlier, Cesare Pavese had already described to me: namely the fascination of young intellectuals in Italy with the 'other America' of the poor and the outcasts as discovered through novelists like Steinbeck, Faulkner and Dos Passos; or through American neo-realist films, New Orleans Jazz and the Roosevelt era's Farm Security Administration documentation. (It was, of course, exactly this sort of complex of influences – plus Woody Guthrie, the Weavers, Pete Seeger and the Pioneer Revival Singers in the USA – which helped to spark off the now flourishing folk revival in Britain and other parts of Europe.)

Pioneering work in the field of 'oral history' was taking place before the outbreak of the Second World War – the Mass Observation project in Britain was part of the same movement – but the very phrase 'oral history' seems to have been an American invention. In Joseph Mitchell's *McSorley's Wonderful Saloon* (New York 1938) there is a rather moving description of one Joe Gould – 'Professor Sea-gull' – a maverick Yankee Bohemian of impeccable New England ancestry, who devoted his life to amassing materials for an enormous book to be called *An Oral History of Our Time*. Joe wrote – and slept – in parks, doorways, flop-houses, lobbies, cafeterias, on benches, on 'L' platforms, in subway trains and in public libraries. He described what he was aiming to do in the following terms: 'What we used to think was history – all that chitty-chat about Caesar, Napoleon, treaties, inventions, big battles – is only formal history and largely false. I'll put down the informal history of the shirt-sleeved multitude – what they had to say about their jobs, love affairs, vittles, sprees, scrapes, and sorrows – or I'll perish in the attempt.'

Joe Gould makes a fleeting appearance in early twentieth-century American poetry, by courtesy of e.e. cummings, who wrote (*Collected Poems*, no. 261): 'a myth is as good as a smile but little joe gould's quote oral history unquote might (publishers note) be entitled a wraith's progress or mainly awash while chiefly submerged or an amoral morality sort-of-aliving by innumerable kind-of-deaths.' (This must be one of the earliest references in literature to a now popular academic discipline.)

An essay of Gould's, printed in the April 1929 issue of *The Dial* had (according to Mitchell) a curious effect on American literature. A second-hand copy of the review was bought a few months later by the 20-year old William Saroyan, who was greatly struck by Gould's work.

To this day, I have not read anything else by Joe Gould. And yet to me he remains one of the few genuine and original American writers. He was easy and uncluttered, and almost all other American writing was uneasy and cluttered. It was not at home anywhere; it was trying too hard; it was miserable; it was a little sickly; it was literary; and it couldn't say anything simply.

These words of Saroyan's bear a curious resemblance – as we shall see – to a passage in Togliatti's 1938 tribute to Gramsci, when he refers to the sterile inflated rhetoric of much Italian literature and speechifying.

While Gramsci in prison was writing – and sometimes (as the variations in successive drafts of the Variorum edition show) revising and elaborating his thoughts on high art and folk-culture – Joe Gould was amassing at high speed his huge unpublishable Rabelaisian/Urquhartian report on the 'subaltern culture' of the USA. One can well imagine what Gramsci would have thought of a good deal of this, if it had come to his notice. And yet, in the solitude of his barely furnished cell, his thoughts constantly returned to the gorgeous resilient folk-culture of his native Sardinia, and he plied his correspondents (mother and sisters) with questions about festas, folksongs, banners and ballads. Can one doubt that this was a conscious effort to add sap and savour to a life given point only by indomitable cerebral obduracy: to counter the rigours of an existence whose staying power was based (as he put it in one letter) exclusively on the will.

Indeed the conviction grows, as one reads and re-reads his cultural writings, that these memories constituted one of the principal holds on reality which sustained him as the agonising years dragged on; that he felt the exorbitant human need, as Diego Carpitella expressed it, to define and occupy 'one's own territory'. The gradual building-up by others of a micro-history of the nation – 'of all that concerns people' – might also surely come to seem a 'communist and revolutionary act'!

However, the 'negative' attributes of folk-culture, which Gramsci clinically examined, were what initially worried and sometimes antagonised Italian folklorists. When the late Ernesto de Martino 'went out there to see what was happening' (Leydi's words) – in other words, to undertake invaluable anthropological fieldwork in southern Italy – he felt himself to a certain extent 'put on the spot' by these same 'disparaging' passages . In his book *La Terra del Rimorso* (Milan 1968) he provides a curious and frank account of the moral and methodological dilemma that, in effect, Gramsci's view of folklore posed for him and his co-workers.

Ernesto de Martino died in 1965. Younger scholars, building on his self-questionings, as well as on his researches, confronted the problem by examining 'the persistence and "refunctionalization" of traditional folklore forms ... in the context of the change towards industrialisation' and the modern consumer society (Clara Gallini, *Un filone specifico degli studi antropologici Italiani*: manuscript of paper delivered in Alexandria, Egypt in 1980). These scholars 'saw the need to get away from a too radical application of the dichotomy "hegemonic" and "subaltern" which would define the world-view of subaltern classes mainly in terms of the positive attributes which a hegemonic world-view has and which it lacks. In ways and degrees that varied from one scholar to another, they sought in Gramsci's philosophy, or in their development of it, a belief in the alternative value of subaltern culture and society' (Byrne, *International Folklore Review*, p. 73).

In short, the possibilities of a political utilisation of folklore – of the fostering of an *alternative* to official bourgeois culture, seeking out the positive and 'progressive' aspects of folk culture – were explored energetically by Italian folklorists. Some explicitly rejected the Gramscian concept 'national-popular' – the idea that the masses could achieve a 'higher' national socio-cultural unity on the basis of a rejection of folkloric and 'provincial' values. Combatting this general idea, Gianni Bosio contended that working people's culture had the quality of 'autonomy', 'otherness', alternative values, and continuity with the older peasant culture, and was not to be contaminated by the qualities of bourgeois 'higher' culture. Pointing to models in the USA and in Britain, Roberto Leydi (in successive numbers of *Il Nuovo Canzioniere Italiano* in the early 1960s) stressed the value to the working-class movement of songs taking their inspiration from folk traditions, and highlighted especially the anti-Polaris songs like 'Ding Dong Dollar' which were sung on the Holy Loch marches. His example sparked off a new wave of field collecting, and young singer-songwriters contributed some excellent new protest songs to the Italian folksong revival. Inside and outside the universities, research into oral history proceeded apace. Summarising these developments, Ms Byrne describes Gramscian theory as 'a complex system – a system which raises questions and stimulates a constant identification of one's "reasons" and "means". Identification, and continual reexamination, of reasons and means is particularly essential to any folklore studies which address a contemporary reality marked by a new complexity of rapidly changing interrelationships between different levels of culture.'

Reading again the scattered remarks on folklore in the prison notebooks, one realises afresh that there is an unresolved but creative clash of contradictions in Gramsci's approach. If 'all that concerns people' is the rightful pre-occupation of the working-class intellectual, of the 'self-taught man', then this must surely include the most ancient patrimony of human exploit and dream.[7]

In the *Guardian* of 1 September 1987 there is a moving account of a woman lawyer's struggle in Canada to defend Indian rights. According to Leslie Pinder, the lawyer,

> the judge had never met an Indian person, and I think he was a bit scared about being taken into a different world. At the beginning we explained that they were a huntergatherer society, who hunted through their dreams, and that their dreams became maps. The judge stopped me and said, 'Every society must have leaders. Are you telling me this society doesn't have leaders?' I explained that they have experts, but that it's not a hierarchical society. He said, 'That's not possible.'

The *Guardian* report continues:

> Incomprehension mounted as elderly Indians delivered testimony in their own language, describing how the world was created, and the relationship between man, the animals and spirits. 'They talked about their prophets. The judge asked whether that was spelled "profits". It was an incredible struggle from beginning to end'.

Ms Pinder, who is still awaiting the outcome, has worked almost exclusively on Indian cases for the past decade. She is much taken with Laurens van der Post's view that the tribulations of aboriginal people represent the destruction of our 'darker' side. 'Our rational, materialistic side has tried to kill an aspect of ourselves that is natural, intuitive, spiritual and creative. When you go beyond government policies, that's the heart of the matter.'

This news item recalls passages in Bruce Chatwin's fascinating book *The Songlines* (London 1987). 'In theory, at least', says Chatwin, 'the whole of Australia could be read as a musical score.' A musical score of stunning complexity and numinous significance, of which the learning is the most imperative business in the world for the aboriginal inhabitants of that continent. Chatwin quotes Heidegger (*What are Poets For?*): 'the song still remains which names the land over which it sings'. He concludes his last section of 'Journey Notes' as follows:

Trade means friendship and co-operation; and for the Aboriginal the principal object of trade was song. Song, therefore, brought peace ... I have a vision of the Songlines stretching across the continents and ages; that wherever men have trodden they have left a trail of songs (of which we may, now and then, catch an echo); and that these trails must reach back, in time and space, to an isolated pocket in the African savannah, where the First Man opening his mouth in defiance of the terrors that surrounded him, shouted the opening stanza of the World Song, 'I AM!'

Small wonder that Gramsci, fighting to assert his continued existence, and his will to execute a lasting work, *für ewig*, should have asked his mother (in a letter sent from Milan prison on 3 October 1927):

When you are able, send me some of the Sardinian songs that the descendants of Pirisi Pirione of Bolotana sing in the streets; and if they have poetry competitions at some festa or other, write and tell me what the set themes are. What about the festa of San Costantino at Sedilo and the festa of San Palmerio? Are they still celebrated, and if so, what are they like nowadays? Is the festa of San Isidoro still a big occasion? Do they carry in procession the flag with the four Moors' heads on it,[8] and are there still captains dressed in the uniforms of bygone days? You know these things have always interested me a lot, so please give me the information I need, and don't think they are silly things unworthy of attention.

Gramsci would no doubt have been interested (and probably delighted) if he could have been accorded a precognitive glimpse into the future, and known that a song *Quadernos Iscrittos in d'una Cella Oscura* ('Notebooks written in a dark cell') would be recorded in Sardinia under the auspices of the Istituto Ernesto de Martino 32 years after his death. The text of this song was composed by Peppino Marotto. Here is a rough prose translation:

Notebooks written in a dark cell by a wise man light up the world. Life is still hard because exploited people don't yet fight to the end for their sacred rights. Gramsci left his mother in Sardinia, his master in Turin, his wife in Russia. With immortal fame, more than any star, shines forth the light of unity that he established. Through the merit of Lenin, every nation wants communism to lead them to glory. Against the aggression of imperialism, the victory will lie with the forces of Ho Chi Minh.

The recording was made in Orgosolo, Nuoro district, Barbagia province. The singers were Peppino Marotto himself and Umberto Goddi, Sebestiano Piras, and Pasquale Marotto. The manner of performance was a kind of polyphony traditional in the central plateau of Sardinia. It is presumed to be ancient. It consists of a lead voice ('*sa boghe*'), a bass, a 'contra', and a middle voice. While *sa boghe* sings the words, the choir comes in on the last note with a series of 'nonsense' syllables intoned rhythmically, and harmonises on the foundation laid down by the bass.

The poems, called *Mutettus*, are made up of a first part on an ABCD/BCDA scheme, and a second part in which some of these lines are repeated in a different order, but which – and this demonstrates the skill of the author or improvisor – come together to make complete sense.

The background to the song is not without interest. Till about 1965 the Orgosolo region was extremely backward, poverty was extreme and life was deeply conservative and traditional. The economy was pastoral. Then the great cheese-making concern of Galbani, in search of cheap sources of supply and labour, set up factories in and around Orgosolo. The life of the shepherds and goatherds was violently altered, and they found themselves pitchforked into the twentieth century, into a world of time-clocks, production lines and labour disputes. The political consciousness of the neighbourhood developed very rapidly, and the changes in the content of the folklore quite outstripped the changes in form. Hence the appearance of entirely modern texts set in remarkably archaic frameworks, as illustrated by the Gramsci song.[9]

The passage from the letter to Gramsci's mother quoted above, and others like it, served to a large extent to neutralise the effect of the long series of negative attributes which passages in the *Quaderni* attribute to folklore. In the past decade a certain equilibrium, a synthesis of speculation and experience, has been achieved in this whole disputed area, and some of the lesser-known remarks of Gramsci have acquired a fresh relevance. In addition, folklorists outside Italy have begun to tackle the job of examining their field of study from a class perspective, and the fresh controversies and 'flytings' which will inevitably surface can only benefit from the vigorous intellectual battles already fought.

Before his death, Benedetto Croce wrote, in a tribute to Gramsci, that he ranked with Giordano Bruno, with Machiavelli, with Vico – and, by implication, with Croce himself – as one of the greatest of Italian thinkers. Certainly, nearly all major writers, artists and film-makers of post Second World War Italy were to a greater or lesser extent influenced by his mighty presence in the recent past. To mention only a few: Pier Paolo Pasolini wrote *Le Ceneri di Gramsci* (The Ashes of Gramsci);[10] Elio Vittorini celebrated the Gramscian cultural heritage in the pages of *Il Politecnico*; Riccardo Bacchelli, writing *Il figlio di Stalin* (The Son of Stalin) tackled the dreadful subject of totalitarian contempt for humanity, of which Gramsci was an outstanding victim; and Renzo Galeotti painted his extraordinary series of Gramsci studies – *Omaggio a Gramsci* – 'Homage to Gramsci: the life of a martyr for the working class represented in the manner of Sacred Art'. As for post-war Italian film-makers, from Roberto Rossellini ('the patron saint of neo-realism') onwards, there cannot be one who has not, to a greater or lesser extent, come under the spell of Gramsci's memory and intellectual heritage.

To be sure, many of these intellectuals were only marginally Marxist, but Gramsci's influence drew them irresistibly in the direction of the same hegemonic umbrella. As James Joll put it in his excellent short study *Gramsci*:

> Because of their variety as well as their fragmentary nature [the notebooks] provide texts to support many different views of Gramsci's message, as well as raising unnumerable questions to which, on account of the circumstances of his life, Gramsci could not give an answer. His range of interests, the extraordinary breadth of his own reading and of his historical and philosophical culture, as well as the enforced detachment with which he was writing his more theoretic work make him unique among Marxists. At the same time the fact that he remained rooted in the Italian and the European idealist cultural tradition so that, however much he reacted against them, Vico and Hegel, Sorel and Croce were in some ways as important for him as Marx and Lenin, means that it is easier for the non-Marxist to conduct a dialogue with Gramsci than with any other Marxist writer of the twentieth century.

This reflection brings us up against one of the charges which were being levelled against Gramsci by his prison mates in his own lifetime – that he was a 'Crocean idealist and a social democrat'. When this was reported to him by Mario Garuglieri, he replied,

> I respect Croce as we should respect men who are high intellectuals (*di alto pensiero*); Croce is a serious scholar; in his historical criticism he proves how solid his thought is, and how profound his culture. As a philosopher he marks the highest development in Italian thought, but as a politician he is the latest expression of a liberal doctrine which defends a society which is at the end of its tether. My comrades will realise how Crocean I am when they see the work about Croce that I am going to produce.

However, as Alastair Davidson recounts (*Antonio Gramsci: Towards an Intellectual Biography*, p. 251) he was sufficiently upset by a campaign waged against him by some comrades to suspend the series of discussions he had been conducting in the exercise yard.

Henceforth, the prison was divided into two groups: those for and those against Gramsci. Gramsci showed no readiness to break off contact with the Socialist, Pertini, with whom he had cordial relations, much as he had refused to be anything but friendly with Bordiga when they were confined at Ustica three years earlier.

The feelings against Gramsci among members of the hostile group did not express themselves in words only: on at least two occasions there were despicable acts of attempted physical violence. Nevertheless, he did not succumb to pressure, for there was no way he could go along with the sterile, myopic and totally unrealistic dogmatism of 'The Third Period', from 1928 onwards: the fable, that is, that in the immediate future the imperialist world would enter a new period of crisis and economic collapse, and that this would lead automatically to a renewed series of revolutions in Europe. Gramsci maintained that the idea of an imminent insurrectionary outbreak against Fascism was a dangerous illusion, and he also seems to have expressed reservations about the equating of social democracy with 'social-fascism' – the self-destructive line which in Germany undoubtedly facilitated Hitler's rise to power. These disagreements would almost certainly have led to his expulsion from the Party if he had been a free man, but – as Victor Serge (a supporter of Trotsky) wrote sardonically – 'reclusion saved him from exclusion'.[11] (C.L.R. James's book *World Revolution 1917–1936*, published in 1937, is still one of the most concise expositions of the deformations and distortions that a principled Marxist revolutionary had to combat in the period when Stalin was consolidating his power. Unfortunately, it contains very little about the repercussions of the power struggle in Italy.)

For almost a year and a half – June 1931 till December 1933 – there were no political-theoretical references to Gramsci in the publications of the Italian Communist Party in exile. As Spriano explains:

Ernesto Ragioneri correctly linked this silence with the whole atmosphere of the Comintern during the Stalinist emphasis on the struggle against 'social-fascism', and with Stalin's famous piece on the historiography of the Bolshevik Party in November 1931, which laid down criteria wholly different from those which Togliatti had endeavoured to provide for an historical rethinking of the experience of the party. (*Antonio Gramsci and the Party: the Prison Years*, p. 73)

It is hard to resist the conclusion that if Gramsci had indeed been released in this period, and had been able to make his way to the Soviet Union, he would eventually have been the target for suppression or 'liquidation'. Even if he had escaped with his life, it is highly unlikely that he would have been able to continue work on his prison notebooks in Vorkuta.

With the outbreak of the Spanish Civil War, and the coming of the new 'line' on Popular Fronts against Fascism, this whole picture changed dramatically. In Tom Nairn's words, 'Gramsci's stubborn anti-sectarianism and openness had altered in retrospect; from near-treason it had become clear-eyed prophesy.' In the article 'Antonio Gramsci, Leader of the Italian Working Class', which Togliatti wrote in May/June 1937, and contributed to the 1938 collection of tributes and recollections published in Paris under the title *Gramsci*, he painted an unforgettable picture of his great comrade as the thinker to whom Italian socialism owed the most profound modification it had undergone in the course of its history. One of the passages in his article became famous:

Not strong physically, gravely wounded in his physical being by nature, Gramsci had an incomparable fighter's spirit. His whole life was subject to his iron will. He radiated energy, peace, optimism; he was able to impose on himself the toughest work discipline, but could enjoy life in all its aspects. As a man he was a pagan – a relentless scourge of all imposture, of all false sentimentality, of all flabby weakness. He used the weapon of laughter and derision in an unrivalled way, to expose the vanity and duplicity of those preaching morality to the people in the interests of the ruling class. He had a profound knowledge of the life and customs of the Italian people, of the legends and stories which have been created by the people, and in which the people have expressed in ingenuous and intuitive form their needs, their aspirations, their dreams of liberty and justice, their hatred of the possessor classes. From this intimate contact with the people he drew inexhaustible and ever new elements of polemical power in the struggle against every form of oppression, not only in the economic-political field, but in the field of intellectual and moral life. The great Italians – from Giuseppe Boccaccio and Giordano Bruno to Giuseppe Giusti and Garibaldi – who fought to liberate the people from the chains of hypocrisy, servility and cant which an age-old tradition of domination by the Catholic church and foreign overlords had imposed on them, found in him an heir and a continuer. He was a bitter enemy of the inflated tinselly eloquence which vitiates such a large part of Italian literature and culture, and has choked in so many literate Italians the fresh bubbling sources of popular inspriration.

Having mentioned Ken Currie's 'The Self-taught Man' at the outset, I would like to conclude by quoting two or three stanzas of what is (in my view) one of the finest Communist poems of the century: 'The Seamless Garment' by Hugh MacDiarmid, which was published in *First Hymn to Lenin* in 1931. Gramsci could not have got to know of this masterpiece, which is a mortal shame, for we can be sure he would have recognised its worth. (MacDiarmid himself grasped immediately the world-significance of Gramsci when I read parts of the present translation to him in 1949; he was later to refer – in *In Memoriam James Joyce* – to

> That heroic genius, Antonio Gramsci,
> Studying comparative linguistics in prison,
> For, as he said in his *Lettere dal Carcere*,
> 'Nothing less! What could be more
> Disinterested and *für ewig*?'

He also intuitively recognised the similarity between Gramsci's ironic use of language and the techniques of the great Austrian satirist Karl Kraus, mentioned a little later in the same poem.)

In 'The Seamless Garment', the poet is talking, in easy colloquial style, to a cousin of his who works in a tweed-mill in the Border town of Langholm (Langholm, the 'Muckle Toon', was MacDiarmid's birth place).

> You are a cousin of mine
>   Here in the mill.
> It's queer that born in the Langholm
>   It's no' until
> Juist noo I see what it means
> To work in the mill like my freen's.
>
> I was tryin' to say something
>   In a recent poem
> Aboot Lenin. You've read a guid lot
>   In the news – but ken the less o'm?
> Look, Wullie, here is his secret noo
> In a way I can share it wi' you.

MacDiarmid compares Lenin's political sure-footedness

> A' he'd to dae wi' moved intact,
>   Clean, clear, and exact

to Rilke's 'Seamless Garment o' music and thought', and calls on the Border weavers to pay heed to the produce of these other looms. The language of the poem is, for the most part, lightly sketched-in Scots dialect readily comprehensible to an English-speaking reader, but at one point the great makar reverts to a richer canon of old Scots speech – much as Gramsci might have needed a full measure of Sardinian to express his deepest feelings. This passage occurs in the penultimate stanza, and means (approximately): 'Lord, how the old "glad rags" of the past are cast off and discarded.'

Hundreds to the inch the threids lie in,
  Like the men in a communist cell.
There's a play o' licht frae the factory windas.
  Could you no' mak' mair yoursel'?
Mony a loom mair alive than the weaver seems
For the sun's still nearer than Rilke's dreams.

Ailie Bally's tongue's keepin' time
  To the vibration a' richt.
Clear through the maze you een signal to Jean
  What's for naebody else's sicht.
Short skirts, silk stockin's – fegs, hoo the auld
Emmle-deugs o' the past are curjute and devauld.

And as for me in my fricative work
  I ken fu' weel
Sic an integrity's what I maun ha'e
  Indivisible, real,
Woven owre close for the point o' a pin
  Onywhere to win in.

Notes

1. This, at any rate, is the reason for his hump-back given by his younger sister Teresina in an interview published in *Gramsci Vivo* (Milan, 1977); the same explanation was given to the present writer by Antonio's younger brother Carlo in 1950. However, it has been suggested that this condition was due at least partly to the attack of rickets he suffered as a small child.
2. But Piero Gobetti saw things somewhat differently; see his 1924 Profile of Gramsci reprinted here.
3. I'd like at this point to express a personal debt of gratitude to Piero, who gave me a lot of help when I was translating the prison letters in 1949 and 1950 – as did Carlo, Antonio's younger brother, when I visited him in Milan.
4. 'Savage indignation' stilled for ever, Gramsci was laid to rest in the Protestant 'cemetery of the English' in Rome, under the shadow of the pyramid of Caius Cestius; the remains of Keats and Shelley lie not far away.
5. *Per Gramsci* is the Italian version of her *Pour Gramsci*, published in the same year in Paris; the passage quoted is expressed with considerably more force in the Italian version than in the French.
6. Rather too common currency, sometimes, one might think, seeing 'hegemony' scattered around in blithe ubiquity over article after article, rather like 'Islamic' on the lips of Muslim fundamentalists. An article 'Italy's Fading Dream', about the PCI losses in the June 1987 election, appeared in *Marxism Today* of August 1987; it was sub-titled 'Hegemony in Tatters'.

7. Many of these problems are likely to be discussed at the International Seminar on 'Tribal Culture in a Changing World' organised by the Institute of Oriental and Orissan Studies, Orissa, India (9-12 December 1988). The Institute has already published *Folk Culture* (5 vols), which presents 200 papers on Folk Culture and Literature; Folkways, Religion, God, Spirit and Men; Folk Arts and Crafts; Folk Music and Dances and Folk Culture and the Great Tradition.

8. In the 1965 edition of *Lettere dal Carcere* the word *Mori* (Moors) is wrongly transcribed *Mari* (seas).

9. I am indebted for much of the above information to the late A. L. Lloyd.

10. An English translation of the title poem by Christopher Whyte appeared in *Bananas*, no. 23 (London, October 1980).

11. According to Fiori (p. 253), Gramsci's brother Gennaro, who visited him in prison in June 1930, reported to Togliatti in Paris that Gramsci agreed with the new 'line' and supported the expulsion of three dissident comrades, but this was not the truth. 'Had I told a different story, not even Nino would have been saved from expulsion.' However, Spriano (*Antonio Gramsci and the Party: The Prison Years*, pp. 56-9) quotes a statement by Luigi Longo (*Gramsci Vivo*, p. 76) that tells a somewhat different story; according to Longo, Gennaro 'told us that Antonio had not wished to say anything regarding the political communications transmitted to him.'

There is certainly a difference of emphasis, but the implications of his refusal to express an opinion are nevertheless quite clear.

Further Reading
The reader is referred to the following works which the present writer has found useful:

Selections from the Prison Notebooks, edited and translated by Quintin Hoare and Geoffrey Nowell-Smith, London 1971. (Still an indispensable introduction for the English-speaking reader.)

Joseph V. Femia, *Gramsci's Political Thought*, Oxford 1981.

Jacques Texier, *Gramsci et la Philosophie du Marxisme*, Paris 1966.

Anne Showstack Sassoon, *Gramsci's Politics*, London 1980; *Approaches to Gramsci*, London 1982.

Roger Simon, *Gramsci's Political Thought*, London 1982.

James Joll, *Gramsci*, London 1977. (The best short introduction for a reader coming new to Gramsci.)

Christine Buci-Gluckmann, *Gramsci and the State*, London 1980.

For Gramsci's early life, introduction to politics and political development, the reader is referred to the following:

Guiseppi Fiori, *Antonio Gramsci* (translated Tom Nairn), London 1970.

Alastair Davidson, *Antonio Gramsci. Towards an Intellectual Biography*, London 1977.

John M. Cammett, *Antonio Gramsci and the Origins of Italian Communism*, Stanford, California 1967.

Martin Clark, *Antonio Gramsci and the Revolution that Failed*, Yale 1977.

Gwyn A. Williams, *Proletarian Order. Antonio Gramsci, Factory Councils and the Origin of Italian Communism*, London 1975. (Much of this appeared alongside the present translation of the *Lettere* in the Gramsci numbers of the *New Edinburgh Review* in 1974.)

Maria-Antonietta Macciocchi, *Pour Gramsci*, Paris 1974.

Ed. Giuseppe Prestipino, Antonio Gramsci. *Arte e folklore*, Rome 1976.

Paolo Spriano, *The Occupation of the Factories*, translated and introduced by Gwyn A. Williams, London 1975; *Antonio Gramsci and the Party: The Prison Years*, translated by John Fraser, London 1979. (This latter is a book of the first importance; it clears up a number of difficult questions raised over the years since Gramsci's death.)

Since the appearance of the *Prison Notebooks* in 1971, three further volumes of Gramsci's writings have appeared in English translation: *Political Writings 1910–1920* (1977); *Political Writings 1921–1926* (1978); and *Cultural Writings* (1985), all published by Lawrence and Wishart in London. The definitive Italian Variorum edition of the *Quaderni del Carcere*, spendidly edited by Valentino Gerratana, came out in 1975 (Editori Riuniti, Rome). The 1965 edition of *Lettere dal Carcere*, edited by Sergio Caprioglio and Elsa Fubini, is a monument of modern Italian literature, and supersedes the earlier 1947 selection (which won the Viareggio Prize when it appeared). An enormous literature of comment and criticism has grown up in Italy relating to Gramsci's career, thought and influence: I have space to mention only the volume of papers given at the first Gramsci Studies Conference, held at Rome from 11 January to 13 January 1958: *Studi Gramsciani*, published by Editori Riuniti, Rome 1958. Articles about Gramsci appear with increasing frequency in British reviews and journals; a concise thought-provoking survey of his political thought by Paul Tritschler appeared in *Radical Scotland*, 20th issue, April/May 1986. A two-volume edition of the prison letters appeared as a supplement to *L'Unità* of 14 February 1988; this edition, not commercially available, was reserved for subscribers to and readers of *L'Unità*. It contained 28 new letters and prefaces by Paolo Spriano (Vol. 1) and Valentino Gerretana (Vol. 2), but carried only a bare minimum of notes.

Gramsci
A 1924 profile by Piero Gobetti

TRANSLATED BY HAMISH HENDERSON
AND TOM NAIRN

Antonio Gramsci is going into the new fascist-dominated Chamber as representative of the workers of the Veneto. One might say it's a case of the Revolution, defeated, going into Parliament to predict doom for the victors. Gramsci is the first revolutionary to enter Montecitorio! And not to smash voting urns or provoke noisy scandals, either! Bombacci and Misiano were like photographic copies of Enrico Ferri: theirs was fashionable revolution, not much good for anything but the diary columns of the bourgeois press.[1] The ideological level and style of these agitators strangely resembled that of Mussolini himself.

If Gramsci does in fact speak at Montecitorio we shall probably see the fascist deputies quiet and attentive for once, as they strain to hear the inflections of that thin muffled voice, and experience the novel sensation of intellect at work.[2] Gramsci's dialectic does not inveigh against the swindles and intrigues of bourgeois government, it looks down from the pure heights of the Hegelian Idea and coldly demonstrates their inevitability. His speeches will be metaphysical condemnations, his invective will be shot through with glimpses of palingenesis.

To understand his hatred of society, one must take into account his whole cultural formation during his years at the University of Turin.

Gramsci's hate is one of the most convincing examples I know of proud nobility and wounded dignity. His socialism is first and foremost an answer to society's insults against the loneliness of a Sardinian emigré.

His ascetic sociology, the philosophical absoluteness of his Jacobin attitudes, are nourished by personal suffering. It is a suffering which has taken on such an intimately aristocratic character that it can deride all the self-indulgences of bourgeois morality, and document the barefaced cruelties of philanthropy. It would be hard to find anywhere a more characteristic example of thorough-going Marxism, of proud unyielding proletarian consciousness which rejects all compromise.

But Gramsci despised this whole semi-bourgeois world already, instinctively: his instincts developed in an island countryside where political opinions quite logically lead on to cattle-stealing or even to vengeance-killing.

A hundred years ago Tuvieri demonstrated to the republicans of the peninsula how, if hypocrisies were disregarded, logic lay on the side of the monarchists; Gramsci too lays down conclusions true to his premises, without half measures. He seems to have left the rural world in order to forget its traditions, in order to replace the sick inheritance of Sardinian anachronism with a single-minded inexorable drive towards the modernity of the city. He bears in his own physical person the marks of one who has turned his back on country existence, and violently superimposed a programme founded on and sustained by the force of desperation; one powered, moreover, by a spiritual compulsion deriving ultimately from the rejection and betrayal of a native innocence.

Antonio Gramsci has the head of a revolutionary; his features look as if they have been modelled by his own overmastering will, carved rudely at the behest of some ineluctable necessity which could brook neither question nor discussion; the brain has overwhelmed the body. The head which lords it over the sick limbs seems to incarnate the logical imperatives of that great salvationist utopia, whose power endows it with a rough-hewn impenetrable gravity. The eyes alone – lively and ingenuous, yet self-contained, and often veiled in bitterness – give an occasional hint of the pessimist's kindness and good nature, to soften the overall impression of granite-hard rational rigour. His voice has a critical, destructive edge, and its tone of irony can turn in no time into a blow-pipe of lethal sarcasm; dogma lived out with tyrannic logic cannot allow itself the saving grace of humour. Behind his open sincerity one can sense an accumulation of inaccessible anger: confined in a solitude which disdains all confidences, he has arrived at the painful acceptance of responsibilities stronger than life itself, and as hard as historical destiny. Rebellion, in his case, springs partly from resentment, and partly from the deeper pent-up grudge of the islander unable to open out except in action, unable to free himself from age-old slavery except by investing his missionary authority with something peremptory, even tyrannical. Impulse and emotion take a back seat, once a disciplined life-style, austere and logical in all its manifestations, is acknowledged to be the first necessity; when organic unity and harmonious serenity are just not possible, the will takes over and imposes its own diktat. Ideas are then masters, and natural human expansiveness goes by the board.

His love for categorical and dogmatic clarity (typical of the ideologue, the visionary) prevents him from getting these ideas across with the sort of easy persuasiveness and sympathy which might gain them readier acceptance – and therefore, behind all the industrious fervour of reports and research projects and statistical summaries, and behind the ethical preoccupations of the Party programme, one can detect an arid rigour, a sense of cosmic tragedy allowing no breath of indulgence. As a student Gramsci managed to find an outlet for the rhetoric innate in our race, precisely by denying fruition to his own undoubted literary gifts, and by leaving behind the ascetic by-ways of glottology (a subject for which he had earlier displayed a lively predilection). Today the utopian imposes his categorical imperative on the *instruments* of modern industry, and regulates the turning of factory wheels with infallible logic; he is like a manager impassively making his deadpan calculations, or a general *counting* the military formations available to him for a given battle. Victory as such does not enter into his calculations, and there are no prognostications on that score, because victory will be a sign from God – the mathematical sum total of revolutionary *praxis*. Here his ethical awareness is sustained by tolerance and silent certitude; it is the bourgeoisie itself which is busy working for the victory of the proletariat.

More than a tactician or a combatant, Gramsci is a prophet. In the only way possible today, that is: unheard except by fate. Gramsci's eloquence will overturn no ministries. His catastrophic polemic, his desperate satire can expect no facile consolations. The whole of humanity, the whole of present-day here and now is suspect in his eyes. He demands justice from a ferocious avenging future.

1. Gobetti refers here to the demagogic strain in the old left wing of the Italian Socialist Party, typified by Ferri (1856–1929). The latter is described as 'a bizarre figure who typified the worst in Italian socialism ... His flowing hair, wide-brimmed hat and theatrical poses fascinated adoring audiences' (C. Seton-Watson, *Italy from Liberalism to Fascism 1870–1925*, pp. 264–5). Mussolini had of course himself emerged from the same tradition. The histrionic Nicola Bombacci (1879–1945) eventually became a Fascist, and was one of the Duce's closest advisers in the period of the 'Social Republic'.
2. In his *Antonio Gramsci* (NLB 1970) Giuseppe Fiori comments: 'Prophetic words. Velio Spano remembers how, as Gramsci spoke, "all the deputies thronged round the benches of the extreme left, in order to hear the faint, inflexible voice. One of the Rome papers published a large picture of Mussolini leaning forward with his hand to his ear ..." '(p. 193).

Piero Gobetti – see note 3 to letter 142 – was the principal figure among the young liberal intellectuals influenced by Gramsci in the immediate aftermath of World War I. Born in 1901 at Turin, he was already at the age of eighteen an enterprising editor; his fortnightly *Energie Nuove* (New Energies) served as a mouthpiece for the youthful avant-garde of his native city.

The 'Two Red Years' of Turin, and the concomitant growth of fascist reaction, brought him close to the working-class movement. First of all he became dramatic critic of Gramsci's paper *L'Ordine Nuovo*, and then (in February 1922) he launched the weekly *La Rivoluzione Liberale*, a magazine of formidable intellectual calibre, which had the explicit aim of rallying the liberal intelligentsia in a front against fascism. Gobetti called for the political fight to be carried on 'with ferocious intransigence', and after the murder of Matteotti he helped to carry the war into the camp of the temporarily rattled and demoralised fascists. His courage led to his being viciously beaten up by a fascist gang (5 September 1924), but *La Rivoluzione Liberale* continued to appear on the bookstalls until November 1925, when the police ordered it to cease publication.

Gobetti left Italy for Paris on 6 February 1926, and he died there on the 16th of the same month, not yet twenty-five years of age.

The profile of Gramsci, which was published in *La Rivoluzione Liberale* on 22 April 1924, is of quite exceptional interest, being the work of an observer who, although a close friend, was capable of standing back and viewing his subject dispassionately, even clinically. No-one reading the later prison letters of Gramsci can doubt that Gobetti had already put his finger, with prescient insight, on one of the principal reasons for Gramsci's tragic estrangement from his wife which is documented in such heart-breaking detail in the Letters.

Historical Note: The profile was published a month before Gramsci returned to Italy from Vienna, and two months before the assassination of Giacomo Matteoti.

The Letters

1

Rome Prison, 20 November 1926

My darling Julca,

Do you remember one of your last letters? (At least, it was the last letter of yours that I received and read.) You wrote that we two are still young enough to look forward to seeing our children growing up, all of us together. You must strongly remember this; you must think of it with courage every time you think of me and associate me with the children. I am sure you will be strong and brave, as you have always been. You must be even more so now than in the past, so that our children can grow up well, and be worthy of you in everything. I have thought much, very much in these last few days. I have tried to imagine what your future life will be like, because I shall certainly be without news of you for quite a long time; and I have thought again of the past, drawing from it reasons for infinite strength and confidence. I am and will be strong; I love you so much, and I want sooner or later to see our little children once again.

My dearest wife, I don't want to worry you in any way whatsoever; I am a little tired, because I sleep little, and so I cannot write all I would like in the way I would like to. I want to let you feel strongly, so strongly, all my love and all my confidence.

Give everyone in the family a warm embrace from me; and you, my dear, I press to my heart most tenderly, together with our children.

Antonio

2

Ustica, 9 December 1926

Dearest Tatiana,

I arrived in Ustica on the 7th, and the following day I received your letter dated the 3rd. In future letters I shall describe all the impressions of the journey, as soon as the various memories and emotions disentangle themselves in my head and begin to sort themselves out; also when I have had a bit of rest after all this strain, and my wretched insomnia.

Apart from the peculiar conditions in which it took place (as you will understand, it isn't very comfortable, even for a man of robust health, to undergo hours' and hours' travel by train and steamer wearing handcuffs, and linked by a chain to the handcuffs of the other travellers), the journey was exceedingly interesting, and rich in diverse motifs; these latter ranging from the Shakespearean to the downright farcical. I am not sure for example if I'll ever be able to reconstruct a night scene which I experienced while we were in transit through Naples: an immense gorge of a room, crammed to the ceiling with fantastic zoological specimens. I think that only the grave-digger scene in Hamlet could equal it.

The most difficult stretch of the journey was the crossing from Palermo to Ustica: we attempted the crossing four times, and on three of these occasions we had to return to the port of Palermo, because the little steam-launch couldn't stand up to the fury of the storm. But even so – do you realise that I have got fatter this last month? I have been quite astounded myself to feel in such grand fettle, and to have such an appetite: I am sure that within a fortnight, after I have had a bit of rest and made up for lost sleep, I shall have got rid of this migraine altogether, and shall start off on a fresh lap of my physical existence.

My first impression of Ustica is excellent from every point of view. The size of the island is five square miles, and it has a population of about 1,300 inhabitants. Of these, 600 are ordinary convicts – that is, criminals with several convictions to their name. The population could not be more courteous: we are all treated with great correctness.

We political prisoners are kept quite separate from the ordinary convicts, whose life it would be hard to describe in a few lines.

Do you remember Kipling's story 'The Strange Ride of Morrowbie Jukes' in the French translation of *The Phantom 'Rickshaw'*?[1] It came back into my mind all of a sudden, because I really seemed be living it.

At the time of writing we are fifteen in number. Our life is perfectly calm and uneventful: we are busy exploring the island, which is big enough to allow of several fairly long walks of about five or six miles. The countryside is most attractive, with sudden vistas of the sea, and marvellous dawns and sunsets. Every two days the steam-launch arrives, bringing us news, magazines, papers, and more friends, one of whom is Ortensia's husband.[2] I was pleased to see him. Ustica is much more beautiful than anyone would think from looking at the picture postcards which I shall send you: it is a little town on the Moorish pattern – picturesque and full of colour. You can't imagine how happy I am to be able to stroll all over the village and the island from end to end, and to breathe the sea air after this month of being pushed around from one prison to another – and especially after the sixteen days in Regina Coeli, which I spent in complete solitary confinement. I think I shall become the champion of Ustica at 'throwing the stone', because I have already beaten all my friends.

I am writing this letter by fits and starts, just as ideas come into my head, because I'm still a little tired. Dearest Tatiana, you can't imagine how I felt when at Regina Coeli I saw your writing on the first bottle of coffee I received, and when I read the name of Marietta[3] I positively felt like a little boy once again ... Do you know this: these days, realising it's a certainty that all my letters are being read by the prison officials before they are despatched, I have noticed in myself a sort of modesty: I don't care to write about certain feelings, and if I try to tone them down, in order to conform to the needs of the situation, I feel as if I were acting as a sort of church elder.

So for now I will restrict myself to a description of certain aspects of my stay in Regina Coeli, taking my cue from the questions you put. Yes, I received the woollen jacket, which has been very useful, and also the stockings etc. Without them I would have suffered severely from the cold, because I left Rome with nothing but a light overcoat, and in the grey hours of early morning, when we were attempting the Palermo–Ustica crossing, it was devilish cold. I received the plates as well, but unfortunately I had to leave them behind in Rome, the reason being that I was obliged to stuff all my baggage into the one kit bag (which incidentally has given splendid service) and I was sure I would break them. I haven't received the Cirio,[4] nor have I had the chocolate and the gingerbread, which were all forbidden: I saw them ticked off on the list, but with the note added that it was not permitted to hand them over. Similarly I wasn't given the little tumbler for the coffee, but I have provided an alternative myself by making a table service with half-a-dozen egg shells proudly mounted on pedestals of dry breadcrumbs. I see you are getting worried because the meals were always cold: there was no harm in that, because after the first day or two I invariably ate at least double the amount I was used to eating in restaurants, and I never had the slightest stomach trouble. All my friends were sick in one way or another and used too many purgatives. I am beginning to convince myself that I'm really much stronger than I ever thought, because unlike all the others I went through these ordeals and got off with nothing worse than a little fatigue.

I assure you that, with the exception of a few hours of black depression one night, when they removed the electric light bulbs from our cells, I have always been in great good spirits; the pawky humour which invariably lets me see the comic or grotesque side of everything was always uppermost and kept me in a merry mood in spite of everything. I've been doing a lot of reading (mostly illustrated reviews and sporting papers) and I've started to build up a library once again. I've drawn up the following programme:
1. to keep myself in good trim, so that my health will continue to improve.
2. to study German and Russian with method and continuity.

3. to study economics and history.

Between us we'll go in for some intellectual gymnastics, etc.

My dearest Tatiana, if I haven't written to you up till now you mustn't imagine even for a single instant that I've forgotten you or haven't been thinking of you. The expression you used is exact, because everything I received and in which I saw evidence of your dear handiwork was more than a greeting: it was a loving caress. I would rather like to have Marietta's address; maybe it would be nice to write to Nilde too – what do you think? Would she remember me, and be pleased if I sent her my greetings? The writing and receiving of letters has become for me one of the most intense pleasures of my life.

Dearest Tatiana, I have written a little confusedly. I am afraid that today (the 10th) the steamer won't be able to make the crossing, because a furious wind has been blowing all night and didn't let me sleep a wink – in spite of the unaccustomed softness of the bed and the pillows. It's a wind which blows through all the cracks in the windows and the balcony, and comes swooping under the doors with whistlings and trumpet blasts which are very picturesque but extremely irritating.

Write to Giulia and tell her that I am really quite all right from every point of view and that my stay here – which I don't think in any case will last as long as the decree orders – will probably clear up all my old bodily ailments. Maybe a period of absolute rest was actually a necessity for me.

My dearest, I embrace you tenderly – because with you I embrace all my dear ones.

Antonio

1. Published in Paris in 1901, with the title *L'homme qui voulut être roi* (The Man who Wanted to be King). *The Strange Ride* is a story about the legendary Indian village of the 'Dead who did not die'- i.e. the supposed corpses who recovered from a trance or catalepsy before being burnt on the ghât.
2. Bordiga.
3. Marietta (and Nilde who is mentioned later in this letter): friends of Tatiana Schucht who often visited Gramsci's lodgings in Rome.
4. A brand of tinned vegetables.

3

Ustica, 19 December 1926

Dearest Tania,

I wrote you a postcard on the 18th to let you know that I had received your registered letter of the 14th: before that I wrote you a long letter and addressed it care of Signora Passarge;[1] it should have been delivered on the 11th or the 12th. Here's a report on all the principal events up to now.

I was arrested on the 8th at 10.30 at night and taken straight to prison; I left Rome in the very early morning of 25 November.

The spell in Regina Coeli was the worst period of my imprisonment – sixteen days of absolute solitary confinement in my cell, and the most rigorous discipline. It was not till the last day or two that I managed to get a room 'on payment'. The first three days I spent in a cell which was fairly bright in the daytime and was lighted during the night; the bed however was pretty filthy – the sheets had already been used, and every conceivable kind of insect swarmed all over the place. I wasn't able to get anything to read, not even the *Sport Gazette*, because it hadn't been ordered; I ate the prison *minestra*, which was not at all bad. I was then transferred to a new cell, darker by day and unlit by night: the one good thing about it was that it had been disinfected with petrol fumes, and the bed had laundered linen on it. I started buying things from the prison canteen; candles for the night time, milk for the morning, *minestra* with meat broth and a piece of boiled meat, cheese, wine, apples, cigarettes, papers and illustrated reviews. I passed from the ordinary cell to the room 'on payment' without warning, which resulted in my spending an entire day without food. The reason turned out to be that the prison provides food only to prisoners in the ordinary cells; those in the rooms 'on payment' have to 'provide their own victuals' (prison term). The 'paid' room brought with it an extra woollen mattress and a pillow *idem* which were added to the horsehair palliasse; furthermore, the cell was furnished with a washstand, a basin and a jug; it also contained a chair. I should have had a small table as well, and also a clothes stand and a little cupboard, but the administration was short of 'barrack accessories' (another prison term). I also had electric light in the room, but there was no switch, and so the whole night long I kept twisting and turning from side to side to protect my eyes from the light.

This is how the day's routine went: reveille at 7 in the morning and cleaning of the cell; towards 9 o'clock milk, which became coffee and milk when I began to receive food from outside the prison. When the coffee reached me it was usually still lukewarm, but the milk was always stone cold. In any case, I broke bread and made an abundant soup out of both of them.

Between 9 o'clock and mid-day we had an hour's exercise: the hour might be from 9 to 10, from 10 to 11, or from 11 to mid-day. We were brought out one by one, and strictly forbidden to speak to anyone else or even to say a word of greeting; we were shepherded into a circular courtyard divided into segments, with very high walls between each, and a railing separating it from the rest of the courtyard. A guard posted on a small terrace which overlooked the spokes of this cartwheel kept us under surveillance; there was also a second guard who marched up and down in front of the gate. The whole courtyard was shut in by massive high walls, and on one side it was overlooked by the low chimney of a small prison workshop. Sometimes the air was all smoke; and once, just for a bit of variety, we had to stay out for about half-an-hour under a downpour of rain.

Around mid-day we got our dinner; the *minestra* was usually still lukewarm, but the rest of the meal was always cold. At 3 o'clock there was the inspection, which included the testing of the iron bars of the gratings. This inspection was repeated at 10 at night, and at 3 in the morning. I slept for a while between these two final inspections; but once, after I had been wakened up by the 3 o'clock visit, I didn't succeed in getting to sleep again. Even so I was obliged to stay in bed from 7.30 in the evening until dawn. The only distraction in this existence was provided by the different voices one heard, and the scraps of conversation which occasionally filtered through from the neighbouring cells, or cells across the corridor. I was lucky enough to escape extra punishment: Maffi, on the other hand, got three days of bread and water in a punishment cell. I really never felt out of sorts for a single instant; although I never managed to get through all the pasta, I always set to with a better appetite than in the days when I ate out in restaurants. As for utensils, I had nothing but a wooden spoon – I possessed neither fork nor tumbler. But I did have a jug, and an earthenware pot for water and wine; a big earthenware bowl for soup and another for use as a wash basin – this before I succeeded in getting a room 'on payment'.

On 19 November, I was informed of the decree which condemned me to five years' colonial exile. There was no other explanation of any sort. A day or two later the rumour reached me that I was to leave for Somaliland. It was not till the evening of the 24th that I learnt indirectly that I was to serve the sentence on an Italian island. Not till I got to Palermo was the exact destination disclosed to me; Ustica was a possibility, but so were Favignana, Pantellaria and Lampedusa. The Tremiti were out of the question, because to reach them I would have had to travel from Caserta to Foggia.

I left Rome on the morning of the 25th with the first Naples train; we got to Naples about 1 o'clock. I travelled together with Molinelli, Ferrari, Volpi and Picelli, all of whom, like myself, had been arrested on the 8th. At Caserta Ferrari was detached from the rest of us as he was bound for the Tremiti. I say 'detached', because even in the railway carriage we were linked together by a long chain. From Rome on I was always in company with the others; this caused an appreciable change for the better in my morale. We were able to chat and joke together in spite of the fact that we were a sort of chain gang with our wrists jammed into handcuffs, and that we had to eat and smoke in this elegant rigout. Even so, we managed to light matches, to eat and smoke; our wrists got a bit swollen, but one realised in one's own body how perfect the human machine is, how ably it can adapt itself to even the most unnatural circumstances. Within the limits of the rules and regulations, the *carabinieri* acting as escort treated us with great correctness and courtesy. We remained for two days at Naples, in the Carmine Prison, still together; then we continued our journey by sea on the evening of the 27th, on the calmest of calm seas. At Palermo we were given a very clean and airy room, the windows of which commanded a most beautiful panorama of Monte Pellegrino; we found other friends destined for the islands, the maximalist deputy Conca from Verona and the lawyer Angeloni, a Republican from Perugia. Others arrived later – among these Maffi, who was bound for Pantelleria, – and Bordiga, bound for Ustica.

I was due to leave Palermo on the 2nd, but we did not succeed in leaving it behind till the 7th. Three attempts to make the crossing failed because of the tempestuous seas. This was the most unpleasant stage of the journey. Just think: reveille at 4 in the morning, the formalities of handing over money and various valuables and other objects to be deposited; then, handcuffs on, a Black Maria to the harbour, the climb down to the boat which carried us to the steam-launch, then climbing up the ship's ladder to get on deck, and descent of another ladder to get down to the third-class compartment; all this wearing handcuffs, and linked by a chain to three others. At 7 o'clock the steamer leaves and for an hour it sails towards Ustica, pitching and rolling and gambolling about like a dolphin; then it turns back because the captain considers that the risk in continuing the journey is not justified. The whole series of ups and downs, etc. is gone through in reverse; we are sent back to our cells; meanwhile it is already mid-day, and there is no time to order a mid-day meal – we don't eat until 5 o'clock, and this after leaving in the morning without having a bit of food. This whole caper four times, with one day's interval.

Four friends had already arrived at Ustica: Conca, Sbaraglini, the ex-deputy from Perugia, and two from Aquila. For a few nights we all slept in one bedroom; now we have a house all to ourselves: there are six of us, myself, Bordiga, Conca, Sbaraglini, and the two from Aquila. The house consists of a room on the ground floor where two of us sleep: also on the ground floor there are the kitchen, the latrine, and a small closet which we have turned into a communal wash-house. On the first floor, four of us sleep in two rooms: three in a fairly big room and one in a little room off the corridor; above the bigger of the two rooms is a wide terrace which overlooks the beach. We pay a 100 lire a month for the house, and 2 lire a day for the bed, the bed laundry and the other domestic fittings (2 lire a head). The first few days we spent a lot on meals; not less than 20 lire a day. At present we spend 10 lire a day on mid-day meal and supper; we are in process of organising a communal mess, which will maybe allow us to live on the 10 lire a day which the government has allotted us; already we political prisoners number thirty, and there may well be more to come.

The rules which govern our daily life are varied and complex. The one which makes itself most felt is that which forbids us to leave the house before dawn and orders us to be back indoors at 8 in the evening. We are not allowed to go beyond certain fixed limits which broadly speaking are identical with the perimeter of the inhabited area. However we have already obtained permission to go for walks all over the island; with the obligation of returning 'inside limits' at 5 in the afternoon.

The island has about 1,600 inhabitants, of whom 600 are ordinary convicts – that is criminals. The people are Sicilians, very decent and hospitable. We are allowed to mix with the population.

The convicts are under a very strict regime. Because of the small size of the island the great majority are unable to find any job to do, and so they have to live on the 4 lire a day which the government allots them. You can imagine what happens: the *mazzetta* (which is the term used for the government allotment) is spent mostly on wine; meals are cut down to a little pasta with green vegetables and a little bread; malnutrition leads to the most depraved alcoholism in the shortest possible time. These convicts are shut up in special large sized rooms at 5 o'clock in the afternoon, and are together all night (from 5 in the afternoon till 7 in the morning) cut off from the world outside; they play cards, sometimes losing several days' *mazzetta* at one go, and soon they find themselves caught in an infernal vicious circle which spins downwards to infinity.

From this point of view it's a real shame that we are not allowed to have contacts with human beings reduced to such an exceptional existence; I think one would be able to do some really unique research in the realms of psychology and folklore. Everything elemental which survives in modern man comes irresistibly to the surface, once these shattered molecules have reformed into a particular pattern – a pattern which corresponds to the essential nature of the most submerged social strata.

There are four fundamental divisions: the Northerners, the Central Italians, the Southerners (including the Sicilians) and the Sardinians. The Sardinians hold themselves completely apart from the rest. The Northerners have a certain solidarity among themselves, but no organisation as far as I can see. They regard it as an honourable thing to have been a burglar, a pickpocket or a swindler, but they have never used the knife. Among the Central Italians, the Romans are the best organised; they denounce none of their own people – not even spies or stool pigeons – to those of the other regions, but keep them at arms length. The Southerners are organised to a marvellous degree, as far as one can make out, but among them there are subdivisions: the Neapolitan 'State', the Apulian 'State' and the Sicilian 'State'. For the Sicilians the point of honour consists in not having robbed, but having drawn blood with the knife.

The above information I obtained from a convict who was in Palermo Prison, doing a stretch for a crime committed while serving his other sentence: this fellow was very proud (cf. the above-mentioned catalogue) of having inflicted a wound to the depth of 10 centimetres – measured, according to him – on the boss who was treating him badly: it had been attested as a wound of 10 centimetres, and 10 centimetres it was, not a millimetre more or less. This was his masterpiece, and it filled him with intense pride ... Believe me, my reference to Kipling's short story was by no means exaggerated, even though it was suggested merely by the first day's impressions ... Dearest Tatiana, I embrace you affectionately.

Antonio

1. Gramsci's landlady in Rome.

4

Ustica, 8 January 1927

My darling Julca,

I have received your letters of the 20th and the 27th, and the postcard of the 28th, carrying Delio's signature. I have tried to write to you several times, but I could never manage to. From your letters I can see that Tania has explained the reason for this to you – it's rather a childish reason, I grant, but anyway it has been completely inhibiting up till now ... I had decided to write a kind of diary for you, a series of sketches giving you an idea of the whole of my life in this odd period, which is interesting enough in all conscience: this I shall certainly do. I want to try and give you all the materials so that you may be able to get a picture of my life in the round, together with all the most notable details. You should try and do the same for me. It would please me so much to know what sort of relationship is developing between Delio and Giuliano: how Delio conceives and expresses his position as elder brother, the one who has the most experience.

Darling Giulia, ask B.[1] what was the source of the report which reached him saying that I was not in a satisfactory state of health. The truth is I never suspected that I had such a reserve of physical energy as it now turns out that I possess. Neither I nor Bordiga have had anything wrong with us from the moment we were arrested; all the others in one way or another, have suffered from nervous crises – some of these very serious – which were all of the same nature. In Palermo Prison Molinelli fainted three times in the one night while asleep, and he fell into acute convulsions lasting for as much as 20 minutes: the whole of which time it was impossible to call for assistance. Here in Ustica an Abruzzese friend who sleeps in the same room as I do, woke up continually during the night; he was a prey to wild nightmares which made him howl and jump about in his bed in the most frightening manner. Myself, I haven't had even the slightest thing wrong with me – except that I can't sleep much; however this is no new thing as far as I am concerned, and anyway it can't have the same ill effects as before, considering the enforced idleness to which I am reduced.

Also, you must take into account the fact that the journey was all the more difficult and uncomfortable because the stormy seas three times prevented us from making the crossing to Ustica. I have become very proud of this quality of physical resistance which I never thought I possessed; it's for that reason I mentioned it. It's a valuable thing in my present situation, and certainly not the most contemptible of possessions.

I'll write again at much greater length, and give a minute description of my life here. You must write to me too (or get Genia[2] and your mother to write) describing the sort of life the children are leading, and your own life as well: you must be very busy and tired.

I feel that all of you are very close to me.

I embrace you tenderly.

Antonio

1. B. Vincenzo Bianco, a Turin worker who was a friend of Gramsci and his family. Bianco had emigrated to Moscow some time previously.
2. One of Giulia's sisters.

5

Ustica, 15 January 1927

Dearest Tania,

The last letter you sent me is dated the 4th January. That means you've left me eleven days without news. In my present condition that is a thing that worries me a great deal. I think it ought to be possible to come to some agreement about regular correspondence: you might make it a rule to send me at the very least a postcard every three days. I've already started to follow this system. When I haven't the material for an actual letter – and that, nowadays, is the usual state of affairs – I will at any rate send you a postcard, in order not to let any chance of communicating slip. Life drags on here, unchanging, uniform, with no relief to the monotony.

Maybe I should rough out some vignette of peasant life here – that is, if I am able to muster enough good humour. For example, I could describe the arrest of a pig which was found having an unlawful feed in the village street and was led off to prison like a common malefactor; the whole thing tickled me immensely, but I am sure that neither you nor Giulia would believe me if I told you about it; perhaps Delio will believe me when he is a few years older, and hears the story, along with others of the same sort (the one about the green spectacles for example) which are equally true, and also to be taken quite seriously. The way of arresting the pig was most amusing too; they got hold of it by its hind legs and pushed it forward like a wheelbarrow – the beast screaming the while like all the foul fiends. I haven't been able to get any precise information on how it was possible to identify this pig as the one which had committed the crimes in question. However, I suppose the guardians of public welfare know all the village livestock intimately.

Another detail which I have never mentioned to you is that I haven't in the whole island seen any means of locomotion whatsoever barring the donkey – which on Ustica is a really splendid animal, large sized and extremely tame: this last characteristic is a tribute to the kindliness of the inhabitants. In my village the donkeys are half-savage and don't allow anyone to come near them but their own master. While we are talking of animals: yesterday I heard a magnificent story about horses told by an Arab who is in exile here. The Arab's Italian was a bit odd in places, and often difficult to understand; but taken as a whole his story was full of colour and descriptive force. This reminds me, by a curious association of ideas, that I have learnt that it is quite possible to find the famous Saracen wheat in Italy:[1] Venetian friends tell me that it's common enough in the Veneto for the people to make *polenta* with it.

Well, I've now exhausted my stock of usable subjects. I hope I've made you laugh just a little; it seems to me that your long silence must be interpreted as the result of melancholy and tiredness, and that it was really necessary to make you smile. Dear Tania, you must write to me, because it's only from you that I receive letters: when there's no letter from you for such a long time I feel all the more isolated, I feel as if my connection with the outside world were broken off altogether.

I embrace you affectionately.

Antonio

1. i.e. buckwheat. Gramsci calls it 'famous', possibly because it is mentioned in Manzoni's novel *I Promessi Sposi*.

6

Ustica, 15 January 1927

My darling Julca,

I want to describe my daily life in its essentials, so that you may follow it, and be able to fill in some details every now and then. As you know, for Tania must have told you already, I am living together with four other friend, one being the engineer Bordiga from Naples, whose name you may possibly have heard. There are five of us, therefore, in the three bedrooms which make up the house; we have at our disposal a splendid terrace from which we can admire the boundless sea during the day, and a magnificent sky at night. The sky, which is quite free of the most distant hint of city smoke, increases our keen delight in all these marvels. The colours of the sea water and of the sky are truly extraordinary in their variety and depth: I have seen rainbows which are quite unique of their kind.

In the morning I am usually the first up; the engineer Bordiga says that at this particular time my step has a special distinctive quality: it's the step of a man who has not yet drunk his first cup of coffee, and who is looking forward to it with a certain impatience. I make the coffee myself – that is, if I haven't persuaded Bordiga to make it, in view of his well-known culinary aptitudes. I make the coffee myself. Then our life begins: we go to school, either as teachers or pupils. If it is 'post day', we go down to the shore and wait anxiously for the arrival of the steamer; if because of bad weather the post doesn't arrive, the day is ruined because a certain melancholy settles on every face. At mid-day we eat our dinner. I am a member of a communal mess, and it's my turn today to act as waiter and orderly: I don't yet know whether I've got to peel the potatoes, get the lentils ready or wash the salad before it is served up. My debut is awaited with great curiosity; several friends offered to act as substitute, but I was firm in my resolve to do my share. In the evening we have got to be back inside the house by 8 o'clock. Occasionally there are inspections to make sure we are actually back. Unlike the ordinary convicts, we are not locked in. Another difference lies in the fact that our right of free entry holds good up to 8 o'clock, not 5: furthermore, we might be able to get passes out for the evening if it should happen to be necessary for something or other. In the evening, back inside the house, we play cards. I've never played cards before; Bordiga assures me that I have it in me to become a dab hand at the game. I have already reassembled a miniature library, and it's possible for me to read and study. The books and newspapers that arrive for me here have been the cause of an amicable rumpus between me and Bordiga; he maintains – quite wrongly – that I am very disorganised, and he gets my things into a real mix-up, out of sheer mischief: the excuse being that they should be arranged symmetrically, with architectural precision! However, the truth is I can never manage to find anything in the frightful symmetrical mess he gets them into. Dearest Julca, write to me at length about your life and the children's life. As soon as possible please send me a photograph of Giuliano. Has his hair grown again? And has the illness left any ill effects behind it? Write a lot about Giuliano. Has Genia recovered?

I embrace you tightly – so tightly.

Antonio

7

Milan Prison, 19 February 1927

Dearest Tania,

It is now a month and ten days since I last heard from you: I haven't an earthly what the reason can be. When I wrote to you a week ago, just as I was about to leave Ustica, the boat had not called for around ten days: the steamer which took me back to Palermo could have brought at least a couple of your letters to Ustica, and these should by now have been redirected to Milan. But among the letters I have received since returning from the island there was nothing of yours. Dearest Tania, if the sin of omission is yours and not (as is possible and probable) the result of some hitch in the office work of the prison, you should be careful not to leave me in suspense for so long. In my present state of isolation, things which one doesn't expect and which don't fall into line with the normal routine of events lead to tormenting and agonising conjectures.

Your last two letters, which I received at Ustica, were really rather worrying; what are these 'preoccupations about my health' which are almost making you ill? I assure you that I have been keeping pretty well the whole time and what's more that I have stores of physical energy inside me which will not readily be exhausted, in spite of the surface appearance of weakness. Do you think that there's no virtue in the fact that I've always led a very sober and hard life? I now realise what it means never to have had a serious illness and never to have dealt my own body a major blow. It's true that I can get horribly tired, but a little rest and nourishment soon brings me back to normal. Indeed I don't know what to say in order to make you look at things with calm and serenity: must I have recourse to threats? I might always stop writing, you know, and let *you* feel what it means to have no news at all.

I imagine you serious and gloomy, without even a fugitive smile. I must try and brighten you up. What about my telling you a few stories? I'd like, for example (as an intermezzo in the description of this journey of mine through the world which seems so awesome and terrible) to tell you something really unusual about myself and my 'fame'. I'm not known outside a fairly restricted circle; because of this my name gets muddled up in all manner of unlikely ways: Gramasci, Granusci, Grámisci, Gránisci, Gramásci, even Garamáscon, with every bizarre intermediate stage you can think of. At Palermo, during a wait while the luggage was being checked, I met in a cloakroom a group of Turin workers bound for provincial exile; among their number was a formidable type of ultra-individualistic anarchist, known by the soubriquet *l'Unico*,[1] who refuses to give anyone, and least of all the police and the authorities in general the details of his name, date of birth, birthplace etc. 'I'm *l'Unico* – that's enough for you' is his reply.

Well, in the crowd which was waiting there *l'Unico* recognised a Sicilian friend of his among the ordinary criminals who were members of the Mafia. (*l'Unico* must be a Neapolitan, or from further south still.) Accordingly, we started introducing ourselves. I told the company my name: the other looked me up and down for a while and then he asked: 'Gramsci, Antonio?' 'Yes, Antonio,' I replied. 'That can't be right' – he declared – 'because Antonio Gramsci must be a giant of a man and not a little runt like you.' He said no more, but retired to a corner, sat down on an appliance I won't name and remained there brooding over his own lost illusions like Marius over the ruins of Carthage. He studiously avoided speaking to me during the rest of the time we remained in the same room, and did not say goodbye when we separated.

Another and rather similar episode occurred a little later; it is, I think, even more interesting and complex. We were just about to leave. The *carabinieri* of the escort had already put our handcuffs on and chained us together; I had been handcuffed in a new and very disagreeable manner, because the things were keeping my wrists in a stiff and painful position; my wrist bone was outside the bracelet and was rubbing against the iron most painfully. In came the commander of the escort, an enormous sergeant major: he read the muster roll, and when he got to my name, stopped short and asked if I was any relation of the 'famous deputy Gramsci'? I answered that I was the man; whereupon he gave me a look full of compassion, and murmured something incomprehensible. At every stop I heard him talking about me in the middle of the little groups which always form around the prison carriage, and he was always referring to me as 'the famous deputy'. (I should add that he had given orders for my handcuffs to be put on a bit more bearably.) He did this so often that, remembering the way the wind is blowing now, I was afraid that on top of everything I might get a beating up from some fanatic. After a certain time the sergeant major, who had been travelling in the second prison carriage, came through into the first, where I was, and started a conversation. He was an extraordinarily interesting and odd type; full of 'metaphysical longings', as Schopenhauer would say, but only capable of satisfying these in the most comical and disordered manner you can imagine. He told me that he had always imagined my body to be 'Cyclopean', and confessed that from this point of view he was very disillusioned. He was at that time reading a book by M. Mariani called *The Equilibrium of Egoisms*, and had just finished a book by a certain Paul Gilles which 'refuted Marxism'. I carefully omitted to inform him that this Gilles was a French anarchist without any scientific or other qualification whatsoever; it amused me to hear him talking with great enthusiasm about so many disparate and disconnected notions. He discussed things in the way you might expect from a self-educated man, intelligent but lacking in discipline and method. At a certain point he started calling me 'master'. This tickled me no end, as you can imagine. And in this way I experienced what it is to be 'famous'. What do you think of that?

I've almost finished the sheet. I wanted to give you a detailed description of my life here. I shall do it in the form of a timetable. I get up at 6.30 in the morning, half-an-hour before reveille. I make myself a good hot cup of coffee (here in Milan the 'Meta' fuel is permitted, very practical and useful stuff). Then I clean out the cell and the toilet. At 7.30 I receive half a litre of milk, which is still hot when it reaches me, and I drink that immediately. At 8 I take the air: that is, I go on exercise which lasts for two hours. I take a book with me, stroll around, read, smoke a cigarette or two. At mid-day I receive dinner from outside, and in the evening supper; I don't succeed in eating everything, although I eat more than I used to in Rome.

At 7 in the evening I go to bed and read until about 11. During the day I receive five daily papers: *Corriere, Stampa, Popolo d'Italia, Giornale D'Italia, Secolo*. I have two subscriptions for the library and am entitled to eight books a week. In addition I buy the odd review and also *Il Sole*, an economic and financial journal published in Milan. The result is I am always reading. I have already read *The Travels of Nansen*, and other books of which I will speak another time. I haven't suffered from any kind of disorder, apart from feeling the cold in the first few days. Write to me, dearest Tania, and send me news of Giulia, Delio, Giuliano, Genia and all the others: and your own news, your own news!

I embrace you,

Antonio

1. The 'Unique'.

8

Milan Prison, 26 February 1927

Dearest Tania,

For about one and a half months now I have had no news of yourself, of Giulia and of the children. I am sure though that you have written to me. I don't know what to make of the fact that your letters don't reach me. One explanation might lie in the fact that some letters have been addressed to me at the 'Military Prison', and that on the envelopes of these 'Not known' had been written in pencil. It's possible that some other letters may have gone astray for the same reason. But it doesn't seem to me possible that 'all' your letters should go astray, so I think that there must exist some mysterious order which prevents a part of my correspondence from reaching me. I am not even sure in any case that my own letters reach you. If they do, please remember this: if in your own letters there has been any reference, no matter how remote, to this regulation about my correspondence, please avoid the slightest reference to the matter, even the vaguest and most indirect reference, and restrict yourself entirely to family matters.

Dearest Tania, if this letter of mine reaches you, write to me at once and tell me how you are getting on, and about Giulia and the children; forget about the preceding letters which you have certainly sent me, and repeat all your news. This business is my only worry just now, and I can't tell you how much it's getting on my nerves.

Dearest Tania, I embrace you affectionately.

Antonio

9

Milan Prison, 19 March 1927

Dearest Tania,

This week I have received two postcards from you, one dated 9 March and the other the 11th. On the other hand, I have not received the letter which you mentioned. I thought I would receive those letters of yours which have been redirected from Ustica: in point of fact I did receive a package of books from the island, and the post clerk who gave me them told me that in the package there were closed letters and postcards as well which had still to pass through the censorship office. I hope to receive these in the next few days. Many thanks for the news you send me of Giulia and the children; I just can't manage to write to Giulia direct until I have received the letters from her; these too have been much delayed. I can imagine what her state of mind is like (quite apart from her physical condition) for a whole mass of reasons. The boy's illness must have caused her a great deal of anxiety. Poor Delio; from scarlet fever to influenza in such a short time!

Write yourself to grannie Lula[1] and tell her to write me a long letter in Italian or French, whichever comes easier (in any case she could send me a translation) and give me a really good and complete description of the lives of the children. I am quite convinced that grandmothers know better than mothers how to describe children and their ways in a real and concrete manner; they are more objective, and they have behind them the experience of an entire life cycle. It seems to me that the tenderness of grandmothers has more substance in it than that of mothers. (Giulia mustn't be offended and think me wickeder than I really am!)

I really don't know what to suggest to you as far as Giuliano's present is concerned; in this line of country I have already failed once before with Delio. Perhaps I'd be able to make something suitable if I were actually with him. Choose whatever you think is best, and send it to him in my name. In the last few days I've been making a papier mâché ball which is nearly dry; I think I shall be able to send it to Delio. However the snag is that I haven't as yet thought of a way of varnishing it, and without varnish it would easily fall to pieces the first time it got wet. My life here is one of unrelieved monotony. Even studying is much more difficult than one would think. I have received a few books and it's true that I read a great deal (more than a volume a day, not counting the newspapers) but it's not just that I mean: I am getting at something else. You see, I am haunted – and this, I think, is a phenomenon quite familiar among prisoners – by an idea: that it is necessary to do something *für ewig*,[2] this last being a complicated and difficult concept of Goethe which I remember much tormented our own Pascoli. In short, I want, according to a prearranged plan, to occupy myself intensively and systematically with some subject which will absorb me and provide a central channel for my inner life. Up to now I have thought of four subjects, and that in itself is an index of the fact that I have not succeeded yet in collecting my ideas. Here they are:

1. Research into the formation of an Italian public spirit in the last century: in other words, research into the nature of the Italian intellectuals, their origins, their groupings according to the cultural currents of the time, their diverse modes of thought etc. It's a subject full of possibilities, but which I would naturally only be able to sketch in broad outline, given the absolute impossibility of having at my disposal the immense mass of material which would be necessary. Do you remember my rapid and entirely superficial essay on Southern Italy and the importance of Benedetto Croce? Well, I'd like to amplify and develop the thesis which I sketched out then, from a 'disinterested' standpoint, *für ewig*.

2. A study of comparative linguistics! Nothing less! For what in the world could be more 'disinterested' and *für ewig* than that? It would, of course, only be a question of handling the methodological and purely theoretical side of the subject, which has never been dealt with exhaustively and systematically from the modern point of view of the neo-linguistic school as against the neo-grammatical school. (I'll give you gooseflesh, dear Tania, with this letter of mine!) One of the major intellectual 'regrets' of my life is the profound sorrow which I caused my dear Professor Bartoli of the University of Turin: this gentleman was convinced that I was the archangel destined to rout the 'neo-grammatical school' for good and all – because he, of the same generation as themselves and bound by millions of academic threads to this rabble of infamous men, did not wish, in his

pronouncements, to go beyond a certain limit fixed by convention and by the deference due to the ancient graveyard monuments of erudition.

3. A study of the plays of Pirandello and of the transformation in Italian theatrical taste which Pirandello represented and helped to determine. Do you know that it was I who, long before Adriano Tilgher, discovered and helped to popularise the plays of Pirandello? Between 1915 and 1920 I wrote enough on Pirandello to fill a volume of 200 pages, and at that time my observations were quite original and without precedent. Pirandello was either amiably tolerated or else openly derided.

4. An essay on ... serial stories in the newspapers, and popular taste in literature. The idea came to me while I was reading the notice on the death of Serafino Renzi, leading actor in a company of barnstormers (the equivalent in the theatre of the serial stories) and remembering the pleasure I had every time I went to hear him. For in fact the performance was a combined effort: the anxiety of the public, the emotions let loose, the intervention in the play of the working class audience, was certainly not the least interesting performance of the two.

What's your opinion about all this? At bottom, if you look carefully, there exists a certain homogeneity which binds these four subjects together: the creative spirit of the people, in its diverse phases and degrees of development, underpins each in equal measure. Write and tell me your impressions; I have great confidence in your good sense and in the validity of your judgements. Have I bored you? Do you know, writing is now my substitute for conversation; I really feel that I am speaking to you when I write; it's just that everything is reduced to a monologue, because your letters either don't arrive or don't correspond to the conversation already started. Write to me then, and at length; letters, as well as postcards; I shall write you a letter every Saturday (I am allowed to write two a week) and write myself out. I shall not take up the thread of narrative about my vicissitudes and I shan't continue my travel impressions, because I'm not sure if they interest you; to be sure they have a personal value for me, in so far as they are bound up with certain definite states of mind and certain definite sufferings; but to make them interesting to others it would perhaps be necessary to set them forth in literary form. You see, I've got to write without preparation, in the short time in which pen and ink pot are at my disposal.

I embrace you, my dear. As you love me, write to me.

Antonio

1. Delio's and Giuliano's name for their maternal grandmother.
2. For eternity.

10

Milan Prison, 23 March 1927

Dearest Teresina,

... Franco looks very lively and intelligent; I should imagine he'll be able to speak well by now. What language does he speak, though? I hope you will let him speak Sardinian, and not go on at him to speak 'properly'. I thought it was a big mistake not to let Edmea [his brother Gennaro's daughter] speak Sardinian freely when she was a little girl. It damaged her intellectual development, and put a straitjacket on her imagination. You musn't make the same mistake with your own children. Remember Sardinian isn't a dialect but a real language, although it can't boast of much of a literature. It's good that a child should learn more than one language, if that's possible. After all, the Italian you would teach him would be a poor, crippled speech,[1] consisting of nothing but those few words and phrases he got from you – a mere childish mixter-maxter. He wouldn't make contact with the world around him, and would finish up not with a language but with just a couple of jargons. An Italian jargon when he's 'talking proper' with you, and a Sardinian jargon, picked up in dribs and drabs, to use when talking to other children, or to people he meets on the square or in the street. I really do entreat you, from my heart, not to make the same mistake; allow your children to suck up all the 'Sardism' they want, and let them develop spontaneously in the natural environment they were born into. I assure you this won't be a stumbling block for their future development – quite the reverse.

Antonio

1. *una lingua povera, monca*: 'monco' means one-handed, maimed, defective, incomplete.

11

Milan Prison, 26 March 1927

Dearest Tania,

This week I have received neither cards nor letters from you. However, I have been given your letter of 17 January (together with Giulia's letter of the 10th) forwarded on from Ustica. Therefore, in a certain sense and up to a certain point, I am satisfied; I have seen Giulia's handwriting once again (but how little she writes, this bad girl, and how good she is at justifying herself by talking about the din the children are kicking up around her!). I have conscientiously got your own letter by heart. I began by finding a few mistakes in it (I study these little things, too, you know) and I got the impression that this letter of yours wasn't 'thought' in Italian, but was translated badly and in a hurry, which means that you were tired and felt ill and were thinking of me only by an indirect route; maybe when you wrote you had just received news of Giulia's and the children's influenza. Anyway, among these mistakes there was to be found an unpardonable confusion between St Anthony of Padua, whose day falls in the month of June, and that other St Anthony who is commonly surnamed 'of the pig'; the latter is my very own saint, because I was born on 22 January, and I am very attached to him for countless magical reasons.

Your letter made me think once again of my life on Ustica, which was certainly very different from your imaginings of it; perhaps at some future date I shall take up my narrative of the life of those days and round off the description I gave of it; today I don't want to, and I feel a bit tired. I asked for the grammar book and the Faust to be sent on from Ustica; the teaching method is good, but involves help from a teacher, at any rate at the beginner's stage. For my purposes though it's excellent, seeing I only want to revise my previous knowledge and get a bit of practice. Another thing I've had sent to me is Pushkin's *The Gentle Peasant Girl*[1] in the Polledro edition: text, interlinear and literary translation and notes. I get the text by heart; Pushkin's prose I judge to be very good, and for that reason I've got no fear of burdening my memory with stylistic barbarisms. This method of learning prose by heart I consider excellent from every point of view.

In the batch of stuff sent on from Ustica there was a letter from my sister Teresina; she encloses a photograph of her son Franco who was born a few months after Delio. I don't think there's any resemblance between the two; Delio, on the other hand, is very like Edmea.[2] Franco's hair is not curly, and from the photo I would say it's dark brown. Anyway Delio is undoubtedly the handsomer of the two. Franco's features are even now rather too strongly pronounced, and this makes it probable that as he grows older they will become rather hard, exaggeratedly so perhaps. In addition, the seriousness of his general expression is quite marked: there's a certain melancholy in his face which is not in the least childish and which gives one quite a lot to think about. Have you sent the boy's photograph to my mother, as you promised? It really would be a good thing to do; the poor woman has suffered a great deal because of my arrest, and I think she suffers all the more because in our villages it's difficult to understand that a man may be sent to prison without being a thief, a swindler or a murderer; she has been living in a condition of permanent alarm ever since the day war broke out (three of my brothers were at the front). She had then, and still uses, a phrase of her own: 'They'll slaughter my sons', which in Sardinian is more savagely expressive than in Italian: *faghere a pezza*.[3] '*Pezza*' is butcher's meat, whereas for human flesh the word is '*carre*'. I honestly don't know how to comfort her, and make her understand that I am in a fairly good condition and am not in danger in any of the ways she imagines. It's really very difficult, because she always suspects that one is trying to hide the truth from her and because she can't get her bearings in present day life. We have got to remember that she has never travelled, has never even been in Cagliari; I suspect that she considers many of our descriptions of life outside to be just so many beautiful fairy tales.

Dearest Tania, I can't manage to write to you properly today; once again they've given me a pen which scrapes the paper and makes me go in for what I can only describe as manual acrobatics.

I'm expecting your letters. I embrace you.

Antonio

1. 'Gentle' has the sense of 'Gently born', as in Allan Ramsay's *The Gentle Shepherd*.
2. Franco's cousin.
3. Make mince-meat out of.

12

Milan Prison, 4 April 1927

Dear, dear Tania,

Last week I received two of your postcards (of the 19th and 22nd March) and the letter dated the 26th. I'm terribly sorry to have caused you pain; I am afraid you didn't properly understand my state of mind, because I didn't express myself well – I'd hate it if there were any misunderstandings between us. Let me assure you that the thought never even crossed my mind that you could forget me, or lose your affection for me; certainly if such a thought had been present in my mind, even remotely, I would not have written to you at all. My character has always been like that and because of it, I've cut a number of old friendships short in the past. I would need to see you face to face in order to explain the reasons for the nervous trouble which overtook me after I had been without news of you for two whole months. I'll not even try to do it in a letter so that we shan't stumble into other misunderstandings, as painful as the first one.

Anyway that's all over now, and I don't want even to think about it. A few days ago I changed my cell and 'radius' (the prison is divided into radii) as you can see from the heading of this letter. I was originally in the thirteenth cell of the first radius; now I am in the twenty-second cell of the second radius. As far as the actual prison conditions are concerned, I seem to be better off. My life, however, drags on in just the same way as before. I'll describe it to you in detail; so that every day you'll be able to imagine what I'm doing.

The cell is about as big as a student's bed sitting room. At a rough estimate I would say that it's 10 feet by 15, and 12 feet in height. The window gives on to the courtyard where we take the air; it's not an ordinary window, of course, but a so-called *bocca di lupo*,[1] with the bars on the inside. All one can see from it is a stretch of sky, one can't look on to the courtyard, nor can one see anything to left or right. The position of this cell is not so good as that of the first one, which faced South-South-West (the sun put in an appearance at 10 o'clock and at 2 o'clock a band of sunlight at least 2 feet wide lay across the centre of the cell); in my present cell, which must face South-West-West, the sun doesn't show up until about 2 o'clock. It stays in the cell till quite late, but the band of sunlight is only 10 inches across. But in this season, the weather getting warmer, things will maybe get better. Another thing: the present cell is situated just over the prison workshop, and one can hear the throbbing of the machines; but I'll get used to that. The cell is very simple and very complicated all at once. I have a camp bed up against the wall with two mattresses, one woollen: the sheets are changed about once a fortnight. I have a small table, a sort of cupboard-cum-night-table, a mirror, a basin and an enamelled iron jug. I possess a number of aluminium articles; these I bought at the Rinascente,[2] which has organised a stall in the prison. I have a few of my own books; every week I get eight books from the prison library (double subscription).

In order to let you get an idea, here's this week's list, although I should say at once it's exceptional so far as the quality of the books is concerned:

1. Pietro Colletta, *History of the Kingdom of Naples* (excellent).
2. Alfieri's *Autobiography*.
3. Molière, *Selected Comedies*, translated by Signor Moretti (a ridiculous translation).
4. Carducci, two volumes of the *Complete Works* (very mediocre, among the worst of Carducci).
5. Arthur Levy, *Napoleon: an Intimate Study* (a curious book – it's a vindication of Napoleon as a moral being).
6. Gina Lombroso, *In South America* (very mediocre).
7. Harnach, *The Essence of Christianity*.
8. Virgilio Brocchi, *Destiny in the Hand*, a novel (enough to set the dogs howling).
9. Salvator Gotta, *La Donna Mia* (just as well she's his, because she's a shocking bore).

In the morning I get up at 6.30, at 7 the reveille sounds; coffee, *toilette*, clearing out of the cells; I get half a litre of milk and eat some bread with it; at about 8 o'clock we go on exercise, this lasts two hours. I stroll around, study German grammar, read *The Gentle Peasant Girl* of Pushkin and learn by heart about twenty lines of the text. I buy *Il Sole*, a newspaper of industry and commerce, and read the economic news (I've read all the annual reports of the limited companies). On Tuesday I buy 'The Children's *Corriere*', which amuses me; on Wednesday the 'Sunday *Corriere*'; on Friday the *Guerin Meschino*, an allegedly humorous weekly. After exercise, coffee; I receive three papers, *Corriere*, *Popolo d'Italia*, and *Secolo*. (These days *Secolo* comes out in the afternoon, and I shan't go on buying it, for it's no longer worth a damn.) The mid-day meal arrives at irregular hours, somewhere between 12 and 3; I warm up the *minestra* (which is either soup or *pasta asciutta*), eat a little bit of meat (if it's veal – I haven't succeeded as yet in eating beef), a bit of bread, a piece of cheese (I prefer it to fruit) and a quarter litre of wine. I read a book, walk up and down, reflect on all manner of things. At 4 or 4.30 I get two other papers, the *Stampa* and the *Giornale d'Italia*. At 7 I have supper (supper arrives at 6 o'clock); *minestra*, two raw eggs, a quarter litre of wine; I never manage to eat the cheese. At 7.30 the bell rings for silence; I go to bed and read books until 11 or 12. Starting two days ago I have been drinking a cup of camomile about 9 o'clock.

(To be continued in our next, because I want to tell you some other things.) I embrace you.

Antonio

1. lit: Wolf's mouth.
2. A big store rather like Woolworth's.

13

Milan Prison, 11 April 1927

Dearest Tania,

I have received your postcards of 31 March and 3 April. Many thanks for the news you send me. I am looking forward to your arrival in Milan, but I must confess I am not allowing myself to count on it too much.

I've decided that to continue the description of my present routine which I started in last week's letter would not be very agreeable. It will be better if every time I just write what comes into my head, without any prearranged plan. I should add that writing has become a physical torment to me because they give me horrible pens which scratch the paper and make me pay a maddening amount of attention to the mechanical side of writing. I thought that I'd be able to obtain the permanent use of a pen and had thought of writing the things I mentioned previously; however, I didn't obtain permission, and I don't care to press the matter. Because of this I can only write in the two-and-a-half or three hours in which the weekly correspondence is hurried through (two letters); naturally I can't make notes, which means that in reality I cannot study in an ordered manner and with profit. I read bits and pieces. Nevertheless the time passes very quickly – much more so than you would think. Five months have gone by since the day of my arrest (8 November), and two months since the day of my arrival in Milan. It doesn't seem true that so much time should have gone by. However one must bear in mind the fact that in these last five months I have been pushed around from pillar to post; and I have had the strangest and most exceptional experiences of my life.

Rome: 8 to 25 November: absolute and rigorous solitary confinement. 25 to 29 November: Naples, in company with my four comrade deputies (three, rather, not four, because one was detached from us at Caserta, and sent to the Tremiti) embarkation for Palermo, and arrival at Palermo on the 30th. Eight days at Palermo: three trips in the direction of Ustica, rendered fruitless by the stormy weather. First contact with the Sicilians, arrested for activity in the Mafia: a new world which before I only knew intellectually. I check and verify my opinions on this subject, and find them on the whole fairly exact. On 7 December arrival at Ustica. I am introduced to the world of the convicts: fantastic and incredible things. I get to know the colony of Bedouins from Cyrenaica, also political exiles: a very interesting Oriental picture. The life of Ustica. 20 January: I leave the island. Four days at Palermo. The crossing to Naples with ordinary convicts. Naples: get to know a whole series of types of the greatest interest – especially for me, because of the Southern Italian Provinces I knew only Sardinia at first hand. At Naples, among other things, I am present at an initiation ceremony of the *camorra*: I make the acquaintance of a convict (a certain Arturo) who leaves an indelible impression on me. Four days later I leave Naples; a halt at Cajanello, in the barracks of the *carabinieri*; I get to know my new chain gang comrades, who are to accompany me as far as Bologna. Two days at Isernia, together with these characters. Two days at Sulmona. One night at Castellamare of the Abruzzi, in the barracks of the *carabinieri*. Two further days, together with about sixty prisoners. Entertainments are organised in my honour; the Romans improvise a marvellous evening of recitations, the poems of Pascarella[1] and popular sketches of the life of the Roman underworld. Apulians, Calabrians and Sicilians organise an evening's entertainment of knife duelling, according to the rules of the four 'States' of the Southern Italian criminal world (the Sicilian, the Calabrian, the Apulian and the Neapolitan); Sicilians against Apulians, Apulians against Calabrians. No matches are arranged between the Sicilians and the Calabrians, because the hate between the two States is tremendous, and if they fought together even an entertainment might turn into bitter and bloody earnest.

The Apulians are the masters of this art: invincible with the knife, they possess a technique full of secrets and absolutely deadly. It has been developed with an eye to meeting and overcoming all the other techniques. An old Apulian of sixty-five, very respected but without official 'rank' in his own State, discomfits all the champions of the other States, and then (as *clou*) fences with another Apulian – this latter a young lad, of magnificent physique and amazing agility, who ranks high in the Apulian hierarchy and exacts obedience from all. For half-an-hour these two give a display of the art of fencing with the knife, together with every known variation. It is a really grandiose and unforgettable scene for all of us, for actors and spectators alike: and it revealed to me a whole subterranean world, immensely complicated, with its own authentic life and its own sentiments, points of view and points of honour. Also with its own cast-iron hierarchies ... The arms used were quite simple: spoons scraped against the wall, so that hits appeared on the duellists' clothes as white chalk marks.

After all this, two days at Bologna with fresh scenes of interest: then Milan. Certainly these last five months have been crowded with incident, and have left me with enough varied impressions to chew over for a year or two.

Now I'll explain to you how I pass the time when I'm not reading.

I think over all these things, analyse them minutely and get drunk on this Byzantine lucubration. Moreover everything which happens around me and which I succeed in taking in becomes of surpassing interest to me. To be sure I'm keeping an untiring watch over myself, because I don't want to fall into the monomanias which characterise the psychology of prisoners. I am helped in this by a certain ironic spirit, a certain fund of humour which never deserts me ... And you – what are you doing, and what are you thinking about? Who buys adventure stories for you now that I'm not there? I'm sure you must have reread the admirable tale about Corcoran and his good-tempered Lisotta.[2] Are you going this year to the lessons at the Policlinico? Professor Caronia – is he the same man who discovered the measles bacillus?

I have been reading about his misfortunes, but I didn't succeed in gathering from the papers whether or not Professor Cirincione has been suspended as well. This whole affair is bound up, at least in part, with the problem of the Sicilian Mafia. It's incredible how the Sicilians, from the highest to the lowest, maintain a solidarity amongst themselves; and how even scientists of undeniable standing skate along the edges of the Penal Code because of this sentiment of solidarity. I am convinced that in reality the Sicilians form a community quite on their own; there is more resemblance between a Calabrian and a Piedmontese than between a Calabrian and a Sicilian. The accusations which the Southerners in general level against the Sicilians are terrible: they even accuse them of cannibalism. I would never have believed that such feelings among the people could exist. I think it would be necessary to read many books on the history of the last few centuries, and especially on the period when Sicily was divided from the rest of the South during the reigns of Joseph Bonaparte and Joachim Murat at Naples, in order to find the origin of these feelings.

... Here's another exceedingly interesting subject for analysis: the Prison Regulations, and the psychology which develops among the prison staff – a psychology deriving from the Regulations on the one hand and from the contacts between warders and prisoners on the other. I used to think that two masterpieces (I mean this quite seriously) concentrated between their covers the thousand-year old experience of man in the field of mass organisation: the Corporal's Manual[3] and the Catholic Catechism. I now see that one must add to these the Prison Regulations – even though the latter operate in a much more limited field, a field furthermore of quite exceptional character – because they contain real treasures of psychological introspection.

I am waiting for Giulia's letters: I think that after I've read them I shall be able to write to her directly. Please don't think that I'm just being childish.

An important piece of news: for a few days now I've been eating a good deal; however I still can't manage to eat greens. I've honestly made an effort to do this but have given it up because it revolts me horribly.

I haven't forgotten that maybe you'll come, and that maybe (alas!) we'll be able to see each other once again, even if it's only for a few minutes. I embrace you.

Antonio

1. Roman dialect poet.
2. Assollant, 'The Adventuress of Captain Corcoran' – an adventure story for boys. Lisotta is a tigress, the Captain's inseparable companion.
3. The manual corresponding roughly to the British *Infantry Section Leading*.

14

Milan Prison, 25 April 1927

Dearest Tania,

I've received your letter of the 12th, and I have decided, coldly and cynically, to make you angry. Do you know that you're a presumptuous woman? I undertake to demonstrate this objectively, and am already having a lot of fun imagining your wrath (don't get too annoyed though; I wouldn't like that).

The letter you sent me when I was on Ustica was all wrong, that's certain: still you can't be held responsible for that. It's impossible to comprehend the life of Ustica and the whole environment of Ustica because it's absolutely exceptional, and clean outside every normal experience of human society. How could you possibly have imagined things like the following? Just listen. I got to Ustica on 7 December, in the first boat to reach it after eight days of storm; that is, after four attempted crossings. I was the fifth political prisoner to arrive. As soon as I got there I was warned to lay in some cigarettes, because the stock was almost exhausted; I went to the tobacconists and asked for ten packets of Macedonia (16 lire), putting on the counter a 50 lire note. The woman behind the counter (a young lass who seemed absolutely normal) was thunderstruck at my request and asked me to repeat it; she took the ten packets, opened them, started to count the cigarettes one by one, lost count, started again, took a sheet of paper, did long sums with a pencil, interrupted this mental labour, took the 50 lire note, looked at it from every angle; finally she asked me who I was. Hearing that I was a political prisoner, she gave me the cigarettes and handed back the 50 lire, explaining that I could pay when I had changed the note. The same story was repeated everywhere I went, and this is the explanation: Ustica knows one economy only, that of the *soldo*:[1] everything is sold in *soldi*: one never spends more than 50 centesimi. The 'economic man' of Ustica is the convict who gets 4 lire a day; he will already have pledged two of these to the money lender or the wine merchant, and he supports himself on the other two, buying five or six ounces of bread and one *soldo's* worth of ground pepper to sprinkle on it as condiment. Cigarettes are sold one at a time: a Macedonia costs 16 *centesimi*, that is three *soldi* and a *centesimo*; the convict who buys a Macedonia a day leaves one soldo as deposit and the extra *centisimo* comes out of this for five days. In order to calculate the price of a 100 Macedonia, therefore, it was necessary to multiply 16 *centesimi* (or rather three *soldi* plus a *centesimo*) by 100, and no-one can deny that this is quite a difficult and complicated sum. And this was the tobacconist's shop, that is one of the biggest businesses on the island. Well then: the dominant psychology in the whole island is that which has as its basis the economy of the *soldo*, the economy which knows only the addition and subtraction of single units, an economy without the multiplication table.

And now listen to this (I am telling you only of things which have happened to me personally, and only of things which I don't think are likely to be censored). I was summoned to the office by that member of the staff who is charged with censoring the incoming post; he gave me a letter addressed to me, and asked me to explain its content. A friend had written to me from Milan, offering to present me with a wireless set and asking me for technical data; he intended to select one on which I would at least be able to get Rome. To tell you the truth, I didn't understand what the people in the office were getting at, and asked what it was all about; they thought my aim was to try and speak to Rome, and refused permission to send for the set. Later on the *podestà*[2] called me in front of him separately, and told me that the municipality would buy the set on its own account, and therefore that I shouldn't insist; the *podestà* was in favour of my being granted permission, because he had been in Palermo and had seen for himself that it was not possible to send messages with an ordinary wireless set.

... Dear Tania, don't get too angry; I'm very, very fond of you and I'd be terribly sorry if I were responsible for your getting into a real rage. I embrace you.

Antonio

1. A coin worth 1/20th of a lira (5 centesimi).
2. Mayor.

15

Milan Prison, 2 May 1927

Darling Julia,

I think it will probably be better for our correspondence in the long run if I don't keep the promise I made to describe at least the positive aspects of my adventures. I'm really sorry to have to give up this idea, because I've got a horror of being reduced to conventional letter writing, or what's worse, to conventional prison letter writing. I would have been able to tell you such a lot of little stories! Did Tania pass on to you a story about the arrest of a pig? Maybe not, because Tania didn't believe it herself; she thought it was a pure invention on my part to keep her in good spirits and make her laugh. In any case, I don't think you will take these stories (green spectacles, and so on) very seriously; but the beauty of them is that they are true (really true). But then you didn't want to believe that story either about the aeroplanes which catch birds by means of glue, or Loria's account of it,[1] even though the review with Loria's article was there to prove it.

How can I get across to you the way in which I'm living and thinking these days? A big part of my present experience you can imagine for yourself; for example, that I'm often thinking of you and of everyone at home. And as to the way I have to live in the physical sense, you can also imagine that for yourself quite easily. I read a great deal; in the last three months I have read eighty-two books from the prison library, including the most bizarre and extravagant sort (the possibility of choice is practically non-existent): in addition, I have a certain number of books of my own, a little more homogeneous, which I read with greater attention and method. Apart from this I read five newspapers a day and a few reviews. Furthermore I am also studying German and Russian ... but, to tell you the truth I've realised that, contrary to what I had always thought, it's impossible to study well in prison, for a great number of reasons, technical and psychological.

Last week I received your letter of 15 March. I wait for your letters with great anticipation, and am very happy when I get them. I wish you could find time to give me a special description of your own life and Delio's. But I realise how busy you must always be. There are so many things that I would like to be told.

Do you know this: when I received the letter in which you refer to the famous Atlas, I had only a few days before returned *Guerin Meschino* to the library. This is a very popular Italian romance of the days when knights were bold; it is much read, especially by the peasants of the south. I would have liked to transcribe a few of the more diverting geographical descriptions contained in it (Sicily, for example, is packed off to the Polar regions) to reassure you that at least one person has existed on the earth who knew less of geography than you do. Not to speak of history – because in that case one would have to quote the above-mentioned Loria, who once during a conversation gave one to understand that he believed Venice was already in existence in the days of Julius Caesar, and that the 'sweet dialect of the Lagoon' was already spoken there (the only evidence for which being his own impudence and his fertile imagination).

My dear, I'll try and write as much as I possibly can about things which I think won't hold up the letter: you must do the same, and write nothing but trivialities of this sort. I embrace you strongly, ever so strongly.

Antonio

1. Gramsci is alluding here to an article by Achille Loria called 'The Social Effects of Aviation (Truth and Fantasy)' published in *Rassegna Contemporanea*, 1 January 1910. In this article Loria expounds the theory of the emancipation of the working class from wage slavery by means of aeroplanes covered in glue. According to him, the squadrons of birds stuck to the sides would provide food for all.

16

Milan Prison, 23 May 1927

Dearest Tania,

Last week I received a postcard from you, and one of your letters, together with Giulia's letter. I want to reassure you on the score of my health; I'm really quite well, and I mean that. This last week I've been surprised at the appetite I've had for my food; I manage to arrange that nearly all the food sent into me should be the sort of thing I like, and it's my belief I've actually got fatter. In addition, for some time now I've been dedicating a little time every day, morning and afternoon, to gymnastics: indoor gymnastics, which I don't think have much to recommend them, but which are doing me a lot of good – or such, anyway, is my impression. This is what I do: I try to carry out movements which will bring into play every limb and every muscle, in a definite order: every week I try to increase the number of movements by a new group. That this is useful is borne out, in my opinion, by the fact that on the first few days I felt sore all over my body and I wasn't able to carry out a certain movement more than a very few times; by now, however, I've succeeded in trebling the number of movements without feeling the least ill effect. I think that this innovation has been of great help to me, psychologically as well as physically, because it has served to coax me away from a lot of futile reading which I was doing with the sole aim of killing time.

You mustn't go thinking that I'm studying too long, either. Study in the full and proper sense of the word is, I think, impossible for various reasons – not only psychological but technical as well. It is very difficult for me to sink myself completely into a subject or a theme and go really deep into it, the way you have to when you study seriously, assembling all possible elements bearing upon the subject and relating them harmoniously the one to the other. Maybe something positive in this sense is beginning to emerge from my study of languages, which I am trying to carry through systematically, that is not overlooking any specific point of grammar. I never used to do this in the past, for I contented myself with knowing only what was necessary for speaking and especially for reading. For this reason I have not asked you up till now to send me any dictionary; Kohler's German dictionary which you sent me when I was on Ustica has been lost for me by my friends down there; I'll ask you to send me the other dictionary, that Langenscheid method, when I have studied all the grammar. At the same time I'll ask you to send me Goethe's Gespräche with Eckermann, which I intend to use more as a manual of style than as reading matter. At the moment I am reading the *Tales of the Brothers Grimm* which are absolutely elementary.

I have come to a definite decision to make the study of languages my main occupation; after German and Russian I am going to take up English, Spanish and Portuguese once again. These are all languages which I have played around with in the last few years; now I shall study them systematically. And Rumanian too, which I studied at the University but only in connection with the Romance part of its vocabulary; I now contemplate studying it in its entirety: that is, taking in the Slav part (which accounts for more than 50 per cent of the Rumanian vocabulary) ... As you can see, all this demonstrates that I am perfectly calm, in the psychological sense as well as in every other; in fact I no longer suffer from nervous tension and no longer succumb to bouts of dull rage, as in the earlier period. I am acclimatized, and time passes at a fair speed; I measure it in weeks, not in days, and Monday is the point of reference – because on that day I write and have a shave, two operations which are eminently topical.

... I wanted to get all this down on paper, because it seems to me that the best way of giving yourself and Giulia at least an approximate idea of my life here, and of the normal course of my thoughts. Above all, you mustn't think that I'm completely solitary and isolated; every day, in one way or another there's some activity. In the morning there's exercise: when I manage to get a good position in one of the small courtyards, I watch the faces of the other prisoners as they go past. Then those newspapers arrive which are permitted reading for all the prisoners. When I am back in my own cell they bring me the political papers which have been authorised in my case. Then comes the time for ordering the supplies, after which the things ordered the previous day are delivered. Then lunchtime. And so on, and so on. In short we are always seeing new faces, each of which conceals a personality to guess at ... By the way, if I gave up reading the political newspapers, I might be able to pass four or five hours a day in the company of other prisoners. I gave a certain amount of thought to this, but finally I decided to remain on my own, and go on with reading the papers; an occasional hour spent in company would keep me amused for a couple of days, possibly even for a few weeks, but then, in all probability, I wouldn't succeed in getting back again to reading the papers. What do you feel about this dilemma? Maybe company, in and for itself, would seem to you a psychological advantage which should be given precedence. Tania, you as a doctor must give me a real professional opinion, because it's possible that I'm not in a position to judge such matters with all the objectivity which is required.

This, then, is the general structure of my life and of my thoughts. I don't want to speak about my thoughts in so far as they are directed towards all of you, and towards the children; that part you must imagine for yourself, and I'm quite sure you can.

Dear Tania, in your postcard you say once again that you may come to Milan and that we might possibly be able to see each other again and have a talk. Is it really true this time? Do you know that I haven't seen any one of the family for more than six months now? This time I'm expecting you in good earnest.

Kisses,

Antonio

17

Milan Prison, 4 July 1927

Dear Berti,

I have received your letter dated 20 June. Thank you for writing to me. I don't know whether Ventura has received the numerous letters I sent to him, because I have received no letters from Ustica for a good while. At present I am going through a period of moral fatigue, because of certain family matters. My nerves are on edge, and I'm very touchy; I can't succeed in concentrating on any subject, even an interesting subject such as the one you bring up in your letter. Apart from this I have lost all contact with your environment, and I have no idea what sort of transformations have been going on in the exile community.

One of the most important activities, in my opinion, for the teaching body[1] to embark on would be that of registering, developing and coordinating their own experiences and observations; only if this work is continued uninterruptedly can there arise the type of school and the type of teacher which the environment requires. What a fine book could be made out of these experiences, and how useful it would be! My views being along these lines, it's difficult for me to give you advice and even more to 'pour out', as you express it, a series of 'brilliant' ideas. I think that 'brilliance' had better be ditched; what is needed is method, combining the most detailed study of experience, and the most dispassionate and objective self-criticism.

Dear Berti, don't think I want to discourage you or to increase the confusion in which – according to your letter – you now find yourself. I would say, looking at the thing in broad outline, that the school should be divided into three grades (these being the basic divisions; every grade could be subdivided into courses); the third grade would include the teachers and those students of equal standing with them. It should function rather as a study circle than as a school in the ordinary sense. Every member, that is, should be in duty bound to contribute his share as teacher or lecturer on certain specific subjects, scientific, historical or philosophical – or (most important) on the art of teaching itself. As far as the course on philosophy is concerned I think – still tackling the thing in broad outline – that the historical explanation should be in the form of a résumé, and that the main effort should be devoted to one concrete philosophical system, the Hegelian; this you should analyse thoroughly, criticising it in all its aspects. I would be inclined to institute a course in logic, getting right down to *barbara, baralipton*[2] etc., and a course on dialectics. But we can talk of all this again, if you send me another letter.

Dear Berti, give all our friends my best wishes, and take for yourself my cordial greeting.

Yours,

Antonio

1. The political exiles on Ustica had organised courses in general and political culture. The teachers were selected from among the exiles themselves.
2. Terms of scholastic logic.

18

Milan Prison, 8 August 1927

Dearest Tania,

I have received your letter of 28 July, and Giulia's letter. I had received no letters after 11 July and I was terribly anxious; so much so that I did something which you will think properly foolish: I don't want to tell you now what it is though – I'll tell you when you come to visit me.

I'm really sorry that you feel in a state of moral fatigue. And all the more sorry because I'm convinced I helped to bring it on. Dear Tania, I'm always dreadfully afraid that you are not keeping as well as you make out in your letters, and that perhaps you may get into a serious condition, all on my account. This state of mind is part of my make up, and there's just nothing to be done about it. It is deeply rooted in my nature. Do you know this, that in the past I've always acted the part of a bear with a sore head just because of this part of my character: I hated the thought of someone else being saddled with any of my own misfortunes. I tried to make even my own family forget me, writing home as little as possible.

Enough of this. I'd like to write something that might at any rate make you smile. I'll tell you the story of my sparrows. You must know then that I have a sparrow, and that I had another who is dead – poisoned (I imagine) by some insect, a cockroach or a centipede. The first sparrow was a much more likeable type than the second. He was very proud, and very lively. The one I have now is exceptionally timid; his nature is servile and he lacks initiative. The first one immediately became master of the cell. I think he had an eminently Goethean spirit, to use an expression I've read in a biography (about the subject of the biography). *Über allen Gipfeln!*[1] He conquered all the summits to be found in the cell, and he would sit on them for minutes at a time drinking in their sublime peace. It was his constant ambition to climb up on to the cork of a bottle of syrup; because of this urge he once fell into a jug full of the leftovers from the coffee pot, and came very near to drowning.

What pleased me about this sparrow was that he did not like being touched. He would protest fiercely, his wings outspread, and peck my hand with great energy. He was tame, but he did not permit too many familiarities. The curious thing was that his relative friendliness was not an affair of gradual growth, but came on all of a sudden. In the early days he fluttered about the cell, but always in the opposite corner to the one I was in. To coax him nearer I offered him a fly in a match box; he would only take it when I was at a distance. On one occasion I had not one, but five or six flies in the box; before eating them he danced round them like a Dervish for a few seconds. This dance was repeated every time there were a number of flies inside the box. One morning, when I returned from exercise I found the sparrow had settled quite near me. He did not beat a retreat; from then on he always stayed near me, from time to time coming up to peck my shoes, in the hope of being given something. But he never allowed himself to be picked up without at once rebelling and trying to escape. He died a slow death: one evening he received an accidental blow while he was tucked away under the table. He gave a scream just like a child, but didn't die until the following day; he was paralysed on the right side and dragged himself painfully around to get the bread and water I put out for him. Then suddenly he died.

The sparrow I have now, on the other hand, is nauseatingly tame; he wants to be spoon-fed, even though he can eat by himself perfectly well. He climbs on to my boots, and gets into the turn-ups of my trousers. If he had a serviceable pair of wings he would fly on to my knees – you can see he wants to do it because he stretches and quivers, and then comes to rest on my boots. I'm afraid he'll die too, because he has a habit of eating the burnt heads of matches; in any case, a diet consisting exclusively of soft bread is bound to do for these little birds in no time.

For the moment he's healthy enough, but he's not lively; he doesn't run around, but stays near me all the time.

Already I've given him one or two involuntary kicks.

And that is the story of my sparrows ...

Antonio

1. Over every peak: first line of one of Goethe's poems.

19

Milan Prison, 8 August 1927

My Dear Berti,

I've received your letter of 15 July. I assure you that my health is no worse than in the past few years; indeed I think it's a trifle better. Besides

I'm not doing any work; you can't call reading work when it's purely and simply reading for pleasure. I read a great deal, but unsystematically. I receive a few books from outside, and I read the books from the prison library week after week, taking whatever I get from the farthing dip.

I have the capacity, a happy one under the circumstances, of seeing the interesting side even of the lowest products of the intellect – such as serial stories for example. If I had the opportunity, I would accumulate hundreds of thousands of notes on certain aspects of mass psychology. For example: what was the origin of the 'Russian steamroller' myth in 1914? In these novels you find hundreds of revealing things which go to explain such questions: this means that there existed a whole ramification of superstitions and fears deeply rooted in the broad masses of the people in all countries: and that in 1914 the governments were using these to initiate what could be called their campaigns for nationalistic agitation.[1] Along the same lines you will find hundreds of small points which illuminate the hatred of the French people for England; these are bound up with the peasant tradition of the Hundred Years War, with the burning of Joan of Arc and then in modern times with the Revolutionary Wars and Napoleon's exile. They say that after the Restoration the French peasants believed Napoleon to have been a descendant of Joan of Arc; don't you think now that that's really exceedingly interesting?

As you can see, I'm reduced to rooting around among the farm-middens. But every now and again some interesting book falls into my hands. At the present moment I am reading *L'Eglise et la Bourgeoisie*, which is the first volume (300 pages in 8 volumes) of a work by a certain Groethuysen called *Origines de l'Esprit Bourgeois en France*. The author, whose name is new to me, but who must be a follower of the sociological school of Paulhan, has had the patience to subject to a thorough analysis the collections of sermons and works of devotion which appeared before 1789: this with a view to reconstructing the attitude, the beliefs and the ideas of the new ruling class then in process of formation.

On the other hand, Henri Massis's much puffed book *Défense de l'Occident* was a great intellectual let-down: I think that Filippo Crispolti or Egilberto Martiri would have written a better book if either of them had taken it into his head to tackle the subject. What makes me laugh is the fact that this egregious Massis, who is consumed by a mortal fear lest the Asiatic idealogy of Tagore and Gandhi destroy French Catholic rationalism, doesn't realise that Paris is in a fair way to becoming a colony of the Senegalese intelligentsia, and that in France the number of half-castes is multiplying. It would be a great joke to make out in reply to his arguments that if Germany is the advanced outpost of Asiatic ideologies, then France is the threshold of darkest Africa, and the jazz band the first harbinger of a new Eurafrican civilisation!

Many thanks for trying to provide the pages missing in my copy of

Rosselli's book.[2] Have you read it? I don't know Rosselli, but I'd like to tell him that I do not understand what place all this acrimony has in an historical work. That is a general comment. In particular: the initial thesis of his book seems to me dramatic to the point of histrionics (naturally the *Giornale d'Italia* reviewer got hold of this point and played it up with the maximum vulgarity). Furthermore, Rosselli does not even mention that the famous meeting of 1864 in favour of Polish independence had been advocated for several years by the Neapolitan societies, and was convened as a result of an explicit letter from a Neapolitan Society. It seems to me a point of first importance. In Rosselli one finds what, for him, must be regarded as a strange intellectual deformation. The moderates of the Risorgimento – the same men who had sent an address of homage to Francis Joseph just after the events of Milan in February 1853 and a few days before the hanging of Tito Speri – at a certain moment, especially after 1860 but even more after the events of Paris in '71 these gentry got hold of Mazzini and made a defence-work out of him, even against Garibaldi (see Tullio Martello, for example in his *History*). This tendency has persisted right up to the present day and is now represented by Luzio.

But why by Rosselli too? I used to think that the younger generation of historians had liberated itself from these diatribes, and from the acrimony which accompanies them; I imagined that we had substituted historical criticism for *Gesta Dei*.

Apart from this fault Rosselli's book does in fact 'fill a gap'.

I embrace you.

Antonio

1. According to Caprioglio and Fubini, the last part of this sentence (from 'were using these to initiate ... agitation') was 'deleted' by the censor, but the words were still legible.
2. Nello Rosselli, *Mazzini and Bakunin*.

20

Milan Prison, 10 October 1927

Dearest Tania,

After our talk on Thursday I did a great deal of thinking, and I have decided to write and tell you what I didn't have the courage to tell you personally. I think that it would be wrong for you to stop in Milan any longer for my sake. The sacrifice you are making is disproportionate. You will never win your way back to health in this wet climate. For me it's certainly a great comfort to see you; but how can I help remembering continually how pale and ill you look – how can I help feeling remorse, seeing that I am the cause and the object of this sacrifice of yours.

I believe I have guessed the chief motive which impels you to remain here: you think that you'll be able to leave in the same train in which they take me away, and maybe manage to provide some small extra comfort for me. Have I guessed right? Well then: there's really no hope of this idea becoming practical politics. The arrangements for the journey will undoubtedly be very severe, and the escort will never think even for a single instant of allowing 'Christians' to have any dealings with the prisoners. (I should explain, in parenthesis, that convicts and political prisoners divide the public into two categories: 'Christians', and prisoners.) What you propose would be useless and maybe even harmful, because it might end up by making the authorities suspicious; which would mean increased harshness and severity. You would yourself make the journey in the worst conditions, and would be laid up in Rome for another four months; on top of which you would achieve nothing.

Dearest Tania, I think that one needs to be practical and realistic even in kindness. Not that you're wasting your kindness; you are wasting your strength and your energies, and I can't go on allowing that. I have really been thinking for quite a time about this, and would have liked to tell you personally. However, I couldn't summon up the courage when I saw you, for I realised that what I was going to say might cause you more pain.

My dear, I embrace you tenderly.

Antonio

21

Milan Prison, 17 October 1927

Dearest Tania,

The day before yesterday I received your letter of 27 September. I am glad you like Milan, and that you are managing to keep yourself amused in it. Have you visited the museums and art galleries? Because as far as the buildings and streets are concerned, I should think one's interest would tend to evaporate fairly quickly. The fundamental difference between Rome and Milan seems to me to lie in this: that while Rome is inexhaustible as an urban 'panorama', Milan is inexhaustible *chez soi* – the interesting thing about it is the intimate life of the Milanese who are more tightly bound to tradition than is often thought. It is for this reason that Milan is so little known to the usual run of tourists; on the other hand it has always captured the allegiance of men like Stendhal who were able to gain entry into its families and drawing rooms, and so got to know it intimately.

Its most consistent social nucleus is the aristocracy which has managed to maintain a homogeneous unity quite unique in Italy; all the other social groups, including the working class, are in comparison nothing but a congeries of gipsy encampments, without stability or recognisable structure. What's more, they are a hotch-potch recruited from every region of Italy.

That is the strength and weakness of Milan, a gigantic emporium of industry and commerce; it is dominated effectively by an élite of old aristocratic families who have behind them a strong tradition of local government. (Did you know that Milan even has a special Catholic cult of its own, the Ambrosian cult – a thing of which the older Milanese are jealously proud and which is all tied up with the situation I have described?)

Excuse the digression. But you know that I'm an awful windbag, and get carried away easily by any subject that interests me.

Give me some more of your impressions of Milan. I embrace you affectionately, and look forward to your reply.

Antonio

22

Milan Prison, 14 November 1927

Dearest Tania,

I have already received some books – *Quintino Sella in Sardinia* and the Mondadori Catalogue I already have in my cell. The books by Finck and Maurras have arrived, but they haven't been handed over to me yet. Strangely enough, the one about Quintino Sella was one I had asked my mother to send me; I think it's one of the first books I ever read, because it was one of our household books; nevertheless it brought back no memories at all.

... At the time of the Machiavelli Centenary I read all the articles published in the five daily papers which I then read: later I received a number of *Marzocco* devoted to Machiavelli. It struck me that not one of those who wrote in honour of the centenary tried to show the relation between the books of Machiavelli and the development of sovereign states all over Europe in the same historical period. Led astray by the purely moralistic problem of so-called Machiavellianism they did not see that Machiavelli was the theoretician of nation states governed by absolute monarchies; or, in other words that he was reducing to theory in Italy what Elizabeth was at that time doing energetically in England – and what was being done in Spain by Ferdinand the Catholic, in France by Louis XI, and in Russia by Ivan the Terrible. This is still true, even though

Machiavelli himself did not know and could not know at first hand of any of these national experiences: experiences which in reality represented the historic problem of his age, and which he had the genius to grasp intuitively and to expound systematically.

I embrace you, dear Tania – after this digression whose interest for you is probably a bit limited! ...

Antonio

23

Milan Prison, 14 November 1927

My dear Giulia,

I want at any rate to send you a greeting every time I am allowed to write. A year has gone by since the day of my arrest, and almost a year since the day on which I wrote to you my first letter from prison. I have changed a great deal in this period. I think that I've got stronger, and have organised myself better. The state of mind which dominated me when I wrote you that first letter (I don't want even to try to describe it to you, because it would give you the horrors) today makes me smile a little.

I think that Delio in this last year must have received impressions which will accompany him his whole life long. And this is a thought which heartens me. I embrace you lovingly.

Antonio

24

Milan Prison, 21 November 1927

Darling Giulia,

In the courtyard where I go with the other prisoners on exercise we have held an exhibition of the photographs of our respective children. Delio had a great success, and was admired very much.

I am no longer in a cell by myself; for a few days now I have been in a cell together with another political prisoner who has a charming and pretty little daughter three years old, called Maria Luisa. In accordance with Sardinian custom we have decided that Delio shall marry Maria Luisa as soon as the two have reached the age of matrimony. What's your reaction to that? Of course, we are awaiting news of the consent of the two mothers, to make the contract more binding – even though this constitutes a grave breach of the customs and principles of my country! ... I imagine that you

must be smiling, and that makes me happy; it's only with great difficulty
that I can imagine you smiling.

I embrace you tenderly, my darling.

Antonio

25

Milan Prison, 26 December 1927

Dearest Tania,

And so the holy feast of Christmas has passed by. I can imagine how
wearisome it must have been for you. To tell you the truth, I would not
have given its exceptional nature another thought, if it had not been for
the memory of how *you* must be faring: this consideration is the only one
which interests me. Nothing out of the ordinary was noticeable in the
prison apart from a general tension among the prisoners. For a whole week
it had been possible to sense the heightening of the tension. Everyone was
waiting for something out of the ordinary, and this common emotion of
anticipation engendered a whole series of minor signs and indications
which in the aggregate gave this impression of an élan of vitality. For
many the exceptional thing consisted of nothing but a portion of *pasta
asciutta* and a quarter-litre of wine which the prison authorities issue
three times a year instead of the usual *minestra*: but what kind of
exceptional event is that supposed to be, I'd like to know! ... Don't think
that I'm having a laugh at the expense of these lads, or want in any way
to make fun of them. There was a time, perhaps, before I got a personal
experience of prison life, when I might have been tempted to do so. But I've
seen too many pathetic scenes: prisoners eating their bowl of *minestra* with
religious compunction, and supping up with a piece of bread the last
vestiges of grease still clinging to the earthenware! I once saw a prisoner
crying – it was in the barracks of the *carabinieri*, while we were in transit
– because instead of the regulation *minestra* nothing but a double ration of
bread was distributed. He had been two years in gaol, and the hot
minestra was his blood, his very life. Now I understand why, in the Lord's
prayer, there is a reference to 'our daily bread'.

I thought of your kindness and of your self-sacrifice, dear Tania. But the
day went by much the same as all the others. Perhaps we did less talking
and more reading. I myself read a book of Brunetière on Balzac, which was
rather like an extra lesson for naughty children. But I don't want to inflict
this subject on you. Instead I'd like to tell you a story (which is almost a
Christmas story) about my childhood: it will amuse you and will show you
a characteristic side of my life in my part of the world. I was fourteen at

the time, and was in my third year at the secondary school of Santu Lussurgiu, a village about eleven miles distant from my own – as far as I know there's still a secondary school there, but to tell you the truth it's a pretty broken down affair. In order to gain an extra twenty-four hours with my family I set off on foot with another boy on the afternoon of 23 December, instead of waiting for the coach on the following morning. Trudging along on shanks's pony we reached a place about half way to our destination. It was a completely deserted and solitary place; on the left, about a hundred yards from the road, there was a ragged rank of poplars, and clumps of pistachio trees were dotted around.

Suddenly a rifle shot rang out: the bullet whistled about ten yards over our heads. We thought it was just an odd shot, and went on walking as if nothing had happened. But a second and third shot, still over our heads but much lower, made us realise all of a sudden that we were being aimed at; we threw ourselves into the ditch, and remained there for a bit lying doggo. As soon as we attempted to get up, another shot rang out, and this caper continued for about two hours; we made an effort to get out of the danger zone by crawling away, but about a dozen shots came our way every time we tried to get back on to the road. Of course, it was nothing but a bunch of practical jokers who were getting a bit of fun out of putting the wind up the pair of us; but it was a fine sort of practical joke, I must say. We got back home when it was quite dark both pretty tired and mucky; we didn't tell the story to a soul, in order not to cause the family alarm; however it doesn't seem to have frightened us over much because when the next holiday came round we repeated the journey on foot without running into any more adventure ... And look, with this story I've nearly filled all the four pages!

I embrace you tenderly.

Antonio

No, this story is really quite true; it isn't a story about brigands after all.

26

Milan Prison, 26 December 1927

Dear Berti,

I have received your letter of 25 November – it was held up for a short time. I knew that a group of exiles had been sent to Palermo Gaol, but I was ignorant of the precise charges against them. I imagined it was just a matter of a disciplinary trial to be heard in front of a police court magistrate,[1] and assumed that it was to be heard at Palermo, for no other reason than that the capacity of the island prison is strictly limited. Oh well – stick it out, dear Berti!

As far as lawyers are concerned, your knowledge is about as good as mine. I imagine you'll have plenty of time to think about this question if the judicial enquiry runs its appointed course and they pack you off to Rome. I personally have not yet thought about this serious problem – in point of fact, it merely brings a slight smile to my face. On the whole, I would be inclined to dispense with a lawyer's services if only I didn't get such a kick beforehand from imagining what his speech, or rather his harangue, would be like; and also if I did not follow the general principle of availing myself of every legal possibility open to me. The entertainment would be most exquisite if I were able to select as lawyer some freemason-democrat (retired for the duration of the régime) and put him in an awkward position, make him blush ... but unfortunately one has got to ration one's own amusements ... (Imagine for example, the position of one of those lawyers who in 1924–5 maintained in speech and in print that we were in agreement with the government or as near as makes no matter.)

Dear Berti, keep smiling; don't worry about anything but your physical health, for if that holds you can stand up to anything that comes along.

Yours fraternally,

Antonio

1. The real charge was of anti-fascist activity carried on in the island of exile.

27

Milan Prison, 2 January 1928

Dearest Tania,

And so we're into the New Year. The thing to do would be to draw up a programme of New Year resolutions in accordance with the usual practice; but as far as I can remember I've never yet succeeded in drawing up and sticking to any such programme. This has always been one of the great difficulties in my life, right from the very first days when I began to think. In elementary schools, every year just about this time, they used to set the following subject for an essay: 'What will you do with your Life?' A difficult question which I answered the first time, at the age of eight, by deciding to drive a horse and cart. My opinion was that a carter's job combined in a high degree both usefulness and pleasure; he cracked his whip and drove his horse, but at the same time he did a job which ennobles man and allows him to earn his daily bread.

I remained faithful to this vocation the following year as well, but for reasons which I should call extrinsic. If I had been honest I would have admitted that my liveliest aspiration was to become an usher in the local magistrates' court. And why? Because in that year an old gentleman had come to my village as usher in the local court, and this old chap was the owner of a most attractive little dog, which was always dressed up – a red bow on his tail, a little coat on his back, a varnished collar and a muzzle like a horse's harness. I was so enchanted by all this that I could not separate the idea of the little dog from the idea of his owner and his owner's profession. Nevertheless, I gave up these daydreams of a future which seemed so delightful, although it was with deep regret that I did so. I was a very logical little boy, and my moral integrity was enough to make the greatest heroes of Duty blush with shame. Yes, I considered myself unworthy to become a police court usher, and so become the proud possessor of such marvellous little dogs ... I did not know by heart the eighty-four articles of the Constitution of the Kingdom! It was just like that! I had finished my second year at school (the year in which my eyes had been opened to the civic virtues of the carter!) and it was my intention to sit an exam in November which would let me pass straight to the fourth class, skipping the third; I felt equal to anything, but when I presented myself before the director of studies in order to make the official application I was faced with this demand point blank: 'But do you know the eighty-four articles of the Constitution?' I had never given them a thought, these blessed articles; all I had done was to study 'The Rights and Duties of the Citizen' as set out in the text book. This was a terrible warning to me, and left an impression which was all the more lasting because the previous 20 September I had taken part for the first time in the Remembrance Celebration: I had carried a Chinese lantern and had shouted with the others: 'Long live the prophet of Staglieno!'[2] (I don't remember exactly if we shouted the 'prophet' or the 'hero' of Staglieno: both, maybe, for the sake of variety!) Then I was certain that I would pass the exam, thus acquiring my title to civil rights, and finding myself on the highroad to becoming a citizen in the full sense of the word ... and instead, I didn't know the eighty-four articles of the Constitution! What kind of a citizen did that make me? And how could I conscientiously aspire to become a court usher and to possess a dog with a coat and a bow on his tail? A court usher is a cog in the state machine (I imagined that he was a big wheel); he is a depository and a custodian of the law, whose duty it is to defend it against the tyrant who might want to trample it under foot. And I was ignorant of the eighty-four articles!

Because of this I set a limit to my horizons, and once again I exalted the civic virtues of the carter who can own a dog too, even though it may lack a coat and a bow on its tail. So you see how programmes that are drawn up in too rigid a manner end by running up against hard reality and shiver into fragments if a man is cursed with too vigilant a sense of duty!

Dear Tania, do you think I'm starting to ramble? Laugh and forgive me. I embrace you.

Antonio

1. Garibaldi.
2. Mazzini.

28

Milan Prison, 30 January 1928

Dear Berti,

I received your letter of the 13th a week ago, when I had already used up my two letter ration. Nothing new at this end. The same old squalor, the same old monotony. Even reading becomes increasingly a matter of indifference to me. Naturally I still read a great deal, but without interest, mechanically. Although I've got company, I read a book a day or even more. All sorts of books, as you can imagine (I've even reread *The Last of the Mohicans* by Fenimore Cooper) just as they happen to turn up from the prison circulating library. In these last weeks I have read a few books sent on to me by my family, but none of exceptional interest. Here's a list of them, to help you pass the time away.

1. *Le Vatican et l'Action Française*. This is the so-called Yellow Book of the *Action Française*, a collection of articles, speeches and pamphlets with most of which I was already familiar, because they came out in the *Action Française* of 1926. In this book the political substance of the struggle is masked behind seven veils, and seven veils again. All that appears on the surface is the 'canonical' discussion of the so-called *'mystical materia'* and on the 'just liberty' (just according to the canons) of the faithful. You know what it's all about: there exists in France a mass Catholic organisation, along the lines of our own *Azione Cattolica*, under the presidency of General Castelnau. Up to the French political crisis of 1926 the Nationalists were in fact the only political party which had grafted itself organically on to this organisation and exploited its possibilities (a four to five million annual membership, for example). Consequently all the Catholic forces were exposed to the repercussions of the adventures of Maurras and Daudet, who in 1926 had a provisional government ready to be hoisted into power in case the existing government collapsed. The Vatican, on the other hand, which foresaw a new wave of anti-clerical laws of the Combes type, decided to make a great show of breaking with the *Action Française*, and to work for the organisation of a democratic Catholic mass party which would have the function of a parliamentary centre, along the Briand-Poincaré line. In the *Action*

Française, for obvious reasons, only articles of a somewhat obsequious and moderate nature appeared: the violent and personal attacks were reserved to *Charivari*, a weekly which has no opposite number in Italy and which was not officially a Party publication; but this side of the polemic is not reprinted in the present book. I have noted that the 'orthodox' have published a reply to the Yellow Book, compiled by Jaques Maritain, Professor at the Catholic University of Paris and recognised leader of the orthodox intellectuals: which means that the Vatican has registered a notable success, because in '26 Maritain had written a book to defend Maurras, and had earlier signed a declaration to the same effect. Today, therefore, there exists a schism between these intellectuals, and the monarchists must find themselves in ever greater isolation.

2. R. Michels, *La France Contemporaine*. A complete swindle. It's a collection, without unity, of a number of articles on certain very fragmentary aspects of French life. Michels believes, because he was born in the Rhineland (a transitional zone between the Latin and the German worlds) that he is destined to cement the friendship between the German and the Romance-speaking peoples, uniting in himself the worst characteristics of both cultures: the haughty scowl of the Teuton philistine and the gormless fatuity of the Southerner. All in all, this fellow, who displays like a cockade his renunciation of the German race and who boasts that he has called one of his sons Marius in memory of the defeat of the Cimbri and the Teutons, leaves on me the impression of the most refined hypocrisy serving the ends of academic careerism.

... Write to me when you can: but I think that your possibilities are even more restricted than mine.

Antonio

29

Milan Prison, 20 February 1928

Dear Teresina,

I have received your letter of 30 January, and the photograph of your children. Thank you very much – I'll be very happy to receive some more letters from you.

The worst drawback of my present life is boredom. These days which are always the same, these hours and these minutes which follow each other with the monotony of water dripping from a tap have finally succeeded in getting on my nerves. At any rate the first three months after my arrest were full of movement; pushed around from one end of the peninsula to the other (in conditions which caused me a good deal of physical suffering, it's true) I had no time to get bored. There were always new sights to observe, fresh exceptional types to catalogue; I really felt as if I were living in some fantastic novel. But now for more than a year I have been stationary in Milan, in enforced idleness. I can read; but I can't study, because I've not received permission to have pen and paper at my disposal – not even under strict surveillance, in the manner laid down by the governor in view of the fact that I am considered a terrible individual capable of setting fire to the four corners of the country or worse. Correspondence is my chief distraction. But only a very few people write to me. To make matters worse, my sister-in-law has been ill for a month and I no longer have my weekly chat with her.

My mother's state of mind worries me a good deal; what's more, I don't know what to do to reassure her and console her. I should like to convince her that I'm absolutely calm – as in point of fact I am – but I can see that I have little success. There's a whole zone of feelings and ways of thought which constitutes a kind of abyss between us. For her my imprisonment is a terrible disaster, and not a little mysterious in the concatenation of its causes and effects. For me it's just an episode in the political struggle which has been fought and will continue to be fought not only in Italy but all over the world, for who knows how long yet. I have been made prisoner, in the same way soldiers might be captured during the war, fully aware that this might happen and also aware that things a good deal worse might happen too ... But I'm afraid that you probably feel much like mother about all this, and that these explanations look to you like a riddle phrased in an unknown tongue.

I have been taking a good long look at the photograph, comparing it with the ones you sent me earlier (I've had to interrupt the letter to have a shave; I don't remember what I intended to write and I don't feel like thinking about it. Let's hold it over to some other time). Affectionate greetings to all. I embrace you.

Ni

30

Milan Prison, 27 February 1928

Dearest Tania,

By the happiest conjuncture of favourable stars, your letter of the 20th was handed over to me on the 24th, together with Giulia's letter. I much admired your cleverness in diagnosis but I have not been caught in the subtle snares of your literary cunning. Don't you think it's more to one's advantage to show off one's cleverness at other people's expense rather than at one's own? (Not that I have any desire to wish bad luck on my neighbour – that is, if one can use the term neighbour in this case. Have you read Tolstoy with care, and made a study of his thoughts? I'd like you to confirm for me the precise significance which Tolstoy gives to the Gospel concept of 'one's neighbour'. It seems to me that he is abiding by the literal, etymological meaning of the word: 'the people most near to you – those of your family, that is, or at the very most those of your village'.) In short, you haven't succeeded in foxing me with all these cards up your sleeve; demonstratively displaying your own skill as a doctor in order to make me think less about your condition as a patient. Furthermore, I have acquired a very special stock of knowledge about phlebitis, because in the last fifteen days of my stay on Ustica I was forced to listen to the long discourses of an elderly lawyer from Perugia who suffered from it, and had had four or five publications on the subject sent to him. I know that it's a fairly serious and very painful illness; will you really have the patience necessary to get well again without hurrying the cure? I do hope so. I can maybe help you to be patient, writing you longer letters than usual. If my gossiping gives you pleasure, this will entail little extra effort and won't cost me anything to speak of. Then again I'm much more at ease now than I was.

Since I got Giulia's letter I've been a good deal calmer in my mind. I'll write her a separate letter, a fairly long one, if I can manage to that is, because I don't want to start reproaching her, and I don't see yet how I can write to her at length without reproaching her. Does it seem right to you in point of fact that she shouldn't write to me when she's not feeling well or when she's suffering or worried? I think it's exactly at these times that she should write to me at greater length ... but I don't want to turn this letter into a series of reproaches. To pass the time away, I'll tell you about a little discussion among the 'prison inmates' which I have been carrying on sporadically. A character who is, I think, an Evangelical or a Methodist or a Presbyterian (I was reminded of him by my own reference to 'one's neighbour' above) was waxing very indignant because certain poor Chinese are still permitted to circulate in our cities – I mean the vendors of those little objects which are certainly mass-produced in Germany but which give buyers the impression that they are entering into the possession of an authentic fragment of the folklore of Cathay. According to our 'nonconformist', they represented a grave threat to the homogeneity of beliefs and ways of thought in Western civilisation; according to him, it was an attempt to graft Asiatic idolatry on to the tree trunk of European Christianity. The little images of Buddha would end up by exercising a special fascination which might act as a reagent on European psychology and help to bring into being new ideological formations totally different from the traditional ones. That an element in society like this Protestant should in all seriousness entertain such preoccupations was certainly very interesting, even if his worries had a pretty remote origin. It wasn't difficult, however, to prod him forward into an ideological maze, which for him contained no exit, by expounding as follows:

1. The influence of Buddhism on Western civilisation has much deeper roots than would appear, because right through the Middle Ages, from the invasion of the Arabs up to about 1200, the life of Buddha circulated in Europe as the life of a Christian martyr, sanctified by the Church. It was only after the passage of several centuries that the Church became conscious of the error committed, and 'de-consecrated' the pseudo-saint. The influence that such an episode must have exercised in those days, when religious ideology was at its liveliest and constituted the only mode of thinking for the masses, is incalculable.

2. Buddhism is not idolatry. From this point of view, if a danger there is, it is to be found rather in the music and the dance imported into Europe by the negroes. This music has actually conquered an entire stratum of the cultured European population; indeed, it has created a real fanaticism. Now can one seriously maintain that the continued repetition of the physical gestures that the negroes make when dancing around their fetishes, and the syncopated rhythm of the jazz band in one's ears can remain without ideological results?

(a) We are dealing with a phenomenon which is enormously widespread, which touches millions and millions of people, especially young people;

(b) It is a matter of very energetic and violent impressions, impressions therefore which must leave profound and lasting traces;

(c) musical phenomena enter it; phenomena that is which express themselves in the most universal language existing today, a language which is communicating with the utmost rapidity complete images and impressions of a civilisation which is not only extraneous to our own, but which is less complex than the Asiatic. It is (I assured him) a primitive and elemental civilisation – one therefore which on the strength of its music and dance can be easily assimilated and popularised all over the world.

To cut a long story short, the poor Protestant became rapidly convinced that whereas he had been afraid of becoming an Asiatic, he was actually without noticing it turning into a negro; also that the said process was terribly far advanced, at least as far as the halfcaste stage. I'm not sure what results have been obtained; I doubt however if he'll be able to give up his cup of coffee, even though it is drunk to the sound of a jazz band. Which means that from now on he'll always be looking anxiously into the mirror to detect the coloured pigments in his blood.

Dear Tania, I wish you a happy and a swift recovery.

I embrace you.

Antonio

31

Milan Prison, 27 February 1928

My darling Giulia,

I have received your letter of 26 December 1927, together with the postscript of the 24th and the enclosed note. Getting these letters of yours made me really happy. In any case I have felt much calmer for some time now. These long months have wrought many a change in me. There was a time when I believed that I had become apathetic and inert. I now think I was wrong in this analysis of my own condition. What's more, I don't think that I was ever actually disoriented. What was happening was this: I was going through a series of crises of resistance to the new mode of life. And this new mode of life was imposing itself implacably. I was being subjected to the pressure of the entire prison environment with its rules, its routine, its privations and its necessities – an enormous complex of little things which follow each other mechanically day after day, month after month, year after year, like grains of sand in a gigantic hour glass. The whole of my constitution, both mental and physical, put up a tenacious resistance, in every fibre of its being, to the process of absorption into this external environment; but every now and again I had to recognise the fact that a certain amount of the pressure had succeeded in overcoming the resistance and in modifying a corresponding zone in my own personality. Following which I would stage a rapid counterthrust with all my forces, aiming to throw back the invader at one go. Today a whole cycle of changes has already taken place, because I have come to the calm decision not to oppose what is necessary and ineluctable with the same means and weapons as before, for these were both inefficacious and inept; I have decided to dominate and control the process with the help of a certain ironic spirit.

In any case I'm sure that I run no risk of ever becoming a perfect Philistine. At any moment I shall be able to throw off with a single shake the coat (half donkey hide and half sheepskin) which grows over one's true and natural skin under the influence of the environment. Maybe there's one thing I shan't be able to restore to my skin – my real skin – the famous 'smoked' colour. Varia will never be able again to call me the 'smoked' comrade. I'm afraid that Delio, notwithstanding your own share in his make-up, will by now look even more 'smoked' than I do. (Do I hear protests?) This winter I went for almost three months without seeing the sun, except in some distant reflection. The light which gets through to the cell is halfway between the light of a cellar and that of an aquarium.

On the other hand you mustn't think that my life drags by as monotonously and uneventfully as might at first sight appear. Once you have got used to this aquarium existence, and your sense organs are attuned to the reception of the dull twilight impressions which flow quivering through it – I'm still looking at things from a somewhat ironic standpoint – a whole world begins to swarm and crawl around you, with its own particular vivacity, its own peculiar laws, its own essential being. You get the same sort of impression if you take a look at an old tree trunk half rotted by time and the elements, and then gradually find your attention held to an ever increasing extent by what you see.

First of all you take in nothing but moist fungus, and maybe a snail oozing its hesitant slimy way forward. Then you become aware all of a sudden of whole colonies of little insects busying themselves with their affairs, making the same efforts and following the same route time and time again. If one maintains one's own independent position, if one doesn't allow oneself to become snail or ant, the whole thing ends up by becoming fascinating – and it helps to pass the time away.

Every detail which I succeed in collecting of your own life and that of the children helps me to fit together a larger scale picture of what you are all doing. But these details are too few and far between, and my own experience of life with you is too scanty. And again, the children must be changing too rapidly at the age they are now to make it possible for me to follow all the stages of their development and get a proper picture of it. It's clear that as far as this is concerned I must be pretty disoriented. But that's inevitable, I suppose.

I embrace you tenderly.

Antonio

32

Milan Prison, 5 March 1928

Dearest Tania,

... I read your letter with great interest because of the observations contained in it, and your new experiences. I imagine it's hardly necessary to remind you that forgiveness is necessary in these matters: not only 'practical' forgiveness but (if I may use the term) 'spiritual' forgiveness as well. I have always been convinced that there is an unknown Italy which is not visible, and which is very different from the apparent and visible Italy. What I mean to say is this: that although we are dealing with a phenomenon which may be observed in every country, the gap between what one sees and what one does not see goes deeper in Italy than in any of the other so-called civilised countries. In this country the *piazza* with its shouting, its verbal enthusiasms, its vainglory overshadows the *chez soi* much more (relatively) than in other countries. Because of this a whole series of gratuitous prejudices and opinions have come into being: with reference to the solidity of our family structure, and the dose of genius which Providence is supposed to have meted out to our people etc. In a recent book of Michels I found the statement repeated that the average Calabrian peasant – even if illiterate – is more intelligent than the average German university professor. This is the sort of reasoning which gives a lot of people the comforting reassurance that they need not do anything about putting an end to illiteracy in Calabria.

I am of the opinion that family relationships in our cities cannot be judged in abstraction from the overall general situation in the whole country, given the recent formation of the urban centres in Italy. The situation in the country at large is still pretty deplorable, and for our present purposes can be summarised as follows: an extreme egotism in that part of the population between twenty and fifty years of age which makes itself felt at the expense of the children and the old people. I do not mean that these two latter categories are scarred with the permanent stigmata of social inferiority: the very thought would be stupid, absurd. It is a phenomenon historically conditioned and explicable which will undoubtedly be overcome when the general standard of living is raised.

The explanation will in my opinion only be found when one has analysed the population of Italy or of any other given country demographically. Before the war Italy had to carry 83 non-productive persons for every 100 workers, whereas in France, which is enormously richer, the ratio was only 52 to every 100. Too many old people and too many children in comparison with the intermediate generation, impoverished numerically by emigration. This is the basis of that egotism of the middle generations which at times assumes features of the most revolting cruelty. Seven or eight months ago the newspapers carried the following shocking information: a father had slaughtered his entire family (wife and three children) because, on returning home from his work in the fields, he had found that the famished brood had eaten up his scanty supper. At about the same period the trial took place in Milan of a husband and wife who had caused the death of their little son, aged four, by keeping him tied to a table leg by a length of wire. From the proceedings one could gather that the man had had doubts about his wife's fidelity, and that the latter, rather than lose her husband by defending her son from ill treatment, had connived at the little boy's murder. They were condemned to eight years' imprisonment. This is a type of offence which at one time was considered in the Annual Statistics of Crime under a special heading. Senator Garafalo was of the opinion that the average of fifty sentences a year for similar crimes was no more than a hint of the widespread character of such crimes, because the guilty parents more often than not succeeded in escaping any sort of punishment. According to him, the reason for this laxity was to be found in the general custom of paying little attention to the hygiene and health of children; and also in the widespread religious fatalism which regards the assumption of new child-angels into the heavenly choir as a particular benevolence of Providence. This, alas, is the most widespread ideology, so there's no wonder that it is still reflected (although in weak and watered down forms) even in the most progressive and modern cities. So you see that charity is not out of place here – at any rate for those people who refuse to believe in absolute principles where such things are concerned, but do believe in the feasibility of their progressive improvement, in conjunction with the improvement of living conditions generally.

All the very best of good wishes.

I embrace you.

Antonio

33

Milan Prison, 9 April 1928

Dearest Tania,

I have received your letter of the 5th with a promptness which befits the coming of Easter. I have also received the lock of Giuliano's hair, and am very happy to have the news you send me. To tell you the truth, I am unable to draw much of a conclusion from it. As regards the speed (or lack of it) with which children begin to speak, I have nothing to contribute but an anecdote about Giordano Bruno. It is said that Bruno did not speak until he was three years old, although he understood everything that was said. One morning, about the time for getting up, he saw a big snake moving towards his cot from a crevice in the wall of the house where his family lived. He immediately called out his father's name, which he had never up to that moment uttered. He was saved from the danger which threatened, and from that day he began to speak – and went on speaking, even to excess, as even the Jewish pedlars at the Campo di Fiori will tell you.

A few days ago I received the *Economic Perspectives* and the *Literary Almanac*. Every year, from '25 onwards, I used to give Giulia this Almanac. I shall not do so this year. It has sunk pretty low. It even contains mottoes, supposedly humorous, of the sort that used to be the exclusive preserve of the semi-pornographic weeklies – favourite reading matter for youthful recruits having their first taste of city life. In my opinion it's worthwhile making and putting on record even so slight an observation as this.

I have just remembered that Delio will be four on 10 August, and that he is already big enough to receive a real present, a present that means something. Signora Pina has promised to send me the Meccano catalogue; I hope that the various sets are listed not only in order of price (from 27 to 2,000 lire!) but also in relation to their simplicity and the children's age. The principle of Meccano is certainly excellent for modern children; I'll choose the set which appears to me to be the most suitable and will write to you about it. There's time enough before August.

I don't know what Delio's present bent is – assuming, that is, that he has already given a clear sign of it. When I was a boy, I had a natural aptitude for the exact sciences and for mathematics. These went by the board during my school years, because the teachers I had for these particular subjects weren't worth a dried fig. And so I dropped mathematics after my first year in the secondary school and plumped for Greek instead. (It was possible at that time to opt for one or the other.) However, in my third secondary school year I gave unexpected proof of having retained a considerable 'capacity' for these subjects. It turned out during this third year that if one wanted to study physics one had to know the elements of mathematics, which the pupils who had chosen Greek were under no obligation to know. The physics master, who was a very capable character, got great amusement out of putting us in an awkward spot. In the final exam of the third term he asked me some questions on physics which demanded a knowledge of maths, telling me at the same time that my total mark for the year would depend on my answers – that is, my promotion with or without an exam would also depend on it. It was great fun for him watching me at the blackboard, where he left me working for as long as I liked. Well then: I stayed for half an hour at the blackboard, covering myself with chalk from head to foot. I had a go, rubbed the thing out, had another shot, wrote more figures, and went on crossing them out, until finally I 'invented' a demonstration which was declared first rate by the master, in spite of the fact that it didn't exist in any text book.

The professor knew my elder brother at Cagliari, and for ever after until I left school he kept tormenting me with his teasing, his name for me being the 'Grecian physicist'.

Dearest Tania, away with gloomy thoughts, and send me plenty of letters. I embrace you.

Antonio

34

Milan Prison, 30 April 1928

Darling Mother,

I am sending you the photograph of Delio. My trial is fixed for 28 May; this time I am likely to leave almost immediately, I think. At any rate I shall try to send you a telegram. I am keeping fairly well. The fact that my trial is to take place so soon has put me in better spirits, because it will at least make a break in this monotony. Don't worry yourself about me, and don't be cast down no matter how heavy a sentence they give me. I think it will probably be from fourteen to seventeen years, but it might even be more, for the simple reason that they have no proof against me: What sort of terrible crimes may I not have committed if I haven't left any evidence behind me?

Be of good heart.

I embrace you.

Ni

35

Milan Prison, 30 April 1928

Dearest Tania,

... I don't know if they've told you that my trial has been fixed for 28 May, which means that they'll probably move me pretty soon. I have already had a chat with the lawyer Aris. I am quite excited at the thought of these new developments so close at hand; however, it's a pleasurable sensation. I feel myself more vibrant with life; there will be quite a battle, I imagine. Even though it's only for a few days I shall be in a different environment from the prison one.

I want to register a protest against your deductions re the ... goats' heads! I am a mine of information on this particular trade. In 1919 I did some thorough-going research into it at Turin, because the Town Council was boycotting Sardinian lambs and kids in favour of their Piedmontese rabbits. Now at that time there were in Turin about 4,000 Sardinian shepherds and peasants on a special mission,[1] and I took advantage of their presence to obtain some information on the subject. The lambs and kids from the South arrive up here without heads, but there's a small percentage of local traders who supply the heads as well. That they are difficult to obtain is illustrated by the fact that the kid's head promised for the Sunday, did not turn up until the Wednesday.

In any case I'm not sure whether it was actually a kid's or lamb's head, although it was very succulent. (In my view at least; it turned Tulli's stomach. It looked a pretty queer sort of kid; the brain had been removed and one of its eyes too – what was left looked like the head of a wolf run over by a tram. For goodness sake don't tell all this to Signora Pina. What a tribe they are, these butchers!)

I am very sorry that Giulia was without news of me for such a long time – shall we be able to see each other again before my departure? I don't imagine so. You mustn't do anything rash; you must take care and get properly well again. It's only if you do this that my mind will be at rest. Remember that from now on I shall only be able to write to you at long intervals.

I embrace you.

Antonio

[The trial of Gramsci began in Rome on 28 May 1928 and ended on 4 June.]

1. The 4,000 soldiers of the Sassari Brigade, a formation renowned for its exploits on the Alpine fronts during World War I. They had been sent to Turin to repress the working-class movement, and Gramsci had carried out most effective propaganda among them.

36

Rome Prison, 27 June 1928

Dearest Tania,

No fresh development in sight up to the present. I don't know when I shall leave. However it's on the cards that my departure may take place in a few days from now. I might get orders to move this very day. A few days ago I got a letter from my mother. She tells me that she hasn't received my letters of 22 May; which means that she has received nothing since my last days in Milan. From Rome I have written home at least three times – the last of these letters I sent to my brother Carlo. Write a letter to my mother yourself, and explain that from now on I shall only be able to write very occasionally, only once a fortnight, and that I shall have to distribute the two monthly letters between her and yourself. On the other hand there is no limit to the number of letters I can receive: my mother has got it into her head that there is such a restriction. Give her the facts about the hold up of my departure for Portolongone after a special visit from the doctor, and about the probability of my being assigned to a more tolerable destination. Try and reassure her about the whole position; tell her that I am in no need of words of comfort to sustain my morale – tell her that I am perfectly calm and serene. This is a point on which I have never had any notable success with my mother: she has got a horrific adventure story conception of my plight as a gaolbird, and imagines that I am permanently plunged in gloom, a prey to desperation etc., etc. You might write to her that you have seen me recently and that I am the very reverse of downcast and desperate etc.: tell her I show a confirmed inclination to laugh and joke about the whole thing. She may believe you: if I write to her along these lines, she thinks I am just doing it to comfort her.

Dearest Tania, I am sorry to burden you with yet another letter-writing commission. In any case I decided to write this letter to you, and I don't want to fall behind the prearranged plan. I hope that I shall see you before I leave.

I embrace you tenderly.

Antonio

37

Turi Prison, 20 July 1928

Dearest Tania,

Yesterday morning I arrived at my destination. I found your letter of the 14th lying here, and a letter from Carlo with 250 lire. Please write to my mother and tell her the things which you think will interest her. From now on I shall only be able to write one letter a fortnight; that means that my conscience will have to cope with a number of dilemmas. I shall try to be orderly about it, and to use the available paper to the very best advantage.

1. The journey Rome-Turi was horrible. It's now clear that the pains I felt in Rome and which I put down to liver trouble were actually the early symptoms of an inflammation which was just about to develop. I suffered in the most excruciating manner. At Benevento I went through two absolutely hellish days and nights; I twisted around like a reptile. I had no rest sitting down, standing up or lying down. The doctor told me that it was 'St Anthony's fire'[1] and that there was just nothing to be done about it. During the stage Benevento-Foggia the pain died down, and the boils with which I was covered on my right side dried up. At Foggia I remained for five days, and after the first two I felt much better. I managed to sleep for a few hours and could lie out flat on my back without being pierced with pain. There are a few boils which are still not completely dried up, and I feel a certain amount of pain in the loins, but my impression is that it's nothing really serious. I don't know how to account for the period of incubation in Rome which lasted for eight days and which made its presence felt with piercing internal pains on the right side of the body.

2. I cannot write anything as yet about my future life. I am going through a first stage of 'quarantine', prior to being assigned definitely to a section of

the prison. I doubt if you'll be allowed to send me anything apart from books and laundry effects; we are not permitted to receive anything in the food line. So never send me anything [2] unless I have previously asked for it.

3. The books from Milan (that is, from the Bookshop) should be sent direct; there's no point in you incurring expenses sending things that have got to be stamped anyway.

4. The *Memoranda* book wasn't there; I had to bring it with me.

The cherries were very useful, although I personally didn't taste one of them; they helped me on the journey.

... I embrace you tenderly.

Antonio

1. Erysipelas. The older name is used by Rabelais (*Gargantua*, Chap. XIII) *Le feu du sainct Antoine te ard*, which Sir Thomas Urquhart translated 'St Antonie's fire seize on thy toane.'(*Toane*, Gaelic *tòn* = buttocks.)
2. Underlined by the prison governor.

38

Turi Prison, 6 September 1928

Dearest Tania,

I received your letters of 31 August, and of the 1st and 3rd September after sending off my last letters to you. So I've asked permission to send you this special letter in order to dam the flood of precipitate actions which you've suddenly let loose. What in the world has taken possession of you? As soon as I got to Turi I wrote telling you 'never to send me anything unless I asked you for it'. The Prison Governor, in an interview, has told me that he underlined this phrase to give it more emphasis. You wrote back saying you agreed, and you promised to stick by this rule; so why have you changed your mind and started doing the reverse?

And the same problems crop up in connection with the Soriano[1] affair. First of all you refer to the idea, and assure me that you will do nothing without my prior consent; then you tell me that you have spoken about it to the Ministry. Why do you act like this? Today my anger has evaporated, because I've received the four packages, and I couldn't help laughing over your lovable naïveté – but I assure you that in the last few days I've been feeling properly aggrieved about it. My not being able to write to you, and to forestall in time some catastrophic gesture (as, for example, making me travel in my present condition) filled me with real fury, I assure you. I felt myself a prisoner twice over, because you too seemed to have decided not to fall in with any wish of mine. You seemed resolved to order my life just as ideas came into your head, and to pay no need to my opinion – although I'm the one that's in prison! I know what it is to be in gaol! I've got the painful marks of it on my skin.

How can you still cherish illusions about 'special conditions for travelling', when you see the way I have been treated up to now? Listen, Tania – I don't want a change for anything in the world, no, not even if they were to buy me a ticket for a sleeping car; I am opposed on principle to any change which isn't necessary and made for some definite purpose. We had quite a brisk exchange of opinions on this subject once before in Milan; you promised then not to re-open the subject.

And then ... oh dear, Tania – what am I to say about the things you've sent me, and the things which you tell me you still want to send. Today I had a good laugh, but honestly there's more reason to be glum when one realises what you think I'm allowed to have. It means that you've no idea what prison is, and that you're unable to get a clear picture of my real position. It sounds as if you think I've retired on a pension, or something similar. Listen: I am not allowed to have anything of my own, barring my books and personal laundry. Nothing else. Have you understood now? No suit of clothes, no overcoat, etc. etc. Nothing metal, not even a vaseline tin. You must not send me anything unless I have asked for it previously, and you must not undertake any action without obtaining beforehand my explicit approval. There are no exceptions of any kind to these rules. Otherwise you'll make my prison life harder to bear, instead of making it easier for me.

I embrace you tenderly, but please don't make me angry again. Give me the credit for having a rational mind: what I do I do after giving it a great deal, a very great deal of thought.

Antonio

1. Tatiana had been trying to arrange for Gramsci to be transferred to Soriano prison, near Viterbo, which was – like Turi – reserved for 'infirm' prisoners. The reason, presumably, was that Soriano would be more accessible than Turi, which is in the 'heel' of Italy.

39

Turi Prison, 19 November 1928

Dear Giulia,

I have been very bad with you, and to be honest, the reasons for that are not as sound as they might be. After my departure from Milan, I got terribly tired. My living conditions generally got much harder. Prison life has cut deeper into me. Now I'm a bit better. The fact that my routine is once again stabilised, that my life is once more governed by certain set rules has helped in a sense to bring the course of my thoughts back to normal.

I was delighted to receive your photograph, and that of the children. When too long a time elapses between one visual impression and another the gap is filled with ugly thoughts; in Giuliano's case especially I was quite in the dark. I had no sort of image to give substance to memory. Now I am really happy once again.

Speaking generally, I have for several months felt myself more isolated and cut off from the life of the world than before. I read a great deal, books and reviews; of course, 'a great deal' is a relative term – the intellectual life possible to prisoners is obviously limited. But I have lost much of my taste for reading. Books and reviews can only give general ideas, mere sketches of the general intellectual current in the life of the world (some more successful, some less); but they cannot give you the immediate, direct, living impression of the life of Peter, Paul, John, of single real individuals – without the understanding of which one has no hope of understanding what is universalised and generalised.

Many years ago, in '19 and '20, I knew a young worker, very ingenuous and very likeable. Every Saturday evening, after coming out of work, he used to make straight for my office in order to be among the first to read the review I was editing.[1] He always used to say to me: 'I haven't been able to sleep, I was so oppressed by the thought: What will Japan do?' Japan was a proper obsession of his, because in Italian papers Japan is only mentioned when the Mikado dies or when at least 10,000 people are killed in an earthquake. Japan was a concept that eluded him; for this reason he never succeeded in getting a balanced picture of the forces in the world, and so it seemed to him that he understood nothing about anything. In those days I used to laugh over such a state of mind, and I would tease my friend on the strength of it. Now I understand him perfectly. I too have my 'Japan': it is the life of Peter and Paul, and also the lives of Giulia, Delio and Giuliano.

What I lack is the direct living impression; so how can I possibly manage to gain an insight into the life of the whole round world – even an entirely superficial one? I feel as though my life were frozen up and paralysed. How, though, could it be otherwise, seeing I lack sensible contacts with your life, and that of the children? Then again, I'm always afraid of being overcome by the prison routine, a monstrous machine which crushes and grinds with definite method. When I see the actions and hear the words of men who have been in prison for five, eight or ten years, when I observe the spiritual deformations which they have undergone, it honestly gives me a cold shiver, and I begin to doubt my own power to watch over myself. I feel that the others too have thought (not all, but some at least) that they wouldn't allow themselves to go under; and instead, without even realising it – the process is so long and minute – they have been changed and don't know it. They have no means of gauging the thing, because they have been changed utterly. To be sure, I shall put up a resistance. But, to give you one example, I notice that I can no longer laugh at myself as I used to – and that's a serious matter.

Dear Giulia, does all this havering of mine interest you? And does it give you some idea of the life I'm leading? In spite of everything, you know, I can still muster interest in what goes on in the world. Recently, I've been reading a number of books about the political activity of the Catholic Church. There's another 'Japan' for you: through what phases will French Radicalism pass before it splits and gives birth to a French Catholic party? This problem 'robs me of my sleep', as used to happen to my young friend. And I should think it's robbing certain others of theirs, too.

Do you like the paper knife? By the way, it cost me nearly a month's work, and at the end of it my fingers were half worn away. My darling, write to me about yourself and the children – and spread yourself generously. You ought to send me photographs of yourselves at least once every six months, so that I can follow the children's development and see your smile more often.

I embrace you tenderly, my dear.

Antonio

1. *L'Ordine Nuovo.*

40

Turi Prison 14 January 1929

Darling Giulia,

I am still waiting for your reply to my last letter. When we have managed to start a regular conversation once again (even if it's at long intervals) I'll tell you ever so many things – about my life, my impressions etc. etc. In the meantime you ought to tell me how Delio is getting on with the Meccano. This is of real interest to me, because I have never been able to decide whether Meccano is the best modern toy for children or not, seeing that to a certain extent it seems to me to rob boys of their own inventive spirit. What do you feel about this – and what is your father's opinion? In general my feeling is that modern culture (American pattern), of which Meccano is an expression, has the tendency to make man rather dry, machine-like and bureaucratic, and to create an abstract mentality (using 'abstract' in a different sense from that current in the last century). The old 'abstraction' was determined by metaphysical intoxication: it is mathematical intoxication which determines the new. How interesting it must be to observe how all these educational principles work out in practice in the case of a little boy – and our own little boy, to whom we are bound by feeling immeasurably different from mere 'scientific interest'.

My darling, write me a long letter.

I embrace you strongly, ever so strongly.

Antonio

41

Turi Prison, 24 February 1929

Dearest Tatiana,

I have received your three postcards (including the one with Delio's doodlings on it); and also the books which I had with me in Milan Prison. You will be pleased to hear that your English suitcase has given miraculous service; it has survived the long drawn-out journey undaunted, and in spite of all its rough handlings has suffered no permanent damage. Apart from the things listed above I have received the two pairs of mended stockings which I left behind with you in Rome, and the *Memoirs* of Salandra. Thank the lawyer for the trouble he has had in despatching the books, even if he did stuff them into the trunk like so many potatoes. So far I have not been able to carry out a detailed check on them; I think there are a few books missing – anyway, it doesn't matter.

Your story about Innocenzo Cappa's lecture much amused me. That creature acts the part of the parsley in all Milanese intellectual sauces – although on second thoughts the metaphor is too favourable to him! Parsley in a sauce fulfils a dignified and useful function, whereas Cappa is to the world of culture what moth is to one's wardrobe. Once upon a time he was the cry-baby of Lombard democracy. Indeed a fine name was invented for him in those days; as Cavallotti had been called the bard of democracy Cappa was dubbed its *bardotto*[1] – *bardotto* being a sort of mule which is born from the crossing of a horse and a she-ass. A figure intellectually null and morally questionable.

Here it seems that the weather has definitely improved; at last we seem to have the smell of spring in our nostrils. Which reminds me that we are getting near the mosquito season; last year they caused me a great deal of bother. For this reason I would greatly appreciate a bit of mosquito netting; it would come in handy for protecting the face and arms as soon as that turns out to be necessary. Not too big, of course, because otherwise it might not even be allowed; I think about one and a half yards square would do the trick. And while I'm about it, I might as well list one or two other needs: first of all, a ball of wool for mending stockings. I've had a look at the darning on the two pairs already received, and it seems to me that I could tackle the job myself. Another item is a bone needle which I could use for wool.

I meant to tell you, but have always forgotten, not to send me the little *meta* stove, because I've already got one made of aluminium; so far I haven't asked to have the use of it in my cell because I knew that permission had been refused to others. In any case it wouldn't be much use to me. I have kept it, because I am sure that sooner or later the things will be permitted in every prison: they have already gained entry into some, and are actually provided by the administration itself.

My dear, I embrace you affectionately.

Antonio

If you can, send me the seeds of some beautiful flower as well.

1. Hinny.

42

Turi Prison, 25 March 1929

Dearest Tania,

... I have received a postcard from Signora M. S., asking me to recommend some books on philosophy for her husband. Tell her that I cannot send her a reply direct, that I am keeping well enough etc. etc., that I send cordial greetings to her husband etc. Then transcribe this paragraph:

'The best manual on psychology is that of William James, translated into Italian and published by the Libraria Milanese; it must cost a good deal now, because before the war it cost 24 lire. No treatise on logic exists, apart from the usual textbooks for secondary schools. I gain the impression that S. still tends to judge things overmuch by the scholastic yardstick; he appears to be under the illusion that he will find in such books more than they can in point of fact give him. Psychology, for example, has already become almost completely detached from philosophy, and has become a natural science like biology and physiology: indeed, in order to make a profound study of modern psychology it is necessary to have a good knowledge of such subjects as physiology. In the same way, formal abstract logic does not today find many champions – outside the seminaries in which Aristotle and St Thomas Aquinas are studied exhaustively. Moreover dialectics – by which I mean the shape of thought which we may term historically concrete – has not as yet been reduced to manual form. In my opinion, the right way for him to go about improving his knowledge of philosophy would be:

1. To study a good manual on the history of philosophy – for example, the *Summary of the History of Philosophy* by Guido de Ruggiero (published by Laterza of Bari, costing 18 lire).

2. To read a few of the classics of philosophy, even if only in extracts: as for example those put out by the same publisher Laterza of Bari in the *Little Library of Philosophy*, which includes slim volumes of selected passages from Aristotle, Bacon, Descartes, Hegel, Kant etc. etc., with notes appended. To gain a knowledge of the dialectic he would have to read some bulky tome of Hegel, although this would be a wearisome undertaking. There is the *Encyclopedia* in Croce's admirable translation; however, this now costs a lot – about 100 lire. Croce's own book on Hegel is also good, although it must be borne in mind that in it Hegel and the Hegelian philosophy go one step forward and then two back: the metaphysical side is got rid of, but there's a backward march as regards the question of the relation between thought on the one hand, and natural and historical reality on the other. In any case this seems to me the road to follow. No new manuals (Fiorentino's is sufficient); instead, reading and personal criticism of the great modern philosophers.'

It seems to me that that should suffice.

... My dearest, I embrace you affectionately.

Antonio

43

Turi Prison, 22 April 1929

Dearest Tania,

... The rose has gone down with a terrible sunstroke; all its leaves, and its most tender parts are burnt and blackened; it looks desolate and woebegone, but it is putting out fresh buds. At any rate it isn't dead yet. The sunstroke was inevitable, because I had no other covering for it but paper, which the wind blew away; the best thing would have been a good-sized bundle of straw – straw being a bad heat conductor, and at the same time serving as a protection from the direct rays. In any case the prognosis is favourable, provided no extraordinary complications supervene.

The seeds have been very slow to come out in fresh flowers; a whole series of them insist on living the *podpolie*[1] life. It's true they were old seeds, and a bit moth-eaten. The ones that have worked their way through into the world are developing slowly. When I told you that a number of the seeds were excellent, I meant that they were good to eat. Oddly enough, in point of fact, some of the little plants look more like parsley or little onions than flowers. Every day I am tempted to pull them out a little to help them to grow, but I remain undecided between the two conceptions of the world and of education: whether to be Rousseau-esque and leave matters to Nature, which never makes a mistake and is fundamentally good; or on the other hand to be 'authoritarian', and to force Nature, introducing into evolution the expert hand of man, and asserting the principle of authority. So far I am still undecided, and the two ideologies are fighting it out in my head.

The six chicory plants made themselves at home straight away and showed no fear of the sun; already they are putting out the shoots which will provide seeds for future harvesting. The dahlias and the bamboo are sleeping underground, and so far have given no sign of life! The dahlias in particular are, I believe, properly done for. And while we are on this subject, I would like to ask you to send me four other kinds of seeds:

1. parsnips, which are a pleasurable memory of my early childhood: at Sassari you can buy the sort that weigh about a pound. Before the war they cost a *soldo*, and rivalled liquorice in popularity.
2. peas
3. spinach
4. celery

I want to put four or five seeds of each kind in a square foot of earth, and see how they do. You can get them in Ingegnoli's shops, one of which is in the Piazza del Duomo and the other in Via Buenos Aires; you might ask for the catalogue too, because it tells you which months are best for sowing the seeds.

I have received another note from Signora M. S. Pass the following lines to her:

'I understand the financial problems involved in getting hold of the books I mentioned in my previous letter. As you'll no doubt remember I did touch on this difficulty as well, but my job was to reply to certain specific questions. Today I shall answer a question which, although not put to me, was implicit and which I realise only too well is the outcome of the general needs of any prisoner, i.e., "How can one make sure one uses time to advantage, and does get some sort of study done?" It seems to me that the first thing to be done is to rid oneself of the mental overcoat of academicism, and not cherish the vain illusion that one can pursue regular and intensive courses of study; that sort of course is out of the question, even for people in less difficult circumstances. The study of modern languages is certainly among the most rewarding subjects; all you need is a grammar, which may be purchased for a few pence on a second-hand book barrow, and one or two books (possibly second-hand as well) in the language selected for study. Of course, you can't learn the pronunciation in this way, but you can learn to read and that is in itself no mean accomplishment. It should be noted too, in passing, that many prisoners underestimate the value of the prison library. To be sure prison libraries are, in general, pretty disjointed: the books have been gathered together any old how – gifts from patrons who receive unsold stocks from publishers, or books left behind by released prisoners. There's an abundance of works of devotion and third-rate novels. Nevertheless it's my opinion that a political prisoner must find ways and means of squeezing blood from a stone. The main thing is to do one's reading with a certain end in view, and to take notes (if one is allowed to write).

'Let me give you two examples: in Milan I read a certain number of books of all kinds, mostly "low-brow" novels, until the prison governor gave me permission to go into the library myself, and make a selection from books which hadn't been issued for general circulation; also from those which – because of some particular moral or political tendency – hadn't been permitted to the average run of prisoners. Anyway, I found that even Sue, Montépin, Ponson du Terrail etc., served my purpose if looked from this point of view: "Why is this reading matter the most read and the most published? What needs does it satisfy? To what aspirations does it respond? What sentiments and points of view are represented in this tripe to make it so popular with wide masses of people? Why is Eugene Sue different from Montépin? And does not Victor Hugo also belong to this class of writers when one considers the subjects with which he deals? And *Scampolo* or *L'Aigrette* or *Volata* by Dario Nicodemi – are not they too the direct progeny of this debased romanticism of 1848?" Etc., etc., etc.

'The second example is this: a German historian, Groethuysen, published recently a large volume in which he studies the links between French Catholicism and the bourgeoisie in the two centuries before 1789. He has made a study of the entire devotional literature of these two centuries: collections of sermons, catechisms from the different dioceses etc., etc., and has put together a magnificent volume. It seems to me that in itself should be enough to show that one can squeeze blood from a stone. Every book, especially if it has a bearing on history, can be of interest. In every trashy little book you can find something which will serve its turn ... especially when you find yourself in our position, and time cannot be measured with the normal yardstick.'

Dear Tania, I have written a great deal; this'll oblige you to enter for a handwriting contest. By the way: remember to see that no more books are sent to me unless I ask for them. If by any chance books are published which you think might be of use to me, put them on one side and send them when I ask you to.

My dearest, I really do hope that the journey didn't tire you too much. I embrace you affectionately.

Antonio

1. Underground (Russian).

44

Turi Prison, 20 May 1929

My dear Giulia,

Whoever told you I could write more letters? Unfortunately it isn't true. I can only write twice a month; it's only at Easter and Christmastime that I have the right to a special letter.

Do you remember what B. told you in '23, when I left? B. was right, he had his own experience to back him up; I had always had an unconquerable aversion to letter-writing. Since I have been in prison I have written at least twice as many letters as in the preceding period; I must have written at least 200 letters (what a ghastly thought!). So it isn't true that I am not calm; in point of fact I am more than calm, I am passive and apathetic. This state of mind holds no mystery for me, and I'm not making even the slightest effort to get out of the bog of inanition.

In any case, this is maybe a sign of strength, and not a state of confusion. There were long periods during which I felt myself very isolated, cut off from every life other than my own. I suffered terribly; a delay in correspondence, any failure to reply to questions I had put, brought fits of irritation which made me very tired. Then time passed, and the landscape of this earlier period receded into the distance. Every casual and ephemeral thing which still kept a foothold in the zone of feeling and desire gradually faded away, and what remained were the essential and permanent motifs of life. And it was natural that that should happen, don't you think? For a certain length of time it's inevitable that the past and the images of the past should still be dominant; but, in the end of all, this constant searching of the past becomes comfortless and unprofitable.

I think that I have overcome the crisis which everyone goes through in the first years of prison life, and which often results in a clean break with the past, in the most radical sense. To tell you the truth I have seen and felt this crisis more in others than in myself; it made me smile, and that in itself was a kind of victory. I would never have thought that so many people could have so great a fear of death; you see, it's in that very fear that you can find the root of all the psychological phenomena of prison life. In Italy they say that a man becomes old when he starts to think of death; it seems to me a very sensible observation. In prison this psychological twist takes place as soon as the prisoner feels that he is caught in the vice and can't get away. A swift and radical change takes place which is all the more serious if the person concerned has not taken his own ideas and convictions very seriously.

I have seen people quite incredibly degraded by this process. And the sight has been of use to me, in the same way that the sight of the degradation of the helots was of use to the Spartan boys.

So now I am absolutely calm, and not even the prolonged lack of news can cause me anxiety – although I know that this could be avoided, given a modicum of good will ... on your part as well as on that of others. Then of course there's Tania who sends me all the news that comes her way. For example, she has passed on to me your father's description of the characters of the two children – a description so interesting that it provided food for thought for several days. And other news too, together with her own graceful comments. But don't take all this as a reproach to yourself! During the last few days I have reread all the letters you've sent me from a year ago up till now, and reading them made me feel your tenderness afresh. Do you know this – when I write to you I sometimes feel that I'm too dry and dour, in comparison with you, who write to me so naturally. It makes me feel as I did those few times when I made you cry; especially that first time (do you remember?) when I was really bad with you, and on purpose too.

I would like to know what Tania has told you about her journey to Turi. The reason is that I am afraid Tania has got a much too arcadian and idyllic picture of my life here, and this causes me more worry than you might think. She doesn't seem capable of getting it into her head that I'm forced to stay within certain fixed limits, and that she mustn't send me anything unless I have previously asked for it, seeing I haven't got a personal supply store at my disposal. Now she's announcing the imminent arrival of a number of absolutely useless things, things which I shall never be able to use, instead of keeping strictly to what I've asked for.

Antonio

45

Turi Prison, 20 May 1929

Dear Delio,

I hear that you're going to school, that you're three feet six inches tall and that you weigh three stone. That means that you're getting a big boy now, and that soon you'll be able to write me some letters. Before that time comes, you can make your mamma write letters to me at your dictation, like when you used to get me to write pimpos[1] for your granny when we were in Rome. And so you'll be able to tell me how you get on with the other children at school, what you learn and what fun you have playing with the other boys. I know you make aeroplanes and trains and that you're taking an active part in the industrialisation of the country. But do these aeroplanes really fly, and do the trains really run? If I were with you, I'd put my cigarette in the funnel, so that at any rate we'd have a bit of smoke!

What's more, you ought to tell me something about Giuliano. Don't you think that would be a good idea? Does he help you in your work? Is he a builder too – or is he still too little to deserve the name? The truth is I want to know a whole heap of things about you, and now you're such a big boy – and, as they tell me, a bit of a gas-bag too – I'm sure you'll write me a long, long letter (even though for now it's only with your mamma's hand) giving me all this news I want, and a lot more into the bargain. And I'll send you news about a rose I've planted, and a lizard that I want to train. Kiss Giuliano for me, and your mamma too and everyone at home; then your mamma will give you a big kiss from me.

Your Papa

I've just thought that maybe you don't know what a lizard is. It's the same sort of thing as a crocodile in appearance, but quite tiny.

1. pimpos = private language of Gramsci with Delio(?).

46

Turi Prison, 3 June 1929

Dearest Tania,

I've got here in front of me two letters of yours and five postcards (the latest is dated 23 May) and I ought to reply to all of them in order, like a good boy. But I won't. Did you get the letter sent from my home, and the other one for Giulia? Going by what my mother says, you must have received the first one very late.

The change of season and the heat – which is already considerable – have depressed me, and I'm getting into a stupor. I feel an enormous tiredness weighing on me; this leaves me in a condition of general weakness, in spite of the fact that I am continuing to take restoratives; however, I don't think it'll last. It's no new thing, and so I'm not letting it worry me ... The whole thing's a bore, nevertheless, because it makes me lose my taste for reading, and blunts my memory and my sensibility all round.

On Saturday I received your parcel, which was handed over to me by special dispensation. Many thanks. But I thought that inside it I would find wool for mending stockings etc.: so I was very disappointed and worried. I really mean it. Let me plead with you not to let yourself get carried away by your imagination or by abstract ideas of the 'useful' or the 'necessary'; keep your eye fixed on the concrete fact of *prison* – by which I mean the things I have asked you to send me. Your postcards give the effect of some story-book plot, with desires, proposals, repentances, cruel dilemmas, wishful thinking etc. Wouldn't it serve a better purpose if we decided to be more resolute and self-controlled? It's true that your way of doing things amuses me, but that's no justification (for you anyway). It amuses me, because it proves to me that you are the least practical of persons, in spite of all the claims you've often flaunted to that effect. As for me, I've usually been the most practical man in this world. I did not do a number of things for the simple reason that I didn't give a damn for them; and so I seemed not to be practical just because I was practical – even to exaggeration!

And I wasn't understood! A really tragic thing.

I think it's now possible to draw up a final and fairly exact balance sheet on the flower situation. All the seeds have failed except one; I'm not sure what it is, except that it's probably a flower and not a weed. The chicory is all in flower and will provide a lot of seed for the coming season. The bamboo-cane has already put out a leaf as large as a hand, and another is under way: it seems to be taking well. The dahlias are still in the incubation stage, and nothing is known about them; however we may presume that they'll be born into the world some day or other, but I don't know their season of flowering. The rose is starting to bud, after being reduced (or so it seemed) to a cluster of dry sticks. But will it succeed in winning through the summer heat lying ahead? I think it's too weak and sickly to amount to much. It's true that in the last analysis the rose is nothing but a wild briar, and therefore ought to have staying power. We shall see.

I would have liked to send you a chicory flower, but on second thoughts I decided not to, for I doubt if it's good for anything except starting a *stornello*.[1]

You say in the postcard of 14 May that you'd like a new list of the books which I asked for when you were here. As far as I can see, I have received all of them. It doesn't matter if something is missing; if it's important I shall remember it. Don't send me any translation which is not published by Slavia, however important and authoritative it may look.

Antonio

1. Tuscan folk song which usually starts with the name of a flower (cf. the snatches of song in Browning's *Fra Lippo Lippi*).

47

Turi Prison, 1 July 1929

Dearest Tania,

... Apropos of this: believe it or not, the rose has completely revived (I say 'apropos of this', because rose-watching has now taken the place of twiddling my thumbs all day). From 3 June up till the 15th it began quite unexpectedly to show little peeps of leaf; these became leaves, until at long last it was flowering green again. By now its little branches are as much as six inches long. It even tried to produce a tiny little bud, but this, alas, started to repine after a while, and now it's sicklying over with yellow. At any rate it's not out of the question that a timorous little slip of a rose might still win its way through to fullness this very year. The thought of this pleases me, because for a year now cosmic phenomena have interested me much (perhaps, as they say at home in Sardinia, my bed is well placed in line with the direction of the terrestrial fluid, and when I'm resting, my body cells revolve in unison with the entire universe). I have been awaiting the arrival of the summer solstice with great impatience, and now that the earth is inclining (in point of fact it's straightening up after inclining) towards the sun, I am happier. (The question is bound up with the matter of the light which they bring me in the evenings, so it's not hard to track the 'terrestrial fluid' to earth!) The cycle of the seasons, the progression of the solstices and the equinoxes, I feel them as if they were flesh of my flesh; the rose is living and will certainly flower, because the heat leads in the cold, and under the snow the first violets are already trembling. In short, time has seemed to me a thing of flesh ever since space ceased to exist for me.

Antonio

48

Turi Prison, 1 July 1929

Dear Giulia,

Tell Delio that the news he sent me interested me enormously, because it really is a serious and important matter. Still I hope that someone managed with the help of a little gum to repair the mischief done by Giuliano, and that the hat didn't just become waste paper. Do you remember how in our Rome days Delio used to think that I could mend anything that was broken? Certainly he'll have forgotten that by now. Does he show any signs of a tendency to patch things up himself? That, in my opinion, would be an indication of ... constructive ability, much more so than making things with his Meccano.

You are wrong if you think (as appears from your letter) that from my childhood onwards I always showed literary and philosophic tendencies. On the contrary, I was an intrepid pioneer, and never went out of the house without carrying in my pockets grains of wheat and matches done up in little bits of oil cloth, just in case I should happen to get cast away on a desert island and left to my own devices. Furthermore I was a gallant builder of ships and handcarts, and knew all the naval nomenclature from A to Z and back again. My greatest success was when one of the village characters asked me to make a paper model of a proud double-decker schooner so that he could reproduce it in tin. Indeed I was obsessed by these things, because by the age of seven I had already read *Robinson Crusoe* and the *Mysterious Island*. I am rather afraid that a childhood like my own of thirty years ago is no longer possible today: today children when they are born are already eighty years old, like the Chinese Lao-Tze. The radio and the aeroplane have destroyed forever Robinson Crusoe-ism which was the food for the daydreams of so many generations. The invention of Meccano in itself shows how the child of today is rapidly becoming more intellectual. He can no longer take Robinson as his hero, what he'll prefer is the detective or the scientific thief – at any rate, in the West. And so your opinion, once it's stood on its head, can be regarded as quite right ... Or am I wrong?

You tell me Giuliano's weight; you don't add how tall he is. Tatiana told me that Delio when he weighed three stone was three and a half feet tall. This piece of news is of great interest to me, because it enables me to get a concrete impression; you send me all too few items of news like that. I hope that Tatiana will continue to be much more industrious than you and will send me loads and loads of news when she is with you – news about the children, and news of you too.

My dear, I embrace you together with the children.

Antonio

49

Turi Prison, 30 July 1929

Dear Julca,

I have received your letter of the 7th. The photographs have not reached me yet: I hope that your own will be among them too. Of course I want to see one of you too, at least once a year, in order to have an up-to-date impression of your appearance; otherwise all sorts of stupid thoughts might start entering my head – for example, that you had greatly changed physically, that you were weaker, that you had a lot of white hairs, etc., etc. Incidentally, I must send you my loving greetings for your birthday well in advance; maybe the next letter would get you in time, but I can't be sure. If a photograph of you arrives, I'll send you the greetings twice over. Of course I would like to see you in a group with the children, as in last year's photograph, because a group gives a livelier, a more dramatic impression; one gains an idea of relationships, and this one can elaborate, carry over into other groupings and transform into episodes of real life, leaving the photographer and his carefully aimed camera behind. To be sure, I think I know you well enough to imagine you in other scenes; but I haven't sufficient basis for an imaginary picture of the children, and of their actions and reactions when they are together with you. I mean the living actions and reactions, face to face, and not the interplay of feeling and character in a general sense; the photographs tell me little, and my childhood memories are small help to me, because in my view they are too individual. I imagine it must be quite different now, in a new world of feeling and with a difference of two generations (one might even allow for more, because the difference between a child brought up in a Sardinian village, and a child brought up in a great modern city is one of at least two generations, having regard to that single fact alone).

Do you know this, that sometimes I should like to write about you, and about your strength which is a hundred times greater than you think; and yet I've always hesitated, because the picture I get of myself is that of a slave-dealer feeling the limbs of a beast of burden. There it is in writing, as I have so often thought it. But anyway – if I've thought it, so much the better if I've written it. I shouldn't let myself think in that way; if I do, the reason must be that many rejected conceptions still survive in my mind, though repressed below the surface: conceptions overcome on a critical level, but not yet altogether obliterated. It's certainly true that many times the thought has obsessed me that the heaviest burdens of our union have fallen on you; the heaviest in an objective sense, to be sure, but that's an idle distinction. The upshot is that I can't fix my thoughts on your strength, which I have admired so many times (even though I haven't always told you so); I'm constrained to think of your weakness, of the tiredness that you probably feel, and this with a great upsurge of tenderness which would express itself in a caress, but only brokenly in words.

Another thing you must realise is that I'm very jealous, because I am debarred from enjoying the first freshness of the impressions of our children's lives, debarred from helping you to guide them and educate them. I remember many little episodes of our life in Rome with Delio, and also the principles according to which you and Genia intended to bring him up; I think them over again and again, and try to develop them and adapt them to new situations. I always arrive at the same conclusion – that you have been greatly influenced by Geneva, and by the environment saturated with Rousseau – and with Dr Fulpius,[1] who must have been typically Swiss, Genevan and Rousseau-ite. But I've wandered rather far (maybe another time I'll write you a letter on this subject, if it interests you); and maybe I've pinked you with the mention of Rousseau which on another occasion (do you remember?) made you so angry.

My dear I embrace you.

Antonio

1. Charles Fulpius, who taught in a school in Geneva, was author of *Cours de morale sociale basé sur l'evolution* (Geneva, 1905).

50

Turi Prison, 26 August 1929

Dear Tatiana,

I have received the photograph of the children, and it made me very happy, as you can imagine. One reason it pleased me so much was that I was able to see with my own eyes that they have bodies and legs; for three years I've seen nothing but their heads, and the suspicion had begun to take root in my mind that maybe they had turned into cherubs – cherubs minus the little wings behind the ears. All in all, I've now got a much more lifelike idea of them. Of course I don't completely share your enthusiastic opinion. I take the more realistic view that their attitude is determined by the need to pose in front of the camera: Delio's position is eloquent of his mood – it suggests one who is obliged to perform some boring but necessary *corvée* and who is taking himself very seriously. Giuliano, on the other hand, is staring at that mysterious object, not altogether sure that there isn't some dubious surprise behind it all – an angry cat might spring out any moment, or maybe some magnificent peacock. For what other reason could they possibly have asked him to look in that direction and not to move? You're right when you say that he bears an extraordinary resemblance to your mother, not only about the eyes, but in the whole line of the upper part of face and head.

Have you guessed? I'm writing this letter reluctantly, because I'm not sure that it will reach you before you leave. What's more, I'm again feeling very low. It has rained a great deal, and the temperature has dropped; that's had a bad effect on me. I get neuralgia, pains in the loins and my stomach refuses food. But all that is normal as far as I am concerned, and so it doesn't worry me too much. However I'm eating two pounds of grapes a day, and so it's out of the question that I'll die of hunger: I'm fond of grapes, and these are of the very best quality.

I had already read an article by the publisher Formiggini about bad translations, and the measures which should be taken to counter this epidemic. A writer had even proposed that publishers should be held personally responsible for the absurdities published by them; Formiggini's reply was to threaten to shut up shop, because even the most scrupulous publisher can't avoid publishing a few howlers. With considerable wit he drew a picture of a policeman arriving and telling him: 'get up and come along with me to the station. You're wanted for assault on the Italian language.'[1] (Sicilians speak somewhat after this fashion, and many policemen are Sicilians.)

The question is a complex one, and no solution for it will be found. Translators are paid badly, and translate worse. In 1921 I asked the Italian representative of the Society of French Authors for permission to publish a novel as a serial. For 1,000 lire I obtained the permission – and also the translation, which had been done by a certain lawyer. The office was reassuringly well appointed, and the lawyer-translator seemed to be an old hand at the game, so I sent the copy to the printers and told them to set up the material in ten instalments ready for use when the occasion arose. However the night before publication was due to begin I resolved to cast an eye over it just for safety's sake and sent for the proofs. After reading a few lines I jumped clean out of my chair: I had discovered that on the top of a mountain there was a large-sized vessel. It wasn't a case of Mount Ararat and Noah's Ark; the mountain was in Switzerland, and the 'ship' was a big hotel.[2] The whole translation was like that: *morceau de roi* was translated 'little bit of king', *goujat* 'little fish', and so on, in even more humorous vein. When I protested, the office deducted 300 lire from the fee to compensate for the compositor's wasted work, and the correction of the translation that was necessary. But the cream of the whole thing was that as soon as the lawyer-translator had got his hand on the remaining 700 lire which he was supposed to hand over to the manager, he ran off to Vienna with a girl.

On the other hand translations of the classics at least have until recently been done with care and scruple, if not always with elegance. But nowadays horrifying things are encountered even in this field. For a collection of Greek and Latin classics which is almost national in character (the state is subsidising it to the tune of a 100,000 lire), the translation of the *Germania* of Tacitus has been entrusted to ... Marinetti – who, by the way, took a degree in Letters at the Sorbonne. I have read in a review a list of the vulgarities perpetrated by Marinetti, whose translation has been much praised by ... journalists. *Exigere plagas* (examine the wounds) is translated: 'Exact the wounds'. That single example is, I think, sufficient: any schoolboy could see that it's a senseless outrage.

Quite a while ago I asked you to get for me a slim volume by Vincenzo Morello (Rastignac) on the Tenth Canto of Dante's *Inferno* which Mondadori published some years ago ('27 or '28): does mention of it bring the thing back to you? I have made a small discovery about this Canto of Dante which I think interesting; it might do something to correct in part a thesis of Benedetto Croce on the *Divina Commedia* which he sustains too uncompromisingly. I won't dilate on the subject just now because it would take up too much space. I think that Morello's lecture is the last in point of time on the Tenth Canto, and therefore it may be useful for my purpose; I want to see if anyone has forestalled me in these observations. I doubt if anyone has, because in the Tenth Canto everyone is hypnotised by the figure of Farinata. Commentators confine their research – and their praise – to Farinata, and Morello (who is not a scholar but a purveyor of rhetoric) will undoubtedly have stuck to the tradition. In any case I would like to read him. Then I shall write my 'Note on Dante', and maybe send it to you in homage, written out in my very best handwriting ... All this is said to a certain extent with my tongue in my cheek, because in order to write a note of that sort I would have to take a second look at a fair amount of material (for example, reproductions of the paintings at Pompeii) which is only to be found in the larger libraries. What I'm getting at is that I would have to assemble the historic data which prove that, as a matter of tradition, from classical art right up to the Middle Ages, painters refused to reproduce sorrow in its deepest and most elemental forms (e.g. the sorrow of a mother). There is at Pompeii a picture of Medea cutting the throats of the sons she had by Jason; in the picture she is shown with her face covered by a veil, because the painter considered it superhuman and inhuman to show the expression on her face.

I shall jot down a few points, anyway, and maybe complete the preliminary draft for a future note.

... My dearest Tania, I embrace you affectionately.

Antonio

1. 'Si levasse e venisse con me in Questura. Dovessi rispondere di oltraggio alla lingua italiana.' These matted subjunctives make a somewhat uncouth impression in Italian.
2. The translator had rendered 'bâtiment' (building) as 'bastimento' (ship).

51

Turi Prison, 30 December 1929

Dear Giulia,

I didn't remember to ask Tatiana, when I had a talk with her a few days ago if she had sent on to you my two last letters to her. I think she must have done, because I did ask her to. You see, I wanted you to know about the state of mind I was in, even at the risk of causing you some anxiety. Since then my black mood has grown less oppressive, but it hasn't as yet altogether disappeared.

I read with great interest the letter in which you gave me an idea of the stage of development Delio has reached. If I make one or two observations on it, these must of course be considered with one or two limiting factors kept well in mind:

1. that I know almost nothing of the development of the children in that very period when the formation of mind and character can be observed at its most revealing: that is, after they have reached the age of two, when they begin to speak with a certain assurance, and get beyond images and pictures to the forming of logical nexi.

2. that the best judge of the direction in which a child's education should move is, and must be, a person who knows him intimately and can follow him in his whole process of development – provided, of course, that this person doesn't allow himself to be blinded by sentiment. (If he does so, he will lose every criterion, and abandon himself to what is purely and simply aesthetic contemplation of the child, the latter being degraded to the position of a substitute for a work of art.)

So, bearing in mind these two criteria, which are really one single one in two coordinates, I would say that the stage of mental development which Delio has reached – as I can apprehend it from what you write – makes him seem very backward for his age, and too infantile altogether. When he was two, in Rome, he had a go at playing the piano; which means that he had already grasped how the notes are graded on the keyboard by comparing them to the voices of animals: the chicken on the right and the bear on the left, with a variety of other animals in between. In a child less than two years old this behaviour was quite normal and to be expected; but at five and a few months the same behaviour applied to getting one's bearings is very retarded and infantile. (Of course, it might be argued that in the second case we are dealing with a very much bigger space – but this has less force than might appear, for the four walls of the room limit this space, and make it concrete.)

I remember very clearly that at less than five years of age, and without ever having left my native village – and therefore still having a very restricted idea of extended space – I was able to find the village where I lived on the map with a stick. What's more, I had an idea of what an island was, and I could find the principal cities of Italy on a big wall map. This means that I had a conception of perspective, of space in the round, and not only of abstract lines of direction; I had an idea of a system of connected measurements, and of orientation according to the position of points of reference (top-bottom, left-right) as absolute space values, quite apart from the exceptional position of my arm. I don't think I was exceptionally precocious in all this; quite the contrary. In general I have observed that 'grown-ups' easily forget their childhood impressions, which at a certain age disintegrate and merge into a complex of sentiments, regrets, mawkish comicalities or other deforming evasions. Because of this they forget that a child's intellectual development is a very rapid affair. From the very first days after birth he absorbs an extraordinary quantity of images which are still remembered after his first years, and which guide him in that initial period of logical thought which is made possible by his learning to talk.

Of course I am really unable to give any general opinion or judgement on this matter because I lack specific data in sufficient quantity; I am ignorant of almost everything if not everything that matters, because the impressions you sent me have no connecting link between them, and don't show any development. But from the mass of these data I have the impression that your own conception (and that of other members of your family) is too metaphysical, by which I mean it presupposes that the whole man is already potentially present in the child, and that it's a case of helping him to develop what already lies latent within him; of forgoing coercion, letting the spontaneous forces of nature do their work, and what have you. I for my part believe that man represents a whole historic formation, obtained by coercion (though that word is to be understood not merely in the sense of brute force or external violence) and I remain firm in this opinion: the only alternative is to fall back into a sort of transcendentalism or immanency. What is believed to be latent force is actually for the most part nothing but the inchoate and indistinct complex of images and sense-impressions of the first days, the first months, the first years of life; images and sense-impressions that are not always the best that could be imagined. This mode of conceiving education as the unwinding of a pre-existing thread had its importance in the days when it was propounded in opposition to the Jesuit school – that is, when it negated a philosophy which was still more harmful – but today it has in its turn been superseded. To refuse to 'form' the child merely means allowing him to pick up the motifs of life chaotically from his general environment, and letting his personality develop in a haphazard way. It's strange and interesting that Freud's psychoanalysis is now creating, especially in Germany (as far as I can gather from the reviews I have read), tendencies similar to those which existed in France in the eighteenth century; it is well on the way towards forming a new type of 'good savage', corrupted by society – that is, by history. The result of this is a new kind of intellectual disorder which is really exceedingly interesting.

All these things came into my mind as I read your letter. It's possible – indeed, it's very probable – that some of my judgements may be exaggerated, or even definitely unjust. It was all very well for Cuvier to take a tiny bone and reconstruct out of that a megatherium or a mastodon; the danger's always there that one might start with a piece of a mouse's tail and end up by reconstructing a sea-serpent.

I embrace you lovingly.

Antonio

52

Turi Prison, 13 January 1930

Dearest Tania,

... Thank you for the news about the family which you sent me. As far as my state of mind is concerned, I don't think you have as yet understood it perfectly. However I may say it's difficult for anyone at all to understand these things perfectly, because too many elements have gone together to form them, and many of these it's almost impossible to imagine; even less, then, is it possible to imagine the complex of which they all form part.

By a queer coincidence, I have just been reading a book 'From 1848 to 1861' which is a collection of letters, writings and documents relating to Silvio Spaventa,[1] an Abruzzese patriot. He was a member of the Neapolitan parliament in '48, was arrested after the failure of the national insurrection, condemned to imprisonment and set free in 1859 as the result of pressure by France and England. In the ensuing years he was a Minister of the newly-formed Kingdom, and until 1876 was one of the most significant figures of the right-wing Liberal Party. It seems to me, that, in spite of the language of his day which was nothing if not sentimental and romantic, he expresses perfectly in many of his letters certain states of mind similar to those which I am constantly going through. For example, in a letter to his father dated the 17th July 1853, he writes:

From yourself I have had no tidings for two months; four months and maybe more have passed since I had word from my sisters; and it is long since Bertrando [his brother] wrote to me. None will find it strange that a man like me, whose heart (as I deem) is affectionate and ever youthful, should feel stricken beyond measure by this cruel privation. I do not think I am loved less now by my family than I always was; but the effects of misfortune are chiefly these, that it often quenches in others all affection for the unfortunate, and not less often quenches in the unfortunate their affection for their fellow beings. I do not fear the first of these two effects in you as much as I fear the second in me; I feel, sequestered as I am here from all human commerce and love, that the immense tedium, the long drawn-out imprisonment, and the suspicion that I have been forgotten by everyone are slowly making my heart bitter and barren.

As I said, leaving aside the style which is a product of the sentimental climate of the age, the state of mind of the writer stands out in clear relief. And, a thing which comforts me a great deal, Spaventa was certainly not a weak character, a cry-baby like some of the others. He was one of the few (about 60) of the 600 condemned in '48 who never once consented to make an appeal for mercy to the King of Naples; neither did he take refuge in religion. Indeed, as he often writes, he became all the more convinced as the years went by that the philosophy of Hegel was the only system and the only conception of the world which seemed reasonable, and worthy of the intellectual progress of those days.

Do you realise, though, what the practical effect will probably be of this discovery of the resemblance between my own state of mind and that of a political prisoner of '48? That from now on it'll seem a bit comical to me, and ridiculously anachronistic. Three generations have passed, and big steps forward have been taken in every field. What was possible for the grandfathers is no longer possible for the grandchildren (I'm not talking about our actual grandfathers, of course, because my own grandfather – I've never told you this – was actually a colonel in the Bourbon gendarmerie, and he was probably one of those who arrested Spaventa, the anti-Bourbonite and partisan of Charles Albert). I mean that objectively, of course, subjectively, individual for individual, things have certainly changed.

... By rights this letter should have been to my mother. Please write to her yourself, so that she won't get alarmed through not receiving my news.

My dear, I embrace you.

Antonio

1. The paternal uncle of Benedetto Croce, whose guardian he became in 1883, after Croce's parents had been killed in an earthquake.

53

Turi Prison, 10 February 1930

Darling Giulia,

It came into my mind, while I was thinking over a number of things from past years, that you once told me that the State Library not only remunerates the translators of foreign books, as is obvious, but also gives a certain sum to people who suggest books for translation, in those cases where the suggestion is acted upon. So it has occurred to me that I might suggest a few of these books to you, together with those details which in my present circumstances I am capable of providing – details which will necessarily remain fragmentary and approximate. This will mean, too, that I shall more easily find subjects to talk about in my letters; I get fed up with writing the same old inanities, and my present life does not provide me with many entertaining or interesting themes. And incidentally I shall offer you a few observations on the currents of intellectual life in Italy, in its most enduring and most genuine manifestations.

Last year a new edition came out of a book which already had a place in European culture: 'Capitalism in the Classical World. A History of the Roman Economy'[1] – 204 pages in 16°, published by Laterza of Bari. The first edition came out in 1906 in French, a translation having been made straight from the Italian manuscript. The book had a great success, and was at once translated into German by Karl Kautsky: I think it was also translated into Russian and other languages. It was a counterblast to the tendency initiated by Mommsen to attach the label 'capitalistic' to every 'monetary' economy. (Marx reproved Mommsen for this error; Salvioli takes up the theme and develops it critically.) This tendency has today assumed the proportions of a disease, thanks to the work of Professor Rostovtzev, a Russian historian who teaches in England; and (in Italy) thanks to Professor Barbagallo, a disciple of Guglielmo Ferrero. Salvioli was a very competent scholar (he died last year while he was giving a lecture at the University of Naples); he accepted the theories of historical materialism, in the form they have assumed in Italy through the 'revision' of Benedetto Croce – that is, as a practical canon of historical research, and not as a total conception of the world. The present Italian edition is a complete rewriting of the earlier book; it has been brought up to date from the scholarly point of view and shorn of those polemical elements which were in place in 1906. In short, it's a new book. The author died before adding the final touches to it. It calls for a Russian translator who knows Italian exceedingly well, and who consequently is capable of understanding even Salvioli's syntactic distortions and his rather laboriously stitched-together periods.

Another recent book is that by Francesco Ercole, at present a member of Parliament: 'From Commune to Principality',[2] essays on the history of public law during the Italian Renaissance (published by Vallecchi of Florence, 1929; 381 pages). It consists of four studies, which are of varying interest from the point of view of non-Italian culture. One that would certainly be of interest outwith the borders of Italy is the first 'The Class Struggle at the End of the Middle Ages',[3] which would make an admirable little book on its own, or alternatively could appear as an article in a big review. It is not free from traces of a certain historical naïveté, e.g. the author's satisfaction that the movement of the Ciompi failed in Florence, because this 'made possible the cultural efflorescence of the Renaissance'; however it contains information which is of great interest and which is unknown to the general public (the original documents relating to the subject were published during the war in editions which, as far as the uninitiated were concerned, were as good as clandestine). It's all about certain attempts made in Florence between 1340 and 1350 to organise the workers of the industries, who were excluded from the craftsmen's guilds; also the odd political repercussions that followed, etc.

Ercole, too, belongs to the same school as historians like Salvioli, the so-called economic-juridical school which has to a certain extent injected fresh life into the writing of history: it has had its effect on the rhetorical historiography of academic tradition, and also on the purely erudite and philological brand, which is admittedly the better of the two.

I don't know whether these notes will be of any use to you, or whether you will have the desire or the opportunity to do something with them; in any case they have given me a chance to write about something other than the weather and the state of my nervous system. Subjects like these are the only things which interest me, and which help me to pass the time as best I may.

Why don't you write to me about Giuliano's intellectual development as well as Delio's?

I embrace you tenderly.

Antonio

1. *Il Capitalismo antico. Storia dell' economia romana* by Giuseppe Salvioli.
2. *Dal Comune al Principato.*
3. 'La lotta delle Classi alla fine del Medioevo'.

54

Turi Prison, 24 February 1930

Dear Carlo,

I have allowed two letters to slip by without remembering to write about an affair which, to a certain extent, interests me 'intellectually' – and maybe 'morally' as well. I was meaning to ask you to approach the Special Tribunal for the Defence of the State (in the Chancellery) and ask for a copy on unstamped paper of the sentence pronounced against me on 4 June 1928, explaining that it is needed in view of a possible appeal for its revision. This should entail no expenditure apart from the transcriber's fee – also the cost of the stationery, which shouldn't amount to much.

I shall tell you what I intend doing, because you already know what my opinions are on the result the thing will probably have in practice.

First of all I want to read the sentence. Originally I was under the impression that in view of the abbreviated procedure of the Special Tribunal, the sentences pronounced by it consisted merely of the penalty and no more; I now know that on the contrary they are pretty detailed, and that they summarise the chief points in the trial, attempting to coordinate them. As it will be the same in my case too, the formal reasons for the appeal can be set out more plainly if they are based on the 'considering that' paragraphs in the sentence. I shall send you this material, together with the sentence itself, and you can submit it to some lawyer whom you know to be a man of good will: he can give an opinion on it, and (if the latter is favourable) can draw up the appeal in the correct legal terms. I didn't want to have anything to do with the lawyer Nicolai; it was for that reason that I got so angry with Tatiana, seeing she addressed herself to him without giving me any warning. When the sentences had been pronounced, the lawyer Nicolai, after the manner of his kind, insidiously advised us to appeal: whereupon Terracini made application to the Court of Cassation, seeing that no definite procedure had been laid down by the law of November 1926. (This provided for the right of appeal but did not say to whom the appeal should go.) Now Nicolai should have got in touch with Terracini, who after all was a client of his; that was his clear duty. I had no hand in it, and I was unable to get in contact with him. But the lawyer, who in 1928 was so convinced of the advisability of appeal had changed his tune by 1929, when the application had gone forward and the appeal was a practical possibility. There are also other reasons too, which I shall not go into here.

As I have no means of finding out what the others who were sentenced with me have decided to do, I consider myself from now on free to act irrespective of anything they may have undertaken: and therefore I want to study the sentence and see if an application for revision seems possible on legal grounds. As a general principle I hold that in a situation like mine, it is one's duty to leave no legal possibility unexplored; not, of course, to harbour any illusions about the probable result, but to be able to say that one has done everything legally possible to show that the sentence pronounced against one has no ground in law.

Please copy out the articles of the code of military law which have to do with the revision of sentences, in order that I may have an exact picture of the possibilities which exist. Write and tell me what you do, and when you do it: don't hesitate to inform me how your own affairs are going. Maybe as far as the request for a copy of the sentence is concerned – in any case it should come from me – you could get into touch with Tatiana if she happens to be in Rome. If she is, she might be able to get your case dealt with more quickly.

I embrace you, together with all the family. My best wishes for the quick recovery of Teresina's children; Mamma wrote to tell me that they hadn't been well.

Affectionately.

Antonio

55

Turi Prison, 10 March 1930

Dearest Tania,

... Nothing honestly irritates me more than the 'wishful thinking' which takes the place of concrete decision; it irritates me in people for whom I have no sentimental attachment, and who as far as I am concerned are 'useless'; it grieves me deeply in people I am fond of, whom I could not and would not judge by any utilitarian yardstick, people I would like to wake up and stimulate. I have known quite a number of types of such daydreamers, especially at the university, and I have followed since then the tragi-comic progress of their existence. Put it this way: I have a number of models of such types in my memory, all clearly outlined and profiled, and they can still make me bristle when, thanks to some quirk of memory, they intrude into my thinking. Yes, they can still make me furious even now. It's because of this that I get so angry when some psychological trait of your own recalls a motif which I associate with one of these prototypes. I know that on such occasions I am capable of being really bad with you. But, believe me, it's my love which urges me on to scold you just as if you were a child: these states of mind really *are* childish. In my opinion we should always be very practical and concrete, and not go in for daydreaming; we should set ourselves moderate objectives which we are confident of reaching. Therefore it is necessary to have a clear idea of one's own limits – otherwise there is little hope of enlarging them or going as far as they allow.

All this appears to me so obvious and banal that I almost feel like a village priest who's taken it on himself to read you a scolding lecture.

My dear, don't be offended at all these things I say to you. I didn't understand the observation you made about *The Little Flowers of St Francis* in your postcard of the 7th. I think the *Little Flowers* can be very interesting, but this depends rather on the point of view of the reader, and also on how much he knows of the cultural history of that period. Artistically they are lovely, fresh, immediate; they express sincere faith and an infinite love for Francis, whom many held to be a reincarnation of God, a second appearance of Christ. That is why they are more popular in

Protestant countries than in Catholic countries.

Historically they prove what a powerful organisation the Catholic Church was and still remains. Francis came forward as the founder of a new Christianity, of a new religion, and raised enormous enthusiasm on all sides as in the first centuries of Christianity. The Church did not persecute him officially, because this would have anticipated the Reformation by two centuries; but it neutralised him, disbanded his disciples and reduced the new religion to a simple monastic order at its service. If you are reading the *Little Flowers* with the idea of making them a guide through life, you have no understanding of them whatever. Before the war Luigi Luzzatti published in the *Corriere Della Sera* a 'Little Flower' which he believed had never before appeared in print, and he accompanied it with a long social-economic refutation which was enough to make you laugh yourself sick. But today nobody could think of such a thing: not even the Franciscan friars, whose rule has been completely transformed even in the letter, and who in any case have fallen in prestige compared to the Jesuits, the Dominicans and the Augustinians – i.e. the religious elements who specialised in politics and culture. Francis was a comet in the Catholic firmament; but the ferment of development was still working in Dominic (out of whom comes Savonarola) and above all in Augustine, from whose order there emerged first the Reformation and then, later, Jansenism. St Francis did not go in for theological speculation; he tried to realise in practice the principles of the gospel. His movement was popular as long as the memory of the Founder lived on, but already in Fra' Salimbene da Parma, who lived a generation later, the Franciscans are depicted as 'merry friars'. Not to speak of the literature in the vulgar tongue;[1] Boccaccio is at hand to show us how far the Order had fallen in public estimation. All Boccaccio's friars are Franciscans.

My dearest, I've ended up by giving you a lesson in religious history. But maybe it will help you to enjoy the *Little Flowers* even more. I do hope I'll soon hear you're completely recovered – and with your will-power, too, in grand condition!

I embrace you tenderly.

Antonio

1. i.e. Italian.

56

Turi Prison, 7 April 1930

Dearest Tania,

... *The Devil at Pontelungo*[1] is 'historical' enough in the sense that the experiment of the Baronata and the Bologna episode in 1874 really took place. As in all the historical novels in this world the general framework is historical, not the individual characters or the isolated events taken singly. What makes the novel interesting, apart from its notable artistic qualities, is the almost complete absence of sectarian bitterness on the part of the author. In Italian literature, if we leave aside Manzoni's historical novel, there is an essentially sectarian tradition in this sort of production which goes back to the period between '48 and '60. On the one side there's Guerrazzi, who started the fashion; on the other there's the Jesuit, Father Bresciani. For Bresciani all the patriots were canaille, cowards, assassins, etc., while the defenders of throne and altar – as they were called in those days – were all little angels come down to earth 'as a sign and a wonder'.[2] For Guerrazzi, I need hardly say, the whole thing is neatly turned upside down; the supporters of the Pope are all sacks of the blackest coal, while the champions of unity and national independence rank with the noblest and purest heroes of legend. This tradition was maintained until a very short time ago by the two camps; it flourished in the thrilling instalments of newspaper serials. In the so-called cultivated or art literature the Jesuit faction held the monopoly. Bacchelli in *The Devil at Pontelungo* shows himself to be independent of both, or very nearly; his humour, which rarely becomes *parti pris*, lies in the things themselves rather than in an extra-artistic *parti pris* of the writer.

There's a novel, *Gironda* by Virgilio Brocchi, which takes up the story of the daughter of Costa and the Kuliscioff woman; I don't know whether you've read it. It's not worth much – very insipid, all milk and honey, along the lines of Georges Ohnet's novels. It relates the events which led up to the marriage of Andreina Costa to the son of the Catholic industrialist Gavazzi, and describes the succession of contacts between the two worlds, Catholic and materialist. Finally the points of friction are rubbed out: *omnia vincit amor*. Virgilio Brocchi is the Ohnet of Italy. D'Herbigny's book on Soloviev is very antiquated, although it's only now that it's been translated into Italian. However d'Herbigny is a Jesuit monsignore of great ability; at present he's the head of the Oriental section of the papal Curia which is working for the reconciliation of Catholics and Greek Orthodox. The book on *L'Action Française et le Vatican* is also out of date now; it's just the first volume in a series which may still be coming out, for Daudet and Maurras are indefatigable in dishing up the same old left-overs with different sauces. However, it's exactly for that reason that this book may still be interesting, for it expounds general principles. I don't know if you've succeeded in grasping the great historic importance which the conflict between the Vatican and the French monarchists has for France: it corresponds, within certain limits, to the events leading up to Italian Concordat. It is the French form of a profound reconciliation between Church and State: the French

Catholics, organised *en masse* in the French equivalent of Catholic Action, are splitting away from the Monarchist minority, and are therefore ceasing to represent the potential popular reserve for a legitimist coup d'état; they are tending instead to coalesce into a vast Republican Catholic party which aims at absorbing – and will certainly absorb – a considerable part of the present Radical Party (Herriot and company). It was typical, during the French parliamentary crisis of 1926, that while the *Action Française* was announcing the coup in advance, and publishing the names of the ministers destined to form part of the provisional government which would recall to the throne the Pretender John IV of Orleans, the leader of the Catholics agreed to take part in a Republican coalition government. The livid rage of Daudet and Maurras against Cardinal Gasparri and the Papal Nuncio in Paris is due to nothing other than the clear realisation that their political power has diminished by 90 per cent, at a conservative estimate.

I embrace you tenderly.

Antonio

1. *Il Diavolo al Pontelungo* by Riccardo Bacchelli. Bacchelli's most famous work is the trilogy *Il Mulino del Po*.
2. 'a miracol mostrare' (lit. 'to show forth a miracle'). This is a quotation from Dante's sonnet in the *Vita Nuova* which begins:
   Tanto gentile e tanto onesta pare
   La donna mia ...

57

Turi Prison, 19 May 1930

Dearest Tatiana,

I have received your letters and postcards. Once again the curious conception you have of my situation as a prisoner made me smile. I don't know if you have read the works of Hegel, who once wrote: 'the criminal has a *right* to his punishment.' By and large you seem to think of me as one who insistently vindicates his right to suffer, to be martyred, and who refuses to be defrauded of one iota or one single instant of his punishment. According to you I am a second Gandhi whose desire it is to bear witness before gods and men of the sufferings of the Indian people; or another Jeremiah or Elijah – or God knows what other prophet of Israel – that went down into the streets and ate filth in order to offer himself as an oblation and a sacrifice to the God of Vengeance, etc., etc.

I don't know what put this idea into your head; I can only say it's very ingenuous as far as you personally are concerned, and unjust towards me, unjust and inconsiderate. I've told you that I'm eminently practical; I don't think you understand what I mean by the expression because you make no effort at all to put yourself in my shoes. (As a result I suppose I must seem like a sort of actor to you.) My practicality consists in this: in knowing that if a man beats his head against the wall it's his head that breaks and not the wall. Very elementary, as you see, and yet very difficult to understand for someone who has never been in a position when he might begin to feel like beating his head against the wall – the sort of person, that is, who imagines that all you need say is 'Open, Sesame!', and the wall will open.

Your attitude is unconsciously cruel; you see a prisoner tied up (or rather you don't see that he's tied, and are just incapable of imagining what bonds are), and this prisoner doesn't want to move because he can't move. You think that he doesn't move because he has no desire to – what you don't see is that he has already gone through the motions, and the fetters have cut into his skin. Accordingly you set to work trying to goad him into moving with the help of red-hot irons. And what's the result? You make him writhe, and to the fetters which have drawn blood from him you add the agony of the burns ... However I'm afraid that this gruesome illustration from a penny dreadful about the Spanish Inquisition won't persuade you; you'll just go on as you were doing before. And as the red-hot irons are themselves purely figurative I shall doubtless carry on with my 'policy' of not breaking down walls by cracking my skull against them (it aches badly enough as it is without my indulging in similar pastimes). I shall also go on leaving on one side the problems I can't solve because I haven't got the necessary data to do so. This is my strength, my only strength, and it's exactly this that you want to deprive me of. The trouble is that it's a strength which, alas, one can't give to others; one can lose it, but it can't be given away as a present, nor can it be transmitted. You, I think, haven't given enough thought to my position, and therefore you are not yet capable of seizing the essentials of it. I am subject to a number of prison regimes: there is the prison regime which consists of four walls, bars, the *bocca di lupo*[1] etc., etc; I had already allowed for that, and unless I am much mistaken I had already succeeded in getting the better of it, seeing that the primary possibility from 1921 to November 1926 was not prison but death. What I had not allowed for was the other prison which has been added to the first: it consists in being cut off not only from the life of society, but from family life as well.

... I embrace you tenderly.

Antonio

1. Type of window in Italian prisons. See letter dated 4 April 1927 and note.

58

Turi Prison, 2 June 1930

Dearest Tania,

... I'd like to write to you about a question which will either make you angry or will make you laugh. Dipping into the *Petit Larousse* I was reminded of a rather curious problem. When I was a little boy I was never tired of hunting lizards and grass snakes, which I gave as food to a beautiful falcon which I had tamed. During these hunting expeditions in the country round about my village (Ghilarza), I happened three or four times to find an animal resembling the common snake, except that it had four little legs – two near its head, and two a good distance from the others, near the tail (if you could call it a tail); the animal was two to two and a half feet long, and very thick in comparison to its length – about the same thickness as a snake four or five feet long. Its legs didn't seem to be much use to it, because when it moved away it crawled along the ground very slowly. In my village this reptile is called a *scurzone*, the literal meaning of this being 'shortened' (*curzo* is the Sardinian for short). The name is certainly due to the fact that the beast looks like a snake cut short. (By the way don't confuse it with the blindworm or slow-worm, which, although short, is proportionately slender.)

At Santu Lussurgiu, which was where I spent my three final school years, I asked the Natural History master (a former engineer who was a native of the place) what the Italian for *scurzone* was. He laughed and told me that it was an imaginary animal, the asp or basilisk, and that he knew of no such animal as the one I described. The local lads of Santu Lussurgiu explained that in their village *scurzone* was in fact the word for basilisk, and that the animal I had described was called *coluru* (the Latin *coluber*): the word for 'snake', on the other hand, was the feminine noun *colora*. However, the master declared that it was all an old wife's tale, and that snakes with legs didn't exist.

Now you know how furious it makes a child when a grown-up tells him he's wrong, and he knows perfectly well all the time that he's right. In this case I was being held up to ridicule as a superstitious fool, although I had been talking about something out of real life. I suppose the reason I still remember the incident is because of the indignant reaction I felt against authority at the service of self-opinionated ignorance. What's more, in my village I had never once heard tell of the maleficent qualities of the *scurzone*-basilisk, although in other villages it was dreaded, and its name wreathed round with legend.

And now I've noticed among the pictures of reptiles in Larousse a saurian, the *seps*, which is nothing but a snake with four little legs

(Larousse says that it inhabits Spain and Southern France, and belongs to the family of the *scindides*, whose typical representative is the *scinque* (maybe the newt?).) The shape of the *seps* is a well-proportioned snake, fairly long and slender, and its legs make a harmonious whole with its body. The *scurzone*[1] on the other hand, is a repulsive animal; its head is very big, not small like that of an ordinary snake; the 'tail' is very conical; the two legs at the front of its body are too near its head, and incidentally they're too far away from its back legs. These latter are whitish in colour, and unhealthy-looking, like those of the proteus; they give the impression of monstrosity, of abnormality. It lives in damp places – I myself never saw it except on occasions when I had rolled away big stones. All in all, the beast makes a deformed, clumsy impression – not like lizards and snakes, which apart from the innate aversion man feels for reptiles, are at bottom elegant and graceful creatures.

What I would like to know now, from your experience in Natural History, is whether this animal has a name in Italian, and whether it's known that this species, which must be of the same family as the French *seps*, exists in Sardinia. It's possible that the legend of the cockatrice or basilisk has prevented people from looking for the thing in Sardinia. The master at Santu Lussurgiu wasn't a fool; quite the reverse. What's more, he was a keen worker, and made mineralogical collections etc.; but even so, he didn't believe that the *scurzone* existed as a plain pedestrian reality, minus a poisoned breath and incendiary eyes. To be sure this animal isn't very common: I haven't seen it more than half a dozen times, and every time under some sort of rock – whereas I've seen thousands of snakes without having to bother to move stones.

Dear Tatiana, don't get angry at all these meanderings of mine.

I embrace you tenderly.

Antonio

1. There is in English a fairly rare word 'scorzonera', which the *Concise Oxford Dictionary* defines as 'black salsify or Viper's-grass, a plant with parsnip-like root used as a vegetable', and gives the derivation as: Italian, probably from *scorzone*, adder, 'because it doth heale the bytinges of this beast'. The OED, however, calls its *scorzone* 'some kind of venomous snake', and adds that the Spanish *escorzon* (Catalan escorcu) is 'some kind of toad or lizard deemed venomous'. Webster derives 'scorzonera' from the Spanish *escuerzo*, a 'kind of toad'.

Italian lexicographers are equally vague about the *scorzone*; Fanfani defines it as 'a kind of snake, black in colour and very venomous'. Cappuccini gives its habitat as America.

The 'basilisk' or 'cockatrice' of the Bible is also a 'venomous serpent not identified' (Webster). In Coverdale's translation the Hebrew *tsepha* (Isaiah xi, 8); which in the Vulgate becomes *basiliscus* and *regulus*, is translated 'cockatrice': ('He shall put his hande in to the Cockatryce denne'). The Authorised version follows Coverdale and has 'cockatrice's'; the Revised Version has 'basilisk's', and a note: 'Or, adder's'. And so the chain of definitions, allusions and cross-references describes a complete circle.

For a general disquisition on the 'basilisk', see Sir Thomas Browne's *Pseudodoxia Epidemica*. A drawing of the *seps* appears on the page illustrating *Reptiles et Batraciens* in pre-1960 editions of the *Petit Larousse*.

59

Turi Prison, 16 June 1930

Dearest Tatiana,

A short while ago I had a discussion with my brother, and that has set up a zig-zag course in my thoughts. His visit was a totally unexpected experience, and I wasn't in the slightest degree prepared for it; I'd never have thought it possible that I'd see my brother again at Turi. I was very pleased indeed to see him, because I was always much closer to Gennaro than to the rest of the family ... However, I'm not sure what to say to you about it. I'll limit myself to quite a small thing. I learned from Gennaro that you're not eating very much at all; this struck him immediately, and he mentioned it quite spontaneously. (I assure you it wasn't due to any guile on my part, and I never even asked him about your eating habits, so his reaction is a serious matter: you eat practically nothing, and it shows. That's bad.) ... You'll have to mend your ways if you're to have any right at all to preach at me.

A thing in your last postcard that gave me a good laugh was the remark that you knew I particularly like to receive greetings on my *onomastico*.[1] I don't know who can have revealed this secret to you; I have kept it carefully hidden in the darkest recesses of my most profound subconscious – so hidden and so secret, in fact, that from the age of six onwards I altogether forgot that it was tucked away there. (It was only up to the age of six that I received presents for my *onomastico*.) I'm quite frightened: God knows what other hidden scars of mine you'll uncover! Maybe my ambition to become a Trappist monk, or a member of the Society of Jesus. (There's only one secret desire that I would like to reveal to you. It has always tormented me; I have never succeeded in satisfying it, and I'm afraid I'll never satisfy it my whole life long. It is this: to eat a mixed grill of the kidneys and brains of a rhinoceros and a babiroussa.)[2]

In any case, dear Tatiana – many thanks for your good wishes. The only thing to add is the fact that the St Anthony who protects me is not the one whose day falls in June, but the one whose day falls in January, and who is commonly associated with the European species of the babiroussa.[3] Unfortunately the babiroussa only lives in the Sonda islands, and therefore is very difficult to get hold of – especially in the shape of fresh brains and kidneys.

Dearest Tatiana, many thanks for the further instalment of news which you have sent me.

I embrace you tenderly.

Antonio

1. Name-day, i.e. day of the Saint whose name one bears.
2. Asiatic wild hog.
3. St Anthony 'of the Pig', see Letter dated 26 March 1927.

[This is the celebrated letter which sets down Gramsci's immediate reaction to his brother Gennaro's visit. Gennaro had been entrusted with a mission by the leaders of the Party in Paris (see Introduction); he was to give his brother the facts relating to the expulsion of three dissident comrades – Tresso, Ravazzoli and Leonetti – who opposed the *svolta* ('turn') in the party line after the Sixth Congress of the International. Spriano refers to the first sentence of this letter as 'an exceptionally sybilline allusion' to the political news from Paris (*Antonio Gramsci and the Party: The Prison Years*, p. 57).]

60

Turi Prison, 14 July 1930

Dearest Tatiana,

These last few days have brought one small item of news – but an item of genuine interest. I have been informed that my sentence has been reduced by one year, four months and five days: the stretch has thus been reduced to nineteen whole years, and the day of my liberation is now 20 January 1946 instead of 25 May 1947. In the communication there was a reference to a declaration of the Special Tribunal of May 1930 which followed the decree of 1 January, which refers to the measures taken on the occasion of the marriage of the Crown Prince. As you can see, it's a novelty in every sense of the word, because the conviction had become rooted among us that the January decree did not apply to those condemned by the Special Tribunal: nevertheless we have had our sentence reduced, and I – like many others, I imagine – have been granted not just a year, but no less than one year, four months and five days!

What is the explanation of all this? My guess is: in the case of the sentences for supposed crimes committed before the Special Law was passed, and therefore pronounced under the old Zanardelli code, there are several headings for the various charges: I was charged under six headings which taken together carried a penalty of thirty-one years and eight months – between prison and detention. This was reduced by virtue of the maximum penalty law to twenty years, four months and five days. I think the Tribunal must have applied the decree of a year's remission to three or four or maybe even five of the headings in the text of the sentence; in which case they will have recalculated the reduction according to the maximum penalty law, and allowed me sixteen months and five days.

I have explained all this at length, because I am very curious to know if my hypothesis is correct; to know, in fact, to what headings in the sentence the reduction was applied. Would you like to find out for me? As soon as you are fully restored to health, you might go along to the office of the Tribunal and ask for a little light on the above points; I'm not sure if there's any other way of finding out. Maybe you could ask P.[1]

... I embrace you affectionately.

Antonio

1. P.: Piero Sraffa, lecturer in political economy in the University of Cambridge. Gramsci had met him when he was a student at Turin, and had formed a close friendship with him. During Gramsci's ten years in prison, Mr Sraffa did everything he humanly could to help him; he corresponded regularly with Tatiana Schucht, undertook several journeys to Italy and succeeded in having a number of talks with Gramsci. He also interested a number of leading British personalities in Gramsci's fate.

61

Turi Prison, 28 July 1930

Darling mamma,

The two little photos that Nannaro[1] brought me pleased me very much indeed: even though they are not terribly good from a technical point of view, they do succeed in conveying quite a reasonable impression of your appearance, and of your facial expression. It seems to me that in spite of your years, and all the rest of it, you've kept young and strong; you can't have more than a few white hairs, and your expression is very lively – even though it is, how shall I put it ... a bit matronly. I'll bet that you'll live to see your great grandchildren, and see them growing up, into the bargain! One day in the years to come we'll get a big photograph taken: all the generations will be in it, and yourself in the middle to keep us all in order.

Mea[2] has grown a lot, but she's still very *spabaiada*.[3]

Nannaro, going by what you wrote to him, must have thought that his daughter was God knows what sort of monster of wisdom and genius. And now, because of this, he's swung back to the opposite extreme, and has forgotten that the child is only nine or ten years old. However it's true that he's got hold of something when he remarks that at her age we were more mature, and more developed mentally. It's a thing that has struck me too. In fact, it seems to me that Mea is too childish for her age – yes, even taking into consideration what a little girl she still is. She doesn't appear to have any ambition apart from looking nice; she doesn't seem to have an inner life, and as far as her sentimental needs are concerned, they all seem to be of the animal variety (vanity etc.). Maybe you've spoilt her too much, and haven't obliged her to discipline herself. It's true that neither I myself nor Nannaro – or the others either if it comes to that – were obliged to discipline ourselves, but we did it of our own accord. I can remember that at Mea's age I would have died of shame if I had made so many spelling mistakes; do you remember how I used to read till late on into the night, and how many subterfuges I had recourse to to get hold of books? Teresina, too, was like that, although she was a little girl just like Mea – except that she was certainly prettier physically. I'd like to know what Mea has read up to now; I should think, judging by what she writes, that she can't have read anything but her school books. To sum up, you ought to try to get her used to working in a disciplined way, and make her cut down on her 'mundane' life a little: fewer successes which gratify her vanity, and more substance and seriousness. Ask Mea to write to me; tell her to describe her life to me etc.

Kisses to all. I embrace you tenderly.

Antonio

1. Gennaro Gramsci, one of Antonio's brothers.
2. Mea (Edmea): daughter of Gennaro Gramsci.
3. Dreamy, scatterbrained (Sardinian).

62

Turi Prison, 22 September 1930

Dearest mamma,

I received Carlo's insured letter on time, with the 200 lire enclosed. I am not ill, and have not been down with any illness; the absence of letters was due to other causes. I haven't received a letter from Nannaro which Carlo told me to expect.

I really do hope that, as Carlo says in his letter, you are at any rate managing to take the doctor's orders seriously. Do you know this – I'm always afraid that you may put too much trust in your robustness of bygone days, when you hardly ever suffered from any illness, and are on that account not too punctilious about obeying the doctor's orders; in short, I'm afraid you're neglecting your health. Carlo and Grazietta ought to force you to get cured, and they ought to stop you tiring yourself, even if it means tying you down in your chair. But Grazietta is probably not energetic enough, and Carlo too will let himself be persuaded: the result is that you'll continue maybe to stand in front of the kitchen range and then likely walk out into the courtyard when you're overheated etc. Ah, Peppina Marcias – what you need is a son like me beside you to make you stick to what the doctor tells you, and not let you dodge around all over the place like a ferret in the warrens.

Darling mamma, write to me – or get someone to write to me, and tell me how you are keeping. Kisses to all at home, and to yourself lots of loving embraces.

Antonio

63

Turi Prison, 6 October 1930

Dearest Tania,

I was glad to get a visit from Carlo. He told me that you have made a good recovery, but I'd like to have more precise information about your health. Many thanks for all you've sent me. The two books have not yet been handed over to me: I mean the Fascist Bibliography, and the short stories of Chesterton. The latter I am very keen to read, for two reasons. Firstly, because I imagine they will be at least as interesting as the original series, and secondly because I shall try to reconstruct in my mind the impression they will probably have made on you. I confess that the latter will be my chief delight. I remember exactly your state of mind when you read the first series: your temperament is such that you have the happy knack of receiving the most immediate impressions – those less muddied with cultural sediments. It had hardly even begun to dawn on you that Chesterton doesn't write detective stories in the proper sense of the word so much as deliciously delicate caricatures of the detective story. Father Brown is a Catholic who makes fun of the Protestants' mechanistic manner of reasoning, and the book is fundamentally an apology for the Roman Church as against the Anglican Church. Sherlock Holmes is the 'Protestant' detective who unravels the plot of each crime starting from the outside, and basing himself on science, on the experimental method, on induction. Father Brown is the Catholic priest who has behind him all the refinements of psychological experience provided by the confessional, and by the laborious subtleties of the moral casuistry of the Fathers; although not neglecting science and experience, he bases himself especially on deduction and introspection. The result is that he knocks Sherlock Holmes into a cocked hat, makes him appear like a pretentious little schoolboy, and shows up his narrowness and meanness. Furthermore Chesterton is a fine artist, whereas Conan Doyle was a mediocre writer – even though he was made a baronet for 'literary merit'. Consequently one can detect in Chesterton a stylistic remove between the subject (the sleuth at work) and the form; hence one finds in him a subtle irony towards the subject he is treating, and that adds a tang to the stories ... Or maybe you disagree? I remember that you read these stories as if they were chronicles of real events; you thought yourself into them so well that you were capable of expressing frank admiration for Father Brown, and for his marvellous acumen – all in a manner so naive that I got a great deal of amusement out of it. You mustn't be offended at that, because for all my amusement I secretly envied your capacity for what one might call a fresh and candid impressionism.

... I embrace you affectionately.

Antonio

64

Turi Prison, 6 October 1930

Darling Giulia,

I have received two of your letters; one of 16 August, and the other a later one, I think written in September. I would have liked to write you a good long letter about them, but I can't; in certain moments I just can't manage to make the link between my memories and the impressions I receive when reading your letters. Unfortunately, however, I'm able to write only on certain days and at hours not fixed by myself; hours which sometimes coincide with moments of nervous depression.

That part of your letter gave me great pleasure where you say that having reread my letters of '28 and '29 you could see how exactly alike our thoughts are. I'd like you to tell me, though, in what circumstances and in connection with what particular subject has this likeness been especially borne in on you? What is lacking in our correspondence is precisely an effective and concrete 'correspondence'; we have never succeeded in getting a 'dialogue' going; our letters are a series of 'monologues' which do not always manage to correspond, even along general lines. If in addition to this you take into consideration the time factor, which makes one forget what one has written previously, the impression of a pure 'monologue' is reinforced. Do you agree?

I am reminded of a Scandinavian folk tale. Three Norse giants live as far distant from one another as great mountains. After thousands of years of silence the first giant shouts to the other two: 'I hear the lowing of a herd of cattle.' Three hundred years later the second giant declares: 'I've heard the lowing too.' After another three hundred years have passed the third giant gets his word in: 'If you go on making a row like this, I'm leaving.'

Oh, I really can't bring myself to write; there's a sirocco blowing all over the place – you'd think it was drunk.

My dear, I embrace you tenderly, together with our children.

Antonio

65

Turi Prison, 4 November 1930

Dearest Tatiana,

... My state of health is still about the same, and I'm doing all I can at any rate to maintain the present equilibrium. The major problem is insomnia, which being determined to a large extent by mechanical external causes, more or less inherent in prison life, and only partially by organic causes, cannot be cured by therapeutic means; at the most, it can be palliated. I have drawn up a statistical table for the month of October: on two nights only did I get five hours' sleep; nine whole nights I did not sleep a wink; the other nights I slept for varying lengths of time, but never as much as five hours. That gives an average of little more than two hours per night. At times I'm lost in wonder myself that I still have so much power of resistance; it amazes me I haven't suffered a general collapse. I am taking the Sedobrol regularly. I am taking it, I repeat, in order to try to keep my physical condition at least at its present level.

... My dear, I embrace you tenderly.

Antonio

66

Turi Prison, 4 November 1930

My darling Giulia,

I don't know whether you're still at Sochi (if you are, this letter will have to be forwarded on to you), or whether you've already returned from the rest cure. Being uncertain on this point, I shan't as yet inflict a long letter on you after the manner of Doctor Grillo which I had planned to write – I had it all worked out in sections and paragraphs like an academic dissertation. Let's leave that till next time. But meanwhile I must warn you that 'all is discovered', that there's no more mystery for me

– in short, that I've been informed about your real state of health right down to the last detail. To tell you the truth, it was what in Italy is called an 'open secret', in the sense that I had understood that you were fairly ill, or at the least that you were going through a psychological crisis which was bound to have a physiological basis. I would have been a pretty poor 'man of letters' if I had not understood this reading your letters – because after the first 'disinterested' reading, in which only my love for you guides me – I reread them from a literary critical and psychoanalytical point of view. For me literary expression (linguistics) is a relationship between form and content: analysis shows me, or helps me to understand, if there is complete adhesion between form and content, or if there exist gaps, fissures, disguises etc. It's possible to be mistaken, especially if one tries to deduce too much, but if the critic has a certain criterion to judge by, he can comprehend a good deal – at any rate the general state of mind. I'm writing all this to let you know that from now on you can and should write to me with extreme frankness.

I have received some photos of our children, which are rather poor from a technical point of view – but of the greatest interest for me just the same.

I embrace you lovingly.

Antonio

67

Turi Prison, 17 November 1930

Dearest Tatiana,

I have received your postcard of 10 November, and the letter of the 13th. I shall try to answer your questions in order. For the present don't send me any books. Keep those you have on one side, and wait till I ask you to send them. I want first of all to clear out all the old reviews that I've been accumulating for four years: before sending them I am going through them again, taking notes on the subjects which interest me most; naturally this takes up a good part of the day, because the notes are accompanied by cross-references, comments, etc.

I have decided on three or four principal subjects, one of which is that of the cosmopolitan function which the Italian intellectuals had up to the eighteenth century. This theme can be broken down into various sections: the Renaissance, Machiavelli, etc. If I were able to consult the necessary material, I think that a really interesting book could come out of it, a book which as yet does not exist; by a 'book' I mean actually an introductory essay and a certain number of monographs, because the question presents itself differently in different periods, and in my view it would be necessary to go back to the time of the Roman Empire. In the meantime I am writing notes, for this reason among others that reading the relatively scanty material which I have makes me remember the reading I did in the past. In any case the thing isn't completely new to me, because ten years ago I wrote an essay on Manzoni's ideas on language; this demanded a certain amount of research into the organisation of Italian culture from the time when the written language (the so-called Middle Latin, i.e. the Latin written between AD 400 and AD 1300) broke away completely from the spoken language of the people – which, once the Roman centralisation ended, was fragmented into innumerable dialects. This Middle Latin was succeeded by 'the vulgar tongue', which in its turn was submerged by the Latin of the humanists, thus giving place to a learned tongue 'vulgar' in vocabulary but not in phonology, and even less in syntax which was reproduced from Latin. So a double language continued to exist – the popular or dialectal language and the learned tongue, the language of the intellectuals and the cultured classes.

Manzoni himself, when rewriting *I Promessi Sposi* and when composing his treatises on the Italian language, was in reality only taking into account one single aspect of language, the vocabulary; he did not consider syntax which is actually the essential part of every language: so much so that English, although 60 per cent of its vocabulary consists of Latin or Romance words, is a Germanic language, and Rumanian, although Slav words account for over 60 per cent of its vocabulary, is a Romance tongue. As you can see, the subject interests me so much that I've let it run away with me.

... I embrace you.

Antonio

68

Turi Prison, 17 November 1930

Dearest Teresina,

I have received your letter of the 11th with the photograph of your children. The kids are very attractive and nice-looking, and I should say they were also strong and healthy. I'm really amazed to see how much more robust Franco looks. Some time ago you sent me a photograph of him in which he seemed thin and delicate – but this one shows as clear as day that he's not only strong, but sunny and lively into the bargain. I'm really pleased with it, and I would be grateful to you if you would send a copy of the same photograph to Tatiana, who will send it on to Giulia. I sent her a few copies of the other photographs myself (although from a technical point of view they were pretty shocking) and she wrote to me that Delio and Giuliano were very interested in them and were asking such a lot of questions.

I have been very worried because for over a month I have had no news of mother: Carlo has not written since his trip to Turi (or at any rate I have not received his letters); and Nannaro, in spite of all his promises, has not written to me once. (Though in his case it's probable that the letters haven't reached me.) You should really make a resolution to write to me a few more times, and in particular to give me a lot of news of your children. That's of real interest to me. The remark you make about Franco, that he writes 'long letters, after his own fashion' which amuse you all, pleases me: it means that he has imagination, that he has something to say, and that he tries to give expression to what comes surging up in his head. Maybe he'll be like the two of us – who knows? Do you remember how fanatically keen we were on reading and writing? Unless I'm wrong you too, when we were getting on for ten and had no more new books to read, ploughed your way all through the Codices. Mimi, on the other hand, doesn't appear to me to have much imagination; she has an astonished expression which makes one feel that she has too much to do wondering at the world to have any time for making things up on her own account. The chief thing I notice about the little girl is that she seems happy to find herself under the protection of the two elder children, and therefore to be able to put a bold face on things in front of the camera, and its *cabbanu*[1] apparatus: she even seems to me to have a certain challenging air with her head cocked at an angle. Or am I wrong? Of course, a photograph can fix and petrify a really quite transient movement or gesture, and it's eminently possible to interpret a single attitude wrongly even when, as in the photograph of your children, that attitude is very dramatic.

Write to me about mamma as well, and tell me how she's really keeping. Don't go under to laziness; don't let the monotony of the office[2] get you down, or the boring chatter of the people who are always hanging around in it. You must become as vivacious as you used to be (not in the physical sense, for vivacious in that sense you've never really been; I mean in the intellectual sense) in order to be able to bring the children up properly out of school hours, and not abandon them to their own devices – as too often happens, especially in the so-called 'respectable' families.

I embrace you affectionately.

Antonio

1. *Moro cabbanu*. (Sardinian). Literally 'black man wearing the hood', a macabre figure resembling the Devil in Scottish folklore (cf. Stevenson's *Thrawn Janet*). The Italian edition translates it in a note as 'lupo mannaro', i.e. 'were-wolf', but this, besides being inaccurate, does not give the picture.
2. The Post Office at Ghilarza.

69

Turi Prison, 1 December 1930

Dearest Tatiana,

I would be glad if you could manage in some bookshop in Rome to get hold of the October number of the review *La Nuova Italia*, edited by Professor Luigi Rosso, and send it to Giulia. It contains a letter which gives an account of the courteous debate between Benedetto Croce and Lunacharsky which took place at the International Congress of Philosophers held recently at Oxford.[1] The question under discussion was this: does there exist, or can there exist, an aesthetic doctrine of historic materialism?[2] The letter is maybe by Croce himself, or at any rate by one of his disciples, and it is curious. From this letter it appears that Croce's position with regard to historic materialism is now completely different from what it was a few years ago. Today Croce maintains, no more and no less, that historic materialism represents a return to ... the old medieval teleology, to pre-Kantian and pre-Cartesian philosophy. A thing to take one's breath away, and to raise doubts whether Croce too, in spite of his Olympian serenity, may not possibly be beginning to nod too often – more often, indeed, than Homer. I don't know whether he'll write some special essay on this subject; it would be of interest if he did so, and I don't think it would be difficult to reply to it – one could annex all the necessary and sufficient arguments from his own works.

I myself think that Croce has had recourse to a very transparent polemical subterfuge, and that his judgement is not so much an historical-philosophic judgement as an act of will – which means it has a practical end. It is perhaps demonstrable that many so-called theorists of historical materialism have fallen into a philosophic position resembling that of medieval teleology, and have made a sort of 'Unknown God' of the 'economic structure'; but what would that prove? It would be exactly the same as if one were to propose giving an opinion on the religion of the Pope and the Jesuits, and then spoke about the superstitions of the peasants of Bergamo. The present attitude of Croce to historical materialism seems to me to be rather like that of the men of the Renaissance to the Lutheran Reformation; 'Where Luther enters, civilisation disappears', said Erasmus – and yet the historians, and Croce himself, recognise today that Luther and the Reformation were the beginning of the whole of modern philosophy and civilisation, including the philosophy of Croce. The men of the Renaissance did not understand that a great movement of moral and intellectual renewal would be bound – if, like Lutheranism, it incarnated itself in the vast masses of the people – to assume at the outset uncouth and even superstitious forms; they fail to see that this was inevitable owing to the very fact that it was the German people, and not a tiny aristocracy of great intellectuals, which was the protagonist and standard-bearer of the Reformation. If Giulia can do so, I would like her to let me know if the Croce–Lunacharsky polemic gives rise to intellectual developments of importance.

My dearest, I have got to hand in the letter. I embrace you tenderly.

Antonio

1. The 7th International Philosophy Congress was held at Oxford, 1-5 September 1930. A. V. Lunacharsky (1875–1933) was People's Commissar for Education from 1917 to 1929. He knew Italy well, and spoke the language fluently.
2. cf. 'The Materialist Conception of History' in Plekhanov' *Fundamental Problems of Marxism*, Lawrence and Wishart, London, 1969.

70

Turi Prison, 15 December 1930

Darling mamma,

I don't know what's happening. Carlo hasn't written to me for over three months. I received the last note you yourself sent me about two months ago. About six weeks ago I received a letter from Teresina to which I replied, but she has not written another letter. (I wrote to Teresina four weeks ago to the day.)

It has occurred to me that Carlo may have had certain unpleasantnesses on my account, and that he does not want to explain to me (or doesn't know how to explain to me) the state of hesitancy and confusion he's probably in. I would like him, therefore, to reassure me on this point, or to get someone else to do it; maybe he could ask Mea to write a letter. I would also like to be informed a little more often about your own state of health. Have you got your strength back? If you haven't the strength to write, get someone else to write the postcard and then just add your signature; that will be enough for me.

Darling mamma, this is the fifth Christmas since my arrest and the fourth that I am spending in prison. Certainly, the conditions under which I spent the Christmas of '26 on Ustica as a political exile were a sort of paradise of personal liberty in comparison with my prison conditions. But don't imagine that there has been any falling away as far as my serenity is concerned. I am four years older, I have many white hairs, I have lost my teeth, I don't laugh as easily as I did once; on the other hand I think I have grown wiser, and that I am richer in experience of men and things. What's more, I haven't lost my taste for life; I am still interested in the wide world, and I am sure that even if I can no longer *zaccurrare sa fae arrostia,*[1] at any rate I wouldn't object to seeing the others *zaccurrare*. And so I haven't grown old yet, have I? We become old when we begin to fear death, and when it displeases us to see others doing what we can no longer do ourselves. In this sense I am certain that you haven't grown old either, in spite of your age. I am sure that you have decided to live for a long time yet, so that you may be able to see us all again, and get to know all your grandchildren: as long as the will to live is there, as long as we have a taste for living and can still look ahead toward some objective, we can put to flight every illness, every disorder.

All the same you ought to keep in mind that it's unwise to tax your strength too much: don't take it into your head that you can still face up to all the stresses and strains you could in your young days. Which reminds me that Teresina, in her letter, mentioned with a touch of mischief that you still insist on doing too much and that you won't give up your supremacy in the housework. But you really ought to give it up and take a rest. Darling mamma, I send you every good wish for Christmas and the New Year: may you enjoy them in laughter and in tranquillity.

With every good greeting and wish to all at home. I embrace you tenderly.

Antonio

1. Crunch roasted beans (Sardinian).

71

Turi Prison, 29 December 1930

Dearest Grazietta,

I have received your letter, and the note from Mea. On Christmas Day I received the parcel. Tell mamma that everything was in good condition, and nothing was spoilt; even the bread was still fresh, and I ate it with great gusto: the taste of the Sardinian maize was very good. *Sa panischedda*[1] I ate with equal gusto: I think it was the first time I had eaten some for fifteen or sixteen years.

Your news about mamma's health has worried me a lot. I'm sure that you'll have a great deal of patience with her, because she has worked for us all her life, sacrificing herself in an unexampled manner; if she had been a different kind of woman, who knows what a disastrous end we all might not have had when mere children. Maybe none of us would be alive today. Don't you agree?

I had seen the photograph of Father Soggiu in two illustrated papers, but had not recognised him; it never even entered my head that it might be him, even though the caption to one of the photos gave his birth place as

Norbello. I looked at it again after reading your letter and recognised the lineaments of his brothers, and especially of his brother Gino, even under the great Franciscan beard. And it wasn't as if he had aged – quite the contrary; even though he became a friar at least twenty-five years ago after taking his degree. He really was a fine man, and he'll have made a grand friar I don't doubt. And so the people of Ghilarza will now have a second local martyr after Palmerio – indeed this one has a better title to the name, because Palmerio had no other 'merit' than that of having made a pilgrimage to Jerusalem. All the same I think that if a Buddhist monk arrived in Ghilarza from China and exhorted his hearers to throw off the religion of Christ and embrace that of Buddha, the people of Ghilarza would assuredly do him in, just as the Chinese have done with Father Soggiu.

Thank Mea for her note; I was glad to get it, but I was sorry to see that she still writes like a little girl in the third class of elementary school (whereas she must be in the fifth, if I'm not mistaken). It really is a shame, because our family had a certain name in the schools of Ghilarza. This Mea must really have been born at Pirri, and she must have been deafened in her cradle by the croaking of the frogs in the marshes: tell her she must have got a frog's brain herself, if she can do nothing but make a noise, and can't think or put two and two together. Pull her ears a wee bit as from me, and tell her to write to me every now and then to let me see how her spelling is coming on. Dear Grazietta, write to me yourself occasionally, I embrace you affectionately, together with mother and everyone at home (including the maid, if she'll let me be so free).

Antonio

1. Sardinian sweetmeat made with almonds, walnuts and unfermented wine.

72

Turi Prison, 26 January 1931

Dearest Tania,

I had intended to devote the whole of this letter to Giulia, but I've at last received a letter from Carlo to which I was bound to reply; in addition I don't feel capable of writing to Giulia as I would like to, because I've a bad headache. So the next letter will be all for Giulia; please tell her therefore not to put any questions in the next fortnight which would need an immediate answer ...

... The affair of the English reviews has also dragged on too long: you could have settled the thing once and for all simply by following Piero's advice. I agree that the supplement of the *Manchester Guardian* (which is called the *Manchester Guardian Weekly*) be substituted for the weekly edition of the *Times*; the subscription to it is only thirteen shillings as against twenty five shillings for the *Times*. In the same way I would agree to the *Domenica del Corriere* being substituted for the *Tribuna Illustrata* (n.b. this is just an example; I don't want either the *D. del C.* or the *T.I.*) By and large Manchester is to London as Milan is to Rome, and the difference makes itself felt even in weeklies like these: the London ones are over full of the births and weddings of 'Lords' and 'Ladies'. I prefer instead four extra pages on the cultivation of cotton in Upper Egypt. Add *Labour Monthly* to the *Guardian Weekly* and the question is settled.

I have received the December number of the *Gerarchia*, but not the earlier numbers from July to November, which weren't sent to me, and which I would like to have.

I am absolutely opposed to the idea of your undertaking a trip to Turi. You're quite certainly exaggerating the strides you've made as far as your health is concerned; eight stone is much too little to weigh, and you oughtn't to set any limit to your weight if you want to get well again. I hope you don't seriously mean you think it was tea which added nearly a stone to your weight! The story of Muscovite merchants' wives who got fat on tea is enough to give anyone a belly-laugh: they lived like geese in a coop, and that will have contributed more than tea to build up their legendary obesity. I doubt if they despised good beefsteaks and butter etc., and maybe they drank a lot of tea to help them digest their abundant meals, much as the Italian merchants' wives of the present day drink a lot of coffee, not infrequently lacing it with rum or cognac. I don't imagine that you with your temperament were ever much inclined to fat; how much did you weigh when you were at the University, in the period when that photograph you showed me was taken? You certainly weren't fat, but you must have weighed nearly ten stone. If you really want to pay your family a visit and be in a condition to stand up to the long journey, with all the strain which it will entail – and that'll be no laughing matter – you must store away a good reserve of physical energy on which you can count. At Turi the weather is dreadful: mist and damp as in Milan, with frequent rain. They say it's an exceptional winter. The thought that you might come, fall ill and remain here six months shut up indoors like last year – the very thought gives me the shivers. You definitely mustn't expose yourself to any such risk: you must wait till you weigh eleven stone and are completely cured of your liver complaint before you even begin thinking of such a thing.

Thank you for your good wishes. I'm afraid this is your way of reproaching me for having forgotten that 12 January was St Tatiana's Day. I really forgot all about it; still I'm just the same about my own so-called feast days, which only you remember every year with such diligence. I assure you that the prison did not issue me with a ham in honour of my *onomastico;*[1] the mayor and the notables of the district likewise forgot to come and wish me the compliments of the occasion. I believe you must still imagine prison to be like a college for orphan girls under the patronage of the Queen Mother. But a little optimism never does any harm: that's my way of looking at it.

I embrace you tenderly. Write and tell Carlo that you've sent me the money order, just to reassure him that I'm not dying of hunger.

Antonio

1. Name day: cf. letter dated 16 June 1930

73

Turi Prison, 9 February 1931

Darling Giulia,

I have received your letter of 9 January, which starts like this: 'When I think of writing – every day – I think of what makes me remain silent, I remember that my weakness is new to you ....'

I too think that up to now there has been a sort of misunderstanding between us, on this very question of your present weakness, and the strength which you were earlier supposed to have, and for this misunderstanding I insist on taking at least the major share of responsibility – it really does fall on me. On one occasion I wrote to you (perhaps you'll remember) that I was convinced that you have always been much stronger than you yourself thought, but that I almost shrank from harping too much on this theme: I appeared in my own eyes like a kind of slave-driver, seeing that the heaviest burdens of our union have fallen on you. I still think that the above is true, but that didn't mean then – and even less does it mean now – that I had made for myself a conventional and abstract image of a 'strong woman': I knew that you were weak, and indeed at times very weak; I knew, in short, that you were a living woman, that you were Julca.

But I have thought much of all these things since I have been in prison – especially of late. (When a man has no chance of making plans for the future, he continually chews over the past, analysing it. Gradually he gets to understand it better in all its aspects. He thinks especially of all the stupidities he has committed, of his own acts of weakness, of everything it would have been better to do or to leave undone or the things he was in duty bound to do or leave undone.)

The upshot of all this musing is as follows: I am now convinced, first that as far as your weakness and strength is concerned I have committed many foolish acts (or so they seem to me now), and I committed them out of excess of tenderness for you; second that this was thoughtlessness on my part; and third that I, who believed myself sufficiently strong, was in reality quite the reverse – that actually I was beyond doubt weaker than you. And so was born this misunderstanding which has had very grave consequences; you wanted to write to me, but you didn't do so for fear of spoiling this image of yourself as a 'strong woman' which you thought was in my mind. The examples I could bring forward to illustrate all this now appear to me so ingenuous that I can hardly manage to think myself back into the state of mind I must have been in, when I was capable of feeling and acting so ingenuously. So I don't feel up to writing to you about them. In any case it would serve little purpose. It seems to me more important that we should now get our relationship on to a normal footing, and make sure that you are never forced to feel an inhibiting restraint when writing to me – and never forced to feel anything like repugnance. To sum up, you need never hesitate to appear different from what you imagine I think you are.

I have told you that I am convinced you are much stronger than you think, and the last letter confirms me in this belief. In spite of the state of depression from which you are now suffering, in spite of the grave loss of psycho-physical equilibrium, you have maintained a notable force of will, a great control of yourself; and that means the loss of psycho-physical equilibrium is not nearly so great as it might outwardly appear; it means that it is limited in reality to the aggravation of a condition which I believe to be permanent in your personality – permanent, at any rate, if one considers it against the background of a social environment which permanently demands an extremely strong tension of the will. It seems to me in short that you are at present obsessed with the feeling of your own responsibility, which makes your strength seem inadequate to the duties which you want to perform; it thus disorients your will and exhausts you physically, diverting your whole active life on to a track which is a vicious circle, and in which your energies – only partially maybe, but in a very real way – begin to burn themselves out: and to no purpose, seeing that they are applied in a disordered manner. But my belief is that in spite of everything you have maintained sufficient will-power to conquer by yourself the difficulties against which you are now struggling. An outside intervention ('outside' only in a certain sense) would make your job easier; for example, if Tatiana were to come and live with you, and you had concrete proof that your responsibilities were diminished in actual fact; that is why I am pressing Tatiana to make the decision to leave for Moscow, and I'm appealing to her to look after her health, so that she may reach your side in a physical condition which will allow her to be active right away. Otherwise I think your whole situation would be worsened instead of bettered. However, I insist on repeating my conviction that you underestimate your own real strength, and that you are capable of surmounting the present crisis by yourself. You have overestimated your strength in the past, and I foolishly let you go on doing so (I'm able now to say foolishly, although at that time I didn't believe I was foolish); now you underestimate it because you're not quite able to match your will to the ends to be reached, and because you don't know which ends to regard as the most important – and also because you're a little harassed mentally.

My dear, I realise only too well how inadequate and cold everything that I'm writing must seem. I am conscious of my own powerlessness to do anything real and effective to help you; I am caught between a feeling of immense tenderness for you which seems to me a weakness that could only be consoled by an immediate physical caress, and the feeling that a great effort of will is necessary on my part if I am to convince you from this distance, with cold and colourless words, that in spite of everything you are still strong, and that you can and must overcome the crisis. And then the thought of the past harries me ... In any case you are right that in our world, mine and yours, every weakness is grievous and every strength a help. I think that our greatest misfortune is that we were together too little, and always in abnormal general conditions, cut off from the real and concrete life of everyday. Our task now, in the conditions of *force majeure* in which we find ourselves, is to make up for these deficiencies in the past, so that we may preserve all the moral stability of our union and salvage from the crisis all the beauty that there certainly was in our past, and which lives on in our children. Don't you feel that I'm right? I want to help you, even in my present condition, to overcome the depression under which you are now labouring; but you must help me a little too; and teach me the best means of helping you effectively, orienting your will, tearing away all the cobwebs of the false ideas of the past which may still be cluttering it. You must help me to get to know the children better and to share in their life, in their formation, in the affirmation of their personalities. In this way my 'fatherhood' will become more real and will always be a thing of the present: it will become a living 'fatherhood' and not just a memory in an ever-receding past. Help me to get better knowledge of the Julca of today, who is Julca + Delio + Giuliano – a sum in which the plus sign doesn't just show a quantitative fact, it reveals a new qualitative person.

My dear, I embrace you tightly tightly, and I'm looking forward to a long letter from you.

Antonio

74

Turi Prison, 23 February 1931

Dearest Tatiana,

I don't know the tone you adopted when writing to the bookshop to inform them (following my drawing your attention to it fifteen days ago) that up to that time I hadn't received the reviews. I hope though that you didn't adopt a peevish or scornful tone, as it would appear you did from your postcard. My own opinion is that the service has been fairly good, even though from time to time something does go astray; there's certainly no point in thinking ill of the Germans, because they don't enter into it at all – the manager of the bookshop is an Italian and the proprietors are Italianised Swiss. Possibly you don't know that at a certain period of Italian cultural history, the book trade was a virtual monopoly of Swiss entrepreneurs, who did us a great service, especially at Milan and Turin. The classic example is Hoepli, now very old, who popularised the arts and sciences with his widely-read manuals. A few days after mentioning the thing to you I punctually received all the arrears: I would therefore be very grateful if you would write to the manager of the bookshop and let him know this, thanking him at the same time. This might induce him to forget any too lively expression you may have used in your earlier letter. You could, if you like, remind him that I am in prison, and that therefore all the publications that reach me have to be checked, stamped and signed by the prison governor before being handed over; it would therefore be a good thing if he could make quite sure that dozens and dozens of articles don't all arrive together. The idea being to avoid any excessive loss of patience on the part of the staff. If I remember rightly, it was just about two years ago that seventy-eight books and periodicals arrived together; this necessitated seventy-eight rubber-stampings and seventy-eight signatures – a real *tour de force*, as you can see ... As I have noticed that Professor Giorgio Mortara's *Economic Perspectives* has appeared, I would like you to have it sent to me; I would also like to have Senator Benedetto Croce's latest book, *Ethics and Politics*, published by Laterza of Bari, and the Atlante De Agostini Almanac for 1931.

A while ago, I received Professor Umberto Cosmo's *Life of Dante*, a book that P.[1] thought would interest me. I must say that I was less satisfied with it than I thought I would be, for various reasons, but especially because I got the impression that the scientific and moral personality of Cosmo[2] has undergone a certain process of decrepitude. He seems to have become terribly religious, in the positive sense of the word; by which I mean he must have been going through – doubtless sincerely, and not for snob or careerist reasons – the same crisis which has been observed, it seems, in a number of university intellectuals, after the creation of the University of the Sacred Heart. It is a crisis which would no doubt be trebled and quadrupled if other Catholic universities were founded, with lots more chairs for converts from the Idealism of Croce and Gentile. Ask P. for information on this point, the first time you get a chance.

I still remember a heated discussion which took place in my first year at the University of Turin between Cosmo, who took over from Arturo Graf as lecturer on Italian literature, and Pietro Gerosa, a student from the Ticino canton of Switzerland, about De Sanctis' judgement on Cesare Cantu. Gerosa, who was a fanatical Rosminian and Augustinian, was not to be moved from his opinion that De Sanctis' negative judgement was due to political and religious sectarianism, for Cantu was ultra-Catholic and a federalist-republican (neo-Guelph) whereas De Sanctis was a Hegelian and a monarchist centralist. (It's true, though, that Cantu was nominated a Senator of the Kingdom, which shows that his federalist-republicanism was, to say the least of it, superficial.) Poor Professor Cosmo tried in vain to persuade him that De Sanctis was an impartial and objective critic. In the eyes of Gerosa, who had the temper of an inquisitor, Cosmo too was a diabolical Hegelian, dipped in the same infernal pitch as De Sanctis, and he did not hesitate to maintain this openly, with abundant quotations from Rosmini and St Augustine. About a year ago I noticed that Cosmo and Gerosa had together compiled an anthology of the Latin Christian writers of the first centuries AD which gave me the idea that Hegel had capitulated to St Augustine, the intermediaries being Dante and St Francis. (The second of these had always held an important place among Cosmo's studies.)

Even so, when I last saw Cosmo in May 1922 (he was then Secretary and Councillor to the Italian Embassy in Berlin), he was still trying to persuade me to write a study on Machiavelli and Machiavellianism; it was an *idée fixe* of his from 1917 onwards that I should write a study on Machiavelli, and he would remind me of this in season and out of season, even though Machiavelli doesn't go very well together with St Francis and St Augustine ... It's only right to add that I still remember Cosmo with real affection; I would say with veneration, if that word didn't carry overtones which do not correspond to my feelings. He was, and I'm sure still is, a man of great sincerity and moral uprightness, with more than one streak of that native ingenuousness which one often finds in great scholars.

I shall always remember our meeting in 1922, in the majestic entrance hall of the Italian Embassy in Berlin. In November 1920 I had written a very violent and cruel article against Cosmo, of the sort one throws off only at certain critical moments in the political struggle; I heard afterwards that he cried like a child and remained shut up in his house for several days. Our personal relations, which had up to that time been cordial, as befits master and ex-pupil, were severed. When in '22 the solemn porter of the Embassy deigned to telephone to the diplomat Cosmo in his office and inform him that a person called Gramsci wanted an interview, he was shaken to the depths of his bureaucratic Prussian soul by what followed. Cosmo came down the great staircase at the run, threw himself into my arms, flooded me with his tears and his beard, and repeated over and over again: 'You know why, you know why.' He was in the grip of an emotion which really amazed me; however, it made me understand how I must have wounded him in 1920, and what the friendship of his former pupils meant to him.

You see how many memories have been awoken in me by this *Life of Dante*, and by Piero's mention of it. (Incidentally, Piero was first introduced to me by Professor Cosmo.)

... I embrace you tenderly.

Antonio

1. Piero Straffa.
2. Cosmo's *A Handbook to Dante Studies*, translated by David Moore, was published by Basil Blackwell in 1950.

75

Turi Prison, 9 March 1931

Dearest Tatiana,

Yesterday I received your letter, which reassured me a little. I hadn't heard from you for about twenty days and I had begun to get really worried.

... It isn't true that I have lost faith in medicine, as you say in your letter. That would be childish. But I've realised that in my present condition medicaments (restoratives) not only have no effect but actually accentuate the disturbances. I follow a very rigid diet, but even so the intestinal disturbances intensify, become more and more painful. When I got to Turi I suffered mostly from stomach trouble, I vomited frequently etc., but the intestines themselves gave me no trouble. About a year ago now the stomach trouble had almost completely passed, but intestinal complications came upon me instead. In my opinion these are closely bound up with insomnia; I have observed that if I wake up unexpectedly, acute intestinal pains come on after about half an hour; therefore it seems to me that waking up interrupts my digestion, and so brings on the disturbances. If I manage to sleep a bit more peacefully for a few nights, these complications become less pronounced. I have stopped taking Benzofosfan, because my experiments with it show that it does nothing but bring on fresh complications etc. Don't think that I haven't made every effort to get sound sleep; I just haven't succeeded in getting any. I now have chronic gastritis (or does gastritis only mean an illness of the stomach? Should I use some other term?), and I hesitate before experimenting again; I prefer not to do anything. I am not a fatalist: I believe that oxygen can give life to the lungs; but I'm sure that making a man whose chest is locked in an iron lung inhale oxygen is pretty useless, and is more likely to do harm than good.

I am looking forward to hearing even better news from your end. I embrace you tenderly.

Antonio

76

Turi Prison, 23 March 1931

Dearest Tatiana,

Thank you for remembering to send off a telegram to my mother for her *onomastico*, I, for the second time, had forgotten all about it, and it never came into my head until after 19 March. Mamma will have been very pleased to receive the greetings in my name.

It seems that my last letter gave rise to a lot of fantastic imaginings on your part as to all the conceivable intestinal maladies which might afflict me. It's just as well I haven't gone under to the prison mentality; otherwise I would never have got out of bed again, and would certainly have convinced myself that I really had all the diseases you enumerate. I hope that you never again in your life have cause to write to people in prison; you'd drive them to suicide for fear of illnesses and sufferings caused by mysterious diseases whose existence the medical profession out of sheer malice refuses to acknowledge. In fact, that is exactly how the mind of the common run of prisoners works: they read with great avidity all the articles which deal with illnesses, and send for pamphlets and books of the *Every Man his own Doctor* and *Emergency Treatment of the Sick* variety; they end up by discovering that they have at least 300 or 400 ailments, and detect in themselves the symptoms of all of them. There are queer specimens (even among the political prisoners) who swallow all the pills and medicines which their mates refuse to take, convinced that these medicines cannot fail to do them good, seeing that they are sure to be suffering from the ailments which the medicines in question alleviate or cure.

These fixations occasionally reach marvellous and picturesque heights of absurdity; I once knew a political prisoner who sent for a treatise on obstetrics. This was not, of course, a manifestation of sadism; it was because (as he himself explained) he had once had to give assistance at an emergency birth, and ever since he had been in prison had been haunted by the feeling of responsibility he had on that occasion. He therefore felt it incumbent on him to get hold of all the information available on the subject. What I'm leading up to is this: I don't believe that I have any of the ailments you enumerate, but simply a form of chronic constipation which becomes painful when I don't sleep, and when the weather is wet; when I can change my diet, indeed, it passes off completely; and when I succeed in sleeping, and the weather is dry, it is much less painful.

Don't take it into your head to send me the *gioddu*,[1] or anything similar, because I wouldn't know what to do with it. And if you think it's an easy matter to prepare *gioddu* – which actually in my village is called *mezzuradu*, meaning 'sour milk'; gioddu is a word used in the Sassari district, and is understood only in a small corner of Sardinia – you're making a big mistake. It's such a difficult task that on the mainland it is prepared only by Bulgarian specialists, and is in fact called Yoghurt or Bulgarian milk. The sort they sell in Rome is positively repulsive compared with that made by our Sardinian shepherds.

I assure you that there's nothing grave or alarming about my condition, quite the reverse: for about ten days I have had no more pains, and my headaches have also become less painful. Carlo informs me on the other hand that *you* have by no means put your own house in order, as far as ordinary living is concerned: he says that you only eat when it occurs to you to do so and that sometimes you forget to, etc. This seems to me very blameworthy on your part, because you promised to eat more regularly – in order to lay up a reserve of physical energy which would permit you to make the journey to Moscow. I believed you would do what you promised, and now I regret it: it means that I was ingenuous, as ingenuous as one of the earliest Italian poets who wrote

Molte sono le femmine che hanno dura la testa
Ma l'uomo con parabole le dimina e ammonesta.[2]

Words are not much use: what one really needs is a 'lovely courbash'[3] as a Bedouin exiled to Ustica always used to say when he talked to me of his relations with his wives and the women of his kabila.

... I would also like to know if a complete collection of 'Leonardo' for the year 1926 can be purchased, and if so, how much it costs. You sent me the complete collection for 1925, but only the first number of '26. The first four numbers of 1927 were lost for me by my friends on Ustica. The following years are all complete. I would like to complete the collection, because it constitutes the best single storehouse of general culture of the last few years. It published, for example, a whole series of numbers devoted to the scientific discoveries of the first twenty-five years of this century. These are very useful, indeed indispensible. I would like you, then, to ask the bookshop to provide the missing numbers. If there's any chance of getting the things, it would be best to go along personally and not rely on correspondence ...

I embrace you tenderly.

Antonio

1. Sardinian form of yoghurt.
2. 'Many are the women who are obstinate, but a man with (soft) words masters them, and makes them see reason.' The quotation is from the *Tenzone* (Dialogue or 'Flyting') of Ciullo d'Alcamo, a poet of the Sicilian court who lived in the first half of the thirteenth century.
3. Whip.

77

Turi Prison, 7 April 1931

Dearest Tatiana,

... It doesn't surprise me in the least that Professor Bodrero's lectures on Greek philosophy didn't interest you much. He is professor of the history of philosophy in some university or other (once upon a time he was at Padua) but he is neither a philosopher nor a historian: he is an erudite philologist capable of making speeches of the humanistic-rhetorical variety. Recently I read an article of his on Homer's *Odyssey* which shook even this belief of mine that Bodrero was a good philologist, for he asserted in it that a man who had been a soldier could understand the *Odyssey* better; I doubt whether a Senegalese who took part in the war is for that reason better equipped to understand Homer. And in any case Bodrero forgets that Ulysses, according to the legend, was a deserter, in so far as he resisted his call-up; he was also in a manner of speaking guilty of self-inflicted wounds, because when he appeared before the military commission which had arrived in Ithaca to enlist him, he pretended to be mad. (Correction: not guilty of self-inflicted wounds, but a malingerer aiming at getting down-graded.)

As far as the question of *gioddu* is concerned, neither Sardinian patriotism nor any other parish pump patriotism enters into it. In point of fact all primitive shepherds prepare milk in this way. What matters is that *gioddu* alias *yoghurt* cannot be sent long distances or be kept for any length of time without it spoiling and turning into a sort of cheese. And there's another very important reason: it seems that a certain dose of dirt in shepherd and environment is necessary if the *gioddu* is to turn out genuine. One cannot fix this element with mathematical accuracy – which is a shame, because if it were possible to do so society shepherdesses might try, like snobs, to add the right dash of filth to their get-up. Another point: this necessary dirt must be authentic dirt, that genuine natural spontaneous dirt which makes a shepherd stink exactly like a he-goat. As you can see the question is complex, and so you'd better give up the thought of playing Amaryllis or Chloe in some dainty Arcadian painting.

Dear Tania, I found your letter very interesting and it gave me pleasure. You were quite right not to scrap and rewrite it. Why on earth should you? If you get impassioned about things, it means that there's great vitality and ardour in you. Some of your observations I really didn't quite understand, such as this one: 'Maybe one should always live outside one's own ego in order to enjoy life with the greatest intensity.' I can't imagine how one can live outside one's own ego, always assuming that an identifiable ego exists once and for all, and that it is not a question of the personality in continuous movement – in which case one can be said to be continuously outside (and continuously inside) one's own ego.

For me the question is now greatly simplified, and I have become, in my profound wisdom, very forgiving ... But joking apart, I have devoted a great deal of thought to the questions you raise, and about which you get impassioned. My conclusion is that the blame for many things rests fairly and squarely on me. I say 'blame', because I can find no other word. Perhaps it's true that there exists a form of egotism into which one can fall innocently. I don't think it's a question of the more common form of egotism, that which consists in making others serve as instruments of one's own well-being and one's own happiness; it doesn't seem to me I've ever been egotistic in that sense, because I'm sure that throughout my life I've always given as much as I received. But there is a further question: giving and receiving may balance up in the general reckoning, but do they balance up in single individual cases? When one has harnessed one's whole life to a certain end, when one concentrates towards the achieving of that end the whole sum of one's energies and one's will, is it not inevitable that a few or perhaps many of the items concerned – or maybe just one single one – may remain outstanding? It's easy to overlook that sort of thing, and there comes a point when one pays for the oversight. A man may perhaps discover that he seems egotistic to the very people that he would never have thought could see him in that light. And he discovers the origin of the error, which is weakness – the weakness of not having dared to remain alone, of not having refused to permit himself ties of love, obligations, close relationships, etc.

When we reach a point like this, it is certain that only forgiveness can give us peace: a kind of peace, at any rate, which is not mere apathy or indifference but a peace that can leave us some sort of loophole for the future. I often review the whole course of my life, and it seems to me I'm just like Renzo Tramaglino at the end of *I Promessi Sposi*: I can draw up a balance sheet and can say – 'I've learnt not to do this, not to do the other, etc.' (Although I must admit that this store of learning is not of much use to me just now.) At one time I didn't write to my mother for a matter of years (for at least two years without a break), and I've learnt that one suffers dreadfully through not receiving letters. (Though probably if I were free I'd fall back into these same old sins of omission, and might not even regard them as such: I'd probably ignore them altogether.) And so on, and so on. To sum up: I have already four years and five months of prison behind me, and I have hopes that in a few more years I'll be completely mummified: I shall explain everything, and conclude that everything that did happen had to happen; I shall explain myself to myself, and find that my explanations are absolutely incontrovertible. I shall end up by convincing myself that the best thing would be just not to think any more, not to receive any stimulus from outside that might make me think, to put any letters I receive on one side without reading them, etc., etc. But maybe nothing of the sort will happen at all; and maybe I'll just have made you pout, or pull a long face and feel out of temper for a short while. And which will signify that you are outside your own ego, and that my ego, an unwelcome guest, has taken its place.

Darling Tatiana, don't be angry if I make fun of you a wee bit. I'm very fond of you, and I embrace you lovingly.

Antonio

78

Turi Prison, 20 April 1931

Dearest Tatiana,

I have received the two photos, and the sheet of paper with Delio's handwriting. I couldn't make head or tail of the letter, and it's incomprehensible to me why he should start writing from right to left, and not from left to right. However I'm glad he writes with his hands: that's something anyway. If he had taken it into his head to start writing with his feet, that would have been a good deal worse without a doubt. Seeing that the Arabs, the Persians and those Turks who have not accepted the reforms of Kemal – and perhaps other peoples too – write from right to left, the thing doesn't seem to me terribly serious or dangerous; once Delio has learnt Persian, Turkish and Arabic, the fact that he has learnt to write from right to left will be a great boon to him. There's only one thing that strikes me, and that is that there hasn't been enough logic in this system. Why was he forced, when he was smaller, to dress like other people? Wouldn't it have been more correct to leave his personality free –

not only as far as learning to write is concerned but in such matters as clothing as well. What right did anyone have to bring him up to follow convention so mechanically? Wouldn't it have been better to leave the articles of clothing dotted about the room and then wait for him to choose spontaneously: socks on his head, shoes on his hands, gloves on his feet etc.? Or better still, why weren't a little boy's clothes and a little girl's clothes both laid out near him, so that he could have freedom of choice in that as well? How does that idea strike you?

The two photographs appealed to me, because in both Giuliano's features have been caught when they were at their most expressive. In the earlier photos Delio looked rather weak and sickly, but this impression is corrected by the subsequent photographs taken at Sochi.

... I have read *Michael, Brother of Jerry* by Jack London. From an aesthetic standpoint it is insignificant: it's a piece of propaganda for some society like the Anti-Vivisection League, or the Society for the Prevention of Cruelty to Animals. In Rome I had *Jerry of the Islands* which, as far as I can remember, was very pleasing. In any case the two best stories about dogs by London are *White Fang* and *Call of the Wild*: following the success of these two books London has written far too much about dogs, his later stuff lacking freshness and spontaneity.

I've read a few things about psychoanalysis, chiefly articles in reviews: in Rome R.[1] lent me some material on the subject. I'll willingly read the book by Freud to which P. has drawn your attention: you might order it. It's possible that Giulia will have recourse to a psychoanalytic cure, if her illness has a purely nervous origin. My own opinion is that the practising doctor counts for more than the psychoanalyst; old Lombroso, on the basis of traditional psychiatry, obtained surprising results which I believe were due more to his ability as a doctor than to abstract scientific theory. His scientific prestige was such that many patients, after their first visit to him and before starting on any definite cure, already felt much better, regained faith in themselves and rapidly found their way back to normal. It's possible that psychoanalysis is a more concrete business than the old psychiatry, or at any rate that it obliges doctors to make a more concrete study of single patients – that is, to look at the patient and not the illness. Apart from this, Freud has followed in the steps of Lombroso and attempted to construct a general philosophy on the basis of a few empirical observed criteria.

I embrace you tenderly.

Antonio

1. Ruggero Grieco.

79

Turi Prison, 4 May 1931

Dearest Teresina,

I have received your letter of 28 April. I think you and Grazietta have completely mistaken the meaning of the observations I made about Mea. In the first place, I only knew Mea in '24, when she was very little; I'm certainly not in a position to give any opinion on her qualities, or on the durability of those qualities. In the second place, and as a matter of general principle, I always avoid judging a person on the strength of what is usually called 'intelligence', or 'good nature', or 'quick-wittedness', etc., because I know that such evaluations carry little weight and are frequently deceptive. More important than all these things seems to me to be 'will power', the love of discipline and work, and a constancy in pursuing one's aims. And in making a judgement of this nature I take into account, not so much the child itself, as the adults who are bringing it up, who have the duty of helping it to acquire these habits of mind, although without mortifying its spontaneity.

The opinion that I have formed, going by the accounts of Nannaro and Carlo, is the following: that you are all neglecting to urge Mea to acquire those solid qualities, which are of fundamental importance for her future, and that you fail to realise that later on it will be more difficult for her to acquire them – maybe impossible. It seems to me you forget that at the present day women in Italy are severely handicapped right from their early schooldays; for example, girls are excluded from a number of scholarships etc. For this reason, if women are to stand up to the competition, they must give evidence of qualities superior to those demanded from men, and a bigger dose of tenacity and perseverance. It's evident that my observations were not so much about Mea as about those who are educating her and bringing her up; in this case it seems to me more true than ever that it is the teacher who must be educated.

I read with interest the letter to Ali Camun that you sent me; I was pleased to see that there are no spelling mistakes in it. Apart from that there doesn't seem to be much to it; it's a collection of commonplaces, and I found nothing original or fresh in it. On the other hand, to do the child justice I found nothing infantile or ignorant in the letter either, apart from the lack of logic and the abundance of contradictions. To call the history of a region which has always been subjected to a series of conquerors and which has never had a proper history of its own 'glorious' seems to me an overstatement: even the schoolmaster Cavaliere Pietro Sotgiu never said as much when he made us sing:

Fulminar la superba Aragona[1]
t'han veduto le attonite genti,
rinnovar gli obliati portenti
del romano e del greco valor.

We children, if I remember rightly, couldn't imagine what 'peoples'
these were who were 'astonished' by the heroism of the Marquis of Zuri:
we preferred reading about Pasquale Tola and Derosas who both seemed to
us even more 'Sardinian' than the great Eleanora. I should think Ali
Camun doesn't waste much time on these old pharaohs: he probably has
greater admiration for some modern brigand.

... Dear Teresina, I hope your children keep in the best of health. Send
me more details about Father's accident – I hope it didn't give him too
much of a shaking.

I embrace everyone at home, especially mamma.

Antonio

1. 'The astonished peoples have seen you strike terror into proud Aragon, and
renew the forgotten wonders of Greek and Roman valour.'

80

Turi Prison, 18 May 1931

Dearest Tania,

... This very moment I have received your letter of 15 May, together
with Giulia's letter. I would have preferred it if you had told me what
impression Giulia's letter made on you. For my part I'm still not quite sure
what to make of it. One positive feature may be distinguished, I think:
Giulia seems to have recovered a certain confidence in herself and in her
own strength. But is this confidence deep-rooted, or is it of a purely
intellectual and rational character? I'm afraid that the intellectualistic
character of her state of mind is only too evident; it seems that the
'analytic' moment has not yet become vital force, volitional impulse. One
reassuring thing is this, that Giulia, like most Russians of the present day,
has a great faith in science: I mean faith of an almost religious character,
the kind we Westerners had at the end of the last century, and which we
subsequently lost, partly as a consequence of the criticism of the most
modern philosophy, but chiefly because of the disaster of political
democracy. Science itself has been subjected to 'criticism', and its frontiers
have been limited.

I would never have thought it would be possible to find an individual in
Turi capable of saying something intelligent, as it appears you have done.

But was it so intelligent after all, what was said to you? I don't think it's difficult to find splendid formulas for living; the difficult thing is to live. I read recently that in modern Europe only a few Italians and Spaniards have still maintained a gusto for living – which is always possible, although that kind of general statement is not exactly easy to prove. Occasionally one comes across misunderstandings which are downright funny. Once I had a curious discussion with Clara Zetkin who declared her admiration for the Italians because they still had this 'gusto for living', and imagined that she was adducing a subtle proof of this fact by pointing out that the Italians say *Felice notte!* (happy night), and not 'Quiet night' like the Russians, 'Goodnight' like the Germans, etc. That the Germans, the Russians, and even the French don't think in terms of 'happy nights' is quite possible, but Italians also refer to a 'happy journey' and affairs 'happily concluded', which rather takes away from the significant value of *felice*. Furthermore, Neapolitans refer to a beautiful woman as *buona* (good) – and the word certainly has no malicious overtones, because *bella* (beautiful) is actually the ancient *bonula*.[1]

In short, it seems to me that formulas for living, whether they be expressed in words or spring from the customs of a people, have one value only, and that is to serve as a stimulus and an incitement to people who go in for wishful thinking and who leave their desires half formulated: they can help such people to change their half-formulated desires into confident will. But it must always be remembered that real life can never be determined by the suggestions one receives from one's neighbours, and still less by formulas: it is born from inner roots. In Giulia's case the suggestion that she should 'unravel' herself is quite justified: it implies that she should seek her strength and reasons for living in her own personality; that she should take courage, not let herself be overwhelmed, and above all not set herself ends which are too difficult to reach. And I think that this suggestion holds good for ... you too, because you sometimes think that one should get outside one's own ego in order to make a reality of life!

I embrace you.

Antonio

1. *bonulus* was a colloquial Latin diminutive of bonus (good) which had become *bellus* as early as the third century BC. From the earliest times colloquial Latin abounded in diminutives which were seldom admitted to literary usage.

81

Turi Prison, 1 June 1931

Darling Giulia,

Tania has sent on to me the 'epistle' of Delio (I use the more literary word), which contains his declaration of love for the tales of Pushkin. It pleased me very much, and I would like to know if Delio thought of this expression spontaneously, or if he was remembering something he had read. Incidentally, I note with a certain degree of surprise that Delio's literary tendencies don't seem to cause you any worry; if I'm not mistaken, you were convinced once upon a time that he showed more likelihood of turning out an engineer than a poet. Now you forecast that he will read Dante with real love. I hope that that prophecy will never be fulfilled, although I am very glad that Delio likes Pushkin, and I'm pleased to be given a bit of evidence of the first blossoming of the child's creative life.

By the way, who *does* read Dante with love? Nobody, I should think, but the gaga professors who make a religion of some poet or man of letters, and worship his memory with strange philological rites.

It's my opinion that a modern man of intelligence should read the classics in general at a certain 'remove', prizing them for the aesthetic value only, whereas 'love' implies adhesion to the ideological content of the poetry. One loves one's 'own' poet; one 'admires' the artist in general. Aesthetic admiration may be accompanied by a kind of 'civil' disdain, as in the case of Marx for Goethe. And so I'm glad that Delio likes imaginative literature, and does some imagining on his own account; I don't think that will prevent him becoming a great engineer just the same and building skyscrapers and power stations. It's more likely to do the reverse.

You might ask Delio from me which of the tales of Pushkin he likes best. To tell you the truth, I've only read two: *The Golden Cockerel* and *The Fisherman*. I also know the story about the 'little basin', which includes the adventures of the cushion that jumps like a frog, the sheet that flies away, the candle that goes hopping about and hides under the stove etc., but it's not by Pushkin. Do you remember it? Believe it or not, I still know dozens of verses of it off by heart.

I'd like to tell Delio a folk tale from my own village which I think is interesting. I'll give you the outline of it, and you can fill in the details for him and for Giuliano.

A child is lying asleep. There's a jug of milk ready for him to drink when he wakes up. A mouse drinks the milk. The child, waking up and finding no milk, starts to cry. His mother starts yelling too. The mouse, in despair, knocks his head against the wall; however, he sees that that will get him nowhere, so he runs off to the goat to get some milk. The goat says she'll give him the milk if she can get some grass to eat. The mouse goes to the meadow to get some grass, but the meadow is parched and wants water. The mouse goes to the fountain. The fountain has been destroyed in the war, and its water is running to waste. It needs the help of the master mason, and he in turn needs stone. The mouse goes off to the mountain, and then there ensues a sublime dialogue between the mouse and the mountain; the latter has been stripped of its trees by speculators, and its bare bones are showing everywhere for want of earth. The mouse tells it the whole story, and promises that when the child grows up he will replant the pines, oaks, chestnut trees etc. So the mountain gives the stone, etc., and the child gets so much milk that he can wash his face in it. He grows up, plants the trees and everything changes; the bones of the mountain disappear under fresh humus, the rainfall becomes more regular because the trees hold back the vapours and prevent torrents from devastating the plain etc. In short the mouse conceives and carries through a real *piatiletka*.[1] It's just the sort of story you might expect from a countryside ruined by deforestation.

Darling Giulia, please do tell the children this story, and then let me know what their reactions are.

I embrace you tenderly.

Antonio

1. Five-year plan (Russian)

82

Turi Prison, 15 June 1931

Dearest Tatiana,

... I never told you that Margherita's husband had ever had the slightest reason to be jealous. All I said was that he *was* jealous, and that this fact seemed to me to reveal a trait which took away from his force of character and his capacity for work. That's all there is to it.

I had no reason for believing that he had any ground to be jealous – assuming that there are reasons for being jealous. (In my view, reasons of that sort are reasons for separating, not for being jealous.)

This is another proof of how pointless all these generalisations about the inhabitants of a region or a country are. The Sardinians, who pass for Southerners, are not 'jealous', in the way that the Sicilians and Calabrians are supposed to be. Blood crimes committed from motives of jealousy are very rare, whereas crimes against the seducers of young girls are frequent. Among the Sardinian peasantry, married couples separate pacifically if they can't get on together; or else the unfaithful wife is just turned out of the house. It often happens that a husband separated from his wife by agreement lives openly with another woman of the same village; similarly the wife may live together with another man. Indeed in many Sardinian villages there existed before the war (I'm not sure about nowadays) a system of trial wedding, i.e. the man and woman did not marry until after the birth of a child; in the eventuality of one proving infertile, both re-assumed their freedom. This was tolerated by the Church.

You see what differences can exist in the sexual field, which holds such an important place among the characteristics of the so-called national 'souls'.

I embrace you tenderly.

Antonio

83

Turi Prison, 15 June 1931

Darling mamma,

I have received the letter you wrote to me with Teresina's hand. I think you should often write to me like that. In the letter I could feel unmistakably all your own particular way of thinking: it really was your letter and not Teresina's.

Do you know what came back into my mind as I read it? A clear picture came back of the days when I was in my first or second year of elementary school, and you corrected my homework for me. I could never manage to remember that 'uccello' is spelt with two 'c's, and you corrected this mistake at least ten times. And so, if you helped us to learn to write (and earlier on you had made us learn a lot of poetry by heart: I still remember *Rataplan*, and that other one:

Lungo i clivi della Loira,
che qual nastro argentato
corre via per cento miglia
un bel suolo avventurato.[1]

It's quite right that one of us should serve as your hand for writing a letter when you're not strong enough to do so. Though I'm afraid the memory of *Rataplan* and the Song of the Loire will make you smile.

Another thing I remember is how I used to admire (I can't have been more than four or five at the time) your skill in imitating the roll of a drum on the table when you were declaiming *Rataplan*.

Apart from all this, you can't imagine how many scenes I remember in which you always appear as a beneficent force, full of tenderness for us children. If you give it a bit of thought, all these questions of the soul, of the immortality of the soul, and of heaven and hell, are at bottom nothing but ways of looking at this simple fact: that every one of our actions is handed on to others, according to its power for good or evil. It is passed on from father to son, and from one generation to another in perpetual movement. Since all the memories that we have of you are memories of kindness and strength, and since you have given all your strength to bring us up, you are now and have always been in the only real paradise which exists, and which for a mother must I think be in the hearts of her own children.

Do you see what I've written? But you mustn't think that I want to offend your religious susceptibilities: I believe that we agree on these points much more closely than might appear on the surface. Tell Teresina that I'm awaiting the other letter that she has promised me. I embrace you tenderly, with all at home.

Antonio

1. 'Along the hilly banks of the Loire, which like a silver ribbon runs for a hundred miles through a beautiful and fortunate land.'

84

Turi Prison, 29 June 1931

Dearest mamma,

I have received a letter from Grazietta, with the news of the brilliant results Mea got in the exams which she sat at Cagliari. I am delighted to hear of these, and send Mea my heartiest congratulations. I hope that she'll write to me herself, describing these exams in every detail, and giving me her impressions of Cagliari.

I have been out of circulation for such a long time now that I don't even know what character or object these 'entrance exams' have which children must take before the elementary school-leaving certificate. I should imagine they are the State examinations for entrance to the intermediate schools, instituted with the express aim of making it more difficult for poor children to win their way forward to advanced study. I would like to make Mea a little present, and I'll make sure I do so. I possess a box of crayons and some exercise books with drawing paper which Tatiana sent me some years ago, thinking that prisons cultivate the artistic aptitudes of their charges. The next time I send some books home I'll put these crayons into the parcel for Mea – so she'll have something to remember me by. (You never let me know if the parcel of books which I handed over to Carlo last March – and which Carlo was to despatch by railway – ever reached its destination.) Teresina has not yet written the letter that she promised me.

From Giulia and the kiddies I have received word fairly recently. Delio has tried to write a letter (they've never taught him to write but have left him to learn on his own account when he takes it into his head to do so; it seems that the doctors thought this the wisest course, because the child is of a nervous disposition, and they don't want him to go in for brain work too early). They are all keeping quite well; they were due to leave Moscow just about now to spend a little while in the country.

Let me know your news regularly. I really do hope that, as Grazietta says, you are keeping better now.

I embrace you lovingly with all at home.

Antonio

85

Turi Prison, 20 July 1931

Dearest Teresina,

I have not yet received replies to two of my letters to mamma. This time your silence is leaving its mark on me. Judging by the last letters I received, mamma's health has had a lot of ups and downs of late. It's very wrong of you to leave me in suspense for ages – the way you do. I'm relying on you, Teresina, and I appeal to you from my heart to tell me honestly what's happening, even if it's only in a few words.

I embrace you affectionately.

Antonio

86

Turi Prison, 3 August 1931

Dearest Tatiana,

... You need never fear that the feeling of being personally isolated may plunge me into depression, or into some such state of mind smacking of high tragedy. In point of fact I have never felt the need of any external reinforcement of moral strength to help me live my life with courage even under the worst conditions; so I'm even less in need of such reinforcement today, now I feel that my strength and my will have reached an even higher degree of solidity and worth. But while in the past, as I have said, I felt almost proud to find myself isolated, today instead I feel the meanness, the aridity, the shabbiness of a life which is founded on nothing but the will. This is my state of mind at the present time.

I think you can't have received, or possibly only received after a long delay, a letter of mine of a few weeks ago; there were a few lines in it for you, and a few lines for my sister Teresina. Do you know this: I haven't had any news from home for quite a while, and they don't send me word about Mama's state of health. Consequently, I'm more than a little worried about it. – I've had a glance at Prince Mirsky's article about the theory of history and historiography, and my opinion is that it's an exceedingly interesting and valuable piece of work.[1] I'd already read a few months ago an essay of Mirsky's about Dostoievsky which was published in a single number of *Cultura* dedicated to Dostoievsky. That essay was also very perceptive, and it is quite surprising how ably Mirsky has made himself master of the central nucleus of Historic Materialism, displaying in the process such a lot of intelligence and penetration. It seems to me that his scientific position is all the more worthy of note and of study, seeing that he shows himself free of certain cultural prejudices and incrustations which infiltrated the field of the theory of history in a parasitic fashion, at the end of the last century and the beginning of this one, in consequence of the great popularity enjoyed by Positivism.

... One of the themes which have interested me most in the last few years has been the defining of a few characteristic features in the history of the Italian intellectuals. This interest had its origin, on the one hand, in my desire to make a thorough examination of the concept of the State; and on the other, in my attempts to extend my knowledge of certain aspects of the Italian people's historic development. Although I have kept my research within its essential limits, it nevertheless remains a formidable undertaking. It is necessary, first of all, to go back to the time of the Roman Empire, and of the concentration of 'cosmopolitan' ('imperial') intellectuals which it brought about. Following which one must study the formation of the Christian Papal organisation of 'learned clerks' which inherited the intellectual cosmopolitanism of the Empire, and developed into a European caste of scholars.

In my opinion it's only by going about it like this that one can explain why it is impossible to speak of 'national' Italian intellectuals until after 1700 – that is, until after the first battles between Church and State had been joined, and the jurisdictional question had emerged. Up till that time the Italian intellectuals were cosmopolitan; they exercised a universalistic and a-national function (either for the Church or for the Empire). As technicians and specialists they helped to organise other national states, they offered 'managing personnel' to the whole of Europe, and they did not become concentrated as a national category, as a specialised group within the nation.

As you can see, this theme might well furnish material for a whole series of essays; but in that case properly conducted research would be necessary. My other labours are brought up short at the same obstacle. You must also remember that the habit of severe intellectual discipline, acquired during my University studies, has left me with a large stock – possibly too large a stock – of methodic scruples. Hence the difficulty I experience in quoting books which are of a very specialised nature. Anyway, I append the title of a book I should like to read: *Un Trentennio di Lotte Politiche*[2] (1894–1922) by Professor De Viti De Marco, published by the Collezione Meridionale, Rome.

... I embrace you tenderly.

Antonio

1. Prince Dmitri Mirsky (1890–1939) was a son of Prince Sviatopolski-Mirsky, Russian Minister of Home Affairs, 1904–5. He welcomed the revolution of February 1917, but opposed the October revolution, and fought with the 'Whites' in the Civil War as a staff officer in Denikin's army. He then emigrated to England, where he taught Russian Literature at King's College, London. He became a close friend of Jane Ellen Harrison, the 'Grecian anthropologist' of Newnham College, Cambridge, who wrote *Prolegomena to the Study of Greek Religion* and *Themis*, and was a member of the circle which included Gilbert Murray and the Cornfords (Francis and Frances). He did a great deal for Russian studies in England, and (as Gramsci hints) became converted to Marxism, joining the Communist Party of Great Britain in 1931. In 1932 he decided to return to the Soviet Union, and for some years was one of the most eminent Soviet literary critics. In 1937 he was arrested, when the Writers' Union was 'purged', and given a summary sentence by an NKVD troika; the rest of his life was spent in the camps of the Gulag. According to eyewitnesses, he succumbed to extreme anguish and despair, and is said to have died insane in a camp near Vladivostock in January 1939.

Ironically, it was to him that Hugh MacDiarmid dedicated the title poem of *First Hymn to Lenin* (1931); this contains the following stanza:

As necessary, and insignificant, as death
Wi' a' its agonies in the cosmos still
The Cheka's horrors are in their degree;
And'll end suner! What maitters 't wha we kill
To lessen that foulest murder that deprives
Maist men o' real lives!

The essay to which Gramsci refers is 'Bourgeois History and Historical Materialism', which appeared in *Labour Monthly*, July 1931.

(I am indebted for much of this information to Professor G. Smith, New College, Oxford.)
2. 'Thirty Years of Political Struggle'.

87

Turi Prison, 17 August 1931

Dearest Tatiana,

Last time I wrote I mentioned an ailment which is troubling me greatly. I'd like to describe it to you as objectively as possible, giving all the details which seem to me essential.

It started like this; at one in the morning on 3 August – a fortnight ago to the day – I all of a sudden coughed up blood. It wasn't anything like a real continuous haemorrhage, the irresistible flow I've heard described by others: I felt a gurgle in my breathing like the feeling you have when you get catarrh. An abrupt cough followed, and my mouth filled with blood. The coughing was not always violent, wasn't even particularly pronounced; it was exactly the sort of cough you get when you've got something or other in your throat; it came in isolated throws, without any continuous fits or paroxysms of coughing. This lasted until about 4. In these three hours I coughed up over half a pint of blood. After 4 I got no more mouthfuls of blood, but at intervals I coughed up catarrh mixed with gouts of blood.

The prison doctor, Dr Cisternino, prescribed 'calcium chloride with a trace of adrenalin', and told me that he would keep an eye on my condition. On Wednesday the 5th of August he made an examination of me with a stethoscope, and ruled out the possibility that an infection of the bronchi might be the root cause; he gave it as his opinion that the fever which had come on in the meantime was probably of intestinal origin. The catarrh with gouts of blood (neither frequent, nor copious) continued until a few days ago, but since then they have completely disappeared. Even though now and then I have one or two fits of coughing – occasionally quite severe ones – I have not coughed up so much as catarrh. It therefore must have been a fortuitous nervous cough.

There is a further symptom which makes the intestinal origin of the fever more plausible. Towards the 5th or 6th of August I had a skin eruption: my left forearm was completely covered with red spots; my neck and the left side of my chest were similarly covered, but not so heavily; on my right arm, nothing. Before coughing up the blood I had suffered exceptionally from the heat of the season, and sometimes found myself bathed in sweat, especially at night time. These nocturnal sweating bouts lasted until five or six days ago, then they stopped; they came on again (but not with such intensity) on the two evenings when the fever came back. I think I've given you all the essential information. I ought to add that this hasn't weakened me to any appreciable extent, nor has it had any psychological repercussions. As long as I was still spitting gouts of blood I had a nauseous feeling of something sickly sweet in my mouth, and I felt that every time I coughed my mouth would fill with blood as on the first occasion; but today (that is, ever since the coughing of blood and catarrh ceased) there is no recurrence of this feeling, consequently I don't think it was purely psychological.

So now you can give me all the advice that you think opportune. As you can see there's nothing very worrying about it – although, as the doctor says, we must keep an eye on it.

I read with great interest the letter from Professor Cosmo that you copied out for me. My impressions are very complex. I would hate it if even the remotest suspicion had entered Professor Cosmo's head that I had as much as admitted to my thoughts an opinion which called in question his uprightness, the dignity of his character and his sense of duty. The last few pages of his *Life of Dante* leave one with the impression that the author is himself a fervently devout Catholic. Side by side with this impression I set the fact that Cosmo, in collaboration with Gerosa, has compiled for a Catholic publishing house an anthology of the Latin writers of the early centuries of the Church. The only conclusion I could come to was that Cosmo must have got himself converted. It certainly never entered my head that his conversion might have anything 'opportunistic' about it, and even less anything venal – although unfortunately one cannot say as much for a number of great intellectuals. The fervent Catholicism of Gerosa himself, as I well remember, had more of a Jansenist than a Jesuit streak about it.

In any case, the thing caused me annoyance. When I was a pupil of Cosmo's I did not agree with him on a number of subjects, as was only natural (though in those days I would not have adopted any hard and fast position, and not only because of the feeling of affection which bound me to him). But it seemed to me that both Cosmo and I, like many other intellectuals of the time (I am referring to the first fifteen years of this century), did stand on certain common ground, which was this: we were engaged, to a greater or lesser extent, in the movement for moral and intellectual reform initiated in Italy by Benedetto Croce. Now the first point in Croce's programme was this, that modern man can and must live without religion. By religion I mean revealed or positive or mythological religion, or any other expression you care to use. This point still seems to me today to be the major contribution to world culture of the modern Italian intellectuals, and it seems to me, furthermore, a conquest in the social political sphere which must not be lost. That is the reason why that faintly apologetic tone displeased me, and the above-mentioned doubt came into my head. In any event I would be really sorry if the old Professor had been hurt by what I said, especially since it appears from his letter that he has been seriously ill. In spite of everything I hope to see him again one day, and to resume with him one or other of those long discussions which we used to have in the war years, strolling by night through the streets of Turin.

... You mustn't think that I go without anything I can buy to supplement my rations; the truth is that the goods to buy are wanting. This year fruit has been on sale on a few occasions only, and each time I bought it; fresh cheese has not been on sale for some time. The canteen only sells things which, because of my gastric troubles I am unable to eat; even ham has been forbidden me by the doctor. I keep strictly to what the doctor orders, and take nothing but eggs, milk, and rice cooked with butter – even so, I can't manage to get my inside in order.

... I have received letters from Ghilarza; they've all been down with malarial fevers.

I embrace you tenderly.

Antonio

88

Turi Prison, 24 August 1931

Dearest mamma,

I have received letters from Mea, Franco and Teresina, with news of how you are all keeping. But why do you leave me without news for so long? Even people down with malarial fever can surely write a line or two, and I would be satisfied with a mere picture postcard. Please understand that I too am getting old, and that therefore I'm nervous, and more impatient and irritable than I used to be. I look at it like this: people don't write to a man in prison for one of two reasons. Either they are unfeeling, or else they are lacking in imagination. In your case, and in the case of the others at home I don't think it can be a question of being unfeeling. My own view is that it's due to lack of imagination: you just can't manage to get any sort of picture of what it's like to be in prison, and of the importance which correspondence takes on – how it fills up the blank days, and continues to give a certain savour to life.

I never speak of the negative aspects of my life, for this reason above all others that I do not want to be pitied. I was a soldier unlucky in the immediate struggle, and soldiers cannot and must not be pitied; that is, if they go into action willingly – not forced to do so, but knowing what they are doing and accepting its necessity. But that does not mean that the negative side of my prison life doesn't exist; it weighs heavily, and those who are near to me can make it either heavier or easier to bear. However, this remonstrance is addressed not to you but to Teresina, Grazietta and Mea who might at any rate send me a few postcards.

I was very pleased with Franco's letter, and I liked his little horses, motor cars, bicycles, etc.: naturally, as soon as I can I shall give him a present too, to show him that I'm fond of him and that I'm sure he's a clever little boy – and a good boy too, though I imagine he gets up to mischief often enough. I shall send off the box of crayons to Mea as soon as I can, but Mea mustn't expect anything too inspiring. Teresina hasn't as yet answered a question I asked her, which was whether the parcel of books and reviews that Carlo sent off from Turi last March has arrived. What I want to know is whether these books and reviews are an encumbrance to you, because I've still got loads and loads of them to send off. If they are just going to get lost or be thrown away I might as well present them – or some of them at least – to the prison library. Personally I feel that even if they do cause some inconvenience (bearing in mind the want of space in the house) at any rate they'll be helpful when the children grow up; it seems to me an important thing to lay the foundations of a family library for them. Teresina especially should remember how we used to devour books when we were children, and how we suffered from not having enough at our disposal.

By the way, how do you explain the fact that malaria has got such a hold in the very centre of the village? Or is it only our family that has got it? I think the present members of the council should take it on themselves to construct the sewers, just as their predecessors constructed the aqueduct; an aqueduct minus sewers means malaria as night follows day – widespread malaria in places where before it was only a sporadic condition.

The long and short of it is that whereas in the old days the women of Ghilarza used to be fat and ugly because of the bad water, nowadays they'll be ugly because of the malaria: the men, I don't doubt, will be going in for an intensive wine cure.

Lots of loving kisses.

Antonio

89

Turi Prison, 31 August, 1931

Darling Giulia,

One of the things which interested me most in your letter of 8-13 August was the news that Delio and Giuliano are keen on catching frogs. A few days ago I saw quoted in a review an opinion expressed by Lady Astor on the way children are treated in Russia (Lady Astor accompanied George Bernard Shaw and Lord Lothian on their recent excursion). As far as I can make out from the article, the only criticism that Lady Astor made of the Russians' treatment of their children was this: that they are so anxious to keep children clean that they don't even leave them time to get dirty. As you can see, this illustrious lady is witty and epigrammatic; but even wittier is the writer of the article, who raises his liberal hands to heaven in desperation and exclaims: 'What will become of these children once they have grown up and it's no longer possible to force them to have a bath?' He seems to think that as soon as the use of coercion is out of the question, the kids will do nothing but dive into the muck regardless, as an individual liberal reaction against the authoritarianism to which they are at present subjected.

In any case I am glad that Delio and Giuliano have an opportunity now and again of getting dirty when they're out catching frogs. I'd like to know if these particular frogs are the sort you can eat or not; if they are, it gives the children's hunting a practical character by no means to be despised. I don't know whether you'll fall in with this suggestion, because you've probably got the same aristocratic prejudices against frogs as Lady Astor has (the English have a contemptuous name for the French, 'frog-eaters'), but you ought to teach the children to distinguish between the kind of frogs you can eat and those you can't. The edible variety have a belly which is white all over, whereas the others have a reddish belly. The way to catch them is to put a piece of red rag on the line instead of the hook. The frogs catch hold of this rag in their mouths. You then pop them into a jug, after cutting off head and legs with a pair of scissors. After skinning them you have two alternatives. The first is to make a really exquisite broth with them; in which case you boil them for a good long time with the usual condiments and then pass them through a sieve, allowing everything to pass through barring the bones. Or else you can fry them, and eat them crisp and golden. In both cases they make a very tasty dish; one moreover which is eminently nourishing and easy to digest. I think that Delio and Giuliano could easily pass into the history of Russian culture, even at their present tender age, by introducing this new foodstuff into popular usage: they would thus realise several millions of roubles' worth of new human wealth, wresting it from the monopoly of crows, ravens and grass snakes. I embrace you tenderly.

Antonio

90

Turi Prison, 7 September 1931

Dearest Tatiana,

I have heard from Carlo, who tells me you wrote him a letter about my illness which made it clear you were very perturbed. Doctor Cisternino has also told me that he received a letter from you in which you seemed exceedingly anxious. I was sorry to hear this, because I don't think there was any reason to get as anxious as all that. Let me tell you that once upon a time I died and subsequently rose again, which shows that my hide has always been pretty tough.

When I was four, I suffered from haemorrhages accompanied by convulsions for three days in succession; I was bled white with it, and the doctors gave me up for dead. Until round about 1914 my mother kept the little coffin and the special little shroud that they were going to use to bury me in. One of my aunts maintained that I came back to life again when she bathed my feet in the oil of a lamp dedicated to a statue of the Madonna; and so, when I refused later on to fulfil my religious duties, she reproved me sharply, saying that I owed my life to the Madonna – a reproof which left me cold, to tell you the honest truth. In spite of the fact that I have never been exceptionally robust, I have never from that day to this had any really severe illness, apart from nervous exhaustion and dyspepsia. I didn't get angry reading your arch-scientific letter, because it simply made me smile: it reminded me of a French short story which I shan't tell you in case it makes *you* angry. I have always respected doctors and the medical profession, though I have an even greater respect for vets: vets cure animals which can't speak, and are therefore unable to describe their own symptoms. This forces vets to be very accurate in their diagnosis (animals cost money, whereas a good part of humanity is a dead loss). Doctors, I'm sorry to say, do not always reckon with the fact that a human being can use his tongue to tell lies as well as the truth – or at any rate, to convey mistaken impressions. To come to the point: I have made a very fair recovery (incidentally, I never stayed in bed even half an hour beyond my usual time, and I invariably went out on exercise); the fever has lessened and my temperature is seldom as much as ninety nine.

I would like to reply to a passage in your letter of 28 August in which you refer to my work on the 'Italian Intellectuals'. It's clear you've spoken to P. about this, because there are certain things that only he could have told you. But the situation is different. In ten years of journalistic activity I've written enough words to make up fifteen to twenty volumes of 400 pages each; however they were ephemeral things, written for a particular day, and in my view they had no business to go on living after that day was over. I never gave permission for any collection to be made – not even a collection of modest scope. In '18 Professor Cosmo wanted me to give him permission to make a selection of the articles I was writing daily for a Turin newspaper; he said he would publish them with a commendatory preface, and this would indeed have been an honour for me. However, I did not care to give my consent. In November '20 I allowed myself to be persuaded by Giuseppe Prezzolini, who offered to publish a collection of articles which had in point of fact been written as an organic whole; however, a month or two later (in January '21) I decided it was better to pay for the cost of setting up part of the material – as work had already been started on it – and to withdraw the manuscript. Again in '24 Franco Ciarlantini, a member of parliament, suggested to me that I should write a book on the *Ordine Nuovo*[1] and said he would publish it in a collection of his own which had already published books by MacDonald, Gompers etc. he undertook not to change so much as a comma, and not to tack any polemical foreword or appendix on to the book. To have a book published under these conditions by a Fascist publishing house was very tempting; nevertheless, I refused.

For P. the question was different; every article of his on economics was highly valued, and initiated long discussions in the specialist reviews. I have read in an article by Senator Einaudi[2] that P. is preparing a critical edition of the English economist David Ricardo; Einaudi has much praise for this undertaking, and I too am delighted to hear of it. I hope I shall be in a position to read English with ease when this edition comes out, and so be able to read Ricardo in the original.

The study that I have made on the 'Intellectuals' is very vast in scope; as a matter of fact I don't think that books on this subject exist in Italy. Certainly, a lot of erudite material does exist, but it's tucked away in an infinite number of reviews and local historical archives. Besides, I greatly extend the concept of the 'intellectual', and I do not let myself be limited by the current notion which equates the term with 'great intellectuals'. Furthermore this study leads on to certain definitions of the concept of the State, which is usually regarded as 'political' society (in other words dictatorship, or an apparatus of coercion to control the masses of the people in accordance with the mode of production and the economic system prevailing at a given period) and not as an equilibrium between 'political' society and 'civil' society (i.e. the hegemony of a social group over the entire society of a nation, a hegemony exercised by means of and through the organisations commonly called private, such as the Church, the Trade Unions, the schools etc.). The sphere in which intellectuals mostly operate is 'civil' society (Benedetto Croce, for example, is a sort of lay Pope, and is a most efficacious instrument of hegemony, even though from time to time he may find himself at loggerheads with one government or another). This conception of the function of intellectuals serves, in my view, to throw light on the reason – or one of the reasons – for the fall of the medieval Communes; that is, the fall of the government of an economic class which never managed to create its own body of intellectuals. Its failure to create such a body meant that it exercised a dictatorship only, not a hegemony. The Italian intellectuals never had a popular-national character; their character was cosmopolitan, after the pattern of the Church. Leonardo had no scruples about selling the plans of the fortifications of Florence to

Duke Valentine.[3] The Commune was therefore a syndicalistic or guild State which never succeeded in getting beyond this phase and forming an integrated State. Machiavelli realised as much and pointed out the remedy, but in vain – he wished through the medium of army organisation to organise the hegemony of the city over the countryside. He thus deserves the title of the first Italian Jacobin (the second was Carlo Cattaneo, although he had too many bees in his bonnet).

That is the reason why the Renaissance must be regarded as a movement of reaction and repression in comparison with the development of the Communes.

I have jotted down these few points in order to show you that every period of Italian history from the Roman Empire to the Risorgimento, must be examined from this specialist point of view. In addition, if I can muster up the will-power (and the higher authorities give permission) I shall write you out an abstract of the material at least fifty pages long and send it to you; because naturally I should be glad to have books which would help me in my work and would stimulate me to think. In addition, I shall in one of my next letters write you out a summary of the material for an essay on the Tenth Canto of Dante's *Inferno*: this I would like you to send on to Professor Cosmo, who as a specialist in Dante lore will be able to tell me whether my discovery is a false alarm, or whether it does in fact deserve to be worked up into a contribution – another little stone to be added to the cairn where its million and one predecessors already lie.

Don't think for a moment that I am not continuing to study, or that I get dejected because there comes a point when I'm unable to carry my researches forward. I have not yet lost a certain inventive capacity; for every important thing I read stimulates me to think: how could I get together an article on this theme? I think of a provocative opening and a trenchant conclusion, and then fill in a series of arguments as irresistible, in my own view, as so many straight lefts to the reader's eye. In this innocent way I amuse myself for hours. Of course I don't write such pieces of devilry down; I limit myself to philosophical and philological themes, the sort Heine was thinking of when he wrote, 'They were so boring that they sent me to sleep, but the boredom was so great that it made me wake up again.'

I embrace you tenderly.

Antonio

1. The socialist weekly (later a daily) founded in Turin by Gramsci.
2. Luigi Einaudi, later second President of the Italian Republic (elected May 1948).
3. Cesare Borgia.

91

Turi Prison, 13 September 1931

Dearest Tatiana,

...In one of your postcards, the one in which you told me of your visits to the cinema and especially of the film *Due Mondi*[1] some of the things you said quite took my breath away. How can you possibly believe that these two worlds exist? This is a way of thinking worthy of the Black Hundreds,[2] the American Ku Klux Klan or the German Swastikas. And how can you of all people say that you've got a living example of it in your house? Has a rupture of this kind ever taken place between your father and your mother[3] – are they not united still as closely as they ever were? The film is certainly of Austrian origin, a product of post-war anti-Semitism.

When I was in Vienna I had a room in the flat of an old superstitious petite bourgeoise, who before accepting me as a tenant asked me if I was a Jew or a Roman Catholic; she eked out a living by sub-letting two rooms, taking advantage of the fact that in '18, during the brief Soviet period, a law was passed which laid down that rents paid by tenants to the landlords of houses were not affected by the inflation. I paid her three and a half million crowns a month (that is, 300 lire); while she herself paid at the most 1,000 of these crowns to the landlord. Just as I was about to vacate the room, a secretary of the Embassy whose wife was obliged to stay in Vienna because of the illness of their son, requested me to reserve it for her. That afternoon I spoke to the old lady and she agreed. But early the following morning she comes knocking on my door and says: 'Yesterday I forgot to ask if the new tenant is Jewish: I don't let to Jews.' The new tenant was in point of fact a Ukrainian Jewess. What on earth was I to do? I mentioned the dilemma to a Frenchman,[4] who told me that there was only one solution: to tell the old woman I couldn't decently ask the new tenant if she was Jewish, but that I did know that she was secretary to one of the Embassies. He explained that although the hatred of the petit bourgeois for the Jew is great, even greater is their servile worship of the Diplomatic Corps.

It worked beautifully. After listening to my story the old lady replied: 'If she's in the diplomatic, of course I'll let her have the room: I know you can't go asking Embassy people if they're Jews or not.'

Now do you seriously maintain that you have the same world in common with this old Viennese?

I embrace you tenderly.

Antonio

1. *Two Worlds*. This film was made in 1930 by the German director E.A. Dupont; it dealt with anti-Semitism in pre-World War I Poland.
2. Popular name for the anti-Semitic leagues (League of the Russian People and League of Michael the Archangel) organised by the Okhrana (Czarist secret police) and the Russian landlords in 1905.
3. Tatiana's mother was Jewish.
4. Probably Victor Serge.

92

Turi Prison, 13 September 1931

Darling mamma,

I have received a letter from Teresina, and one from Grazietta with a few lines written by yourself. Many thanks – but if writing is such a painful business for you, dictate the letter to Grazietta or Mea or Teresina, and then just add your signature to it. That would make it easier for you, and you'd be able to write more often.

I shall reply in order to the two letters. To Teresina: as far as my books are concerned I told Carlo not to lend them to people outside the family circle, but to let any one of the family read them who wanted to. The principle involved is this: I don't see why my books should help entertain people who are indirectly responsible for my being in prison. To Teresina I shall send as a personal present one of the finest novels of Leo Tolstoy, *War and Peace*; the heroine is called Natasha and she is a delightful person. Many thanks to Franco for his resolve to become an airman when he grows up, so that he can come and liberate me and bring me back to mamma. It's quite on the cards that when I'm released from prison, fourteen years from now, it may actually be possible in Italy to travel by aeroplane as one travels today by car; Franco's promise may therefore be more realistic than it might appear. And not only that: in fourteen years' time he'll be twenty years of age, and at twenty a boy can be a very fine pilot.

I am sorry that Mima was offended because I didn't promise her a present too. It might have been better if you had promised her something in my name; it's an ugly thing when feelings of envy and jealousy take root among children. So I promise her a present too, and you'll see that I shall keep my word as soon as I possibly can. But tell the children to be patient: you must explain to them that not being able to do everything you want when you want is exactly what being in prison means. I suppose they imagine that I'm in some sort of place like the tower of Ghilarza; tell them I've got a very big cell, bigger maybe than any of the rooms in the house. The only trouble is that I can't get out of it. Just imagine, dear mamma – and I don't think I've ever told you this – I have an iron bedstead with a metal framework, a horsehair mattress and pillow, and a woollen mattress and pillow. I've also got a night table: it's nothing to write home about, as they say, but it's very useful to me.

The things which Grazietta wrote I found very interesting. If malaria tends to lead to tuberculosis it means that the people are suffering from malnutrition. I would like Grazietta to tell me what the following categories of people eat in a week: a family of:

1. *zorronaderis*[1]
2. *massaiosa meitade*[2]
3. small farmers who work their own land
4. shepherds whose flocks are a full-time occupation
5. craftsmen (cobblers or blacksmiths)

(Questions: how many times do they eat meat in a week, and how much? Or alternatively, do they just go without? What do they use to make soup? How much oil or fat do they put in, how much pasta, how many vegetables etc? How much corn do they grind, and how many loaves of bread do they buy? How much coffee or coffee substitute, how much sugar? How much milk for the children etc?)

Darling mamma, I embrace everyone – and take a warm embrace for yourself.

Antonio

1. Day labourers (Sardinian).
2. Sharecroppers (Sardinian).

93

Turi Prison, 20 September 1931

Dearest Tania,

I shall now try to set down that much bruited outline of my essay on the Tenth Canto of Dante's *Inferno*.

Cavalcante and Farinata

1. De Sanctis in his Essay on *Farinata*[1] notes the unevenness which characterises the Tenth Canto by reason of the fact that Farinata, after being shown in heroic vein early on in the episode, in the second half of the Canto turns into a pedagogue. He holds, to put it in Crocean terms, that Farinata ceases to be 'poetry' and becomes 'structure'. The Tenth Canto is traditionally Farinata's Canto, and therefore the unevenness noted by De Sanctis has always seemed plausible. I maintain that in the Tenth Canto there are two dramas, Farinata's and Cavalcante's, and not just the single drama of Farinata.

2. It is strange that the interpreters of Dante to the world have never

noted, for all their painstaking Byzantine labours, that it is Cavalcante who, of all the Epicureans of the fiery tombs, is the most truly punished – I mean the one whose punishment is the most immediate and personal.[2] In this punishment Farinata has an intimate part, and his end is like his beginning – he still 'holds heaven in great disdain'.[3]

The law of retribution in the case of Farinata and Cavalcante is as follows: for having desired to look into the future they are deprived (theoretically) of all knowledge of earthly things for a definite period; i.e. they live in a cone of shadow, from the centre of which they can see into the past beyond a certain radius and into the future beyond a radius of equal length. When Dante appears on the scene, the position of Cavalcante and Farinata is this: they can see Guido alive in the past, and they see him dead in the future. But in this particular moment, is Guido living or dead?

The difference between Cavalcante and Farinata is obvious. Farinata, hearing Dante's Florentine speech, becomes the partisan, the Ghibelline hero: Cavalcante on the other hand can think of nothing but Guido, and when he hears the Florentine speech he lifts himself up to find out if Guido is alive or dead in that moment (the new arrivals being in a position to inform them). The actual drama of Cavalcante's appearance is extremely rapid, but of unspeakable intensity. He at once asks about Guido and hopes that he is with Dante; but as soon as the poet, who is not aware of the above-mentioned detail of Cavalcante's punishment, uses the word *ebbe* (had), the verb in the past tense, he gives a terrible cry, and: *Supin ricadde, e piú non parve fuora.*[4]

3. Just as in the first part of the episode 'Guido's scorn'[5] became the centre for the researches of all the manufacturers of hypotheses and contributions, so in the second part Farinata's prophesy of Dante's exile absorbed their attention. It seems to me that the importance of the second part consists especially in the fact that it illuminates the drama of Cavalcante, and provides all the essential elements so that the reader may relive it.

Can this therefore be called a poetry of the ineffable, the unexpressed? I do not think so. Dante is not trying to get out of bringing the drama before us directly; indeed, that is just the way in which he does bring it before us. We are here concerned with a 'mode of expression' and in my view 'modes of expression' can change with time in the same way that language, in the strict sense of the word, itself changes. (Only Bertoni can think himself a Crocean when he serves up the old theory of 'beautiful' words and 'ugly' words, and imagines it's a linguistic novelty deduced from Croce's *Aesthetics.*)

I remember that when in 1912 I was attending Professor Toesca's course on the History of Art I got to know the reproduction of the picture at Pompeii in which Medea is shown at the killing of the sons she has had by Jason.

She is present, but with her face veiled. Now I seem to remember Toesca saying that this was an accepted mode of expression among the ancients, and that Lessing in *Laokoon* (I am quoting from my memory of these lectures) did not consider this an artifice of impotence but, on the contrary, the best manner of giving an impression of the infinite suffering of a mother. Suffering of this nature, if represented openly, would be crystallised in a grimace. Similarly the expression of Ugolino: '*Poscia più che il dolor poté il digiuno.*'[6] belongs to this language, and the people have understood it as a veil thrown over the father while he is the act of devouring his own son.

There is nothing in common between these modes of expression of Dante, and those employed here and there by Manzoni. When Renzo thinks of Lucia after making for the Venetian frontier, Manzoni writes: 'We shall not try to describe what he felt: the reader knows the circumstances; let him imagine it for himself.' But Manzoni had already declared that there was more than enough love in the world to keep our revered species from dying out; so why talk about it in books and attempt to describe love for practical and ideological reasons. In any event, my contention that Farinata's discourse is intimately bound up with the drama of Cavalcante is confirmed by Dante (the character) when he says finally: '*Or direte dunque a quel caduto, Che il suo nato è coi vivi ancor congiunto.*'[7] (Incidentally, the younger Cavalcante was Farinata's son too;[8] however, the latter, absorbed heart and soul in the wars of the factions, gives no sign of perturbation on hearing the supposed 'news' contained in the word *ebbe*, i.e. that Guido is dead. Cavalcante is the more truly punished of the two, and for him the *ebbe* means the end of the anguish of doubt as to whether at that moment Guido is alive or dead.)

4. It seems to me that this interpretation does vital damage to Croce's thesis on the poetry and structure of the *Divine Comedy*. Without the structure there would be no poetry, and so the structure too has the value of poetry. This question is bound up with another: what artistic importance have the stage directions in plays? The more recent developments in stagecraft, which give ever greater importance to the producer, raise this question in an increasingly sharp form. The author of the play fights to keep his end up with actors and producer, his chief weapon being the stage directions, which enable him to depict his characters in greater detail. The author wants his own sphere of influence to be respected; he wants to ensure that the interpretation of the play by actors and producer (who are translators from one art into another, and at the same time critics) shall be consistent with his own vision. At the end of his *Don Juan*[9] Bernard Shaw provides as an appendix a little handbook supposedly written by John Tanner, the protagonist; his purpose being to delineate the figure of Tanner with greater precision, and to obtain from the actor a greater faithfulness to his own conception. A play without stage directions has more the

quality of lyric poetry than that of a portrayal of living people in the clash of drama; the stage direction has in part incorporated the earlier monologues etc. If in the theatre the completed work of art is a result of the collaboration of writer and actors, unified aesthetically by the producer, the stage directions have an essential importance in this creative process, seeing that they limit the arbitrary freedom of the actor and producer. The entire structure of the *Divine Comedy* has this exalted function; and although in places the distinction may be valid, one must be very cautious and must take each particular case on its merits.

I have written the above off the reel, having nothing beside me but the small Hoepli edition of Dante. I possess the essays of De Sanctis and Croce's *Dante*; in addition, I have read part of the study by Luigi Russo which was published in Barbi's review and quoted in a *Leonardo* of '28. That part which I have read refers to Croce's thesis. I also possess the number of *Critica* which contained Croce's reply. However I have not seen this article for a long time, anyway not since the nucleus of this theory had taken shape in my head, because it's at the bottom of a box kept in the storeroom. Professor Cosmo will be able to tell me if this is a fresh case of somebody inventing the umbrella for the second time; or alternatively, whether there's some point which might be worked up into a note, to pass the time.

I embrace you tenderly.

Antonio

1. Farinata, a member of the noble family of the Uberti and leader of the Ghibellines (faction favouring the Emperor) in Florence, was expelled with his followers in 1258. Two years later he defeated the Guelph army at Montaperti and re-entered Florence in triumph. The other Ghibelline leaders proposed razing Florence to the ground, but Farinata successfully opposed this course.

As a 'follower of Epicurus' he is placed by Dante in the sixth circle of the Inferno – the circle of heretics and atheists – who are imprisoned in open fiery tombs.

2. Cavalcante Cavalcanti, a Guelph (adherent of the Papal faction), was the father of Guido Cavalcanti, one of the most famous poets of the *dolce stil nuovo*, and a close friend of Dante. Boccaccio describes the elder Cavalcanti as 'a rich and elegant gentleman, who was of Epicurus' opinion that the soul does not outlive the body, and that man's highest good is in the delights of the flesh'.

3. *avendo il cielo in gran dispetto*. But this is a misquotation. The full passage in the original is as follows:

Ed ei mi disse: 'Volgiti; che fai?/Vedi là Farinata che s'è dritto:/Dalla cintola in su tutto il vedrai.'/I'aveva già il mio viso nel suo fitto;/Ed ei s'ergea col petto e con la fronte/come avesse lo inferno in gran dispitto.

(*Inferno*, X 31-36)

And he (Virgil) said to me: 'turn round: what are you doing? Look at Farinata who is standing up (in the tomb): you'll see the whole of him from his girdle to his head.' I had already fixed my gaze on his; he was standing erect, and thrusting out his brow and chest, as if he held the Inferno in great disdain.

4. 'He fell backward, and did not show himself again.'

5. When Cavalcante asks 'Mio figlio ov'è? E perche non è teco?' ('Where is my son? And why is he not with you?') Dante replies: 'Da me stesso non vegno,/Colui che attende là per qui mi mena, Forse cui Guido vostro ebbe a disdegno.' ('I have not come here on my own [authority]. My companion, for whom your Guido perhaps felt scorn, is waiting over there; he it is who is guiding me through these regions.')

Why Guido Cavalcanti should have felt scorn for Virgil remains an enigma. The commentators to whom Gramsci refers have put forward scores of solutions, some of them really fantastic. The likeliest solution seems to me that Dante had to find a rhyme for *vegno* (and *ingegno* five lines back); also that the noble line about Farinata 'holding Hell in great disdain' was still ringing in his mind.

6. 'And then my hunger (lit. the fast), proved stronger than my sorrow' (*Inferno,* XXXIII, 75). This popular interpretation is not shared by the cloud of commentators: Olschki, for example, calls it 'geschmacklos' (tasteless). His own interpretation is: 'What sorrow could not do, my hunger did' (i.e. killed me).

7. 'Tell the one who fell back that his son is still among the living.'

8. Guido had married Farinata's daughter Bice.

9. Don Juan = Man and Superman. The title of John Tanner's manual is 'The Revolutionist's Handbook and Pocket Companion'.

94

Turi Prison, 28 September 1931

Dearest Tatiana,

... I'm sorry you haven't yet enlarged on the subject of the Jews, and the 'two worlds'. And I'm also sorry that this old hoodoo has entered your head, especially seeing there has been no anti-Semitism in Italy for a long while now. Jews can become ministers of the crown (not to mention prime ministers, as in the case of Luzzatti); they can also reach the rank of general in the army. Marriages of Jews with Christians are very numerous, particularly in the large cities; and this is not only a working-class phenomenon, for a number of girls of the aristocracy have married Jewish intellectuals. In what way does an Italian Jew (leaving aside a small minority of Rabbis and traditionalist greybeards) differ from an ordinary Italian of the same class? There's a much greater difference between such a Jew on the one hand and a Polish or Galician Jew of the same class on the other. It's true there was a little political anti-Semitism against Toeplitz, the director of the Commercial Bank, and in 1919 the Milan Review (*La Rivista di Milano*) was founded: this was as fiercely anti-Semitic as its circulation was restricted. I can't help being reminded of the Italian (or French) proverb: 'Scratch a Russian and you'll find a Cossack'; many Cossacks used to believe as an article of faith that Jews had tails.

As far as my Dante synopsis is concerned, I'm afraid it will have been of very little interest to you; it's very schematic, and it is more than possible that certain allusions to erudite books may have escaped you.

I embrace you tenderly,

Antonio

95

Turi Prison, 28 September 1931

My dear Carlo,

I received your letter of 12 September, You mustn't be surprised that I didn't answer it last week, as I could have done; I am forced to distribute the space at my disposal among all my various correspondents.

The two books you mention are both worth buying; I know them well, and I can give you an idea in advance of their weaknesses, both internal and external.

The *History of Rome* you refer to is, if I am not mistaken, the one written not only by Hartmann but also by Kromayer. It is good, although by now a bit antiquated – and very clumsily translated (the first edition at any rate). Another grave drawback is that it only covers the period of written history – i.e. that for which documents exist; accordingly it passes over the early so-called 'legendary' centuries in silence. The more modern school of historians is not so rigorous and bigoted in the matter of documentary evidence. Moreover Goethe himself once wrote that the whole history of Rome, including the legendary period, should be taught, because the men who had invented those legends were worthy of being known through the very legends they had created.[1]

The truth is that in more recent years many legends have been shown not to be legends at all, or at any rate to have a certain nucleus of fact, as a result of fresh archaeological discoveries and the coming to light of epigraphical documentation. Wells' book[2] is also very badly translated notwithstanding the high reputation of Laterza as a publisher. It's interesting, because it tends to demolish the ingrained habit Europeans have of thinking that history has only taken place in Europe, especially in ancient times; Wells speaks of the ancient history of China and India, and of the medieval history of the Mongols in the same tone he uses when dealing with European history. He shows that if one takes a world view one must admit that Europe is only a province, and has no right to consider itself the depository of the whole of human culture. Another innovation introduced by Wells, which I like less, is the history of the earth prior to the appearance of man. And a further weakness: the history of the Catholic Church and its influence on the development of civilisation is seriously distorted; one feels that Wells is an Anglican anti-Papist and not an unprejudiced historian.

... Now a word of advice on the learning of languages, seeing you intend to start work on this. Don't get submerged in grammar books; when you read, go to the dictionary for help rather than to the grammar book. Grammar, in my view, should accompany translation and not precede it. Many people begin with the study of grammar books and end by getting hopelessly bogged down; they wear out their memories into the bargain.

I must finish now. A warm embrace.

Antonio

Don't forget to write home.

1. Goethe's *Gespräche mit Eckermann*, 15 October 1825.
2. *A Short History of the World*, published (in English) Nov. 1922.

96

Turi Prison, 5 October 1931

Dearest Tania,

...The fact that you have toned down your assertions on this question of the so-called 'two worlds' does not alter the fundamental erroneousness of your point of view, and does not diminish the force of my assertion that we are dealing with an ideology which belongs, even if only marginally, to the same camp as the Black Hundreds.[1] Of course I understand perfectly well that you wouldn't take part in a *pogrom*; nevertheless, for a *pogrom* to be possible, it is necessary that the ideology of 'two impenetrable worlds', of races etc., should be widely diffused. This helps to create that imponderable atmosphere which the Black Hundreds can exploit, organising the discovery of a child's corpse drained of blood and accusing the Jews of having murdered him in ritual sacrifice. The outbreak of the World War has shown how ably the ruling classes and groups know how to exploit these apparently innocuous ideologies, in order to set in motion the waves of public opinion. The thing seem to me so very surprising in your case, that I would seem to myself lacking in love for you if I didn't try to liberate you completely from every preoccupation with this question.

What do you actually mean by the expression 'two worlds'? That we are faced, as it were, with two planets which cannot draw any nearer to each other and cannot enter into communication? If you do not mean this, and the expression is to be understood only in a metaphorical and relative sense it has little significance, because metaphorical 'worlds' are numberless, and include even that one which is described in the peasant proverb: *Moglie e buoi dei paesi tuoi*.[2]

To how many societies does an individual belong? Hasn't every one of us got to make continual efforts to unify his own conception of the world, in which heterogeneous splinters of fossilised cultural worlds are bound still to be lodged? And doesn't there exist a general historic process which is persistently tending to unify the entire human race? Don't we two, when we write to each other, continually discover grounds for friction, and at the same time don't we try, at times successfully, to reach agreement on certain questions? And does not every group or party, or sect, or religion tend to create a 'conformism' of its own (I do not mean the word in its passive sense of 'falling in with the crowd').

The important thing to remember in connection with this question is that the Jews were not liberated from the ghetto until 1848, and that they remained in the ghetto segregated in every way from European society for almost two millennia. Since 1848 the process of assimilation in the Western countries has been so rapid and profound that one cannot help thinking that it was only the segregation imposed on them which prevented their complete assimilation in the various countries. It should be borne in mind that the Christian religion was the only 'state culture' which (right up to the French Revolution) demanded that Jews should be segregated because of their religious 'incorrigibility'. (This intransigence, incidentally, is a thing of the past. Nowadays they pass from Judaism to Deism pure and simple, or to atheism.) In any case it is worth noting that many characteristics which are taken for racial are actually the result of life in the ghetto. On the other hand the system of ghettos was imposed in different ways in different countries, with the result that an English Jew, for example, has almost nothing in common with a Jew from Galicia.

Gandhi today appears to represent the Hindu ideology: but the Hindus have reduced the aboriginal Dravidian inhabitants of India to the status of pariahs – they were a warlike race, and they could hardly have thrown up a man like Gandhi until after the Mongol invasion and the English conquest. For two millennia the Jews have had no territorial state, and no unity of language or culture or economic life; how then could one expect to find an aggressiveness etc. in them? The Arabs too are Semites, blood-relations of the Jews; once upon a time they had their period of aggressiveness and of attempts at world conquest. And one last point: in so far as the Jews are bankers and holders of finance capital, how can you possibly assert that they do not have their share in the 'aggressiveness' of imperialist states.

I embrace you tenderly.

Antonio

1. See note to Letter 91.
2. 'Wives and oxen from your own villages.' This is a Tuscan proverb: the sense is – Go to your own village (i.e. the place you know best) for your wife and your cattle.

97

Turi Prison, 12 October 1931

Dearest Tania,

I received your postcard of 10 October, which did not mitigate in the least the effect caused by your letter of the 2nd. It was not just harsh, it was positively offensive. Whatever did you mean by saying that I play 'blind man's buff' with you, and that I try to 'get you into a corner'? I really ought to send you back some hard words in exchange; however I think it will be better to avoid any future repetition of these unpleasant incidents, to call them no worse name. Your reference earlier on to my being an ex-journalist is likewise nothing but *imbelle telum sine ictu*,[1] to use a pompous expression. I have never been a professional journalist, the sort that hawks his pen to the boss who pays him most, and is bound to go in for never-ending lying because an ability to lie is part and parcel of his professional qualifications. I enjoyed maximum freedom as a journalist, stood by my own opinions, and was never forced to hide my profound convictions in order to please bosses or yes-men.

You say that you did not like my remark about your having 'toned down' your assertions about the Jews. You are right in this sense, that in practice you have toned down nothing ; as far as your present position is concerned there's a little of everything in it, but the differing views came out in different letters. First of all there was a point of view which led straight to anti-Semitism; then a Jewish Nationalist or Zionist position; and last of all certain opinions which would have been shared by the old Rabbis who opposed the destruction of the ghettos, foreseeing that a decrease in the number of these segregated communities would end by 'denaturing' the race, and relaxing the religious bonds which maintained its personality.

It's clear I was wrong to discuss the question at all; it would have been better to joke about it, and counter your assertions by advancing the theory of English 'phlegm', French 'fury', German 'loyalty', Spanish 'hauteur', Italian 'adaptability', and finally Slav 'charm', all things which are most useful to authors of serials for the newspapers and scenarios of popular films. Or else I could have put this question: who is the 'true' Jew, or 'average' Jew? – or even the 'average man', who is not, I think, to be found in any museum of anthropology or sociology. Or alternatively: what significance is there for the Jews of the present day in their conception of God as the 'Lord of Hosts', and all the language of the Bible about the 'chosen people' and the mission of the Jewish people, which sounds like the sort of talk Kaiser Bill used to go in for before the War. Marx has written that the Jewish question went out of existence at the time when the Christians all became Jews, assimilating the essence of Judaism which is the speculative spirit. Or rather, that the Jewish question will only be solved when the whole of Europe is liberated from the speculative spirit, or Judaism in general. This seems to me the only way of posing the general question, apart from recognising the right of Jewish communities to cultural autonomy (of language, schools etc.), and also national autonomy in any case where a Jewish community succeeded in one way or another in inhabiting a definite territory.

Everything else seems to me false mysticism, good enough maybe for the little Jewish intellectuals of Zionism; it is all one with the question of 'race', when that word is understood in any other sense than the purely anthropological; as early as the time of Christ the Jews no longer spoke their own language, which was reduced to the status of a liturgical language – they spoke Aramaic. When a 'race' has forgotten its native tongue, it means that it has already lost the major part of its inheritance, of its own original conception of the world, and has absorbed the culture (together with the language) of a conquering people. What meaning does 'race' still have in that case? It is evident that we now have to deal with a new community, a modern community which has received the passive (not to say negative) imprint of the ghetto, and which in the framework of this new social situation has grown a new 'nature'.

It's strange that you don't make use of historical method when you discuss the general question, and yet want me to explain historically why certain Cossack communities believed that the Jews had tails. When I mentioned this I was thinking of a joke told me by a Jew who had been political commissar of an assault division of Oremburg Cossacks during the Russian–Polish war of 1920. These Cossacks had no Jews in their territory, and they imagined them to be as the official Tsarist and clerical propaganda had pictured them: monstrous creatures who had murdered God. Consequently they refused to believe that the political commissar was a Jew. 'You're one of us' – they said – 'you're not a Jew. Your body is scarred with wounds from the Polish lances, you fight by our side; Jews are a different thing altogether.'

In Sardinia the Jew is pictured in various guises: there is the expression *arbeu*, which means a legendary monster of evil and ugliness; then there is the *giudeo* who killed Jesus Christ – although the idea of a good *giudeo* as well as an evil one does exist, pious Nicodemus having helped Mary to take the body of her son down from the Cross. However, for the Sardinian the *giudei* are not associated with the world of today; if a Sardinian is told that someone is a *giudeo*, he will ask if the Jew is like Nicodemus; but the general idea in his head will be that of a Christian as wicked as the people who desired the death of Christ. Finally there's the term *marranu*, from the expression *marrano*[2] which in Spain was applied to the Jews who had pretended to get converted; in Sardinia it is an expression of general offensiveness. Unlike the Cossacks, the Sardinians have not been subjected to anti-Semitic propaganda, and do not make a distinction between Jews and other human beings.

As far as I am concerned, that just about settles the question, and I'm not going to let myself be lured into starting others. The question of 'race', outside the realm of anthropology and prehistoric studies, does not interest me. (And so your mention of the importance of tombs to historians of civilisation is of no avail. In any case it's only true for the most remote periods, tombs being the only monuments of such periods that are not destroyed by time; also because objects from daily life were placed in the tombs beside the dead. Even so these tombs give us a very limited picture of the times in which they were built; they illustrate the history of costume, and part of the religious rites. Another drawback is that they present the lives not of the common people but of the rich and the upper classes, who were not infrequently foreign overlords of the country.) I myself have no race: my father is of quite recent Albanian origin (the family left Epirus along with other refugees during or after the war of 1821, and were rapidly Italianised); my paternal grandmother was a Gonzalez, a descendant of some Spanish-Italian family of southern Italy – a large number of these remained on after Spanish rule had ended. My mother is Sardinian on both her father's and her mother's side, and Sardinia was not united to Piedmont until 1847 – before that it was an hereditary possession held in fee by the Piedmontese princes, who got it in exchange for Sicily, which was too far away and therefore more difficult to defend. Nevertheless my culture is fundamentally Italian, and this is my world; I have never felt torn between two worlds – although a two-column article in the *Giornale d'Italia* which appeared one day in March 1920 said as much, and attempted to prove that my political activity in Turin was in part explained by the fact that I was a Sardinian and not a Sicilian or Piedmontese. No capital was made of the fact that I am of Albanian origin, because Crispi[3] too was an Albanian; he was educated in an Albanian college, and spoke Albanian. Besides, such questions as these have never been put in Italy, and nobody in Liguria gets alarmed if a sailor brings home a negro wife to his village. People don't wet their fingers and rub her skin to see if the black comes off; nor do they believe that the sheets will be dyed black after she has slept in them.

I embrace you tenderly.

Antonio

1. An unwarlike weapon devoid of force.
2. The literal meaning of *marrano* in Spanish is pig.
3. Francesco Crispi (1819–1901), the leading spirit of Italian imperialism in the nineteenth century. Inaugurated Italy's colonial enterprises in 1885. Planned the war against Menelik, the Emperor of Ethiopia, but lost power following the disastrous battle of Adowa (1896).

98

Turi Prison, 19 October 1931

Dearest Tania,

... Next time it's likely that I'll want to devote all the space at my disposal to Giulia; I'll write a brief note to you if it's necessary. So don't ask me any complicated questions. I see that De Ruggiero has given high praise in Croce's review *Critica* to a book by Salvador de Madariaga called *Anglais, Français, Espagnols* (*edition de la Nouvelle Revue Française*). Madariaga is a Spaniard who is at present a functionary of the League of Nations; for some time he taught in an English university. So he appears specially competent to define the different characteristics of the three peoples without falling headlong into the prejudices which are usual in books of this sort. Why not read it, and then send it on to me? I would really like you to. Not that De Ruggiero's opinion is a good reason, for De Ruggiero also tends to conceive humanity in terms of national groups of intellectuals; anyway, even from this point of view (once you are critically aware of it) the book may be of interest, especially for what it says about the French and the English. Not so much for what it says about the Spaniards, because Madariaga is a Spaniard, even if an intelligent Spaniard, and Vico in one of his *degnità* (or axioms) in the *Scienza Nuova* writes that 'the vain-glory of nations' is one of the gravest obstacles to the writing of history.

In the time of Crispi a French publicist (I think his name was Ballet[1]) wrote a book called *L'Italie qu'on voit et l'Italie qu'on ne voit pas*. This title might well be given to a book on national characteristics. The people the visitor usually sees are the intellectuals; those he does not see are the peasants. Yet the latter, who make up the greater part of the population, are themselves in a real sense the 'nation', even though they count for little in the government of the State, and are thrust into the background by the intellectuals (apart from the interest that may be aroused by some picturesque trait). This obscurity is the matrix of phenomena like the 'Great Fear' – such as that of 1789–90 in France – when the peasants rise in revolt: they operate like a mysterious and unknown force, like the elemental forces of nature, and they raise the same sort of panic as that caused by earthquakes and cyclones.

I embrace you tenderly.

Antonio

1. Auguste Brachet. His book was published in Paris in 1881.

99

Turi Prison, 19 October 1931

Dearest mamma,

I have received your letter of the 14th, and I am very glad to know that you are much stronger now, and that you'll be going for at least a day to the feast of San Serafino. What a delight I took when I was a little boy in the valley of the Tirso under San Serafino! I used to stay for hours and hours sitting on a rock and admiring that part of the river just under the church where the *nesserzu*[1] that was built lower down the valley forms a sort of lake; watching the moorhens as they left the cover of the surrounding reeds and swam towards the middle; and the fish leaping out of the water to catch gnats. Maybe all that has changed now, if they've started to build the dam that was planned to catch the waters of the Flumineddu. I still remember how once I saw a big snake slide down into the water and come out a wee bit later with a fat eel in his mouth; I killed the snake and took the eel myself, but I had to throw it away because I didn't know how to carry it back to the *muristene;*[2] it had got as stiff as a stick; and it was making my hands stink like the devil.

However did it get into your head that I was ill, and that I was hiding the fact from you? It's true I can't do a dance on one leg, but sometimes I am amazed myself at my own powers of resistance. One drawback is that I've lost all my teeth and can't chew; so I can only eat a certain type of food, and have to leave the rest. I'm especially annoyed about this, because shortly there will be lamb for sale as an extra, and I can't eat it although I'm so fond of it.

I don't remember Maria Porcu, but I must have known her if she lived till she was ninety-seven. Write to me occasionally about Aunt Margaret's family: what has become of Giovannino, Ignazio, Natalina and the other child whose name I've forgotten? Giovannino's sons must be quite big now. And Nennetta Cuba? etc, etc. One time or other you should put all my old acquaintances on parade. Do you remember the eldest son of Tanielle the butcher *su re*?[3] Once I met him by accident in a Milan café: he had got the sack from Farinacci's paper in Cremona (I honestly don't know what he could have been doing on a newspaper, for he still had the same foolish and cretinous air that he had when he was a boy). He spoke to me in a very servile manner, and asked me to find him a job on my party's newspaper. He seemed very much down on his luck, but I couldn't help laughing at this naive request of his.

I am still waiting for the letter that Teresina promised me.

Kisses to all, especially the children and you, dear mamma, I embrace with all the tenderness in the world.

Antonio

1. Weir (Sardinian).
2. Muristene: two-roomed bothy built near isolated country churches or shrines to shelter visitors and pilgrims (Sardinian).
3. *su re*: the King (Sardinian).

100

Turi Prison, 2 November 1931

Dearest Tania,

... I've never remembered to write to you about the applications made by Umberto[1] for a revision of the sentence, copies of which I received and studied some while ago. Reading them through I saw that the grounds for an appeal that I knew of were known to Umberto too; he had in fact set them forth in detail himself. There was one point, however, which, although it was known to Umberto – because I myself suggested it to him after the sentence – had not been exploited by him in all its possibilities. Perhaps I might be able to set forth these particular grounds for appeal, if it were possible to get the exact data to enclose with the appeal through the lawyer concerned (what lawyer is dealing with the question anyway?).

This is the point at issue. One of the most important paragraphs in the indictment against the presumed members of the Central Committee of the Communist Party was that accusing them of having planned an armed rising to take place during 1926; this decision was supposed to have been reached at the Congress of Lyons, and the evidence quoted was a booklet entitled *Regolamento universale della guerra civile*.[2] Umberto rightly calls attention to the fact that this article had already been published in entirety by the review *Politica*, edited by the Minister of Justice himself and by the Academician Francesco Coppola, and he affirms that the booklet mentioned in the accusation is nothing but a literal reprint of that publication. I myself never saw the booklet, and cannot say whether it was just a reprint of this kind; however, this has little importance seeing that the exact truth can be documented. Before the article *Regolamento universale della guerra civile* was published in the Italian review Politica it had appeared in the French *Revue de Paris* at the end of '25 or the beginning of '26. But the *Revue de Paris* did not publish this article alone; in 1926 – I don't remember the exact number – it published an article (which was either an editorial or an anonymous article signed by asterisks) called *La guerre civile et la bolchévisme*; on the cover the title was *La guerre et le bolchévisme*, I remember it exactly. Here the question was summarised as follows: the Universal Guide is nothing more than an article from a review, the review being 'Military Thought' (Voiennii Mysl); it has no official character, and is not obligatory for Communist parties. On the contrary, the article was severely criticised by a whole series of Russian military writers, who pointed out how pedantic, abstract and academic it was etc., etc. The second of the two numbers of the *Revue de Paris* which summarises this discussion is conclusive proof that no Communist party – and least of all the Italian Communist Party! – could possibly publish this article and allow members to regard it as authoritative. Hence the Italian booklet cannot be considered a party document for which members of the Central Committee must take responsibility (surely it was their job to be on top of the question, and not take an article of that sort seriously); the thing must be regarded rather as a publication initiated by irresponsible elements who took it on themselves to produce it absolutely off their own bat. As far as I personally am concerned there is printed evidence of this available. It is contained in an issue of the Communist Party Bulletin which appeared early in 1926; in the second part of that number there will be found a summary – though it's a pretty incompetent one, to tell you the truth – of a speech of mine to the political commission of the Congress of Lyons. In that speech, which I delivered in the name of the outgoing Central Committee as a directive which the Congress was asked to endorse – and endorse it it did – I declared peremptorily that no such situation existed in Italy, and that the job on hand was that of 'political organisation' and not of attempts at insurrection. This bulletin was not quoted at the trial, but I think it's probably filed away among the documents in the case.

Why not show this material to the lawyer who is tackling the appeal and ask his opinion? Of course even if I do appeal myself it won't change matters one iota, but anyway it's probably useful that the thing should be on record. You can find the appropriate numbers of the *Revue de Paris* without difficulty in any library which takes it. In any case the lawyer might be able to make use of this material to back up Umberto's application, for it's probably better that the appeal for a revising of the sentence should go forward in the name of one man.

...If the Jewish question interests you, and you want to get to grips with it scientifically, there are two recent publications which I have seen quoted in a review, and which I would like to recommend to you. These are two reports that were read at the International Congress of Population Research recently held in Rome, and were later published as separate pamphlets. One is by Professor Livio Livi and deals with the entire Jewish population of the world; the other by Professor R. Bachi deals with Italian Jews in particular. Both seem to me, going by the summary given, to be very interesting and instructive. As far as Italy is concerned, it is only in Rome, according to Bachi, that one still finds a relatively compact Jewish nucleus: elsewhere in Italy the phenomenon of dispersion and absorption by the general environment is in progressive development. On a world scale the coherent Jewish nucleus is that of Eastern Europe; around this nucleus the other Jewish communities – those which are allowing themselves to be absorbed by their environment – form a sort of halo. In Rome where the ghetto remained in existence right down to 1870, and where the presence of the Vatican perpetuated a tradition of exclusion, and also in the agricultural countries of Eastern Europe, the segregation of the Jews continues in fact, even without the ghetto.

I am expecting a good long letter from you. You never tell me about your state of health.

I embrace you tenderly.

Antonio

1. Umberto Terracini.
2. Universal Guide to Civil War.

101

Turi Prison, 9 November 1931

Dearest Tania,

I am writing to you on the fifth anniversary of my imprisonment. Five years is certainly a tidy span, and in addition these particular five years are a swathe out of the most important and productive period in a man's life. But there's nothing to be done about it: they've passed by, and I have no desire to tot up the profit and loss, or to cry my eyes out over this stretch of my life that has gone to the devil. I am rather of the opinion that these years have to a large extent coincided with a definite physiological period, i.e. that they have been necessary to get my physical constitution adapted to prison conditions. The ill-health from which I have been suffering for three months is certainly the start of a period in which prison life will make itself felt with greater severity – an ever-present agent operating permanently to destroy the strength of its victim.

I think the package of medicine that you say you sent me has already arrived, and that its contents will be handed over to me within a few days. As the sirocco[1] has started blowing again, I have had fresh bouts of acute agony, and so I am looking forward to being able to use these medicines, which may at any rate give me some relief. I forgot to write and ask you to send me some more cigarette papers. Maybe it's a marvel to you how I can use up so many of these papers, when at the same time I tell you that I have to a large extent cut down the amount of tobacco I smoke. There's no contradiction between these two facts – indeed the one is closely dependent on the other. The secret is that I have learnt how to make a greater number of small cigarettes (three instead of one) by using smaller papers; that is, by cutting them along the top and down the side: this means that you can have a short smoke three times instead of once with the same quantity of fresh tobacco, and that's enough to get rid of the desire.

The other prisoners smoke the same cigarette three times (smoking it in instalments) and then they use the fag-ends. I find this practice disgusting, and I prefer my own solution; the only snag being that you need a lot of cigarette papers – more than you can get along with the tobacco and matches. As far as matches are concerned, the best policy is to follow time-honoured prison practice and split them in two with a needle, thus doubling their number. As a matter of fact, in the period from July till today I have not only succeeded in reducing the amount of tobacco smoked to a mere 40 per cent of what I smoked before (immediately before, that is, because I had already cut down the amount several times) but I think I'll manage to cut it down even more in the future. Indeed my belief is that eventually I shall cut my smoking down to the minimum, even if I don't succeed in giving it up altogether. It's true, though, that the amount you smoke depends on the amount of brain work you have to do; I read little and think less, so my intellectual effort these days is slight. The result is that I smoke less. I can't manage to concentrate my attention on any subject; I feel myself as stultified intellectually as I am worn out physically. This state of affairs will probably last for at least the whole winter: my strength will therefore be just about sufficient to keep me from going further downhill, but not enough to give me any chance of recovery.

I embrace you tenderly.

Antonio

1. Dry, dust-laden wind from the Sahara; arrives in Italy hot and humid; very enervating.

102

Turi Prison, 16 November 1931

Dear Teresina,

Thank you for writing to me. I hadn't had news for over a month. I am looking forward to the letter from mamma that you tell me is on the way.

If Uncle Zaccaria comes to visit me it'll be a pleasure to see him; but I don't imagine he'll come. How long is it since I saw him last? I don't remember. My memories of him are very vague, and date back to the time when he was very young and I was a little boy. I imagine he now looks like Uncle Achille; perhaps a little smoother and more genteel on account of his life in the city. I doubt, though, if he's as likeable.

But who makes the homemade bread these days? Not mamma, and not you either, because you'll have a lot of work in the office.[1] Grazietta won't be able to take on everything. I just can't manage these days to get any concrete idea of what your life is like.

The rhyme.

Una nave che esce dal porto,
Ballando con passo scozzese
E lo stesso che prendere un morto
E pagarlo alla fine del mese.[2]

is not a riddle, but a piece of nonsense which is useful when you want to make fun of types who jumble words together without rhyme or reason, and imagine that they're saying all sorts of profound and mysterious things. It served its turn with several of the village characters (do you remember Signor Camedda?) who, in order to make a display of their culture, picked up high-sounding phrases from the popular novels and stuffed them into their conversation backside foremost to make the yokels gape. Pious old women do the same sort of thing when they repeat the Latin of the prayers in the Filotea;[3] do you remember that Aunt Grazia thought that once upon a time there had lived a very pious woman called 'Donna Bisodia' – so pious that her name was always repeated in the Lord's Prayer. It was the *dona nobis hodie*[4] which she, like many others of her clan, interpreted as 'Donna Bisodia'; the latter she thought of as a lady of the good old days, when everyone went to Church and there was still some religion in this world of ours. One could write a novel about this imaginary Donna Bisodia who was always held up as an example: how many times Aunt Grazia must have said to Grazietta, Emma and maybe yourself as well: 'Ah, you're not like Donna Bisodia, to be sure!' when you didn't want to go and confess on obligatory feast days like Easter.

Now you'll be able to tell your children this story; and don't forget the story of the beggar woman of Mogoro, of the musca *maghedda*[5] and the black and white horses that we have been awaiting for so long.

Dear Teresina,

I embrace you affectionately.

Antonio

1. The post office of Ghilarza.

2. 'A ship that leaves port dancing a Highland reel is like taking on a corpse and paying him at the end of the month.'
3. A devotional book by St François de Sales.
4. 'give us this day' (our daily bread).
5. Gadfly.

103

10 December 1931

Dearest mamma,

I have been waiting in vain for the long letter from yourself that Teresina promised me. I hope that its failure to turn up isn't due to your health making it impossible for you even to dictate. What I would rather think is that you have not had the necessary collaboration from a willing amanuensis.

I've received nothing all this time but a picture postcard signed by Teresina and her children. But who's Diddi? To what 'Christian' name does that correspond? I can well imagine what fun Teresina must have letting her imagination run riot when she invents pet-names for her children; this Diddi could be the name of a brownie or a bogle. Teresina ought to write me out a sort of dictionary, putting on one side the names in the pedestrian form in which they appear in the calendar, and on the other the fantastic derivatives invented by herself; it would be useful, because I can no longer make head or tail of things among all these luxuriant poetical flowerings.

Dearest mamma, this letter should strictly speaking be restricted to the sending of Christmas greetings, and so I'd better send these blessed greetings without further delay. I would like to have definite news about your health – I do hope it's as good as it's reasonable to expect. Does Carlo write to you; he has only written to me once since his journey to Turi. He wrote to Tatiana and told her that he'd write to me as well, but nothing has come of it. He seems to have moved from Milan to a village in the province. And does Nannaro write to you? After all the promises that he made you, he has never written me a word. Even so I keep my end up in the same old way, and am more serene than ever, although I'm getting older in prison.

I embrace you tenderly with everyone at home.

Antonio

104

Turi Prison, 14 December 1931

Darling Julca,

I have received your note of 21 November. Tania has also sent me a copy of your letter to her; and so your note was brought to life, and lost its abstractness and vagueness. In one of your earlier letters you mentioned the fact that you thought of starting to study, and that you had asked the doctor for her opinion; which latter, you said, had been not unfavourable. Allow me, with a certain pedantry, to make a practical proposal to you: let me, so to speak, present some of my 'claims' (I think one can quite well speak of the 'claims' that a prisoner has on free people, because the condition of a prisoner in modern times is intimately linked with that of a slave in classical times; in Italy the words *galera*[1] and *ergastolo*[2] which are used for 'prison' are clear proof of this affiliation).

You intend, you say, to study; by that a number of things could be understood. You might mean you want to go deeper into some specialised subject, or else that you want to acquire the 'scientific habit' – that is, to attain mastery of general methodology and epistemological science (do you hear what pedantic words I'm using?). In the latter case wouldn't it be a good idea to study certain things which interest me too and so start a correspondence with me about material which is of interest to the two of us because it is a reflection of the present intellectual life of Delio and Giuliano? In short, what I would like is this (and here, in general form, is my first 'claim'): to be kept informed systematically of the scientific theories of education according to which the school or schools attended by Giuliano and Delio are run – this in order to be in a position to understand and evaluate the meagre references that you occasionally make to these. The question of schooling is of the greatest interest to me – and it is of great interest to you, too, because you write that 60 per cent of your conversations are about the children's education. To set out your impressions on this subject in an ordered and coherent form is 'study': after your illness it will restore you to a frame of mind which will permit you to regain mastery of your scientific purpose and your faculties of analysis and criticism. Of course you must do a real job of work, and not just write letters: you must do some research, take notes, get the material you gather organised, and set forth the results with order and coherence. I would be very happy if you did that. It would be a pedant's happiness, I admit, but even that is not to be despised.

I would dearly like to know, for example, why it is that the principle of the assault brigades and of 'corners' devoted to specialised subjects[3] has been inserted into the programme of primary schools: what educational end is this meant to serve? The doubt could easily arise that a policy such as this might tend to accelerate the professional aptitudes of pupils in an artificial way, and falsify their inclinations; it might lead to the teachers losing sight of the aim of the school, which is to guide children forward to a harmonious development of all their activities, until such time as the formed personality gives evidence of more deep-seated and permanent inclinations – which are a more reliable guide, seeing that they emerge at a higher level of development of all the vital forces.

For example, I might tell Delio of my childhood experiences with living creatures; or would it seem like a fairy tale to him that I have seen hares dancing – or jumping rather, though the country people see it as dancing – in the moonlight, or a hedgehog family (father, mother and the little hedgehogs) going on an expedition to collect apples by the light of the autumn moon?

What is meant by the 'animals' corner'? I once read something about 70 per cent of the children in big American cities not knowing what a cow is; the writer stated that cows are taken around on show in cages, as bears and monkeys once used to be in Italy. ... Maybe they have a 'cow's corner' in American schools?

Dear Julca, I embrace you tightly, ever so tightly, together with our children.

Antonio

1. The original meaning of *galera* is 'galley': a *galeotto* is strictly speaking a galley slave.
2. From Latin *ergastulum*, the prison in which chained slaves used for hard labour were kept.
3. A feature of the Dalton system of education, then in use in Soviet schools.

105

Turi Prison, 21 December 1931

Darling mamma,

I have received your letter of the 16th, the one written (it seems with a certain mischievousness) by Teresina. I think you were both having a good laugh when Teresina wrote that you like doing yourself well, that you're fond of tasty titbits, and that you never have an appetite but when there's something good to eat. Now that you drink white coffee instead of black of a morning, I'd like to know whether you put a drop of the barley in it, seeing that that's 'refreshing'.

But Teresina hasn't yet told me the proper name of the child she calls Diddi; once upon a time, if I'm not mistaken, her baby girl was called Isa. I honestly don't know where I am among all these pet names: it would be simpler to call the kids Cunegonda, Restituta, Ermengarda etc. As for the boys, what about Baldassare, Napoleon and Nebuchadnezzar?

I'm looking forward to getting the Christmas presents - and thank the children in anticipation, seeing they helped, as you say, to choose the gifts.

I embrace you, together with all at home.

Antonio

106

Turi Prison, 18 January 1932

Dearest Tania,

Through this entire period I have had no acute (or even middling acute) ailment. Indeed, in a relative sense, I think I'm getting along fairly well. It's true that I'm always listless, oscillating between a state of nervous tension and a state of enervation and apathy; but I think this condition of partial weakmindedness is a form of defence mechanism which the body resorts to in order to counter the continuous wearing-down process you undergo in prison – a process which is the sum total of all the little pinpricks and petty annoyances. You end up by becoming a micromaniac[1] (it's possible that I'm further on the way to becoming one than I myself think) as a result of your nerves being constantly filed away by all these pettinesses and niggling thoughts and paltry little preoccupations.

And you're 'had' another way too. Prometheus warring against all the gods of Olympus appears to us a tragic Titan; Gulliver tied up by the Lilliputians makes us laugh. If Prometheus, instead of having his liver devoured daily by an eagle, had been condemned to be nibbled by ants he would have been a target for our laughter too. Jupiter wasn't really very intelligent in his day: the technique of getting rid of one's opponents was at that time in its infancy. A modern writer (I don't remember who, possibly Guelfo Civinini) has a piece about a husband who thinks up a scheme to settle the hash of a beau that his wife showed signs of falling in love with: he shuts him up for the night in an abandoned hut infested by ravenous fleas. You can imagine the look on the lady's face when she beholds the spectacle of this ladykiller riddled by millions of revolting flea-bites.

My dearest Tania, I embrace you tenderly.

Antonio

1. In Italian micromania exists as an antonym of megalomania: it means (i) a mania for (or induced by) trifles or things of no moment, and (ii) insanity characterised by self-depreciation.

107

Turi Prison, 18 January 1922

Dearest Teresina,

I have received your letter of the 14th, together with Franco's letter, his drawings in colour, and the nice little letter from Diddi and Mima. Please thank all your children from me; I don't know what I can do to show my affection for them. I'll give this some thought and see if I can hit on something that I could do for them or send them – there would be no savour to any other sort of present, and it would have no meaning.

Here's a thing I could do. I have translated from the German (as exercise) a series of folktales of the kind we used to delight in when we were children: they do resemble our own ones in part, as a matter of fact, because the origin in both cases is the same.[1] They're a bit on the old-fashioned side, a bit countrified; however, modern life with the radio, the aeroplane, the talkies, Carnera,[2] etc., hasn't yet penetrated to Ghilarza sufficiently to make the taste of present-day children very different from our own taste when we were small. I shall make a point of copying them into a notebook and despatching them – if I'm allowed to do so – as my contribution to the development of the children's imagination. Perhaps when reading them aloud you should add a pinch of indulgent irony as homage to modernity.

But how, in any case, does this present itself in Ghilarza? The girls will have had their hair done *a la garçonne*, I suppose, and the songs will be about Valencia and mantillas of the beauties of Madrid; nevertheless, a few antiquated types like Aunt Alene and Corruncu will still be around, and the stories will thus have an environment appropriate to them. By the way, I don't know if you'll remember, but I used to say when I was a little boy that I'd like to see Aunt Alene on a bicycle – which shows that we used to amuse ourselves by contrasting the 'troglodytes' with the relative modernity of those days; although the latter lay way out on the fringe of our environment, that did not prevent it from seeming pleasant and attractive to us.

Send me some more news about mother, to whom I send loving kisses. Best wishes to all at home.

Antonio

1. Comparative folklore studies were a permanent interest of Gramsci's; cf. letter 9, dated 19.3.27, and his summary of a Sardinian version of an international folktale, letter 81 dated 1.6.31. (This letter belongs among the 'chain tales' involving the eating or drinking of an object, nos. 2025–8 in the Formula Tales section, Antti Aarne and Stith Thompson, 'The Types of the Folktale', Helsinki, 1961.) See also passages from the prison notebooks printed in Antonio Gramsci: 'Selections from Cultural Writings', London, 1985, pp. 188-95.

Among the papers read at the 1st Conference of Gramsci Studies held in Rome, 11–13 Jan. 1958, was one by Raimondo Manelli on 'The Dialect Poetry of Terni'; this takes as its starting point remarks by Gramsci on the study of folksong and folklore ('Studi Gramsciani', Editori Riuniti, Rome, 1958, pp. 183–7).

2. Primo Carnera, heavyweight boxing champion of the world, 1933–4.

108

Turi Prison, 25 January 1932

Dearest Tania,

... You have not yet properly understood what the real psychology of a prisoner is. What makes him suffer most is the state of uncertainty, the doubt about what other people (not the prison staff) are going to do; this merges into the state of doubt and uncertainty which is inherent in prison life itself, and vastly accentuates it. One gets used, after a great deal of suffering and after much cultivated inhibition, to being an object without will or subjective personality – as against the administrative machine which can at any moment pack you off to whatever point of the compass it pleases and can force you at a moment's notice to change deeply rooted habits, etc., etc. If to this machine and its irrational jerkings is added the irrational and chaotic flurryings of one's own relations, the prisoner feels himself absolutely crushed and pulverised. Never make vague and nebulous plans and promises, never do things likely to get on my nerves; otherwise it could happen that even a man like me, patient and capable of a great deal of self-restraint, might become obstinate, and assert 'his own will', and insist on it being respected even in cases of no consequence – just to prove to himself that he's still alive.

I embrace you tenderly.

Antonio

109

Turi Prison, 1 February 1932

Dearest mamma,

I have received Grazietta's letter of 15 January. The news she sends me is pretty vague, and there isn't much of it, but at any rate it reassures me that there's no development of any importance as far as your own general state of health is concerned.

I don't know how the intermediate school is organised at Ghilarza, and what exactly the subjects for study in the whole course are. I read in the *Corriere della Sera* a report of the discussion which took place in Parliament about this type of school, but the whole thing was too vague and generalised to leave me with any definite idea of what it's all about. The only important thing that could be gathered was that the intermediate school is not an end in itself, and that it does allow for the possibility of a further scholastic career. So in Mea's case as in that of others the last word hasn't yet been spoken, and the years up to now won't have been completely wasted. What appears to me essential in her case – and a thing which must guide you all in this question of her education – is the need to make her feel it all depends on her – and on her own willpower, whether or not she uses this extra time to study on her own account, outside the school syllabus. Tell her it's only if she does this that she'll be in a position, if conditions change, to make a leap ahead and embark on a more advanced course of study. The one and only thing that matters is that she should have willpower and ambition, in the better sense of the word. However, the world won't come to an end if she finishes her days at Ghilarza, knitting socks, because she never had a shot at doing something better with her life, something further out of the ruck.

By the way, is she a member of the *Giovani Italiane*?[1] I suppose she must be, although you have never mentioned this in any letter; I should think right enough that her ambitions lie in the direction of parades and suchlike. And so she'll have the same destiny as the other *giovani italiane* – that of becoming good mothers of a family, as the saying goes – provided of course that they find somebody fool enough to marry them. A thing which is by no means certain, because although the fools want stupid little geese as wives, they want them with a little land for the sun to shine on, and money in the post-office savings bank.

Please thank Aunt Maria Domenica's son for remembering me and sending his greetings.

I embrace you affectionately.

Antonio

1. Fascist youth organisation for girls.

110

Turi Prison, 8 February 1932

Dearest Tania,

I have read with interest P.'s[1] comment on our somewhat disconnected and slightly acrimonious discussion on the 'two worlds'. (The phrase reminds me of the 'Hero of the Two Worlds'[2] and other similar ideas of nineteenth century romanticism: the *Rivista dei Due Mondi* was also founded in 1830!) As it is plain that you have shown him my letters, and therefore have informed him of the general tenor of our controversy, I would be grateful if you would let me know his opinion of it. I don't imagine that he will be in agreement either with the old rabbis or with the young Zionists; it would seem though that he accepts the existence, at any rate within limits, of the famous 'two worlds'. His observations, although objectively very interesting, do not seem to me absolutely exact. I don't think the inference is justified that there is an 'evident' tendency to 'force the Jews back into an isolated community'; this tendency seems to me to be rather the 'subjective' one of the old rabbis and the young Zionists. The objective truth seems to be that, as a result of the Concordat, the Jews are in the same position as Protestants. On the other hand there does exist – or will exist – a social category whose condition is very sad in comparison with that of Jews or Protestants: and that will be (or rather is already) the category of unfrocked priests and monks. These latter will be excluded from employment by the State; that is, they will be degraded as citizens. The fact that it has been possible to give the sanction of law to the institution of such a category of civil pariahs seems to me much more important than the status in law of Jews and Protestants – to whom legal prerogatives have been granted that are the very reverse of degrading, in the spirit of the law.

I do not rule out the possibility that an anti-Semitic tendency may yet develop here; I do not see that it exists today. The signs that are taken as substantiating its existence are open to various explanations; moreover, one can set against them facts of equal or greater significance. But the fact that in my opinion is important is this: that one section of the Jews can and does approve measures against other Jews. Professor Levi-Civita of the University of Rome was subjected to certain unpleasantnesses because he did not attend official religious ceremonies; but the unpleasantnesses in question were initiated by the Rector Del Vecchio who is himself a Jew. The question then was not racial but political. A member of the ruling class must pay homage to Catholicism as *instrumentum regni*; it doesn't matter what his own religion is.

And so the line drawn by the Academy and Parliament proves nothing:

scientists of world fame who are not Jews have found and will find themselves on the wrong side of it. The position taken up by Teodoro Mayer in the Credito Mobiliare also seems to me significant. I think that in many cases it is not the Jewish side of things which counts, but so-called 'Jewish' freemasonry – that is, the fact that the freemasons certainly included many Jews in their ranks.

Dearest Tania, I embrace you tenderly.

Antonio

1. Piero Sraffa.
2. Garibaldi.

111

Turi Prison, 15 February 1932

Dearest Tania,

I have received a postcard from you dated the 12th, but I have not yet received the other postcard which you mention. I am not writing to Giulia this week either, for several reasons: firstly, because I'm not feeling very well and can't think as straight as I'd like; and secondly because I have not yet decided on the most opportune and fruitful line to adopt in relation to her own position and her psychological condition. The whole thing seems to me terribly difficult and complicated. I try to unravel the skein but I can't get started, and I'm not sure if I'll be able to get started.

I'd like just for a little to chat to you about this question, so that you can give me a helping hand. It's true that I would have to write an entire volume if I wanted to provide all the necessary material (though what I have has been gleaned solely from my own impressions and experiences, and cannot in the nature of things be other than incomplete). However, we'll just have to do what we can.

My central impression is as follows: that the gravest symptom of Giulia's lack of mental balance is not to be found in the facts, all of these very vague, to which she refers – the facts which purport to be the reason for her embarking on a psychoanalytic cure. The symptom is the fact that she has had recourse to this cure and that she has such inordinate faith in it. To be sure, my knowledge of psychoanalysis is neither vast nor precise, but of the little which I have studied I think there are at least a few points on which I can give a definite opinion: points which remain of definite value after one has stripped psychoanalytic theory of all its phantasmagorical and witch-doctorish elements. The most important point seems to be this: that a psychoanalytic cure can be helpful only to those elements in society which romantic literature used to call the 'insulted and injured'[1], and which are in fact much more numerous and varied than they were traditionally supposed to be. I would describe them as those individuals who are caught up between the iron contrasts of modern life (to speak only of the present day, although every age has had a 'modernity' in opposition to a past) and are unable on their own to stand up to the strain of these contrasts. People, in short, who fail to overcome warring contrasts of this nature, and are incapable of arriving at a new moral serenity and tranquillity; i.e. an equilibrium between the impulses of the will and the ends which the individual can achieve. The situation becomes dramatic at certain definite moments in history and in certain definite environments: when the environment is super-heated to extreme tension, and gigantic collective forces are unleashed which press hard on single individuals – and drive them till it hurts, in order to obtain from them the maximum return of will and determination for the purposes of creation. Such situations become disastrous for exceptionally refined and sensitive temperaments, whereas they are necessary for – and indeed indispensable to – the more backward social elements; for example, the peasants, whose robust nerves can strain and vibrate at a higher diapason without weakening or being worn out. I believe, therefore, that a person of culture (using the word in its German sense), an active element in society (as Giulia certainly is, and not merely for official reasons such as the presence in her bag of a party card which postulates social activity on her part) is and must be his or her own best psychoanalyst.

What, for example, does she mean when she says that she ought to study, etc? It is the duty of everyone concerned in productive activity of some sort at all times to study and to improve his or her own theoretical knowledge and professional capability; why should Giulia think that this is a personal problem of her own, or an index of her inferiority? Every day men and women are developing and unravelling their own personalities and their own characters; every day they are fighting instincts, impulses and tendencies which are harmful and anti-social, and raising themselves to a new level of collective living. In this I find nothing exceptional, nothing individually tragic. Everyone learns from his own neighbours and kindred spirits; everyone gives up and acquires, loses and gains, forgets and accumulates notions, traits, and habits. Giulia writes that if we were together again she would this time have no thought of defending herself against any intellectual or moral influence I might exert upon her; for that reason she feels that her personality is more integrated. But I really don't believe that in the past she did defend herself to the extent – or in the dramatic manner – she seems to think. And isn't it possible, in any case, that I may have tried to defend myself from her influence, and at the same time developed and modified my own personality through contact with hers? I have never theorised about this process in myself, and I have never laid a burden of care on my back because of it; that does not mean, however, that the process has not taken place, and even maybe to my advantage.

Dear Tania, no more of this rambling. A short while ago I received your letter of the 12th, with the transcription of Delio's letter. I'll reply next Monday. The letter gave me pleasure.

I embrace you.

Antonio

1. 'Umiliati e offesi'. This is the usual Italian translation of the title of a novel by Dostoievsky.

112

Turi Prison, 22 February 1932

Dearest Tania,

I have received your two letters of 12 and 16 February. Today I'm replying to Delio too, as you'll see from the enclosed. Maybe I've been too long-winded: I'll have to develop a style which won't weary him when he reads my letters.

...What you write about my outline for an essay on the Farinata Canto reminds me of the fact that I may indeed have spoken to other people about it in the years gone by. I remember now that the first time I thought of that interpretation was when I read the ponderous work of Isidoro Del Lungo on Dino Compagni's Cronache fiorentine,[1] in which Del Lungo fixed the date of Guido Cavalcanti's death for the first time. More recently, and from another point of view, my mind harked back to the theme when I was reading Croce's book on the poetry of Dante: in this the episode of Cavalcante is mentioned in such a way as to make one think that he must have missed the Farinata counterpoint. I recall, furthermore, that Calosso wrote a study on the Tenth Canto of the *Inferno* published in the '*Giornale dantesco*', but I don't remember its exact contents; I am pretty sure, though, that he made no reference in it to the point which I was developing. However, I realise now that I'd forgotten a number of things which your letter brought back into my mind. It's of small importance, because I have never aspired to become a *dantista* and make great hermeneutical discoveries in this field. However, it's been useful to me as a check on my own memory; it's evident that I shouldn't place too much trust in it when so many gaps have been discovered.

As far as the notes on the Italian intellectuals are concerned, I really don't know where to begin: they are scattered through a series of notebooks, mixed up with other variegated notes, and my first job would be to collect them together and get them into some sort of order. This work weighs on me a great deal, because I often suffer from bad headaches which stop me concentrating on the thing as I should do: also, from a practical point of view the job is very laborious because of the conditions under which I have to work, and the restrictions to which I am subjected. If you can, send me some exercise books – but not like the ones you sent me a while ago; those were too big and clumsy to handle. Choose notebooks of normal format, the same kind schoolboys use, with not too many pages – forty or fifty at the most. Otherwise they are bound to turn into a mixter-maxter of miscellaneous jottings and end up as a complete jumble. I'd like to have these little exercise books for the purpose of getting my notes in order, and dividing them by subject matter: this is the only way to make sense out of them. It'll help me pass the time, and will be of use to me personally, in order to arrive at a certain intellectual order.

Recently I have had severe pains in my intestines, but there has been no swelling this time, and there have been no ups and downs of temperature. It has snowed heavily here (eighteen inches) and it has been very cold; nevertheless I have come out of it all fairly well as far as ailments go.

I embrace you tenderly.

Antonio

1. Chronicles of Florence.

113

Turi Prison, 22 February 1932

Dear Delio,

I liked your description of the little 'birds and beasts corner'[1] with the chaffinches and the goldfish. If the chaffinches ever escape from the cage, you mustn't get hold of them by their wings or their legs, as these are delicate and you could easily break them or knock them out of position. The way to hold them is to cup your hand right round them, and not press too hard.

When I was your age I kept lots of birds, and other animals too; hawks, white owls, cuckoos, magpies, crows, goldfinches, canaries, chaffinches, skylarks etc. etc.; and I also at various times possessed a little snake, a weasel, and also hedgehogs and tortoises.

Here's how hedgehogs collect apples.

One autumn evening – it was already dark, but the countryside lay bathed in radiant moonlight – I went with another boy, a friend of mine, into an orchard full of fruit trees, chiefly apple trees. We hid in a bush, facing into the wind. All of a sudden the hedgehogs came out of their holes; there were five of them, two big ones and three little ones. They made their way in single file towards the apple trees, rambled about in the grass for a little and then got down to work: they looked for the windfalls and rolled them together into a clearing, pushing them along with their legs and their little snouts. In this way they built up a hoard, all the apples lying close together. Now it happened that the apples lying on the ground turned out not to be sufficient; so the biggest of the hedgehogs had a look around, with his nose tilted in the air, and then, having chosen a tree which was very bent, he climbed up it, followed by his wife. They perched themselves on a well-laden branch and began to rock to and fro in gentle rhythm. Their movements made the tree rock too, and the rhythm of its rocking increased with sudden jerkings. Many more apples fell to the ground. When these had been collected together in the same place as the others, all the hedgehogs, big and little, rolled themselves up into a ball – and with their spikes bristling they lay down on the apples and pierced the skin of each one. The little hedgehogs hadn't been able to prick many, but the father and mother managed to prick seven or eight apples for each of them.

As they were in the act of going back to their holes, we came out of our hiding place, put the hedgehogs in a sack and carried them home with us. I had the father and two of the little ones for my share, and I kept them for many months in the courtyard, free to roam about where they wanted; they hunted all the little animals and insects, such as cockroaches and maybugs, and ate fruit and leaves of lettuce. They were very fond of the fresh leaves, and so I was able to tame them to a certain extent; they stopped their trick of rolling up into a ball as soon as they saw a human being. They were very afraid of dogs. I used to think it was great fun to bring live snakes into the courtyard to see how the hedgehogs would hunt them. As soon as the hedgehog became aware of the snake's presence, he quickly jumped up on to his four little legs and charged it with great courage. The snake raised its head, put its fangs out and hissed; the hedgehog gave a little squeak, got hold of the snake with its two front legs and bit its neck. He then ate it piecemeal. One day these hedgehogs disappeared: it's certain that someone had taken them away to eat them.[2]

Tatianishka has bought a beautiful big teapot made of white porcelain and has put the doll on it. Just now she is wearing a warm scarf round her neck because it's very cold; in Italy too it has been snowing a great deal. You ought to write and tell her to eat a bit more, because she won't listen to me. I think your chaffinches probably eat more than Tatianishka.

I'm glad you liked the postcards. Another time I'll tell you about the dance of the hares, and about other animals. I'd like to tell you of other things I saw and heard of when I was a boy: the story of the foal, the fox and the horse who only had a tail on feast days; the story of the sparrow and the *kulak*[3]; the story of the kulak and the ass; the story of the weaver-bird and the bear, etc. I believe you already know the story of Kim; do you know the Jungle Books – especially the story about the white seal and Rikki-Tikki-Tavi?

Is Giuliano a *udarnik*[4] too? For what activity?

Kisses.

Papa

P.S. Give Giuliano and mamma Giulia a big kiss for me.

1. Literal translation of the Russian expression *zivoj ugolok* which means a room or part of a room, in which animals and birds etc., are kept.
2. Gypsies regard hedgehog as a delicacy. They roll them in clay, and bake them in the ashes of a fire.
3. Rich peasant.
4. 'Champion worker'.

114

Turi Prison, 29 February 1932

Dearest mamma,

In a letter dated the 11th Teresina told me that a letter from Grazietta and maybe one from Mea were under way; however, I have received nothing. I take it the weather has been very bad in Sardinia, as elsewhere, and has deprived people of the will to write. Here it has snowed a lot; more than in '28–'29, a winter which then seemed exceptional. Thank Teresina for the news she sent me. I would really like to hear Aunt Delogu's endless natterings: I'm sure her stories about her young days must be inexhaustible. Has she still gone on growing enormous seedless tomatoes? God knows what it must have cost her to have to give up those labours of hers which were veritable labours of Urumare! ...

Tell Teresina as well that I'm grateful to her and her children for their intention to send me the Chenale violets and the bulbs of wild cyclamen. Unfortunately I am not allowed to receive these gifts; it would go against the regulation which lays down that prison life must retain its punitive character. I must needs be punished, so no violets, no cyclamen; no cheeky little devil out of rebellious nature must tickle my nostrils with its scent or delight my eyes with the colours of its flowering.

I embrace you tenderly, together with everyone at home. Give Aunt Delogu my best wishes when she pays you a visit.

Antonio

115

Turi Prison, 7 March 1932

Dearest Tania,

... I'd like to explain in greater detail one of my statements regarding psychoanalysis: I can't have done so adequately, because it has occasioned a misunderstanding, as is obvious from your letter of 23 February. I didn't say it was definitely established that a psychoanalytic cure can only benefit the so-called 'insulted and injured' elements in society; my knowledge in this connection is nil, and I don't even know if anyone has hitherto put the question in these terms. All I gave you was a page or two of personal reflections, quite unchecked, on that criticism of psychoanalysis which seems to me the most worthy of attention and the most scientifically grounded; these I outlined to you in order to explain my feelings as regards Giulia's illness. But these feelings are not as pessimistic as you seem to think; furthermore, they are not prompted by phenomena of such a primitive and lowly order as the phrase 'insulted and injured' leads you to assume. I used this phrase merely for brevity and as a general reference point.

Here is my point of view. I think that the only real and concrete thing which can be salvaged from the *échafaudage*[1] of psychoanalysis is the following: thorough observation of the devastation caused in many minds by the contradiction between what seems a categorical obligation, on the one hand, and on the other hand the individual's actual tendencies, which are founded on the sedimentation of old habits and old ways of thinking.

This contradiction manifests itself in an innumerable multiplicity of single cases; indeed, it assumes a strictly peculiar character in every given individual. At every moment of history it is not only the moral ideal but also the ideal 'type' of citizen delineated by public law which is superior to the average man in a given State. This hiatus between the ideal and the real becomes much more pronounced in moments of crisis, as for example this post-war period, either because the level of 'morality' is lowered, or because the standard to be reached is raised (this being eventually expressed in a new code of law and a new morality). In the one case and in the other coercion of the individual by the State increases: the pressure and control exerted by a part over the whole becomes greater and also the pressure of the whole on all the individual cells that go to make it up. Many resolve the problem with ease; they overcome the contradictions by means of vulgar scepticism. Others adhere outwardly to the letter of the law. But for many the question can only be resolved in a catastrophic manner, because it gives rise to morbid outbreaks of repressed passion, which the necessary social 'hypocrisy' (i.e. adherence to the cold letter of the law) has merely benumbed and driven deeper into the subconscious.

This is the central nucleus of my reflections, and I'm quite aware how abstract and imprecise these must seem if taken in a literal sense. But remember that what I am setting down now is nothing but an outline, a sketch giving the general direction of my thoughts; if understood thus it seems to me sufficiently clear and lucid.

As I have said, it is necessary to distinguish very numerous and complex gradations in single individuals and in the various cultural strata. The lowest grade consists of those elements which in the novels of Dostoievsky are referred to as the 'insulted and injured'. This category may be regarded as the inevitable creation of a society in which the pressure of the State and the community on the individual is of the most external and mechanical; a society, what's more, in which the contrast between State law and 'natural' law (to use that equivocal expression) cuts deepest because of the absence of any mediating agency – the sort of agency which existed in the West, and whose personnel was provided by the intellectuals dependent on the State. Dostoievsky certainly did not act as an intermediary between the State law and the individual; he himself was 'insulted and injured' by it.

It is from this point of view that you must understand what I meant when I referred to 'false problems', etc. I believe that, without falling into vulgar scepticism or making oneself comfortable on the cushions of an easy and convenient 'hypocrisy', one can arrive at a certain serenity even in the clash of the most absurd contradictions, and under the pressure of the most implacable necessity. But one can only reach it if one succeeds in thinking 'historically', dialectically, and identifying one's own task with intellectual dispassionateness; one's own, or at any rate some well defined task which one can regard as one's own, and which is within the limit of one's capacity. In this sense, as far as psychological ailments of the above variety are concerned, one can and therefore one must be 'one's own doctor'.

I'm not sure if I've expressed myself clearly or not. But for me the whole thing is absolutely clear. I realise that a more minute and analytical exposition would be necessary to put that clarity over: however, I can't hope to provide this in a single letter, owing to the shortness of time at my disposal and the lack of space. At all events I should warn you not to interpret all this too literally. There's another warning, too, which I would like to give you, in relation to the conception of 'science' in all that concerns these psychological data. It is this. I find it very difficult to accept in this connection any too rigid conception of the natural and experimental sciences. If one did so, one would have perforce to give a great deal of importance to so-called atavism and to the 'mneme' *qua* memory of organic matter etc. My feeling is that much is attributed to atavism and the 'mneme' which is simply historical and acquired during the individual's life in society – which, it should always be remembered, starts as soon as the baby sees the light after leaving his mother's womb, as soon as he opens his eyes and receives his first sense impressions. That man will have a ticklish job who tries to indicate at what point precisely the manchild – who is already equipped at birth to record what he hears and sees – really begins to work over in his conscious or subconscious the first impressions he has received. How then is one to single out and pin down what is to be attributed to atavism and to the 'mneme'?

Dearest Tania, you mustn't think that I have felt or that I feel very ill. I've really got through this winter fairly well; for example I've had no pain whatsoever in my back which always gave me a lot of trouble in the preceding winters.

I embrace you tenderly.

Antonio

1. Ramshackle jerry-built structure. The *Petit Larousse* (a copy of which Gramsci had in his cell) defines its extended meaning as 'a series of ideas combined artificially'.

116

Turi Prison, 14 March 1932

Dearest Tania,

... If you happen to write to P., tell him from me that I'd like to know if any publications relating to Machiavelli's views on economics and political economy are in existence; also whether he could possibly obtain for me, if it isn't too much trouble, the essay by Professor Gino Arias on this subject which was published a few years ago in the *Annali d'Economia* of the Bocconi University.[1] Can it be said that Machiavelli was a 'mercantilist' – if not in the sense that he consciously thought along mercantilist lines, at any rate in the sense that his political thought corresponded to mercantilism; i.e. that he was saying in political terms what the mercantilists were saying in terms of political economy? Or couldn't it actually be argued that in the political language of Machiavelli (especially in the *Art of War*) we may find the first trace of a Physiocratic[2] conception of the State, and that therefore he might be regarded as a precursor of the French Jacobins (though not in the external sense, as in the case of Ferrari and perhaps of Foscolo)?

I embrace you tenderly.

Antonio

1. The Luigi Bocconi Commercial University.
2. French eighteenth century school of political economy: immediate precursors of the classical laissez-faire orthodoxy enshrined by Adam Smith.

117

Turi Prison, 14 March 1932

Dear mamma,

I have received Grazietta's letter of 3 March. I had already written to you some time ago via Tatiana: I don't remember exactly when, but it doesn't seem very long ago. It would be annoying if this letter of mine turned out to have gone astray.

My condition is unchanged. The winter here was very cold and it snowed a great deal, but I got through it fairly well. I received news of Giulia and the children quite recently: there are no new developments of any importance in this sector either. The reason I haven't always written about Giulia and the children is that Teresina once mentioned in a letter that you were getting all their news from Tatiana. I quite understand that Grazietta has a great deal to do and therefore can't always be writing to me; nevertheless I think that with a little goodwill she'd be able to write to me more often. I'd like to have some exact information about the programme of the classes Mea[1] is going to; furthermore, if it's possible to get hold of it – and I think it should be, through the good offices of some schoolmaster or mistress – I'd like to have a copy of the three years' programme of the intermediate school. Tell Franco to write to me about his Meccano and the things he builds with it. I am sure he'll become a great mathematician and engineer.

Let's hope that this bad weather, which is really exceptional, is all over now and that you manage to get back some of your strength. I embrace you tenderly, together with everyone at home.

Antonio

1. His niece, daughter of Gennaro.

118

Turi Prison, 21 March 1932

Dearest Tania,

... I have read Professor Cosmo's observations on the Tenth Canto of Dante's *Inferno*[1]. I would like to thank him for his suggestions, and the list of books I might consult. However, I don't think it's worthwhile getting hold of the copies of the reviews which he mentions: what would be the point of it? If my intention were to write an essay for publication, this material wouldn't be sufficient (or at least, in my present state of mind, which is a compound of gloom and dissatisfaction, it would not seem sufficient to me); and if all I wanted was to write something just to please myself and to pass away the time, it would not be worth while disturbing such solemn monuments as the *Studies on Dante* of Michele Barbi – seeing there's no guarantee that they would in fact yield any necessary material, or even material that might be indirectly useful. The literature about Dante is so prolix, and there's such a plethora of it that one is only justified in adding to it if one has something really new to say, and if one says it with the maximum of precision and the minimum of verbiage. I'm afraid Professor Cosmo himself suffers a bit from the functional malady of the *dantisti*: if I followed his suggestions to the letter I'd have to write an entire volume. Personally I'm quite satisfied with the knowledge that the interpretation of the canto which I have sketched out is relatively new and worthy of more detailed treatment; for a gaol-bird like me this is quite sufficient encouragement. It'll start me off distilling a few pages of notes which won't seem entirely superfluous.

I have also read with due interest the last notes you send me on the question of the 'two worlds', or, if you prefer it, the 'Lion of Caprera'.[2] If the question is posed in this way – that is, well within its proper limits and with every bacillus of racist romanticism and confused Zionism well and truly sterilised – the matter is worthy of attention. And the data you now provide are interesting, because I was totally ignorant of facts such as these.[3] What I wished to establish is this: that for some time now no popular anti-Semitism (which is the classical anti-Semitism, that which has provoked and still provokes tragedies, and has an importance in the history of civilisation) has existed in Italy, and that in no sense do the Jews represent a special culture or have any particular historical mission in the modern world. In short, that they do not in themselves represent a separate ferment of development in the historical process. That was the starting point of our debate, and it is not out of place to recall it, because now we are talking about something else. These particular cases you mention of Italian Jews 'sacrificed' to a greater or lesser extent to the advantage of 'Christians' don't seem to me to constitute a problem of the first magnitude. Analogous cases could be quoted arising out of other examples of discrimination in our social history; for example, in September 1920 a secret circular was published which the Association of Metallurgical Industrialists of Piedmont had sent round to all member firms; the object of this circular, which came out during the war, was to stop firms employing workers born 'below Florence', i.e. central and southern Italians. Nor does it seem to me that one can draw a parallel between 'Jewish Freemasonry' and the state of affairs in Poland, where the Jews were traders and money-lenders, not peasants. In Georgia it was the Armenians who were the moneylenders; consequently, the Armenians were the 'Jews' of Georgia.

In Naples, when the police scent trouble in the air they put guards outside the pawn-brokers' offices, because it is against these that the poor people wreak their fury. Now if these pawn-brokers were Jews and not faithful servants of San Gennaro[4], there would be anti-Semitism in Naples – as there is in a part of the Casalese, the Lomellina and the Alessandrino, where the Jews are agents for the sale of land, and always turn up when there's a 'calamity' in some family or other, and people need to sell their land (maybe for a song). But in these areas anti-Semitic feelings never go beyond fairly modest limits because nobody is interested in stoking the fire ...

Do you know this – I sent no Easter greetings to my mother, and no greetings for her *onomastico*[5] either. This year I haven't got a calendar, so I didn't realise in time that St Joseph's day was approaching at great speed; what's more, this year we weren't allowed a special Easter letter, so my guns were spiked on all sides. Next time I write I'll make a point of apologising. Also I'll take an early opportunity to write to Giulia: maybe it's better to wait till she writes again, or Delio replies.

All the very best – I embrace you tenderly.

Antonio

1. The text of Cosmo's letter to Sraffa, dated 29 December 1931, was conveyed to Gramsci, as usual, by Tatiana. In it the Professor expressed broad agreement with Gramsci's thesis re 'poetry and structure'; discussing the inter-related elements of the 'structure', he remarks that they become 'founts of poetry. Remove them, and the poetry vanishes'. He adds, at the end of the letter: 'I'd like you to tell our friend [Gramsci] that never a day passes without my thinking of him.'
2. Garibaldi, who was known as l'Eroe dei Due Mondi; see letter 110, 'The Hero of Two Worlds'.
3. Piero Sraffa had sent Gramsci, via Tatiana, a lengthy comment on the 'two worlds' controversy; this contained a good deal of pertinent information, new to Gramsci, and also an analysis of the dilemma of 'free-thinking' Jews in post-Concordat Italy, especially as regards the education of their children (an account which in part, recalls Heine's description of similar problems facing Jews in early nineteenth century Germany). Sraffa also refers to the possibility of events in Italy being 'coloured by the example of foreign countries, especially of the Nazis, and similar movements.'
It should be added that Italy's record in World War II with regard to its Jewish population was very good in comparison with that of most other countries allied with or occupied by Nazi Germany.
4. The patron saint of Naples.
5. Name-day: letter dated 16 June 1930. His mother's name Giuseppina ('Peppina') equals Josephine.

119

Turi Prison, 28 March 1932

Dearest Tania,

As you see I have replied to Giulia's letter, but unfortunately my own letter has got rather out of control; it's possible that I've not succeeded in writing in the way I would have liked, or in getting it all down. Maybe the lack of space is to blame.

Your father's postcard interested me a great deal: it springs from a real and concrete way of living, the sort of life one can 'see' physically – or so I would say ...

I have read in the reviews that the Foreign Secretary has announced the forthcoming publication of a work on *The Italian Genius Abroad* which is planned on an ambitious scale: a prospectus has come out, listing the subjects to be dealt with. Do you think you could possibly get hold of this prospectus and send it to me? It's not on sale, but I think it would be possible to obtain it from some senator or deputy. If you have a shot at getting it I'll be terribly grateful but don't waste a lot of time on it if the thing turns out to be difficult. The theme is connected with the history of the Italian intellectuals, a subject which interests me; I'm still jotting down notes and observations every now and then, when my reading or my thinking starts me off.

Dear Tania, I must hurry up and finish, because time's up.

I embrace you tenderly.

Antonio

120

Turi Prison, 28 March 1932

Dear Julca,

A while back I received your letter of January, and a few days ago the one dated 16 March. I didn't write earlier, because – as I've mentioned on other occasions – I feel a certain shyness, a certain restraint when I try to make contact with you. A number of different factors have gone to create this state of mind; it's possible that one of the most important of these is the peculiar psychology which grows on one during a lengthy imprisonment, and the consequent protracted isolation from every kind of society congenial to one's own temperament. However, it's certain that two other factors predominate: first, the fear of injuring you through interfering hamhandedly with your cure; and second, the realisation that these years in gaol have made me more 'bookish' than I used to be, and that I tend sometimes to fall into a preaching or schoolmasterish tone. I laugh at myself when I detect this, but there's one big drawback to self-criticism of that sort: it makes me feel that as a result of it I'm just impelled to talk further nonsense. So you can see I'm more or less in a maze, and feel myself constricted! Apart from that, it's clear from your letters that some of my observations have overstepped the mark and have had 'too great a success', i.e. a harmful effect. You give too great importance to what I said about your personality not being as yet fully developed, and about the need for you to unravel your own real being etc. This makes me feel sure that you've taken my remarks too literally, and haven't fitted them into their appropriate context.

One thing that has certainly slipped your mind is that I've tried time and time again to persuade you to dedicate part of your time to music. I have always believed that it was principally in and through artistic activity that your personality came to its flowering; and if I was right, you have inflicted a kind of spiritual amputation on yourself by subordinating these interests to the claims of practical and immediate living. I would say that there has been a 'metaphysical' error in your life, and that its consequences have been a lack of harmony and a lack of psycho-physical equilibrium. On one occasion I affirmed, to your no small scandalisation, that scientists, in their activity, are 'disinterested'. You came back at me, short and sharp, that they are always 'interested'. Naturally I was speaking in 'Italian' terms, and as far as Italian culture is concerned I was thinking of the philosophic theories of Professor Loria who interpreted the term 'interest' in a derogatory sense – the sense which Marx in the *Theses on Feuerbach* refers to as *schmutzig jüdisch,* sordidly Jewish. Well then – it seems to me that you have planned your life in this 'sordidly Jewish' sense, without being deeply convinced of the rightness of it all – as indeed you couldn't be. My own idea was that your personality needed to emerge from this primordial 'phase', to unravel itself, to bring to fruition many of the characteristics of your early period as a 'disinterested' artist (not disinterested in the sense of living in the clouds, of course). Or if you prefer it, let us say an 'interested' artist, provided it's understood we're not using the word in its immediate practical mechanical sense.

However, I don't want this letter to degenerate into a schoolmasterish lecture. Dear Julca, I hope you'll always feel absolutely free to let me know all your thoughts and feelings. It's a long time since you last sent me a photograph; I think a new one would not only be very dear to me, but would also help me to see how you're really keeping. Another thing you should let me know is your weight. And the same for Delio and Giuliano – please send the best of the recent photographs of them, with a note giving the height and weight of both children.

I embrace you tenderly.

Antonio

P.S. I hope you won't misunderstand the expression 'sordidly Jewish' that I have used above. I mention this because recently I had a controversy with Tania about Zionism which went on for several letters, and I don't want to incur a charge of anti-Semitism because of the use of this word. But wasn't the author of the phrase himself a Jew?

121

Turi Prison, 4 April 1932

Dearest mamma,

I have received Mea's letter, and I was very amused at the story of Signor Sias who deciphers the letters of hens with the aid of various dictionaries. You should advise him to take a photograph of the egg, to enlarge it and to send the enlargement to Professor Taramelli of Cagliari museum.

It may well be true that the language the hen uses when writing its missives is Punic, if the hen is descended from the hens of Carthaginian days. And also, of course, if it reveals the place where some treasure or other is hidden – a treasure of coins of the year dot, fabulously valuable.

The news Mea sent me of the intermediate school is too scanty. I'd like in addition to have some facts about the text books, the Italian composition, the subjects of the curriculum, the timetable etc. I am looking forward to receiving Franco's letter – I hope he'll tell me all about his engineering works with the Meccano.

My life is just the same as ever, and just as monotonous. I'd like you to rummage among the books on the famous bookshelf and see if there's a pamphlet called *La Quistione Meridionale*.[1]

I embrace you tenderly with everyone at home.

Antonio

1. The Southern Question, i.e. the political and economic problems created by the feudal conditions still prevailing in Southern Italy, and the treatment of the South and the Isles as exploitable colonies by the Northern bourgeoisie. For an excellent short account of Gramsci's work in this field, see Maria-Antonietta Macciocchi, *Pour Gramsci*, Edition du Seuil, Paris, 1974, pp. 133–57.

122

Turi Prison, 4 April 1932

Dearest Tania,

... I don't want tobacco – neither *Macedonia*, nor any other brand. I have succeeded, as I told you earlier, in cutting down my consumption of tobacco considerably. The position is at present stabilised at a packet of *Macedonia* every five days; but after I've consolidated these gains, I'll try to cut it down still further by easy stages. Coffee without caffeine is no use to me: I can't use it. Once every now and again I can get some hot water, but it's no good for any purpose other than a foot bath; it's not drinkable because it's out of the big *bain-marie*[1] cooking vessels – but certainly not at boiling point, at 140 to 160 degrees at the most. You, Tania, as I've had occasion to tell you before, are much too ready to build castles in the air if you're given half a chance.

I'm really very sorry to hear that Giacomo[2] is dead; the news is a great grief to me. Our friendship was much deeper and more intense than you can ever have imagined – for this among other reasons, that Giacomo was not on the surface very expansive, and seldom spoke much. He was a rare chap, I can assure you, although in his last years he changed a great deal and his health got very bad. When I knew him in the period just after the war, he was a man of Herculean strength (he had been a sergeant in the mountain artillery, and used to carry heavy gun parts on his shoulder). What's more, he was a man of audacious courage, though completely lacking in rodomantade. Yet in spite of all this his emotional sensibility was quite incredible, and at times betrayed him into touches of melodrama; nevertheless these sprang from sincerity, and could not be called a pose. He knew a great mass of verse by heart, but it was all out of that literature of debased romanticism which the common man is so fond of (stuff in the style of opera libretti, which are written for the most part in a very curious baroque style, full of disgustingly sentimental purple patches, and in spite of that give extraordinary pleasure). He was very fond of reciting this stuff – although he blushed like a child caught in the act of doing something wrong, every time I infiltrated the audience to listen to him.

It's this same memory which returns insistently and remains as the most living trait in his character: the gigantic man declaiming with genuine passion verses in the worst possible taste (although, to do him justice, they usually expressed robust, impetuous and elementary passions) and stopping covered in blushes when he realised that he was being listened to by an 'intellectual' – even though that intellectual was his friend.

I embrace you.

Antonio

1. Originally an adjunct of the alchemist's laboratory, said to have been invented by 'Mary the Jewess'. The apparatus is described in the *Nomenclator* (1585) as 'a double vessel which being set over another kettle doth boile in the heat thereof seething'.
2. Giacomo Bernolfo, a Turinese worker who had been in charge of the security and defence services of the *Ordine Nuovo*, Gramsci's paper. He was bound to Gramsci by ties of the closest affection; he escorted him through the streets of Turin when the Fascist threats of violence were at their height, and considered himself responsible for his leader's safety. After the March on Rome (1922) he had emigrated to the USSR.

123

Turi Prison, 11 April 1932

Dearest Tania,

This week I've only received one postcard from you (the one dated the 6th). You'll certainly have received my own letters of a week ago; so you know that I duly received the package of medicine. I hope you'll read and mark the observations I made in that letter. It's quite possible that my present diet is not too happy a one, but it's the best under the circumstances (a few days ago I switched over from pasta to rice, and I think it's an improvement). A *minestrina*[1] every day would be a good thing, you tell me. However, seeing it's out of the question, what's the use thinking about it? In any case, as I explained, I'll be able to have a plateful every fortnight. Every time you want it you've got to put in for it officially. However, as I also told you, I make use of the peptonised extract which goes very well with rice.

... Dearest Tania, I embrace you tenderly.

Antonio

1. Thin soup.

124

Turi Prison, 11 April 1932

Dear Julca,

I'd like to add a word or two to what I said in my previous letter, which maybe seemed to you a bit disconnected and inconclusive. I should think it's quite likely it did so, because my letters always make that impression on me as soon as I've written them. The trouble is I've got to write at a fixed time, and on a fixed day; I get an obsession that I'll not be able to write all I want to in time, so I end up by writing elliptically, and go in for hints and glancing allusions; I utilise the thoughts that come into my head at the moment of writing, and they get spatch-cocked on to the rough draft which I've already sketched out in my mind before I sit down to write. The result is a *pot-pourri* – or such, at any rate, is my impression.

What I wanted to add is this. Your worries seem to me to be unjustified for a whole crowd of reasons – reasons which are aspects of the question we are discussing. But my own contribution to the discussion was particularly unjustified, because it was badly expressed.

Once again then. I feel that when you evaluate your own contribution to the shaping of your life you don't take account of the fact that at a particular point you gave your personality a new orientation, abandoning artistic activity and taking up activity more immediately practical. In addition I feel that you have always given the concepts of 'utility' and 'practicality' a content which is much too mean and narrow: that is the theoretical error I had in mind when I used the expression 'sordidly Jewish'. The result is that you have been obssessed by a feeling of not being 'useful' enough, and of not being able to be 'useful', in the erroneous sense you accept as the real one. I have gained the impression that the germ of your illness is to be found in this.

Your sensibility was always quite exceptionally acute, and it has been given too fine an edge by the events of the last six years. Now this 'inferiority complex' has started to wear it away still further. In any case, I now believe that I myself am responsible, at least in part, for these problems of yours ...

My darling, I embrace you tightly, so tightly.

Antonio

125

Turi Prison, 18 April 1932

Dearest Tania,

Thank you for transcribing the letter in which Giulia gave you particulars about Delio's state of health.

When I've read Croce's book,[1] I'll be very happy to scribble a few notes of criticism, if that will help you. It won't be a full-dress review, as you propose, because that would be difficult to turn out off the cuff. However,

I've already read the introductory chapters of the book, because they appeared a few months ago, as a separate booklet; so I can start today by listing a few points that may be of use to you as a springboard for research or for the accumulation of fresh facts – that is, if you want to give your work a certain breadth and organic unity.

The first question to raise would, in my view, be this: what are the cultural interests which today predominate in Croce's literary and philosophic output? Are they of an immediate character, or are they of more general import, corresponding to deeper needs not born of the passions of the moment?

The answer is not in doubt: Croce's work can be traced back to relatively distant origins – to be precise, it can be traced back to the period of the war. Before one can understand his most recent works, one must reread his writings on the war, which are collected in two volumes (*Pagine sulla Guerra*,² second edition, with fresh material added). I haven't got these two volumes by me, but I read the articles one by one as they came out. Their essential content can be briefly summarised as follows: a fight against the interpretation given to the war under the influence of French and Masonic propaganda; an interpretation which made the war out to be a war for civilisation, a war of the 'crusade' type with the capacity in it of unleashing the passions of the people and giving these the character of religious fanaticism. After war comes peace: this does not only mean that a new collaboration among the peoples involved should follow the conflict; it also means that peace groupings must succeed the war groupings, and one cannot assume that the two will be identical. Such regroupings, both general and particular, will take place, and there will be scope for fresh collaboration: but how would that be possible if the immediate criteria of utilitarian politics were allowed to assume the role of a universal and categorical principle? It is of great importance, therefore, that intellectuals should resist these irrational forms of propaganda, and (although careful not to court the charge of weakening their country in time of war) should resist demagogy and save the future.

In the moment of peace Croce always sees the moment of war, and in the moment of war that of peace; his efforts are therefore directed towards making sure that every possibility of mediation and compromise between the two moments is not destroyed. From a practical point of view Croce's position has made it possible for Italian intellectuals to resume friendly relations with German intellectuals – a thing which never has been and still is not easy for the French and the Germans. Consequently Croce's activity has been of use to the Italian State in this post-war period, when the profoundest motifs of our national history have led to the cessation of the Franco-Italian military alliance, and to a political realignment against France favouring rapprochement with Germany. So there's nothing strange about the fact that Croce, who has never taken part in militant politics in the party political sense, became Minister of Education in the Giolitti government of 1920-21 ... But has the war finished? And have we seen the last of this impermissible error of raising particular criteria of day-to-day politics to the level of general principles, and the blowing out of ideologies to the size of philosophies or even religions? Certainly not. And so the intellectual and moral battle continues; the conflicting interests are still with us, alive and kicking; we must not abandon the field.

The second question is that of the position occupied by Croce in the field of world culture. Before the war Croce already held a very high place in the estimation of intellectual circles in all countries. The interesting thing is that – notwithstanding the general opinion – his fame was greater in the Anglo-Saxon countries than in Germany or Austria: the editions of his books, translated into English, are most numerous – larger than the figure for Germany, and indeed for Italy itself. Croce, as is clear from his writings, has a high conception of this position of his as a leader[3] of world culture, and of the responsibilities and duties it carries with it. It's evident that his writings presuppose a world public, an élite. It should be remembered that in the final years of the last century Croce's writings on the theory of history provided the two greatest 'revisionist' movements of the time with their intellectual weapons: Eduard Bernstein's in Germany and Sorel's in France. Bernstein has himself admitted that he was compelled to re-elaborate the whole of his philosophic and economic thought after reading Croce's essays. Sorel's close link with Croce was known, but it was not properly appreciated how constant and intimate it was until after the publication of Sorel's letters: in these Sorel reveals throughout his intellectual subordination to Croce in the most surprising manner.

But Croce has carried his revisionist activity still further, during the course of the war and especially after 1917. The new series of essays on the theory of history begins after 1910 with the essay *Cronache, storie e false storie*,[4] and continues right up to the last chapters of the *Storia della storiografia italiana nel secolo XIX*,[5] to the essays on political science and on to the very last literary works – including the *History of Europe* (or so it seems from those chapters which I've read). I think that Croce regards this position of his – as leader of revisionism – as the most important thing of all, and that he intends the best of his present output to be seen against this background. In a short letter, written to Professor Corrado Barbagallo and published in the *New Historical Review* of 1928 or '29 (I don't remember which exactly), he explicitly states that the whole elaboration of his theory of history as ethico-political history (and that means the whole, or almost the whole of his thinking for about twenty years) has as its purpose the completion of his revisionist studies of forty years ago.

Dearest Tania, if notes similar to these can be of use to you in your work, let me know and I'll try to knock a few more into shape.

I embrace you tenderly.

Antonio

1. 'A History of Europe in the Nineteenth Century'.
2. 'Pages on the War'.
3. 'Leader' is in English in the original.
4. 'Chronicles, Histories and Pseudo-histories'.
5. 'History of Italian Historiography in XIX Century'. These essays will all be found in *Theory and History of Historiography* (translated by Douglas Ainslie).

126

Turi Prison, 25 April 1932

Dearest Tania,

... I don't know as yet whether the notes I have written on Croce have been of interest to you, and if they fit in with the plan of your work or not: please tell me, so that I can get a better idea of how to proceed. In any case you must remember that these are merely notes and suggestions, and naturally would have to be developed and completed. I'll write you another paragraph now; the licking into shape you can take care of yourself.

Why have Croce's works enjoyed such a huge success? There you have, in my opinion, a very interesting subject for discussion, for an éclat of such magnitude is not often given to philosophers to enjoy in their own lifetime; moreover, it is almost unique, because it has spread far beyond academic circles. It seems to me that one of the reasons for this must be sought for in the style. It has been said that Croce is the greatest master of Italian prose since Manzoni. Personally I think that that statement is true – with this qualification, that Croce's prose does not derive from Manzoni's so much as from the great scientific prose writers, especially Galileo. The novelty about Croce's style is precisely that its place is in the field of scientific prose: he has the power to express with great simplicity and with great force matters which, when dealt with by other writers, usually appear obscure, distorted, jumbled and prolix.

This literary style is the natural expression of a proportionate style in the moral life of the writer – an attitude of serenity, composure and imperturbable assurance which one might call Goethean. While so many other people are losing their heads and are stumbling around in the dark, hag-ridden by apocalyptic feelings of intellectual panic, Croce has become a landmark for all who wish to arrive at inner strength, because of his unshakeable certitude that metaphysically evil cannot prevail, and that history is rationality.

One must bear in mind, in addition, that for many people Croce's thought does not have the appearance of a massive philosophic system, forbidding and difficult to assimilate. I feel that Croce's greatest quality has always been his ability to get his conception of the world into general circulation; this he does by giving pedantry the go by, and turning out a whole series of short essays in which the philosophy is presented directly, and consequently is absorbed by the generality as 'good sense' and 'common sense', however you like to put it. And so Croce's solutions to a vast number of problems in the end become common currency, and circulate anonymously; they get into the newspapers, and into everyday life, with the result that there are a lot of 'Croceans' who are unaware of the fact that they *are* Croceans, and maybe don't even know that Croce exists. For example, a certain amount of his idealism has got in among the Catholic writers; and the latter are at present trying without success to liberate themselves from it by putting forward Thomism as a philosophy sufficient unto itself, and adequate to the intellectual exigencies of the modern world...

Antonio

127

Turi Prison, 25 April 1932

Darling mamma,

I've had no news for exactly a month; Mea's and Grazietta's letter left Ghilarza on 24 March. I'm hoping that, as the proverb says, no news is good news – or at least that it betokens events of no importance.

A few days ago I received a postcard from Teresina with kisses from Diddi. Tell Teresina that I have at long last eaten the preserve of game in oil which she sent me in the Christmas parcel, and that it was delicious. It had been perfectly prepared; so that I was able to eat it without trouble, although I have no serviceable teeth left in my head. And not only that – the birds were really choice, quite exceptional as far as size and fatness were concerned; I imagine they must have been shot by Paolo, and so I would like to extend to him too my compliments and thanks. In my own life there has been no novelty whatsoever; how could there be? The same unchanging existence; the days make up the same unending rosary of *Ave Marias*, the one following the other in identical ennui.

I embrace you affectionately.

Antonio

128

Turi Prison, 2 May 1932

Dearest Tania,

I have received your letters of the 23rd, and 27th April. I don't know if I shall ever send you the outline I promised of my work on 'the Italian intellectuals'. The standpoint from which I observe the question changes periodically; maybe it's too early yet to summarise it and make a synthesis. The material is still in a fluid state, and has yet to undergo its final elaboration.

Don't take it into your head to copy out the 'programme' of the publication on the Italians abroad; I don't think it's worth the trouble, especially as Marzocco has given a fairly detailed summary of it. If you can get hold of a copy, all well and good; if not, don't bother ... And while we're on this subject, I'm sure I don't need the works of William Petty to help elucidate the question of Machiavelli's economic ideas. The cross-reference is interesting, but I think it's enough to leave it as a cross-reference. What I would rather have, some time in the future, is the edition of Machiavelli's own collected works; maybe you'll remember that I asked for these when I was still in Milan, but the complete set had not then been published.

... There are still a few points about Croce's book (incidentally, I haven't yet read it as a complete volume) which might serve as signposts for your essay. And even if these notes, like the others, are a bit disjointed, I think they'll be useful to you all the same. Of course, you'll have the job later on of getting them in order on your own account for the purposes of your study.

I have already alluded to the great importance which Croce attaches to his theoretical revisionist activity, and mentioned how, on his own explicit admission, the whole purport of his thought in the last twenty years has been directed towards the end of completing the revision and turning it into liquidation. As a revisionist he helped to get the new current of economic-juridical history on the move; it's still moving even now, although pretty diluted – its chief representative today is the academician Gioacchino Volpe. Today he has given literary form to what he calls ethico-political history: the *History of Europe* is intended to be exemplar.

In what does Croce's innovation consist? Has it the significance which he attributes to it, and above all has it this 'liquidating' quality which he asserts that it possesses?

One definite observation that we may make is that Croce, in his historico-political activity, lays stress exclusively on that moment which in politics is called 'hegemony' by consent, i.e. by virtue of cultural direction, as distinct from the moment of force, of restraint, of State intervention through the law and the police. It's honestly hard to understand how Croce can believe in the capacity of this conception of historical theory to achieve a definitive liquidation of any and every philosophy of praxis. In the very same period in which Croce was shaping this so-called 'club'[1] of his, the greatest modern theoreticians of the philosophy of praxis[2] were doing the job of shaping a much more efficient instrument; they were engaged on a systematic revaluation of the concept of the moment of 'hegemony' or cultural direction in opposition to the mechanistic and fatalistic conceptions of 'economism'.[3] Indeed it has been asserted that the essential characteristic of the most modern philosophy of praxis consists precisely in the historico-political concept of 'hegemony'. And therefore it seems to me that Croce isn't up to date[4] with the results of research or with the literature of his favourite studies – either that, or he has lost his capacity for critical orientation. As far as I can see, he relies to a great extent for his information on a notorious book by a Viennese journalist called Fülop-Miller.[5]

This point should be developed extensively and subjected to thoroughgoing analysis, but that would mean writing a lengthy essay. For your own purposes I think these notes are sufficient: in any case it wouldn't be easy for me to develop them at length.

My dear, I embrace you tenderly.

Antonio

1. clava: the original allusion is to the club of Hercules.
2. i.e. Marxism.
3. A term derived from the thesis of a group within the RSDLP (fought by Lenin and the Bolsheviks) which made a fetish of the economic/trade union struggle of the working class. The term was used subsequently in the general sense of 'economic determinism', i.e. where all is seen as 'means of production' and 'means of subsistence', to the exclusion of political/ ideological considerations.
4. In English in the text.
5. R. Fülop-Miller, 'Geist und Gesicht des Bolschewismus' (The Spirit and Face of Bolshevism), Vienna, 1926.

129

Turi Prison, 9 May 1932

Dearest Tania,

... From now on you must keep strictly to this rule; if I need any book I shall ask for it myself. Of late the books sent to me haven't been handed over; I have been told that for each of them I must make a separate application to the Minister – an absurd business, and wretchedly tedious.

Don't you agree? By the way, I asked you to take out a subscription to
Cultura, seeing I had obtained permission to have it; I'm not sure if you've
done so or not. I have just noticed that it is to be published quarterly, and
that the first issue for 1932 is already out.

I have had no news from home for over a month and a half; a fortnight
ago I had a postcard from Teresina, but it carried nothing but greetings.

...As I haven't yet read the *History of Europe*, I obviously can't comment
on its actual contents. What I can do, though, is to jot down a few
observations which might seem to lie outside the subject under discussion,
but in fact do not, as you shall see. I have already pointed out that all
Croce's historical labours of the last twenty years have been directed
towards the elaboration of a theory of history as ethico-political history,
in opposition to economic-juridical history – this being the theory of
history derived from historical materialism following the process of
revision which it had undergone as a result of Croce's own work. But is
Croce's history ethico-political? It seems to me that Croce's history can
only be called 'speculative' or 'philosophic' history, not ethico-political
history: it is for this reason, and not because it is ethico-political, that it
is in opposition to historical materialism. An ethico-political history is
by no means excluded from historical materialism, in so far as it is the
history of the moment of 'hegemony': but 'speculative' history is excluded,
like every 'speculative' philosophy.

Croce says that his philosophic aim has been to liberate modern
thought from every trace of theology, of the transcendental, and therefore
of metaphysics in the traditional sense; following this line he has arrived
at a position where he denies philosophy as a system, for the very reason
that in the idea of a system there is a theological residuum. But his
philosophy is a 'speculative' philosophy, and because this is its nature it
is bound to perpetuate the theological and the transcendental, though
clothing these in the language of historicism. Croce is so deeply immersed
in his method and his speculative lingo that he is incapable of making a
judgement except in terms of these; when he writes that in the philosophy
of praxis the structure is 'like a hidden God', this would be true if the
philosophy of praxis were itself a speculative philosophy – and not, as it
is, an absolute historicism, liberated in reality, and not in words alone,
from every transcendental and theological residuum.

In connection with this point there is another observation I have to
make; it more closely concerns the *History of Europe*, both as regards
conception and composition.

Can you envisage a unitary history of Europe starting in 1815, i.e. with
the Restoration? If a history of Europe is to be written so as to describe the
formation of an historic bloc, it cannot exclude the French Revolution and
the Napoleonic Wars, which are the 'economic-juridical' premise of the
historic European bloc, the moment of force and struggle. Croce takes as his

subject the subsequent moment, that in which the forces previously let loose have reached a state of equilibrium – or, – to put it differently, have undergone a catharsis; he makes this moment a fact existing in and for itself, and so constructs his paradigm of history. He did the same thing with the *History of Italy*: he chose 1870 as its opening year, thus obscuring the moment of struggle, the economic moment, and concentrating attention on the purely ethico-political moment, as if the latter had fallen from the skies.

Of course the truth is that Croce, a master of all the wiles and artful dodges of modern critical jargon, has fathered forth a new type of rhetorical history; speculative history is actually nothing but the modern form of rhetorical history. This stands out even more revealingly if one examines the 'historic concept' which is at the centre of Croce's book, that is, the concept of 'liberty'; Croce, contradicting himself, confuses 'liberty' *qua* philosophic principle or speculative concept with liberty *qua* ideology – that is, an instrument of practical government, an element of moral unity sustaining a hegemony.[1] If the whole of history is the history of liberty, or in other words of the spirit which creates itself (and in this jargon liberty equals spirit, spirit equals history and history equals liberty) why should the history of nineteenth century Europe alone be singled out as the history of liberty? Isn't it more likely that the history of nineteenth century Europe may turn out to be the history not of liberty in a philosophic sense, but of the self-knowledge of that liberty? And also of the diffusion of this self-knowledge under the guise of a religion throughout the intellectual strata – and in the form of a superstition among the masses, who feel themselves united with the intellectuals, and are conscious of participating in a political bloc of which the intellectuals are priests and standard bearers.

'Liberty' as an historic concept is the very dialectic of history, and it does not in practice have distinct and identifiable 'representatives'. History was liberty even under the oriental satraps: in those days, too, there was historic 'movement', and the satrapies have crumbled to the dust. In short, it seems to me that words change, words are maybe said quite well, but the things themselves are not so much as scraped by them.

It seems to me, indeed, that the *Critica fascista* has in an article provided the just criticism, although not explicitly; it observes that in twenty years' time, when Croce sees the present in perspective, he will be able to identify its historic justification as a process of liberty.

Anyway, if you remember the first point to which I drew your attention – that is, the observations about Croce's position during the war – you will understand his point of view better: as a 'priest' of the modern religion of historicism, Croce is living the thesis and antithesis of the historic process. He lays equal stress on both for 'practical reasons', because in the present he sees the future, and he preoccupies himself as much with the future as with the present. To each his own part: to the 'priest' that of safeguarding our tomorrows. But at bottom there's a good large-sized dose of moral cynicism in this 'ethico-political' conception; it's the modern form of Machiavellianism ...

I embrace you tenderly.

Antonio

1. Cf. Croce's *History the Story of Liberty*, translated by Sylvia Sprigge (London, 1941).

130

Turi Prison, 23 May 1932

Dearest Tania,

I have received your postcard of the 17th, and the letter of the 19th. The information Carlo gave you about my state of health seems to have been somewhat muddled. I have not had serious attacks of uric acid trouble, although certainly the continued intestinal catarrh may well be partly due to excess uric acid in the blood. For some time past, on the other hand, I have been suffering from insomnia – if you can call it insomnia; to speak plainly, I don't sleep not because I can't get to sleep, but because my sleep is interrupted due to external causes,[1] and this has induced in me a condition of enormous weariness and exhaustion. It's visible to the naked eye, and Carlo must surely have noticed it. The problem is a complex one, and I'll tell you all about it if you come to see me. I have no particular preferences as regards the date of your visit: you choose the time which is most convenient for you ...

I embrace you tenderly.

Antonio

1. Gramsci's cell was the first cell in the corridor on the first floor. All traffic to and from other parts of the prison, and to and from the sick bay, passed along this corridor. It was only when a warder was on duty who was less bossy and officious than the rest that things quietened down a bit, and Gramsci's sufferings were slightly diminished (Giovanni Lay, *Talks with Gramsci in Prison*, published in *Rinascita* 8, 20 February 1965).

131

Turi Prison, 27 May 1932

Dearest mamma,

I have received Grazietta's letter of 13 May. Carlo told me last Monday that you are keeping a bit better. By now you'll certainly have had Carlo's impressions of the talk he and I had together, because he promised me to write to you straight away. Tell Mea that now, at long last, she is really going to receive the famous crayons I promised her nearly a year ago. Carlo took them with him, and promised me to despatch them without delay. And Teresina will get Tolstoy's *War and Peace* which I have promised her. Carlo also took with him the bundle of books that I got ready; he'll send those on too – after reading them himself, I suppose. The difficulty about sending off these packages is due to the fact that at Turi station they don't accept articles to be forwarded to Sardinia by rail: one has to take them to Bari and despatch them from there. That's why I wasn't able to keep my promise to Mea before.

I read the piece of news Grazietta sent me about the death of Giampietro Sanna. But what is Titino doing these days, and where does he live? I imagine he must have gone completely daft by now: he was well on the way to it when he was in Turin. At that time it seemed as if he was suffering from a serious illness, some sort of epilepsy maybe. At least it always came about that every time I told him he would have to go back to Ghilarza, given his financial situation, and the hard fact that I was unable to go on feeding him indefinitely, he threw himself on the ground in convulsions and foamed at the mouth. I asked myself whether he might not be putting on an act to make me sorry for him; on the other hand, I was bound to set against that the knowledge that in order to stage an attack of that sort one must possess a certain amount of intelligence and will-power, and it didn't seem to me as if Titino had either the one or the other. Of course, he may have got better and settled down to work, because he was very good-natured, and in those days would have fought for me till he was cut to pieces: he escorted me through the streets, came to wake me up with great punctuality, and firmly believed he was performing the most prodigious deeds. He made such a fuss and bother that I always had the impression that they might knock him over the head one fine day.

Dearest mamma, tell them to write to me a bit more often.

I embrace you tenderly with everyone at home.

Antonio

132

Turi Prison, 30 May 1932

Dearest Tania,

I have received your postcard of the 25th and the money order of the 28th. I thank you from my heart, but I assure you that there was no urgency about it at all. As I told you a few months ago, the amount I spend is relatively small, and apart from the fact that it's not possible to buy anything tasty, it's actually better for me to keep within the limits of a fairly rigorous diet; otherwise I'd just get worse. Every change for the sake of variety, and every attempt to increase the quantity of food I get down merely gives me stomach trouble, so I prefer not to do any experimenting. In any case it's not worrying me just now, and I feel no weaker than I normally do.

You mustn't think that I've turned into a fatalist, or that I'm letting the current carry me away *comme un chien crevé;*[1] on the contrary I'm continually chewing things over in the search for reasonable solutions to my various problems. My field of choice is pretty restricted, however, and it shrinks still further after every attempt which turns out to be useless.

But let's talk about more interesting things, things that'll give me a chance of gabbing away about all and sundry as I always love doing. I'd like now to tell you about one or two points I've been turning over in my head, so that if you think it's worth it you can copy them out for Piero, and ask him to supply a few references about books which will help me to enlarge the field of my cogitations and get myself better oriented. What I would like to know is this: does any special work exist (maybe in English?) on Ricardo's methods of research into economics, and on the innovations which Ricardo introduced into critical methodology? I should imagine that on the centenary of his death, ten years ago, a valuable literature on this subject may well have appeared, and that it might be quite possible to find something which exactly suited the research I am engaged on just now.

The train of my thought is more or less as follows: can one maintain that Ricardo has an importance in the history of philosophy, as distinct from the history of economics in which he is certainly a figure of the first order? And can one say that Ricardo helped to put the first theoreticians of the philosophy of *praxis*[2] on the road which led to their overcoming the Hegelian philosophy and constructing a new historicism, freed from every trace of speculative logic? It seems to me that one could make an attempt to prove the truth of these assertions, and that it would be worthwhile undertaking this. I would base myself on the two fundamental concepts of economics, 'market equilibrium' and 'law as a statement of tendency', which I believe we owe to Ricardo, and proceed as follows: is it not possible that these two concepts served as a starting-off point when the attempt was being made to reduce the 'immanentist' conception of history (expressed as it was in the idealistic and speculative language of classical German philosophy) to a realistic, immediately historical 'immanence' - an 'immanence' in which the law of causality of the natural sciences had been purged of its mechanistic character, and left free to identify itself systematically with the dialectical reasoning of Hegelianism?

Perhaps this whole nexus of ideas is still a bit fuzzy and opaque, but it's important that it should be comprehended as a whole, even if only approximately: sufficiently, at any rate, for Piero to be able to tell me whether this problem has ever been perceived or tackled by any student of Ricardo.

It is opportune to remember that Hegel himself, in other cases, was aware of these necessary nexi between diverse scientific activities - and also between scientific and political activities. Thus in his *Lectures on the History of Philosophy*[3] he discovered a nexus between the French Revolution and the philosophy of Kant, Fichte and Schelling, and said that 'only two people, the Germans and the French, although the opposite of each other in so many ways (maybe, indeed, *because* they are such opposites) took part in the great epoch of universal history at the end of the eighteenth century and the beginning of the nineteenth, the reason being that while in Germany the new principle burst forth as *spirit* and *concept*, in France it took shape as effective reality.' If you look up the *Holy Family* you will see that the theoreticians of the philosophy of *praxis* established this very nexus between French political activity and the above-mentioned German philosophy. What I want to find out is how much classical English economic theory (in the methodological form elaborated by Ricardo) contributed to the further development of the new theory, and in what manner it exerted this influence.

That the classical English economic theory contributed to the development of the new philosophy is commonly admitted, but usually one thinks merely of Ricardo's theory of value. It seems to me that we must look a little further and identify a contribution which I would call synthetic (that is, bound up with the intuition of the world and the manner of thinking) and not merely analytical (in relation to a particular doctrine, however fundamental). P., in the course of his work on the critical edition of the works of Ricardo, might collect a lot of valuable material relating to the whole question. Anyway, I'd be grateful if he could find out whether any book dealing with the subject does exist, and thus be of real help to me in my present condition as a prisoner - that is, while I am unable to do systematic research in libraries myself.

Dearest Tania, I embrace you tenderly.

Antonio

1. Like a dead dog.
2. i.e. Marxism.
3. Title of E.S. Haldane's translation.

133

Turi Prison, 6 June 1932

Dearest Tania,

...I shall try to answer all the other questions you put about Croce, although I don't properly understand their significance, and rather feel that I've already answered them in the preceding notes. Reread the passage in which I deal with the attitude that Croce maintained during the war, and ask yourself if the reply to one section of your present queries is not implicitly contained in it.

The break with Gentile took place in 1912, and it was Gentile who broke away from Croce and tried to achieve his philosophical independence. I don't think Croce has changed his position from that time onwards, although he has since defined his doctrines with greater precision. A more notable change is the one which took place between 1900 and 1910. The so-called 'religion of liberty' is not a discovery of recent years, it is the recapitulation, in a single drastic formula, of the entire sweep of his thought right from the moment he abandoned Catholicism. He himself admits this in his intellectual autobiography (*Contributo alla critica di me stesso*[1]).

Nor does Gentile seem to me in disagreement with him over this point either. I think that your interpretation of the formula 'religion and liberty' is inaccurate, as you give it a mystical content (or so one might think, seeing you talk about 'taking refuge' in this religion as if it were a question of a 'flight' from the world etc.). It's got nothing to do with that at all. Religion of liberty simply means faith in modern civilisation, which has no need of the transcendental or of revelation, and contains in itself its own rationality and its own origin. Therefore it's an anti-mystical formula or, if you like, an anti-religious one. In Croce's eyes every conception of the world and every philosophy *is* a 'religion', in so far as it becomes a norm of living, a moral code. Religions in the confessional sense are of course 'religions' as well, but 'mythological' ones and therefore in a certain sense inferior – it's as if they corresponded to the historic childhood of the human race. The origins of this doctrine are already to be found in Hegel and in Vico, and are a common patrimony of the whole of Italian idealist philosophy, Gentile's as well as Croce's.

Gentile's scholastic reform is based on this doctrine, in so far as religious instruction in schools is concerned. Gentile himself wanted to allow religious teaching only in the elementary schools (to restrict it, that is, to the years of actual childhood), and even the government did not want it to be included in the curriculum of the senior classes.

And so I am inclined to believe that you are exaggerating the extent of Croce's isolation at the present time. He is not as isolated as you think. Don't allow yourself to be taken in by the polemical effervescence of writers who are all to a greater or lesser extent irresponsible *dilettanti*. Croce has expounded a fair number of his present ideas in the review *Politica*, edited by Coppola and by the minister Rocco. My own opinion is that not only Coppola but many others as well are persuaded of the usefulness of the position assumed by Croce, the reason being that the latter is helping to create a situation in which it is possible to undertake the education to State service of the new groups of the ruling class which have come to the surface in these post-war years.

If you study the whole of Italian history from 1815 up to the present day you will realise that a small ruling group has succeeded in attracting into its parlour and then methodically absorbing the entire political personnel which the mass movements, the movements of revolutionary origin, threw up. Between '60 and '76 the Action Party, which had been inspired by the ideals of Mazzini and Garibaldi, was absorbed by the monarchy, leaving behind an insignificant residuum which continued to exist as a republican party, but which was of greater interest as folklore than as a political organisation. This phenomenon was dubbed 'transformism'. However, don't run away with the idea that this was an isolated phenomenon; it was an organic process which, as far as the formation of our own ruling class was concerned, corresponded to what had happened in France during the Revolution, and what had happened in England under Cromwell. Indeed the process has continued piecemeal from 1876 right up to the present day.

In the immediate post-war period things began to look serious for the ruling class, because it appeared that the traditional ruling group was unable to assimilate and digest the new forces released by events quickly enough. However this ruling group turned out to be more *malin*[2] and able than one would have thought: the process of absorption was difficult and arduous but it is taking place all the same, in devious ways and by means of a wide variety of agencies.

Croce's activity is one of these ways, one of these agencies; his teaching is secreting perhaps the greatest quantity of 'gastric juices' to help on the work of digestion. If one sets it in its historical perspective – in Italian history, naturally – Croce's work appears as the most powerful machine for 'conforming' the new forces to its vital interests (not only short term interests but long term ones too) which the dominant group today possesses. I believe that the ruling class appreciates this correctly, in spite of surface appearances. If you put together two different bodies from the fusion of which you wish to obtain an alloy, the surface effervescence shows that the alloy is in process of formation – and not the reverse. Moreover, in human relationships of this kind, inner concord always appears on the surface as *discors*, as a struggle or a wrestling match, and not as a stage embrace. However, it's none the less concord, and concord of the most intimate and serviceable.

Dearest Tania, I embrace you tenderly.

Antonio

1. Contribution to the criticism of myself.
2. Sly, cute.

134

Turi Prison, 19 June 1932

Dearest mamma,

I have received the two letters from Grazietta and Mea that were sent off on the 15th, and I would like to send Franco and Mea many hearty congratulations on the brilliant results they obtained in their exams. I am greatly looking forward to Franco's letter; I hope he'll tell me all about his studies now his first year at school is over, and say how he likes his lessons. The first exam is a very important thing in life; Franco can say now that he has made his entry into manly society and has become a citizen, because he has made an effort to let other people see what he has to show for his age; and these others have sat in judgment and their verdict has been favourable. It's a much more important thing than the first communion, in my opinion. And so I hope that Mea too will tell me all about her own lessons. I'm not sure whether Carlo has sent her the crayons yet, or not; it mightn't be a bad thing to give him a prod and tell him to send them off without delay.

Many thanks to Grazietta for the news she sent me; she had already informed me of the deaths of Emilio and Patrizio Carta, but not of Angelico's. I was sorry to hear of all this, chiefly for their mother's sake. I remember her well – she was a very fine woman.

... Things here are just the same as usual.

I embrace you lovingly.

Antonio

135

Turi Prison, 27 June 1932

Dearest Tania,

I have received your postcard of the 20th, and the registered letter enclosing letters from Giulia and Delio. Delio's letters are interesting, don't you think? But what's the meaning of the poem about the spring rain which he puts at the end of the one to me? (I mean, why did he copy it out? Was it because he wanted me to have the pleasure of making its acquaintance?)

Do you think this would be a good time to send him the Italian illustrated edition of *Pinocchio*? There's an edition with illustrations by the painter Attilio Musini[1] (published by Bemporad of Florence). However, as far as I can remember the illustrations weren't terribly good, or at any rate I didn't like them much. When I was a boy I had my own idea of what Pinocchio looked like, and when I saw a drawing of him later on which was different from the Pinocchio of my imagination, it irked me and put me off the thing.

That's why I think it was a very good thing that Florence dropped that project of putting up a Pinocchio monument; it would just have meant that the Florentine children would have had a standard image imposed on them from outside instead of being able to imagine Pinocchio for themselves, as we could. Don't you agree that it's imagining the characters and scenes for themselves that gives children most pleasure when they read books like *Pinocchio*?

... I embrace you tenderly.

Antonio

1. A memory slip: the actual name is Attilio Mussino.

136

Turi Prison, 27 June 1932

Darling Julca,

I have received the pages, dated variously as to month and day, which you sent me. These letters of yours have reminded me of the short story of a little-known French writer, a clerk in some department of the municipality of Paris; Lucien Jean,[1] I think, was his name. The short story in question was called 'A Man in a Ditch'. Let me see if I can remember how it went.

A man had been having a good time one evening; maybe he'd had over much to drink, or else the sight of one beautiful girl after another had gone to his head. Anyway, after leaving the bright lights he staggered along the road on a zigzag course and finally ended up in the ditch. It was very dark, and his body was wedged in tight between boulders and bushes; he didn't move because the drop had put the fear of God in him – also, the ditch being deep, he was afraid of falling down still further. The bushes sprang back into place over his head, and the snails began to slime their way across him, leaving silver tracks. (Maybe a toad came and sat on his heart, to listen to its beating, and make sure that he was still alive.) The hours passed; it drew on towards morning, and when the first glimmerings of dawn were in the sky people started passing by along the highway.

The man started shouting for help. A bespectacled gentleman came walking along the road: he was a scientist, returning home after working all night in his laboratory.

'What's up?' he asked.

'I want to get out of the ditch,' said the man.

'Oho! You want to get out of the ditch. What do you know, I wonder, of the will – of free will or fettered will? You *want* to get out, you want to get out! There's typical ignorance if you like! All you know is this, that you were standing on your feet by virtue of the law of statics, and that you've fallen over in accordance with the law of kinetics. Ah, what ignorance, what ignorance' – and he went on his way shaking his head scornfully.

Soon the man heard other steps, and he again started yelling out. A peasant came up, smoking his pipe; he was leading a pig to market by a string tied to its leg.

'Aha! you've fell in the ditch, eh! You've had a drink or two, you had a good time, and now you've fell in the ditch. Why didn't you go home to bed, like what I did?' And off he went, shuffling along in time with the pig's grunting.

The next passer-by was an artist, who lamented the fact that the man should want to get out of the ditch; he was so beautiful as he was, all silvered over by the snails and with an aureole of grass and wild flowers about his head. He was so pathetic!

After him there came a minister of religion who started railing against the depravity of the City – the City which went whoring after pleasure or snored in a stupor while a brother lay helpless in the ditch. He worked himself up into a great state of emotion, and hurried away to compose a fearsome sermon to be delivered at the next service.

And so the man remained in the ditch – until he looked around him, saw exactly where he had fallen, started wriggling a bit, arched his body, and then, using his legs and his arms as levers, pushed himself upright and so got out of the ditch by his own unaided efforts.

I don't know if I've given you the flavour of the story, nor even if it's very appropriate. However I think it is, in part at least: you yourself tell me that you haven't got much use for either of the two doctors you've recently consulted, and that whereas up till now you've let others make the decisions, from now on you want to stand on your own legs. Such sentiments don't convey the idea of despair in the least: on the contrary I think they're very sensible.

We must hurl all that's past into the flames and build new lives from the ground up. Why should we let ourselves be crushed by the lives we've led up to now? There's no sense in preserving anything at all but what was constructive and what was beautiful. We must get out of the ditch, and throw off that silly toad sitting on our hearts.

Dear Julca, I embrace you tenderly.

Antonio

1. Lucien Jean was the pseudonym of Lucien Dieudonné (1870–1908). Gramsci had published a translation of this story in the *Ordine Nuovo*, 6–13 December 1919.

137

Turi Prison, 12 July 1932

Dearest Tania,

This week I wasn't allowed to read a single word written by you. I know a registered letter from you did arrive, because it was opened in my presence to see whether it contained anything of value, but it hasn't up till now been handed over to me.

Dearest Tania, several times I have mentioned when writing that not infrequently you seem to lose sight of the reality of my present situation; in fact, you appear to forget what being in prison means. On other occasions I have reminded you that too much zeal can be the very reverse of helpful. Perhaps I should have tried to drum this point into you more forcibly, but as often as not I hadn't the heart to, when I realised that you just didn't succeed in grasping what I was telling you. Therefore I don't think it's out of place to send you just once more the following warning:

1. In your letters it's best not to refer to anything but family matters, and that in the clearest and most understandable terms possible. Of course you must remember that clarity in this context does not only mean what's clear in your eyes, but also what's likely to be clear in the eyes of any other person who may chance to read the letter, without knowing a thing about the facts to which you refer. 'Clear' must mean, in short, that nothing is included which might possibly be open to any other construction.

2. Don't send me anything other than things to wear. Not that I want any more underclothes and so on. It's a general warning: I'm not allowed to receive anything from outside the prison – nothing in the food line, no tobacco or cigarette papers, no medicine of any sort. Nothing.

My darling, I have a terrible headache and find it difficult to write. Next week, when I have read your letter and Giulia's, I shall write to you at length and shall also write to Giulia. Please, when you get this letter, send me a picture postcard with nothing on it but words of greeting.

Remember what I have said here, and when you write to me, err where possible on the side of simplicity and baldness rather on the other side, to avoid any possibility of hitches and delays.

I embrace you tenderly.

Antonio

138

Turi Prison, 18 July 1932

Darling Julca,

I have had two letters from you, one dated 24 June and the other 3 July. I have not been feeling very well of late – it's about a year now since I began to get these out-of-sorts spells more frequently – and I just don't feel up to writing you a long letter. But I want to tell you that your last letters have made me happy; I think you've really and truly become stronger and surer of yourself. I am also glad to see that you have got rid of that fixation about a psychoanalytic cure. Although I can't say a great deal owing to the meagreness of my own knowledge it seems to me pretty thoroughly steeped in charlatanry; furthermore I would say that if the therapist doesn't succeed in quite a short time in overcoming the subject's resistance, and levering him out of his depressed state by dint of his own authority, a psychoanalytic cure may very likely aggravate nervous maladies rather than cure them; it will suggest fresh motifs for disquiet to the patient and induce in him a redoubled psychological confusion.[1]

Dear Julca, I think that when your mother told you she would see to it that you became 'as strong as an elephant' she showed herself the most reliable and trustworthy doctor you have ever had.

I embrace you tenderly.

Antonio

1. For a fresh challenging look at this whole question, see Aaron Esterson, *The Leaves of Spring* (Penguin) and *Whither Psychiatry*, Scottish International, Vol VI, no. 5, May–June–July 1973, pp. 16–19.

Cf. also the articles by Esterson and Peter Reid on Mental Health in *Boundaries*, published by the Scottish Council for Civil Liberties (214 Clyde Street, Glasgow), March/April 1974.

139

Turi Prison, 1 August 1932

Dearest Tania,

I have received your letters of 26 and 28 July, together with Giulia's letter and the photos. The photos, notwithstanding their poorness (which you yourself noted), gave me a lot of pleasure just the same. Although it's clear from the photograph that Giulia has suffered a great deal, I would say that her physical condition is by no means so low that she mightn't make a fairly rapid recovery – provided, of course, she takes care of herself. I read her mother's letter with great interest; I thought it bore out the commonly held opinion that grandmothers can write better about children than the mothers themselves.

In the last few days I've felt a bit better. At least I've had a change of illnesses, and I feel more at ease. Not just at this precise moment, however. It's started to get overpoweringly hot, here as elsewhere: every small effort I make bathes me in sweat, and that is disagreeable as well as weakening. The diet I was forced to follow wasn't merely 'liquid', as you thought, but simply 'watery': I ate nothing at all, and drank nothing but an occasional lemonade for about three days, in two successive stints. As for milk, I can't drink more than a very little – let alone six pints! If I drink more than a couple of pints of milk a day, I feel very poorly and my digestion doesn't function. Nevertheless, broadly speaking my digestion has improved – although I've got to be careful to eat very little, if I don't want to let myself in for immediate pains in my innards.

All this leaves me very weak, especially with the heat, the lack of rest and the difficulty I have sleeping. It's an abominable complex of suffering, and you'll agree my stock of patience and my battery of resistance must have been very great, seeing that they have kept me going till now.

I embrace you tenderly.

Antonio

140

Turi Prison, 1 August 1932

Darling Julca,

... What you write about Delio and Giuliano and their respective inclinations has reminded me that a few years ago you thought Delio had a greater aptitude for constructional engineering, whereas nowadays it seems that this last is Giuliano's bent. Delio, you say, is now more interested in literature and in the construction of ... poetry.

To tell you the truth, I haven't much time for such a precocious display of tendencies, and I must admit I haven't much faith either in your capacity for ascertaining what professional aptitude they do in fact tend to reveal. I should think that in both boys, as in all other children, there are likely to be found all sorts of tendencies, towards the practical side, towards theory and towards imagination. Consequently my feeling is that it would be more proper to guide them towards a harmonious blend of all intellectual and practical faculties, confident that specialisation in one or the other of these will inevitably take place in due time on the basis of a personality vigorously formed and totally integrated. Modern man ought to be a synthesis of the qualities which are traditionally embodied in certain national characters: the American engineer, the German philosopher, the French 'political man', thus recreating, so to speak, the Italian Renaissance man, the modern Leonardo da Vinci become 'mass-man' and 'collective man' without sacrificing his own strong personality and individual originality. A tall order, indeed, as you can see. You wanted to call Delio Leo; why on earth didn't we think of calling him Leonardo? Do you think that the Dalton educational system[1] has the capacity in it of producing Leonardos even if only as a collective synthesis?

I embrace you.

1. For further remarks by Gramsci on the 'Dalton method', a development of Montessori's ideas, see *Selections from the Prison Notebooks*, ed. Hoare and Nowell Smith (London, 1971), pp. 32–3.

141

Turi Prison, 9 August 1932

Dearest Tania,

I have received your letter of 4 August, together with Giulia's letters. It seems to me that it's now possible to state quite definitely that Giulia is *uscita fuor dal pelago alla riva*[1] and that a new life is beginning for her.

I can't expect you to provide a long-range diagnosis of my troubles by correspondence. When I write to you I'm just pouring out my heart, and that's all there is to it. You mustn't worry overmuch about these jeremiads of mine. Indeed it's a great pity, not to speak of a waste of effort, when you offer advice which it's plain impossible to follow, but which seems to you reasonable and practicable. This makes me think that you haven't even now got a clear idea of what life in prison is like, and what my conditions actually are. I can assure you that after five and a half years it's not a gay carefree existence. The advice – which you again repeat – to drink thin soup (just to take one example), could be considered either exhilarating or the reverse, depending on one's temperament. And yet you know in your heart that it's nothing but the sort of joke about the medical profession which you can find in any humorous weekly. Time and again you must have seen drawings of doctors prescribing for a beggar a cure in the mountains with chicken and choice wines etc. It's the sort of joke that never fails to get a laugh. But not always, it stands to reason, from the patient himself. On the other hand, the lemonade cure is practical, hygienic, costs little, occasions no disturbance and (it's only fair to add) does the job into the bargain.

What's more, it's of venerable antiquity. Do you know Boccaccio's story about the method employed by the brigand Ghino del Tacco to cure the Abbot of Cluny and make it unnecessary for him to take the waters? If you do, you'll realise that in the days of Ghino del Tacco this was already a well-known cure. It seems therefore that in every man – even in a person reduced to the direst poverty – there's always an Abbot of Cluny tucked away.

I embrace you.

Antonio

1. 'on shore, after emerging from the deep' (Dante, *Inferno* I, 23 adapted).
2. *Decameron*, IX, 2.

142

Turi Prison, 15 August 1932

Darling Julca,

... I've already explained to you in a letter why it is that I can't be of any help to you in the work which you propose undertaking in the immediate future. Your letter of 2 August makes me sure that I was right. How do you think I could possibly be in a position to indicate which significant Italian books of today you should read? I am completely cut off from present-day life, and have been for the six years I've spent in prison. In these last few years (four anyway) I have not read a single book of Italian poetry (or poetry in any other language, if it comes to that); the last books I read of some artistic interest were two novels: *Amo, dunque sono*[1] by Sibilla Aleramo, and *Il Diavolo al Pontelungo*[2] by Riccardo Bacchelli. My baggage, as you can see, is very light, not to say scanty. By and large I labour under the same disadvantage as you do, or maybe even a worse one. The reading I do is very limited, for it's almost always the same books. I read a certain number of reviews, and these contain stories and sometimes a full-length novel; however, in Italy reviews never follow the intellectual currents in the country at all closely, and consequently never offer even the shadow of a complete picture of life, far less of a country's life in all its ceaseless movement. They almost always have a sort of archaeological flavour, and not only as far as literature is concerned. Articles on Giacomo Puccini, on Enrico Panzacchi, on Savonarola, on Machiavelli, on Virgil etc. Apart from this, several of the reviews I have been reading contain articles full of recriminations about the wide remove between art and life, about literature not reflecting the present-day life of the nation, and young men exhausting their talents in formalistic experiments with style, metre and vocabulary.[3] These are recriminations which may well have an intrinsic interest, but which reveal a certain barrenness in the intellectual and artistic landscape.

In any case it appears from this letter of yours – and also from the earlier ones – that you have formed for yourself (or others have formed for you, by giving you inexact information) a too decorative and idyllic conception of my life here. My life is empty, terribly and depressingly empty, and devoid of any content of interest whatsoever; it lacks everything that might serve as an intellectual stimulus and every pleasure that makes life worth living. I barely live at all; I hang on grimly to the outskirts of animal, or rather vegetable existence.

I don't want to plunge you into gloom, but it's useless for you to cherish glossy rose-coloured illusions about the conditions I am living under. Anyway I'm used to them. And I endure. And I have patience (though certainly not resignation). And yet the suspicion that perhaps others may believe the reality of my position to be totally different from what it actually is, and have pictures of me immersed in all kinds of useful and interesting work irritates me to the last degree – and revolts me a little into the bargain. It makes me feel even more cruelly how isolated I am – and how utterly cut off from life ...

... I embrace you tenderly.

Antonio

1. I love, therefore I am.
2. *The Devil at Pontelungo*, see letter dated 7 April 1930, and note.
3. Doubtless the familiar gripes against the *ermetici* (hermetic poets), of whom one, Eugenio Montale, was among the foremost poets writing in Europe at that time. Montale's work was hardly known outside Italy in the 1930s, however, and only to a small avant-garde public in Italy itself. See Ruggero Orlando, *On Modern Italian Poetry* (trans. H. Henderson) in Fred Marnau's review *New Road*, no. 4, London, 1947.

See also Glauco Cambon's introduction to *Eugenio Montale, Selected Poems* (New Directions, New York, 1965): 'We find him actively supporting, or contributory to, alert magazines of the twenties like *Il Convegno* ... Those were, without exception, rallying points for the liberal intellectuals who refused to go along with the Fascist Establishment ... The significance of such élite dissenters can hardly be exaggerated in the context of Fascist Italy. Even when they abstained from overt political opposition, they kept alive the tradition of independent thinking and artistic integrity, which is to say that they made writers like Eugenio Montale possible. It was one of the liberal editors, Piero Gobetti of Turin, who published Montale's first volume of verse, *Ossi di Seppia* (Cuttlefish Bones) in 1925.' This passage is highly relevant in the present context, for it is the brilliant and sympathetic figure of Piero Gobetti which provides a direct link between the worlds of Montale and Gramsci.

143

Turi Prison, 22 August 1932

Darling mamma,

For a while now nobody has written to me, and so I don't know your news. A few weeks ago Tatiana sent me some photos of Teresina's children, and I was delighted with them. It's true that Mimi looks very like Emma did when she was a child. And certainly it's marvellous how strongly marked the family features are in these children (Delio and Giuliano have them very clearly marked too). You'd think, looking at the photos, that you were catching sight again of faces you'd seen hundreds of times, faces surfacing in the memory from out of the depths of the years. I think Diddi looks like Teresina did when we were still living at Sorgono and were going to the nuns' kindergarten; but she hasn't got the blonde curls that Teresina had. The last photo of Delio that I received made me feel that I was looking at a photo of Mario taken when he was eight. Giuliano's little face on the other hand has features which put me in mind of Nannaro and still more of Uncle Alfredo. (To tell you the truth I was never very taken with Uncle Alfredo, although he was so clearly one of us in physical appearance – unlike Uncle Cesare, who seemed an intruder from some other family.) However these are possibly just superficial impressions.

Incidentally, why didn't you let that other person stay in the group with the children? One can see he has just stepped back out of the road. It's Paolo, unless I'm much mistaken.

I'm looking forward to hearing your news. Give Teresina and Grazietta a dig in the ribs, and tell them to write to me. I embrace you affectionately.

Antonio

144

Turi Prison, 29 August 1932

Dearest Tania,

I have received your letter of the 24th with Giuliano's letter enclosed. I have given a great deal of thought to what you write about the possibility of getting a doctor you can trust to give me a thorough examination. It seems to me that broadly speaking your arguments do hold water, and that the project should be given serious consideration.

In my opinion, I've reached a point where my powers of resistance are in danger of complete collapse. In these last few days I've felt worse than I've ever felt before; for more than eight days I haven't slept for more than three-quarters of an hour a night, and some nights I didn't sleep a wink.[1] It's as sure as fate that although enforced insomnia is not in itself the cause of any specific malady, it aggravates the troubles one has to such an extent, and throws in so much incidental discomfort, that life is just not worth living.

Nevertheless, before embarking on the course you suggest, I'd like to make another application to the director of the prison, and if necessary to the superintendent of prisons, to see if it isn't possible to put an end to the conditions which are causing the present state of affairs. It's by no means impossible that this might do the trick, and I'd prefer it that way in order to avoid the considerable expense which a visit from a reliable doctor would entail. Besides, any doctor, however capable, couldn't help coming to the conclusion that the disastrous condition I'm in is due to a great extent to lack of sleep, that the problem presents itself in these terms and that before doing anything else one must solve it. In the worst hypothesis it would only mean postponing the realisation of your project till September.

In short, your suggestion is worthy of being acted upon; carry on with your plans, get the details fixed, and take all necessary steps to see how much the thing will cost. We'll have to decide too which doctor we want, because I rather think that when filling in the application for the authorisation of the visit it will be necessary to insert his name and all relevant particulars.

My dearest, I embrace you tenderly.

Antonio

1. See note 1 to letter 130.

145

Turi Prison, 29 August 1932

Darling Julca,

I've received your letter of the 14th. Today I just don't feel able to write a long letter. I always read your letters with immense interest, and they give me a few hours of serenity and happiness. I am sure that on their birthdays you'll have told Delio and Giuliano many many things in my name as well as in your own. You can do that better than I could myself, because you're familiar with the picture of me which they have in their heads, and can therefore speak in a way that will be convincing.

Darling Julca, I embrace you tenderly.

Antonio

1. Both children were born in August.

146

Turi Prison, 5 September 1932

Dearest Tania,

I've received your letter of 26 August – the one which is almost all taken up with the transcription of Giulia's letter to yourself. You tell me nothing of your own illness, and the cure that you had to undergo. I have started taking Sedobrol again, and I hope that it'll finally put an end to the state of nervous excitement I had got into. It had become so acute that the least little thing caused excruciatingly painful convulsive spasms. I was greatly taken with the letter Giulia wrote to you; I think we may rest assured that her recovery is a reality. I'd like to know if you intend to send her any books, because I might be able to recommend one or two titles which fit in with what I was telling her in today's letter. For example, as I see it, she ought to have a whole collection of specialist dictionaries at her disposal. A dictionary she shouldn't be without is Rezasco's: it's called *An Historical-Administrative Dictionary of the Italian Language*, or some name like that. It's an indispensable work for anyone reading the historical and political literature of Italy, because of all the terms it contains relating to the law, politics, administration, military regulations etc. However this dictionary's out of print, and only to be found in secondhand bookshops, so a copy may cost a fair sum. You might visit some secondhand bookshop in Rome and ask for it; but don't take the price they quote for gospel. Prices in that line of country are very elastic, and it's best to compare a few of them before making a purchase. The best thing to do would be to go to some reputable dealer who is in a position to study the catalogues of the various firms.

In the meantime you might, if you like, send her Francesco De Sanctis's *History of Italian Literature*, which is really a history of Italian civilisation (Treves has issued a cheap edition in two volumes; the price is, I think, 8 lire). This history of De Sanctis is a work of art in itself and is not to be used simply as a manual; a manual does exist, however, which is accurate, precise and exceedingly useful – Vittorio Rossi's *History of Italian Literature*, published by Vallardi in three volumes.

I read very little, I forget things from one minute to another. It's strange that while I remember past events in great detail, I can't remember things that happened the day before or even an hour or two before. Nevertheless I'll read Emil Ludwig's *Talks with Mussolini* with great interest, and the prefect Mori's book about the Mafia. Another book that I'd be very interested to read is one by Professor Adolfo Pagani, called *I braccianti della Valle Padana*[1] (edited by the National Institute of Agrarian Economy). I'd also like to see the annual report of the Banca Commerciale on the Italian economic situation; I always used to get it in the past.

Dearest Tania, tell me how you're bearing up.

I embrace you.

Antonio

1. The Landless Labourers of the Po Plain.

147

Turi Prison, 5 September 1932

Darling Julca,

I'm rereading your letter of 14 August.

... What you write about Leonardo da Vinci doesn't really seem to be correct or accurate; you've probably not had much opportunity to see examples of Leonardo's work as an artist, and even less opportunity to get to know him as a writer and a scientist. But what certainly is inaccurate is the opinion which you attribute to me that 'to love a writer, or other artist, is not the same as to esteem him'. I'm sure that I never wrote anything so banal; the memory of a number of plays, the progeny of universal philistinism, in which these themes of 'love without esteem' and ' esteem without love' have been applied in every imaginable way to married life would have put me off, even if nothing else had. Perhaps I was making a distinction between aesthetic enjoyment and the positive appreciation of artistic beauty, on the one hand – that is, a state of aesthetic and intellectual enthusiasm for the work of art as such – and, on the other, a state of moral enthusiasm, i.e. a feeling of kinship with and participation in the ideological world of the artist. This is a distinction which seems to me just and necessary from a critical point of view. I can admire Tolstoy's *War and Peace* aesthetically without sharing at the same time in the ideological substance of the book; if the two things coincided, Tolstoy would be my vade-mecum, *le livre de chevet*. I could say the same about Shakespeare, Goethe and Dante as well. It wouldn't be accurate for me to say it in the case of Leopardi, in spite of his pessimism. In Leopardi one finds, in an extremely dramatic form, the crisis of transition towards modern man; the critical abandonment of the old transcendental conception but not as yet the finding of a new moral and intellectual *ubi consistam* which would give the same certainty as the jettisoned faith ...

Darling Julca, I embrace you tenderly.

Antonio

148

Turi Prison, 12 September 1932

Dearest Tania,

I've received two cards and two letters from you, dated the 9th and the 10th. I must admit that the second of the two letters exasperated me more than a little. Whenever it's a question of doctors and medicines you at once run riot with projects and fantastic imaginings. How many times have I implored you to be cool and level-headed, and not let your zeal run away with you.

When I was at school (a little communal school at Santu Lussurgiu in which three so-called 'masters' shared between them the teaching load of all five classes, relying more on brazen cheek than competence) I was boarded out in the house of a peasant woman. (I paid 5 lire a month for board, bed linen and very frugal meals, which were cooked for me.) The woman had an old mother who was a little weak in the head, but not actually certifiable; it was this old creature who did the cooking and looked after me generally. Every morning, when she saw me, she would ask me who I was and how it came about that I was sleeping in their house, etc.

However, that's another story. What I'm getting at now is that the daughter wanted to get rid of the mother, and was trying to persuade the town council to lodge her at its own expense in the provincial lunatic asylum. To this end she treated her mother in a harsh cruel way that was positively wicked; it was clear her idea was to provoke the old woman into some desperate act of folly that would give the daughter a chance to claim that she was dangerous.

The poor old creature used to say to this daughter, who addressed her as *voi*,[1] according to custom: 'Call me tu, and treat me decent.'

I'm a bit dubious about the relevance of this anecdote now I come to think of it, but at any rate I feel myself forced once again to ask you to be a little less solicitous, because that's the best way of showing your affection for me, an affection which means a very great deal to me. In short you must do literally nothing but what I ask you to do in my letters and don't flavour the dish with sauces of your own invention, for it can happen that they just make the mouthful go down the wrong way. Don't indulge in fantasies, and don't go in for absurd guesswork.

In any case I'm a bit better now, and am hoping that the improvement continues – and that, you must agree, is the main thing.

I embrace you tenderly.

Antonio

1. 'You' (the second person plural): in Italian it is usually a form denoting respect, and in some regions children still address their parents as *voi*. The sense of the remark is: Call me what you like, but be kind to me.

149

Turi Prison, 12 September 1932

Dearest Mamma,

I've received a letter from Grazietta dated 24 August, giving me news of the harvest, and of the new house where Teresina has gone to live. I remember well the courtyard where I played with Luciano, and the basin of the fountain where I used to manoeuvre my great fleets of paper boats, and boats made of cork, reeds and bamboo canes, and then wreck them with shots from a *schizzaloru*.[1] Do you remember how clever I was at making models of the big sailing vessels, and how I knew all the proper nautical terms? I used to speak of nothing but brigantines, xebecs, three-masters and *schooners*,[2] of hammock netting, of top-gallants and of sky-sails, and I was well up in all the phases of the sea battles of the Red Corsair, and of the Tiger Cubs of Mompracem.[3] The only thing that riled me was that Luciano possessed a simple little craft, very sturdy because it was made of thickish tin, which was capable in four movements of ramming and sending to the bottom my more elaborate galleons, with all their complicated rigging, their bridges and their various sails. But in spite of that I was very proud of my skill.

Darling mamma, I've always forgotten to ask you for news of Giacomino, the son of the surveyor Porcelli, who right from the time he was a tiny little boy, showed a great affection for me and for my falcon, and always wanted to be in my company. There's a Giacomo Porcelli, a very aggressive Catholic, who writes books and articles on French literature; is it the same one? His uncles are sure to know ... But is there anyone of the Corrias family still alive?

Make them write to me a little more often. Why hasn't Teresina ever sent me that letter she promised so many times?

I embrace you affectionately with everyone at home.

Antonio

1. Primitive air-gun made from the branch of an elder tree and fitted with a small piston capable of discharging pellets (Sardinian).
2. English in the text.
3. Characters out of the boys' stories of Salgari, the Henty (or Ballantyne) of Italy.

150

Turi Prison, 3 October 1932

Dear Tatiana,

I have received your postcard of 29 September. It hasn't brought me the least satisfaction ... From now on you must stop taking an active interest in my life as a prisoner,[1] and consequently you must moderate what you write on this subject, if you don't want to interrupt our correspondence altogether. I beg you not to discuss this wish of mine, because otherwise I'd be obliged to return your letters or postcards. I have been master of my own life for a long time now, and I was master of it when I was a child. I started working when I was eleven years old, earning the princely sum of 9 lire[2] a month (which, by the way, meant a loaf of bread a day) and working ten hours a day plus Sunday mornings. The job was moving ledgers which weighed more than I did, and many a night I wept in secret because my whole body was aching. Hardly ever have I known any but the more brutal sides of life, and yet I've always managed to get through for better or for worse. Not even my mother knows the whole of my life and the hardships I've undergone; nowadays, when from time to time I mention our past life, I remind her of nothing but that slender part of it which now in perspective seems carefree and joyous. These memories sweeten her old age, because they make her forget the much graver vicissitudes and more profound afflictions and sorrows she has been through in the same period. If she was aware that I knew everything that I do know,[3] and realised that these events have left their scars, it would poison the last years of her life – years in which it's best that she should forget, and seeing the carefree life of her little grandchildren playing round her, should let the perspectives blur, and think that the two epochs of her life are really one and the same.

Dear Tatiana, I embrace you affectionately.

Antonio

1. On 15 September Tatiana had made an official appeal to Mussolini, in her own name and in Giulia's, asking him to permit an outside doctor, Professor Umberto Arcangeli, to visit Gramsci at Turi and give him a thorough examination.
2. Roughly eight shillings (40p) at that time.
3. See letter 156, note 2.

151

Turi Prison, 10 October 1932

Dearest Tatiana,

I have received your letter of the 7th, with the copy of the application made by you to the Head of the Government. I don't want to make any comment on this. If the application is accepted, and Professor Arcangeli can come and visit me, I shall explain to him exactly how things stand. You'll certainly have received by now the letter I wrote you last Monday. Although my anger has died down now, I beg you to get it into your head that the letter was written very seriously although with great regret and with much grief. One reason I'm very sorry about it all is that from now on I'll have to be so careful what I write to you that I shan't know what to say.

I embrace you tenderly.

Antonio

152

Turi Prison, 10 October 1932

Darling Delio,

I'm told you've been at the seaside, and that you've seen all sorts of lovely things. I'd like you to write me a letter and describe all these lovely things to me. Have you seen any new living creatures? At the seaside there's a whole host of creatures: shrimps, jellyfish, starfish etc. A good while ago I promised to tell you some stories about the animals that I knew when I was a child, but I wasn't able to. Now I'll keep my promise and tell you one or two:
1. For example, the story of the fox and the foal.
They say that when a foal is just going to be born, the fox knows about it and lies in wait. Therefore, as soon as the foal is born, the mother starts trotting around it in a circle, for the little one is defenceless and can't run away if a wild animal attacks it. In spite of this you sometimes come across horses without ears and tails on the roads of Sardinia. Why is that, you may ask. Because as soon as they were born the fox succeeded in one way or another in getting at them and eating their ears or their tails when

these were still as tender as anything.

When I was a little boy, a horse like that belonged to an old peddler who went from village to village, selling his wares, which were olive oil, candles and paraffin (in those days there was no co-op, or any other such system of getting the goods to the people). On Sundays, fearing that the local lads would tease him, this peddler used to put false ears and a false tail on his horse.

2. Now I'll tell you how I saw a fox for the first time.

One day I went with my little brothers to a field belonging to an aunt of mine where there were two huge oaks and a few fruit trees; our job was to collect acorns as food for a wee piglet. The field was not far from the village, but it was quite deserted, and we had to go down into a sort of valley. What should we see as soon as we got into the field but a big fox sitting peacefully under a tree, with his beautiful big tail up in the air like a flagpole. He showed not the least sign of alarm; he showed his teeth, but it looked as if he was smiling and not as if he was threatening us. We kids were angry because the fox wasn't afraid of us – and indeed he wasn't frightened in the least. We threw stones at him, but he hardly bothered to dodge them and just went on looking at us slyly and mockingly. We lifted sticks to our shoulders, and we all went Boom! as if we were firing guns, but the fox couldn't have cared less – he just showed his teeth.

Suddenly a real shot rang out, fired by someone nearby. Then (and then only) the fox made a jump and scampered off in double-quick time. I can still see his yellow body streaking over a dyke, tail still in the air, and disappearing into a clump of thorns.

Darling Delio, tell me about your travels and the new sights you have seen. Kisses to you, and to Giuliano and mamma Julca.

Antonio

153

Turi Prison, 24 October 1932

Dearest Tania,

I'd be very grateful if you'd write and tell my sister Grazietta that I've received the letter of the 19th in which she gives reassuring news about mother's state of health. On the 7th she wrote to me that mamma was dying, that she had already given her last instructions and that there was no hope. Now she writes that mamma has rallied, and the doctor says there's no reason why she shouldn't live for several years yet, given her exceptional strength. I also hear she's eating with a good appetite. Poor Grazietta is terribly sorry to have given me such a fright. But it stands to reason she too must be feeling very poorly after all the trouble and fatigue she's been through.

Another thing I'd like you to do, if you don't mind, is to let the bookshop know that I haven't received the September number of *Problemi del Lavoro*; nor have I received Ludwig's *Talks with Mussolini* and the volume issued by the Commercial Bank. I have, however, received the prefect Mori's book about the Mafia, and the volume about the landless labourers of the Po plain.

I embrace you.

Antonio

154

Turi Prison, 24 October 1932

Darling Julca,

I have received your letters of 5 and 12 October, together with Julik's little letter and the three photographs, which gave me much pleasure. I think it's the first time that I've really got an idea of Giuliano's physical appearance, although the photos aren't awfully good from a technical point of view. Giuliano seems to me to be rather a good-looking boy, and I don't think this is just because I'm his father; it leaps to the eye, or so I'd say, when he's in a group photo near you. Unfortunately you haven't come out at all well yourself.

I'm glad that he wanted to write to me; I don't know how to reply to his request for a photograph. Maybe you've got a photo of me you could give him? It's true that I've changed a lot since those days, and it seems like cheating the boy to give him a ten-year-old photo. Nowadays I've got a lot of white hair, and the loss of my teeth must have made a big change to the look of my face. (I can't say exactly how great, because I haven't had a chance of seeing myself in a mirror for four and a half years, and it's precisely in these years that I must have changed most.)

I was very interested to hear what you had to say about Delio as a schoolboy, the inner seriousness he reveals for all his love of fun. I feel with keen and piercing regret how unlucky I am to have been deprived of the opportunity of taking my share in helping the children to develop in an all-round way; especially as I invariably won the friendship of children in no time, and knew how to keep them interested. I'll always remember a little niece of my landlady in Rome; she was four, and had a very difficult name, of Turkish origin if I'm not mistaken. She would come stealing along to my room, as quiet as a mouse, for her granny had told her she mustn't disturb me, seeing I was always writing. She would try to turn the handle of my door and not quite manage it; then she'd give a timid little knock, ever so soft, and when I asked 'Who's there?' she'd say 'Stlivi. Would you like to play?'

Then she'd come in and offer her cheek to be kissed; after which she'd ask me to make little birds for her, or funny pictures that I made by dropping blobs of ink at random all over the paper.

My darling, I embrace you tenderly.

Antonio

155

Dear Julik,

I have received your letter, and the kitten postcard. What about you and Delca making a shade for the electric light? With 18 inches of copper wire or thin steel wire and with a bit of coloured material – or else with a piece of oil-paper – you can make a most useful lampshade which will stop the light from being too trying to the eyes. You can either make the shade a permanent fixture, so that the light is reduced on all sides, or else you can make it movable, and so direct the light and shade where you want them.

I have received some photos of you, and I'd like you to tell me what exercises you can do on the Swedish wall bars (that's what we call them in this country anyway) where I see you perched among your friends.

Kisses from your Daddy.

156

Turi Prison, 31 October 1932

Dearest Grazietta,

I've received your letter of the 19th, with the reassuring news about mamma's health. I understand what a state you must have been in when you wrote the earlier letter, and so there's nothing to excuse. The first piece of news you sent certainly gave me a bad fright, especially as I wasn't feeling at all well myself at the time, and so I was inclined in any case to think in terms of disasters. However, the good and reassuring news you send has made me as happy now as I was depressed then.

You must see and keep well yourself, because you'll have plenty of work to do; so mind you watch out and look after your health. It's true that, being a branch of the Corrias, we can claim to be a bit *corriazzos*,[1] but even so I doubt if we're as tough as our forefathers were. One has to take into consideration that our generation has been through hard times, our own family particularly. Would we be capable of doing what mamma did 35 years ago? Standing up by herself, poor woman, in the teeth of a terrible storm and bringing seven children safe through it?[2] Her life is assuredly an example to us, and is proof that with enough tenacity you can overcome difficulties that would seem insuperable even to men of the stoutest moral fibre.

Loving embraces to all and especially mamma, from your brother

Antonio

1. leathery (Sardinian). This play on words was a sort of family pun among the Gramscis.
2. Gramsci is alluding here to a calamity which hit the family when he was seven. His father had supported the losing candidate in the parliamentary election of 1897, and the winning faction succeeded in getting Gramsci senior 'investigated'. Charges of financial misconduct were brought against him and, although the sum involved was a trifling one, he was sentenced to over five years in prison. The affair seems, in part at least, to have been a political frame-up.

Her husband's imprisonment was a terrible blow to Peppina Marcias Gramsci. She had seven children to bring up, and with the loss of Francesco's salary the family suffered from acute financial hardship. However, she faced up to the situation with the utmost courage and resolution and, working long hours as a seamstress and making many sacrifices, she succeeded in keeping their heads above water.

The humiliation of having a member of the family in prison was a very real one, and Peppina Marcias tried (probably mistakenly) to keep the truth from her younger children. The discovery of the truth was undoubtedly a traumatic shock for Antonio. In a letter to Tatiana dated 15 December 1930 (pp. 391–2 in the 1965 edition of the *Lettere*, ed. Caprioglio and Fubini) he wrote: 'I can't think why the fact that I'm in prison has been hidden from Delio. Didn't it occur to anyone that he might find out about it indirectly – that is, in the most disagreeable way possible for a child, seeing he naturally begins to doubt the truthfulness of the grown-ups looking after him ... At least, that was my experience when I was a child; I remember it all perfectly ... I remember how every discovery of subterfuges to hide the painful truth from me offended me and made me shut myself up within myself, and draw apart from others.'

157

Turi Prison, 31 October 1932

Dearest Tania,

These days there are a lot of rumours going the rounds, some of them pretty far-fetched, about forthcoming measures of pardon and amnesty which the government is supposed to be drawing up for prisoners. Some even say that the amnesty would be total in the case of prisoners sentenced for crimes committed before the formation of the Special Tribunal; in which case I could look forward to freedom (or rather to exile) in a few weeks at the most. But to tell you the truth, these items of news in the main leave me cold and sceptical. An interesting essay could be written on the changes which news undergoes in prison when it is passed through the filter of the prisoners' own personal desires. In this particular case I do think there's something in it – I believe, that is, that a gesture of pardon would be politically justifiable and useful to the government; but I have my doubts about its probable extent. It's true that when this letter reaches you the thing may already have been decided on and made public, but I'm writing in this strain to stop you harbouring too many illusions; I've observed that it's their relations who usually give prisoners false hopes, making them think that they've ultra-reliable sources of information at their disposal, 100 per cent authentic. I ought to thank you for never having been guilty of that kind of frenzy.

I embrace you.

Antonio

158

Turi Prison, 21 November 1932

Dearest Grazietta,

I have received your letter of the 12th, with your impressions of the news which got around about the amnesty decree. I don't know whether you did well or ill to have mamma on and let her think that I had been set free – and then have to invent details of my journeys and all kinds of complications of that sort. Let me know all the details of this, so that I know what to say when I write. To tell you the truth, that kind of deception – even in the case of sick people – is repugnant to me, because my fear is that in the end it probably causes worse distress than that which it was originally meant to alleviate. In any case please give me clear and full information about the whole thing.

I'm not yet in a position to let you know what definite consequences the decree will have in my case; it's possible that there will be no change in my position, and it's possible too that the stretch I have still to do will be reduced to five years and two months. But even if it were actually so, I don't think the change would be of great importance. Thirteen years and five years are all the same to me, seeing that it's a matter of a period of time that lies outside the scope of calculation.

I embrace you with everyone at home, especially mamma.

Antonio

159

Turi Prison, 28 November 1932

Darling Julca,

I've received your letters of 22 October and of 15 November. I've read with interest your observations on Julik's love of looking at himself in the mirror, but it was the ingenuous and frankly 'womanish' quality of your reasoning which appealed to me. The real quintessence of femininity. Regarding a mirror purely as a means of gratifying narcissism is assuredly the most feminine of things. I've always had a mirror; how else do you think I could have shaved myself all these years? Your observations are profoundly mistaken; they indicate a way of thinking which is anachronistic, out of date and ... terribly dangerous. It's this sort of mental state – negative, and reacting merely to certain psychological degenerations – which is calculated in the end to make a worker break his machine or a clerk fudge his books. It seems to me that there's nothing wrong with Julik not wanting holes in his stockings – quite the reverse. What's the sense in leaving holes in stockings if you can mend them?

I think you're confounding the means with the end, that you're unable to adjust the means to the end in question – i.e. you don't know exactly what practical and immediate ends you want to reach; the ends you set yourself should interlock in a chain, so that you can move without a break from the one to the other.

There's still a 'Rousseau-esque' sediment in your intellectual make-up, and this sediment is the cause of no insignificant part of your psychological trouble – and therefore of your physical ills as well. There's something contradictory in your inmost self, a cleavage which you've not managed to heal, between theory and practice, and between intellection and instinct. Do you agree I'm right? ... Still it isn't all that serious, and in any case it's exactly that which makes you Julca, and not Masha or Valya.

I should have been the one to help you to know yourself better, to overcome these difficulties. Ah, well! I often think about all this, about what I could and should have done, and haven't done. Maybe it's true that I've been too much of an 'egotist', and that aesthetic sensations have meant more to me than moral obligations. Maybe I've been too 'Italian', in the intellectual sense of the word, and because of that have always felt such kinship with ... Leonardo and the Renaissance. I think that now I'm a 'reformed' character and that I've reconciled in my heart both Renaissance and Reformation, to use the two terms which in my view symbolise every movement on the grand scale in the history of civilisation.

My dear, what a lot of nonsense I'm writing. I was pleased to hear the news about Julik and Delio. What a contrast they make! Even so I'm sure that ultimately they'll become integrated, developing together, educating each other reciprocally ... under your guidance.

But *do* you direct them yourself? In what ways do you participate in the formation of their characters? ... How many things there are which I'd like to know and which maybe I shall never know ...

I embrace you.

Antonio

160

Turi Prison, 12 December 1932

Dearest Tania,

As far as the decree is concerned, all I can do is hazard a few guesses, all of these pretty vague and in any case purely arbitrary. They range from the one extreme to the other.
1. The decree may not concern me at all, in which case the legal position remains unchanged (the most pessimistic hypothesis), and
2. By virtue of the decree my sentence may be reduced to five years (the most optimistic hypothesis), and in consequence the legal position may itself be modified in accordance with what the new code lays down concerning the conditional freeing of prisoners. Between these two extremes there are a number of intermediate hypotheses which are all feasible.

As you can see, I'm just stumbling around in the dark. Usually in the case of a pardon or amnesty, the prisoner concerned is eventually informed officially of any change in his position. Such a communication may be delayed for four or five months. But the lack of official information doesn't in itself mean that the amnesty or pardon does not apply in that particular case; it may always be the result of an oversight or an error etc. That's why it sometimes happens that the interested party may have to appeal, demanding that the terms of the pardon be enforced in his case.

As you can see, the question is complex. In any case, it may well be that I shall remain in the dark for months yet about what is to happen to me. It was for this reason that I wrote a few weeks ago, asking you if you would be so good as to pay a visit to the office of the Special Tribunal to get some information – although there was no immediate hurry. Of course in these matters the lawyer's side has no importance whatever. It's possible that the Clerk of the Court himself doesn't know a thing in the case of individual prisoners, because it's obvious that the Tribunal will deal with the various cases in order of urgency, and will leave to the last those prisoners who still have a long sentence to serve – even if the amnesty does apply to them. But it's probable, to say the least of it, that the secretary will know whether the decree does actually apply in such cases or not, seeing that prisoners in the same general position (but with shorter sentences) may already be enjoying the benefits of the decree as free men.

I think I've made things clear enough. In my own case what we need to know, in the absence of other particulars, is whether I have a right to the benefits of the decree or not. How far such benefits go in my case may not as yet be settled – it may not be for some time. But without preliminary information of this nature I couldn't properly put in an application for the enforcement of the decree.

Don't get it into your head that I'm egging you on to get out of doors and run all over the place in order to get hold of this information. I've already told you that there's no hurry. In matters of this kind it makes no odds whether you think in terms of weeks or of months (that is, it makes no odds in my case, more's the pity!). What matters is the accuracy, the precision, the exactness of the news in question. The maybes etc., have no value – or rather they have nothing but a negative value, in that they help to weaken a man's resistance and wear him out. It all boils down to a norm of conduct which I'm set on recommending to you as the most effective. No haste, no impulsiveness: before you decide on a thing, be sure you have in your head all the positive factors making for success – and be sure, too, that you have grappled with and overcome all the negative factors, those making for failure. In certain circumstances the time factor, saving time etc., may be one of the latter, in so far as it may hinder you from gaining a realistic picture of these fundamental data. The common sense of the people has made a synthesis of this kind of experience in the proverb 'More haste, less speed'.[1]

It has been announced that we are entitled to receive 'one' Christmas parcel from home. I imagine you'll already have thought of sending me something. But honestly, I think you'd be far better to hang on to the money for other purposes. If you really are dead set on giving me something for Christmas, seeing that the possibility exists, please don't make it anything lavish. If you really want to, send me something – but just a very little, something quite simple. If you'd like to know the things that would give me pleasure, here they are: a little *panettone*[2] and, if possible, a few pots of that concentrated vegetable extract you once sent me. Please believe that I'm not just being 'polite'; I can hardly digest anything, and I'm incapable of chewing. Maybe you could add a small bottle of bitters. I honestly don't know what brand to recommend: Ferro-china or something of that sort. However, let me assure you again that even if you send me nothing but your own greetings I'll be quite content – maybe even more.

I'd be grateful if you'd write to the bookshop and tell them that I have not received the October numbers of two reviews, viz. *Leonardo* and *La Nuova Italia*.

Dearest Tania, often after I've written to either Giulia or yourself, I think over what I've written, and when I consider the manner of writing or the tone I've adopted I feel that I must weary you both a great deal with my pedantic pedagogue-ish airs. As you see, I'm conscious too of this sort of tone. But I can't write any other way. Every letter, believe you me, is the result of a complex series of efforts of will and acts of self-control, and the resulting compound can't help taking on a shape which often appears ridiculous – even to me! Many's the time I've felt a powerful scorn for what I've written and the way I've written it. Ah well, I must have patience. Be patient too, and love me just the same.

I embrace you fondly.

Antonio

1. The Italian proverb has more humour in it: 'a hasty cat makes blind kittens.'
2. A Milanese sweetmeat.

161

Turi Prison, 19 December 1932

Darling Julca,

I've received your letter of the 2nd but from what Tania tells me it seems you've not received certain letters of mine (for example, one to Delio). To tell you the truth, I'm actually not sorry if some *have* gone astray; but unfortunately this sort of thing depends on blind chance, and can't happen intelligently. What I mean is that sometimes, after writing to you, I myself feel a certain annoyance with what I have written, for I often seem to catch myself out in a pedantic sort of tone – which often enough must seem downright comical to you. This tone is the outcome of a number of circumstances bound up with my prison conditions, and with a number of events of recent years; it is also partly due to the fact that in your own letters there are so few points which call for an answer. You're too abstract and general, whereas what I need is something a lot more concrete. I have lost much of my power of imagination, and I've lost, too, the greater part of my contacts with the flux of real life; my memories, although they're lively, are after all six years old – and how much may I not have changed in those six years? I can't help being 'anachronistic' in everything; and so, because this is always the trouble, I take refuge in pedantry and adopt my preaching tone, seeing that, in spite of everything, I want to say something and pretend to help you, and yet can't do anything effective to help you overcome the problems of this present phase of your life – which I would think is probably a period of convalescence in which you're likely to make a thousand plans of action and not know where to begin. This gives me the idea that there's something anachronistic in you as well; that you, like me (although in a very different way) have remained on the margin of the flood of life, and don't know how to take the plunge into it again (or else think you don't know how, not realising that you've actually been at work again for some time).

Once upon a time I advised you to take up music once again, in the same way that I would start my philological studies afresh if I were able. Seeing that the study of music was a starting point for you, it seemed to me that by returning to it you would in a certain sense relive the past, but with greater critical understanding, and would advance again through the various stages of your development – not just repeating them mechanically but reliving them with intensity, and feeling for the broken ring in the chain (assuming there is a broken ring). I am not sure whether you understood my advice in this sense, or whether you mayn't just have taken it for a stop-gap expedient intended to counteract the state of inertia which, as you say, has possessed you for some time past.

When one surveys one's own past life from the vantage point afforded by all the richness of experience that has accrued, it may well happen that one will make interesting discoveries; one may realise that there has been a slight deviation from the line which would have allowed a greater expansion of one's energies, and consequently a greater contribution to the progress of the vital forces of history. Perhaps what was at the beginning just a slight deviation has become wider and wider, and has modified one's personality; the correction of this might well signify a return to a reality more normal, more fruitful, and more meaningful.

As you can see, these too are abstract and general observations, but they are so of necessity. In any event, please give me some precise information about your new attempt at a cure. I'm glad that this autumn the children didn't go down with any of the illnesses of the season; and I'm very pleased too that you're writing with the pen I sent you. (But watch out – the ink to use is proper fountain pen ink that flows freely, and not the common sort that leaves a deposit and chokes the works.)

I embrace you, my dear, together with our children.

Antonio

162

Turi Prison, 9 January 1933

Dearest Tania,

I've received your postcard of the 2nd, and the money order sent off on the 3rd. I thank you from my whole heart. I too hope that this month I'll be able to spend a little less on medicines, because I feel somewhat better.

In December the amount I spent was exactly 122 lire and 5 centesimi, made up as follows:

medicine	L.60,70. (almost the half)
post	L.8,80.
articles from the canteen	L.52,55. (L.15,08 of which was for tobacco)

In addition there was 1 lire for matches, and 88 centesimi for cigarette papers. On foodstuffs, as you can see, I spent exactly 37 lire and 47 centesimi.

You'll notice I've managed to cut down my consumption of tobacco a good deal; I think it's correct to say that I smoke only a 15th today of what I used to smoke when I was a free man, and as far as the expense is concerned I only spend a 10th or an 11th part today of what I spent then. It's still too much, in my view, but you must remember that it's very difficult to extirpate completely a habit which is so inveterate and deeply rooted.

My state of health is a bit better, although I have the impression that I've again lost some weight. In point of fact my stomach is not so swollen now as it was, and therefore I've digested my food a bit better, but the amount of food I can get down is still small, and the stomach trouble has not disappeared altogether. I sleep for a few hours every night, but never more than three and a half, and so I take the Sedarmit Roche tablets; I never feel properly rested, and very often I have the feeling of being suspended in mid-air without any bodily equilibrium – the sort of condition you're in when you're giddy or when you're drunk. Anyway I feel better and my headaches are not nearly so bad. I feel the cold more, and (what is quite natural) I've had chilblains on my ears. In the past I never suffered from chilblains, not even as a child; in this I was different from my brothers who on certain days, as I well remember, had their hands and feet scratched raw and bloody. That's a complete report on my state of health.

I embrace you tenderly.

Antonio

163

Turi Prison, 16 January 1933

Darling Julca,

For a while now I've had no letter from you (the last was dated 2 December). The day before yesterday I had a talk with Tania who came to pay me a visit; it was the first time we'd seen each other for two and a half years. As you can imagine it made me very happy, and broke the terrible monotony of my life.

In the last few days I've read a few extracts from a diary kept by Cesare Lombroso when he was a boy; I chanced on a few points which bear on what you wrote about Giuliano and his habit of looking at himself in the mirror. Lombroso writes: 'I remember very well the time when I first saw myself in the mirror and *became aware of my presence* – it awoke the liveliest curiosity in me. I was between four and six years of age.'

Lombroso makes a distinction between the period of his childhood when he became aware of his physical existence as a person, and the period during adolescence when he became properly aware of his individual personality (at sixteen). It seems to me that the distinction is a just one and has its importance. Don't you think that in Giuliano's case it may well be a case of something similar? What I mean is that he may have started to think about his existence and his personality in a more concrete manner, and therefore feels impelled to look in the mirror every now and again, almost as if to assure himself that he's still the same – or possibly to see whether something about him mayn't perhaps have changed.

Haven't you ever noticed that grown-ups don't seem to remember what it was like to be a child, and consequently have a tough job understanding the child's way of thinking; they often fail to comprehend the reactions of the children with whom they have to deal. That's why they sometimes just can't manage to make sense of the ideas or attitudes of their children. Quite possibly another complicating factor is the difference between the sexes; I mean, a mother may not understand boys as well as she does girls and vice versa. Write me a few lines on this subject; it really interests me a great deal.

Darling Julca,

I embrace you tightly – ever so tightly.

Antonio

164

Turi Prison, 16 January 1933

Darling Delio and Giuliano,

You haven't written to me any more for such a long time. Why is that? I haven't heard anything more about Delio's pets – his chaffinch and his goldfish. And another thing: has Delio received the book about Pinocchio? Did he like the illustrations? Are they like the picture he had in his head of what the puppet was like? And does Giuliano like the story of Pinocchio? What are you both most interested in just now, at school and at home? Write and tell me all sorts of things, both of you.

Lots of hugs and big kisses.

Antonio

165

Turi Prison, 30 January 1933

Dearest Tania,

I've received the postcards you sent me from Bari and Naples. I hope that by now you'll have had a good rest after your journey, and have got back by now to your normal routine.

I was amused to see that in your card of the 24th you tell me 'to keep in good spirits', as if it were your prescription for the cure of enterocolitis ... In any case, you're quite right. The only remedy is to contrast one's own fate with a fate that's even worse, and console oneself with the thought of the relativity of human fortunes.

When I was eight or nine I had an experience which came back clearly into my mind as I read your advice. I knew a family – father, mother and children – in a village near my own: they were small farmers and kept a dairy. An energetic crowd, especially the woman. I knew (or rather I had heard it said) that apart from her known children, whom everybody knew, this woman had another son whom nobody ever saw, and about whom people used to talk in sighs and whispers: it was said he was a great misfortune for his mother – an idiot, a monster or something lower still. I can still remember how often my mother used to refer to this woman as a martyr, saying how great were the sacrifices she made for this son, and how cruel was the cross she had to bear.

One Sunday morning, about 10 o'clock, I was sent on an errand to this woman's house; I had to deliver some crochet work to her and collect the money. I arrived just as she was closing the house door; she was all togged up, being on her way to High Mass, and she was carrying a bag under her arm. When she saw me she hesitated for a moment, and then made up her mind. She told me to come with her to where she was going, and said that when we came back she would take the crochet work and hand over the money. Our way took us out of the village, as far as a little kitchen garden all cluttered up with refuse and rubble; in one corner there was a sort of pigsty, about three-and-a-half feet high, without a window or a hatch of any kind but with one stout door in the front. She opened the door, and at once an animal-like grunting was heard; inside was her son, a great big lump of a boy, about 19 years of age. The roof was so low he couldn't stand upright, and so was forced to remain seated; when the door opened he shuffled forward on his backside – as far as the chain that was fixed round his middle and made fast to a ring in the wall, would let him. His skin was encrusted with filth, and his eyes were reddish, like the eyes of some nocturnal animal.

The mother emptied the contents of the bag into a stone trough; it was just the household leavings made into a sort of pig swill. Then after filling another trough with water she closed the door and we came away. I told my mother nothing of what I had seen, partly because I was so shocked by the whole thing, and partly because I was sure nobody would believe me. Not even when I heard the same old refrain about the sufferings of that poor mother did I put a different colour on things by telling my story and making known the wretched fate of that poor human derelict who had been landed with such a mother.

And yet look at it another way – what was the woman to do?

... As you see, it's possible to make comparisons, and so console oneself after the manner of *Candide*.

I embrace you tenderly.

Antonio

166

Turi Prison, 30 January 1933

Darling Julca,

I have received your letter – it's quite a long one. I was amused and pleased to hear that Giuliano proposed sending me the first little milk tooth he lost: I thought it showed in a positive sort of way that he feels a real tie between himself and myself. Maybe it would have been better if you'd actually sent me the tooth, so that the thing would have been imprinted on his memory.

The news you send me of the children interests me enormously. I don't know if my own comments are always adequate; perhaps not, for in spite of all the efforts I make, my opinions are bound to be one-sided.

Tania has transcribed one of your letters to her. It seems to me that when you write to me, you avoid telling me a lot of things, maybe for fear of making me sad, seeing I'm in prison. I think you ought to persuade yourself you can be perfectly frank with me and need hide nothing; why shouldn't there be the maximum confidence between us about everything? Don't you agree that not knowing things is bound to be worse, seeing that it's easy for a man to suspect that something is being hidden? Which results in one's never being sure whether the attitude one has adopted is the correct one.

Dear Julca, you really must write to me about yourself and about your state of health as fully and frankly as possible, never hesitating to say anything for fear of depressing me. The only thing which could possibly depress me would be the knowledge that you had thrown in the sponge and abandoned the fight to regain your health: and that you won't do, I'm sure. The future may still be dark, but that's no reason for slackening one's grip. I have been through many nasty moments; many and many's the time I have felt physically weak and nearly worn out; but I have never yielded to physical weakness, and, in so far as it's possible to say these things, I don't think I shall ever yield to it, either now or in the future. Even so there's not much I can do to help myself. Whenever I realise that more unpleasant moments lie ahead of me – whenever I feel weak, and see the difficulties piling up – all the more do I screw myself up to a point at which every ounce of willpower is brought into play.

Sometimes I review these past years. When I think of all that has happened, I realise that if six years ago I had been given a preview of all that I have in fact gone through, I'd never have believed it possible; I would have felt sure that I'd be bound to crack up completely sooner rather than later. It's exactly six years since I passed through – guess where! – Ravisindoli in the Abruzzi,[1] which you've occasionally mentioned because you once went there for your summer holidays. The transport provided was a railway prison truck with metal walls, roof and seats, that had stood all night in the snow; I had neither an overcoat nor a woollen shirt, and I couldn't even move because it was necessary to stay seated owing to the lack of space. I trembled all over as if I had a fever, and my teeth chattered in my head; I honestly felt I'd never manage to survive that journey to the end, I thought my heart would turn into an icicle. And yet six years have passed from that day to this, and I *did* manage to chase that glacier cold from my back. Though it's true that occasionally I have recurrences of those shivering fits – a few got into my bones and stayed there – I laugh now when I remember what my thoughts were at that time; the thing seems child's play to me now.

In short, your letter to Tania was too melancholy and gloomy for my liking. I believe that you, like me, are much stronger than you actually think, and that therefore you ought to steel yourself and move every muscle to overcome the crisis you have been going through, and emerge once and for all as victor.

My darling, I'd like to help you, but often I think that because in days gone by I didn't know exactly how you were, I may just have helped to make you more desperate. Write to me often; make a real effort and write to me more often. Make Delio and Giuliano write to me too.

I've read a letter from Genia to Tania about Delio which to tell you the truth didn't much appeal to me. After having read this letter I don't feel that what you write about Delio's schoolmistress and the mistakes she has made in sizing him up is really very convincing. It seems to me that

Delio is living in an ideological atmosphere which is somewhat too soft and byzantine – an atmosphere which doesn't help him to be energetic. On the contrary it must tend to enervate and weaken him. I'd like to write out some other story about animals for Delio, but I'm afraid of repeating something I've written before; nowadays I forget things very easily.

I embrace you tightly, ever so tightly, my darling.

Antonio

1. When he was transferred from Ustica to Milan (January–February 1927).

167

Turi Prison, 14 March 1933

Dearest Tania,

Just a few lines. In the early morning of last Tuesday, while I was getting out of bed, I fell to the ground and couldn't get up again by myself. These last few days I have been in bed all the time, and have been feeling very weak. The first day I was in a sort of state of hallucination, if that's the right way to express it, and I couldn't connect ideas with other ideas, or ideas with the appropriate words. I'm still weak, but less so than that day.

Please come to visit me as soon as you can get permission.

I embrace you tenderly.

Antonio

[The visit from an outside doctor requested by Tatiana in September 1932 – see letters 119 and 149 – took place on 20 March 1933. After giving Gramsci a thorough examination, Professor Arcangeli wrote and signed the following statement:

Antonio Gramsci, prisoner at Turi, is suffering from Pott's Disease; he has tubercular lesions in the upper lobe of the right lung which have caused two discharges of blood; one of these discharges was copious, and accompanied by fever lasting several days. He is also suffering from arterio-sclerosis, with hypertension of the arteries. He has suffered collapses, with loss of consciousness and partial aphasia lasting several days. Since October 1932 he has lost 7 kilos (over a stone) in weight; he suffers from insomnia and is unable to write as he used to. Gramsci cannot survive long under present conditions. I consider his transfer to a hospital or clinic to be necessary: that is, if it is not considered possible to grant him conditional liberty.

Another eight months was to elapse before action was taken on these recommendations.]

168

Turi Prison, 3 April 1933

Dearest Tania,

I've received a letter of yours dated 27 March, and a postcard of the 30th. I'm very glad the journey didn't fatigue you. My condition is the same as before, with continual ups and downs. I'm still very weak. The only objective fact I can give you is my temperature. Last night I felt a bit worse than usual, and so I wanted them to take my temperature etc. Towards 2 in the morning I felt a certain cardiac insufficiency, together with tightness (not pangs or palpitations, but as if the heart were being grasped inside a hand) and cold shivers; my temperature was 96. Towards 6 in the morning my temperature was 97.3. I didn't get up until 11.30, because I felt weak and was a bit shivery about the arms and hands and the lower limbs. After I had been up for half an hour my temperature rose to 99.

As I have already told you, these symptoms are identical with those which I had in 1922, except that then it was summer time, and consequently at the hour when my temperature rose I was completely bathed in sweat, which made me very much weaker; that, of course, doesn't happen now. It's true though that at that time I was ten years younger, and had a reserve of nervous energy which has since been used up, or very nearly. I had occasional bouts of rage then which were quite ferocious (and that isn't just hyperbole, because I remember that some very nice people who came to visit me and keep me company told me later on that they had been afraid – knowing I was a Sardinian – that I might suddenly knife someone!!!).[1] Nowadays, on the other hand, I feel I've become a sort of jam or jelly.

I've received a letter from Carlo; I'd be very grateful if you'd write him a postcard telling him that I've received his note, and that there's absolutely no need for him to come to Turi.

It doesn't seem to me that Julca's letter refers to my letters: I don't know how you came to that conclusion.

I embrace you affectionately.

Antonio

Please write to the Bookshop and ask them to send me the little volume of Professor Michele Barbi which has appeared recently: *Dante – Vita, Opere, Fortuna* (published by G. C. Sansoni, Florence, 1933). I can't resist the temptation to have this book, even though I probably won't be in a fit state to study it for some months.

1. This was the period when at the suggestion of Zinoviev he was admitted to the Serebranyi Bor (Silver Wood) sanatorium, on the outskirts of Moscow. Gramsci remained in the sanatorium for six months and only left it to attend the 4th Congress of the Comintern in November 1922. He was still ill, and (in his own words) 'found work impossible because of insomnia and amnesia'. See Giuseppe Fiori, *Antonio Gramsci: Life of a Revolutionary*, trans. Tom Nairn, NLB, London, 1970, Chapter 16.

169

Turi Prison, 3 April 1933

Dearest Teresina,

I've received your letter of 26 March. Before I forget, I'd better ask you to give mamma heartiest Easter greetings from me.[1] This year I forgot to send greetings to her on her *onomastico*,[2] and I'm really very sorry about this.

Don't imagine that I've lost one jot or tittle of my serenity (as you call it) even for a single instant. At the very most, when I feel myself physically weak, I lose the desire to occupy myself with anything but my own precious body; it's like when you've got to make a big effort to lift a weight – you grit your teeth and don't talk, for fear of wasting your energy on something other than the job on hand. More or less everybody, at one time or another, has found himself (or will find himself) in similar circumstances.

I think you ought to explain all this to Mea, to show her she mustn't lose heart but must continue studying in every way possible. She may lose a year or two (if the worst comes to the worst) as far as actual time is concerned, but it won't be a complete loss if every day she works to extend the horizon of her knowledge and the scope of her intellectual interests. To tell you the truth, I honestly can't visualise what point she has reached in her studies, because nobody has written to me about this for such a long time.

I embrace you together with everyone at home.

A big hug and kiss for mamma.

Antonio

I received a note from Carlo.

1. Peppina Marcias, Gramsci's mother, had died on 30 December the previous year, but the news had not been broken to him. It was felt – by Tatiana, as well as by the family in Sardinia – that in his state of health he might be unable to stand the shock. The only surviving letter written by Gramsci in 1934 is to his dead mother; it is included in the inclusive (1965) edition of the letters, ed. Caprioglio and Fubini.
2. 'Name-day', i.e. day of the Saint whose name one bears. Peppina's *onomastico* was St Joseph's day (19 March).

170

Turi Prison, 10 April 1933

Dearest Tania,

I've received your letter of the 4th, together with Delio's note and the picture postcard. You were quite right, I think, to say in your letter that I was a bit better. It isn't quite accurate that in my letter of a fortnight ago I said that my condition was worse; at any rate I didn't want to give that impression. I meant that my condition was (and still is) very variable, up one day and down the next: I would not say therefore that a relapse is out of the question, but that there has been none so far.

What is the meaning of 'worse' anyway? Worse than what? Not worse than the crisis of 7 March, that's certain; I can't picture what 'worse' could mean in that context. In point of actual fact the hallucinations have passed off completely, and the contraction and retraction of my limbs – of my legs and feet in particular – has lessened. My hands are still very painful, and I can't do anything with them, or lift any weight – even the lightest. If I try, as an experiment, to do something that demands a slight effort, I once again lose control of my movements: my hands and arms start twitching and jerking spasmodically, because of contractions of the tendons. I'm afraid this will last for quite a time.

It's true that in his little note Delio shows great sureness in forming the letters and in the way he expresses himself. His writing is simple and straightforward: as far as I can see there's only one mistake (he's left out the 'i' in *primula*[1]). I say this because in 1916 I gave Italian lessons to a boy who was in his third year at a secondary school, and I never managed to get him to write down even a simple little sketch a few lines long like this of Delio's.

How in the world did it come into your head to send off that book about Hegel[2] to Giulia? If I remember rightly, it was in 1930 that I mentioned it; at that time there was a controversy about the dialectic – but what purpose could it serve today? It'll likely seem very odd to Giulia.

I embrace you affectionately.

Antonio

1. primrose.
2. Croce's 'Essay on Hegel'.

171

10 April 1933

Dearest Delio,

I've received your letter of 28 March, with news of the goldfish, the rose and the primrose, the beans and the lions. But what sort of lions were those ones you saw? African lions, or lions from Turkestan? Did they have manes, or was the hair round their necks short and smooth? And were the bears like the ones you saw in Rome? You haven't told me yet whether you received the book about Pinocchio, and whether Giuliano liked hearing about the adventures of the famous puppet. I'd like to read the story about the white seal, the mongoose, Rikki-Tikki-Tavi and the boy Mowgli who was brought up by wolves; I think you would, too. In 1922 the State Library[1] was preparing a lovely edition with new illustrations, which I happened to see while the lithograph workers were transferring them to the stone. Ask mamma and Genia[2] if this edition is still available; if it isn't I'll send you the book in Italian or in French.

Kisses to you and to Giuliano.

Antonio

1. In Moscow.
2. Eugenie, Giulia's eldest sister.

172

Turi Prison, 10 April 1933

Darling Julca,

Tania writes that she has sent you in my name a book of a modern Italian philosopher which is a critique of Hegel's philosophy; she wants to know if the book has reached you. I had asked Tania some years ago to send you this book (of which I had two copies); it was at the time when there was a philosophical controversy in the press about the value and significance of the dialectic. It seemed to me then that you might be interested in the Italian philosopher's formulation of the problem; and especially the way in which he tackled the question of the 'distinct' as against the 'opposed'. I'm not sure if this will still interest you – and indeed whether you have as yet received the book which, it seems, Tania did not put in the post until quite recently.

I embrace you tenderly.

Antonio

173

Turi Prison, 17 July 1933

Dearest Tania,

After your postcard of the 11th I have had no more news of you. I hope the journey didn't tire you too much; the last time I saw you, I thought you didn't look as well as you did the previous time. I don't know what to write to you. Up to two days ago I thought I was getting some benefit from the Elastina, and from the fact that at night, even though I can't as yet manage to sleep, I'm at any rate less agitated. But it's all very precarious; yesterday and today I have been feeling as if my hands were full of needles, and if I want to write I've got to form single letters, because my hands are always jerking involuntarily. Even so I think I'm on the upgrade.

They've handed over Giuliano's note; it was written by Giulia really – the child only wrote the heading.

Dearest Tania, I embrace you affectionately.

Antonio

174

Turi Prison, 24 July 1933

Dearest Tania,

I've received your letter of the 20th, together with the letter from Giulia. I think I can say (although you know how fallible such statements are) that I am keeping a bit better. The change of cell[1] and therefore of a few of the external conditions affecting me, did help – in the sense that now at any rate I'm able to sleep. Or at least the conditions which used to prevent me from sleeping even when I felt sleepy and made me wake up abruptly, thus causing violent agitation and excitement – those conditions are a thing of the past. I don't manage as yet to sleep with any regularity, but I *could* sleep, and that's the main thing; in any case, even when I don't sleep I'm not in too excited a state. I think there's ground for satisfaction, allowing for the fact that a shattered organism certainly can't get back to normal all of a sudden; besides, the high blood pressure I am suffering from at present must in itself cause a certain amount of insomnia ...

In a few days' time I am starting on a course of injections; the basis of it is strychnine and phosphorus. The new doctor who has examined me assures me that it will help me a lot. He tells me that it is nervous exhaustion and not any organic complaint which is at the root of my trouble. Apparently I am in need also of psychotherapy. In so far as I can judge, this seems quite likely. I don't know if it's correct to say that arterio-sclerosis is a functional and not an organic phenomenon. My hands are very painful all the time, and I can't even lift the lightest of weights or press with any energy.

On the psychotherapy side I can't say anything very precise. It's quite true that for many months I've been living without any hope for the future, seeing that I wasn't cured and could see no way of escape from the process of gradual wasting away which was consuming me. I can't say that this state of mind is a thing of the past, or that I've managed to persuade myself that I'm no longer in an extremely precarious condition; however I think I can say that this state of mind no longer obsesses me as it did in the past. Now that I'm better, the people who were with me when I was at the critical point of my illness tell me that even in the moments of delirium there was a certain lucidity in my wanderings (which were interspersed with long tirades in Sardinian dialect). The lucidity consisted in this – that, being sure I was going to die, I tried to demonstrate the uselessness of religion, and its inanity, and I was worried lest the priest should take advantage of my weakness and should make me carry out (or carry out for me) certain ceremonies which were repugnant to me, and against which I couldn't see any way of defending myself. It seems that for an entire night I spoke of the immortality of the soul in a realistic and historically-minded sort of way, describing it as a necessary survival of our useful, our necessary actions, and the incorporation of these into the universal historic process, irrespective of our own personal desires. Listening to me was a worker from Grosseto who was dropping with sleep, and who I'm sure thought I was going mad – an opinion shared by the duty warder. In spite of this he remembered the principal points of my harangues, points which I kept on repeating over and over again.

Darling Tania, as you can see, the very fact that I have written these things shows that I am feeling a bit better ...

I embrace you tenderly.

Antonio

1. He had been transferred to a quieter cell on the ground floor.

175

Turi Prison, 1 August 1933

Darling Julca,

There are three letters of yours to which I ought to reply. I have also received three photographs of Giuliano. I don't feel capable of writing at length or in a connected way. There are some points in your letters which have reference to subjects brought up a good while ago, and I don't remember exactly what it was all about. My memory is not very good now. So I'll just write a few lines in order to resume our correspondence – I wish it could be more coordinated.

I'm really very glad that Delio has gone off camping with his fellow pupils; I think he'll soon become independent-minded and get liberated from unwholesome tendencies – the sort which are effeminate in a deleterious sense. I was also much interested in what you wrote about Giuliano, and his way of reproducing the impressions he's received when looking at wild flowers in the country. But don't you think it's a little premature to draw definite conclusions about his leanings from such modest data? Can one really say much about the inclinations of a little boy when he is still in the very first stages of his development? I would say that this way of judging things betrays a fair-sized dose of that mechanistic approach which is characteristic of some school teachers; a good deal too, of – how shall I put it? – bogus science and pedantry. Nevertheless it's very interesting that the schoolmistress does make these observations and attempts to coordinate them. The really important thing is that such data should not be too scanty and disconnected; if they are, they may tempt her to give an artificial importance to motifs which are superficial and the reverse of well-founded.

My darling, I embrace you tenderly.

Antonio

176

Turi Prison, 8 August 1933

Darling Julca,

I ought to write to Delio in reply to the note he sent me some time ago. Could you tell him yourself that he'll get two books sent to him shortly: the *Jungle Book*, which includes the stories about the White Seal and Rikki Tikki Tavi, and *Uncle Tom's Cabin*. I'd be interested to know how Delio got it into his head that he'd like to read the latter? And I wonder if, when he's read it, someone will explain it to him from an historical point of view, and help him to place the sentiments and the religiosity with which the book is saturated in their right context in time and space. This must be an awfully difficult thing to do for a child (to do seriously of course, and not just making use of well-worn generalities and commonplaces). I really doubt if you are very well equipped to do it yourself. What you say about *War and Peace* and Leonardo's *Last Supper* doesn't incline me to think that you are!

I'm not in a condition to write down coherently and logically what I feel about this subject. In general, though, it seems to me that you put yourself in the position of a subaltern and not of a commander (not only in this matter but in others too). What I mean is that the position you adopt is not that of a person who can criticise the ideologies from an historical point of view, dominating them, explaining them, and justifying them as an historic necessity of the past. It is rather that of a person who when put in contact with a particular world of sentiments and ideas may feel himself either attracted or repelled, but will always remain in the sphere of sentiment and immediate passion. That's maybe why music no longer has the attraction it once had for you. My own feeling is that we should experience a catharsis, as the Greeks used to say, by virtue of which sentiments are recreated 'artistically' as beauty, and are no longer felt as passion which is still at work in us, and in which we participate. No doubt this calls for explanation at much greater length, but I think that even these few notes ought to give you an idea of what I'm driving at.

I embrace you tenderly.

Antonio

177

Turi Prison, 23 August 1933

Dearest Tania,

I've received the postcard that you sent from Bari on the 19th. I hope the journey to Rome didn't tire you too much. Here are one or two things I'd like you to do for me:
1. Ask the bookshop to send me Professor Giorgio Mortara's *Economic Perspectives for 1933*, and the volume published by the Commercial Bank on the fluctuations of the Italian economic situation. It must have been published by now.
2. I'd be very glad to have the report delivered a few months ago by Azzolini, the Governor of the Bank of Italy; this year it's particularly important.
3. I'd also like to have the following little work: Santino Caramella, *Il Senso Comune, Teoria e Pratica*, published by Laterza of Bari.
I embrace you tenderly.

Antonio

[On 18 November 1933, Gramsci was informed that he would be leaving the following day for the prison at Civitavecchia, en route for his final destination, the clinic of Dr Giuseppe Cusumano at Formia. Gustavo Trombetti, his cell companion, succeeded in stowing away the 18 manuscript prison notebooks among the other effects in his trunk, while Gramsci himself 'kept the warder talking'.

After three weeks in the prison sick-bay at Civitavecchia, he was sent on to Formia, getting there on 7 December. In this clinic he was subject to grotesquely strict police surveillance; bars were put up outside the window of his room, and carabinieri were on permanent guard there.

A committee had been formed in Paris to draw the attention of the world to Gramsci's plight – Romain Rolland and Henri Barbusse were both members of it – and (partly, at least) as a result of their efforts Gramsci was granted 'provisional liberty' on 25 October 1934. This changed little in his life, however, apart from the fact that the guard was taken away from his room. By that time he was far too weak to derive any real benefit from the 'concession'.]

178

8 April 1935

Dear Delio,

I've received your letter, and I've also had news about how you are getting on at school. Did you like the stories about Mowgli? My life here[1] is a bit monotonous, but it's doing my health quite a lot of good. How sorry I am not to be close to my dear boys, and not to be able to help them with their school work and help them forward on their journey in life.

I saw the result of the chess championship in the newspapers, but chess is a game I've never learnt to play: the only game I can play a bit is draughts.

Kisses.

Your papa[2] Gramsci

1. In the clinic at Formia.
2. Written in Russian.
   [In August 1935 Gramsci was allowed to move to the Quisisana clinic in Rome.]

179

25 November 1935

Darling,

I've received your two letters. I'm calmer now than when I started writing to you again,[1] even though writing is very wearisome to me, and leaves me for a matter of hours (or even for a matter of days) in a condition of excitability which is very trying.

Tania has passed on to me something of what you've been talking about in your letters, and other news she has received. She has told me, with great amusement, that Delio thought it would be a good thing to rub vaseline on an elephant – probably because he had felt its rough hide with his fingers. I don't think there's anything strange about a boy wanting to rub vaseline on an elephant, although I don't think any such idea occurred to me when I was a boy. She has also told me that Julik wants to be given all possible information about me: I think this is because he saw a picture of me in a Park of Culture.[2]

My darling, when I think of all these things, and remember that for so many years (for almost a quarter of my life, and for more than a quarter of yours) your world has been so completely cut off from my own, I don't feel very happy. Even so, we must resist, we must hold fast; we must try and regain our strength. In any case what has happened was in no sense unforeseeable; you who remember so many things out of the past, do you remember that time when I said to you that I was 'going into battle'? Maybe it wasn't said very seriously on my part, but it was true, and I did actually feel like that. And I loved you very very deeply. Be strong then, and do all you can to get better.

I embrace you tenderly, together with our boys.

Antonio

1. For a long period he had written no letters to his wife.
2. A large photograph of Gramsci had been exhibited in one of the principal streets of Moscow, together with pictures of other anti-fascist leaders imprisoned in various countries.

180

25 January 1936

Dear Julca,

Your note puts me in a terribly embarrassing position. I've not yet properly decided whether I ought to write or not. It seems to me that the very fact that I am writing to you will exercise a certain coercion on your will; and although on the one hand the thought of bringing any compulsion to bear upon you, even in what is surely an indirect and innocent manner, is profoundly repugnant to me, on the other hand I can't help wondering (in the cold light of reason) whether in matters such as these compulsion mayn't sometimes be necessary, and perhaps even beneficial. Actually I have been in this sort of position for many years, probably right from 1926; from that period, immediately after my arrest, when my life – brusquely, and with no small brutality – was wrenched away in a new direction dictated by external forces, and the boundaries of my liberty shrank until they enclosed only my own inner life. From that time onwards my will was nothing but the will to resist.

However, I don't want to get too far away from the question which interests us at present – and which certainly interests you too, even though you make no mention of it in the letter – I mean your trip. A trip to Italy, that is, and for any length of time, long or short, which you care to fix; a trip which doesn't commit you to anything, and the principal object of which would be to help you recover and maintain the strength you need for a normal and fully active life. I think it's necessary that you should convince yourself, reasonably and rationally, that this trip is necessary, not only for your own sake but for the sake of the boys as well (seeing that their future, as things stand at present, is dependent on you, and on your own ability to work). And for other reasons too. But if you are to convince yourself of this, the journey must be seen in its proper perspective: as a practical matter, stripped of all unwholesome sentimentality, as an action which will leave you free – yes, maybe free you once and for all from a whole heap of thoughts, of preoccupations, of repressed feelings and I don't know what all in the way of old junk which still obsesses you, and which you need to jettison. I am your friend, to go to the heart of it, and I really need to speak to you as one friend to another, with absolute frankness and open-mindedness.

For ten years now I have been cut off from the world. What a terrible feeling I had, after six years of looking at nothing but the same roofs, the same walls, the same grim faces, when I saw from the train[1] that all the time the vast world had continued to exist, with its meadows, its woods, its ordinary people, its gangs of little boys, certain trees, certain gardens ... and above all what a shock I got on seeing myself in a mirror again after all that time; I at once turned away and went back among the carabinieri ... Don't think I'm writing this just to move you; what I'm getting at is that after such a long time, after so many things that have happened (and the real meaning of many of these may well have given me the slip); after so many years of a life which was mean and cramped, and swaddled in darkness and shabby miseries: after all this it would do me good to be able to speak to you as one friend to another. If I say this you mustn't feel that some awful responsibility is weighing on you; all I'm thinking of is ordinary conversation, the kind one normally has between friends.

Well then: I am perfectly certain that from every point of view this trip would have excellent consequences for the two of us. I am considerably altered, or so I believe, and you yourself will no longer be the same as you were in the old days. Don't worry about the practical problems; I think these can be solved ... I am sure that the project has more positive than negative sides to it, and I can't help wondering now why in the world I didn't think of all this sooner. (The trouble is that I've been all wound up in myself like a silkworm in its cocoon, and I haven't managed to unwind myself even yet.) I'd like you to consider the thing in a quiet, practical, down-to-earth way; and furthermore I want you to be the one to decide, to decide coolly and calmly, not letting yourself be influenced by anyone – not even by me. Do you think that the boys would be unhappy about your coming to visit me, if they knew that I myself couldn't move for reasons of *force majeure*?

Your note opens with a phrase that looks as if it's by D'Annunzio: that doesn't appeal to me much. And there are also words which aren't completed. You must have been feeling rather agitated. Maybe what you were needing was a caress of mine to calm you and bring you rest.

I embrace you.

Antonio

1. i.e. when he was being transferred from Turi prison to Civitavecchia, 19 November 1933.

181

25 January 1936

Darling Julik,

I send you lots and lots of good wishes for success during the rest of the school year. I'd be very pleased if you told me what the difficulties are which you encounter in your school-work. I should think that if you yourself admit having difficulties they can't be terribly big ones, and you'll be able to overcome them. Do you get enough time for study? Maybe you're a bit scatterbrained – you can't pay attention and your memory doesn't work – or you can't make it work! Do you sleep all right? When you're out playing do you think of what you've been studying or is it the other way round? You're a big boy now, so you ought to be able to give me the right answers to these questions. At your age I was pretty disorganised myself; I used to take off and roam around for hours and hours in the fields. In spite of that I was pretty good at my school-work too, because I had a good and quick memory, and I didn't forget anything that was necessary for my school-work – though to tell you the truth (the whole truth) I ought to add that I was cute, and fly enough to get by even when the lesson was difficult and I hadn't prepared it. However, the school system on the island where I spent my childhood was much behind the times; in addition, nearly all my fellow pupils spoke very stumbling and broken Italian,[1] and this gave me a big lead because the schoolmaster couldn't go faster than the class average permitted. So being able to speak fluent

Italian was an advantage which made a great number of things easier (the school was in a village out in the country, and the vast majority of the children were of peasant stock).

Darling Julik, I'm sure you'll write to me regularly and keep me well posted about how you are getting on.

Lots of kisses.

Your Papa[2]

1. The Sardinian 'dialect', their mother tongue, is really a language, and is as different from Italian as Catalan is from Spanish.
2. Here, and in most of the other letters written to the children, 'Papa' and 'Your Papa' are in Russian.

182

6 May 1936[1]

Darling Julca,

I've read your letter over and over again. It's as if I hadn't read a letter of yours for many years, and had started off again with this one.

I have been taking a good long look at the photograph of Julik. I am very pleased with our little boy, and the way he has posed for this picture, but it seems to me he's much changed from the picture I had of him in my mind. I am looking forward to the photo you promise me.

I don't know what to write to you, after having read your letter; maybe there's nothing that I could write or too much ... and all broken and crumbled into a chaos of impressions and memories.

I embrace you tenderly.

Antonio

1. According to Caprioglio and Fubini, this letter was written in July 1933 (i.e. while Gramsci was still at Turi).

183

July 1936

Darling Delio,

I am very glad to know that you weren't offended by anything I've written in my letters. (I've been told that about that time you weren't very well, but I don't know any of the details.) You're right in thinking that no one should be offended when he's told things that are true in a proper tone.

I think I understand now why it was I didn't say anything about the argument you had with the schoolmistress about the works of Chekhov. I think it was because the question, as you outlined it, was too dogmatic for my liking; it was very much the sort of theory which certain people used to stuff their pockets with (to use Engels' expression), thinking that in this way they could dodge having to study history concretely.

But you're only twelve, Delio, and I don't imagine you've got your pockets stuffed full of scholastic dogmas. Anyway you've got all the time in the world to empty your pockets and get your brain well stocked with ideas.

However I don't want to have a discussion with you just now, because I've got an awful headache. All I am thinking of is that you are twelve years old and, although I haven't seen a new photo of you for a long time, I imagine that you've grown a lot and look very, very serious (in front of the photographer, that is).

I've sent you a watch. Are you pleased? Your memory plays tricks on you sometimes, but it doesn't matter. It'll be difficult to find a celluloid ball with a swan inside; the one I had I'd brought from ... Milan.

Lots of kisses.

184

16 July[1] 1936

Dear Delio,

Your little letters are becoming shorter and shorter, and you always say the same thing. I should imagine you've enough time to spare to write longer and more interesting letters; there's no need to wait till the last minute, and then just do a rush job before going out for a walk. Don't you agree? I'm sure you wouldn't like it if your daddy judged you from your letters to be just a silly little juggins whose main interest is his parrot, and who has no more to say than that he's reading some book or other. I think that one of the most difficult things of all at your age is to sit down at a table and get one's thoughts in order (or do a bit of real thinking), and then set the results down neatly, and with a bit of style.

That's an 'apprenticeship' that can be more difficult than that of a young worker whose aim is to get qualified in his trade – and who therefore has to start serving his apprenticeship just about your age.

Lots of kisses.

Papa

1. This should be June, according to Caprioglio and Fubini.

185

Summer 1936

Dear Giulia,

I find it more and more difficult to write to you, but Tatiana insists on my sending you at least a few lines; also she wants me to ask you for detailed information about the reasons which led you to send Julik to a special school. So there's the job done. Actually I had written quite a long letter, but I broke off because on rereading it my own words filled me with repugnance. I'm not sure if I'll send the letters to Julik and Delio. Today the sun has been very strong, and it's been terribly hot; maybe it's because of that that I feel off-colour.

Do please send me the news about Julik, and don't be too put out by my quirks and cranks.

I embrace you.

Antonio

186

August 1936

Dear Delio,

Many congratulations on your recovery. You've never told me if you liked the watch or not. I hope that now you'll write me longer letters, and let me share in everything that interests you.

Kisses from your

Papa

187

November 1936

Darling Delio,

Write to me about Pushkin whenever you like. Remember to think it over carefully beforehand, so you can give me proof positive of your ability to think, to reason and to criticise (that is, to distinguish the true from the false, and the certain from the possible or the probable). But don't get too worried about it: I know how old you are, and the stage you've reached, so I'll be able to judge objectively (even though I love you very, very much indeed, and therefore it's rather difficult to be objective).

It'll be difficult to find the books on Pushkin and Gogol; but in any case what use would they be to you? They're old and out of date; nowadays there's a whole fresh literature on the two writers, a new criticism which has been developed on the basis of discoveries made in the archives open to the young and go-ahead Soviet philology.

I am so glad that you are well, and that you don't get too tired studying. Dear Delio, I embrace you – see and give your mamma a hug for me.

Papa

188

24 November 1936

Darling Julca,

To make you laugh, I'd really like to write a proper schoolmasterly letter, full of pedantry from top to bottom, but I don't know if I'll succeed. More often than not I'm a pedant without meaning to be; I've developed a particular style under the pressure of events, in these ten years of multiple censorings.

I'd like to tell you of a little 'episode' to make you laugh, and help you to understand what I'm getting at. Once when Delio was little, you wrote me a very attractive letter in which you told me how the little chap made his debut in the study of geography and 'direction finding'; you described him lying in bed with his head to the north and his feet to the south, and saying that in the direction of his head there were people who got dogs to pull them along in sledges; on his left was China, on his right Austria, in the direction of his legs the Crimea, and so on.

Now in order to get this letter I had to argue for more than an hour with the prison governor, who suspected that all this was some elaborate kind of super cunning code. And I had to argue, of course, without having read a single word, and trying all the time, from the questions he was putting, to guess what you had written and what on earth you meant by it.

'What's all this about 'Cathay', and how does Austria come into it?'

'The men who make dogs pull their sledges – what does that stand for?'

It was a formidable job to give a plausible explanation without having read the letter, and I don't think I would have been able to pull it off if at a certain point I hadn't lost my patience and demanded: 'But haven't you got a wife yourself? And don't you understand what a mother is likely to write when she wants to send news of a child to a father who's far away?'

When he heard this, he handed the letter over to me without further delay; as it happened, he had a wife, but no children.

The whole thing's laughable really, but it has its significance for all that; I 'knew' that he would be reading my own letters with the same acrimonious and distrustful pedantry he showed when reading yours, and this forced me to adopt a 'prison' style of writing – a style from which I doubt if I'll ever manage to free myself now, after so many years 'constriction'.

I could tell you of other episodes, other things like this, but there's no point, just in the hope of making you laugh, in hanging out a lot of threadbare miseries on the line. I'd probably overstep the mark and merely depress you.

Your letter cheered me up: I would say it's a long time since you wrote with such lightness of touch – and with such a complete ... absence of mistakes. My dear, what about setting to work and writing me a long letter about the children,[1] without bothering to be objective ... By the way, I would say that the following aphorism of yours: 'To write a report (!?) on the children's lives is to take their lives to pieces', is a grandiose piece of nonsense, if ever there was one ... No reports then (I'm no chief constable) but just your 'subjective' impressions.

My darling, I'm so isolated that your letters are like bread for the starving (that's not pedantic, now, is it?). So why do you measure the ration so cannily? ...

Dear Julca, I embrace you tenderly.

Antonio

1. 'Children' is in Russian.

189

24 November 1936

Dear Julik,

I was pleased to see, from your letter, that you're writing better. Your writing is like a big boy's now. Why did you like the film *The Sons of Captain Grant*? You ought to write me a longer letter, describing your life, telling me what you're thinking about, what books you like and so on.

I'm glad you were pleased with the watch; you needn't be afraid to wear it outside as well as indoors. If it's well strapped on to your wrist you can't lose it – unless of course you go in for something pretty energetic when you're out – like boxing for example. What games do you like best?

Dear Julik, I embrace you.

Papa

190

December 1936

Dear Julca,

Your letters always arouse great emotion in me, but ... (these damned buts ...) they leave me a bit confused, with my thoughts spinning around in a vacuum. You know I have a mania for concreteness, that I have great admiration for ... reports (*daklad*) when they're well put together, and descriptions like those written by the very reverend Jesuit fathers about China, which can teach us something even after the passage of several centuries. Dear Julca, my pedantry is really horrific; write as you please, because you always write well, with great spontaneity, and putting the whole of yourself into the letter....

I am very pleased with my sons, and with their last two letters. Julik is laconic, epigrammatic. No adjectives, no padding: his style is almost telegraphic. Delio is very different.

And you my dear – how are you? The picture I have of you in my mind isn't terribly clear, although I'm always thinking of times past. Send me photographs; they aren't much, but they help.

When I was in exile on Ustica, a Bedouin took a great fancy to me (he was in exile from his country too). He used to come and visit me; he would sit down, drink a cup of coffee, and tell me stories of the desert. Then he would be silent for hours, and watch me reading or writing. He envied me the photographs I had, and told me that his wife was so stupid that she would never think of sending him a photograph of their son. (He didn't know, by the way, that Mussulmans are forbidden to draw the human likeness, and he was by no means unintelligent.) You don't want to turn into a Bedouin's wife, now, do you?

My dear, I embrace you with love and tenderness.

Antonio

191

December 1936

Dear Delio,

I'm looking forward to your reply on the question of Pushkin – but take your time. Get organised and do your best. How are you and Julik doing at school? Now you have marks given you every month, it'll be easier to see how you're getting on in general. Thank you for giving mamma a tight, tight hug from me: I think you ought to give her one every day, every morning in my name. I am always thinking of you, so every morning I'll imagine you doing it and say: my sons and Giulia are thinking of me at this very moment. You're the elder brother, and you should tell Julik about the idea too: every day you could have 'Daddy's five minutes'. What do you think of the idea?

Kisses.

192

5 January 1937

Dear Julca,

My memory isn't very good either (in the sense that I forget things that have happened recently, whereas I often remember with great minuteness things that took place ten or fifteen years ago); even so I'm quite certain that what you write very often doesn't correspond to what I've written previously. But that isn't of great importance. The important thing is that you should write just whatever comes into your head ... lightly, spontaneously, without effort. I read your letters several times; the first few times I read them so to speak 'disinterestedly', in the way a man reads the letters of one he loves: my love for you is the only thing I think of, the only thing that matters. Then I reread them 'critically', trying to guess how you were the day when you wrote, etc.; another thing I look at is the handwriting, to see how sure and firm your hand is, etc. In short, I try to extract from your letters every indication and every meaning possible.

Do you think that this is pedantry? I don't think so. Maybe a bit of 'prison-itis' enters into it, but not the old, traditional pedantry – which in any case I would feel like defending bitterly against a certain superficial 'bohemian' slapdashery which has fathered many ills in the past, and still fathers as many. And will father others. Today I prefer *Infantry Section Leading*[1] to *Les Réfractaires*[2] of Vallès ... But maybe I'm wandering from the subject.

Actually you couldn't write better about the two boys than you do; my oft-repeated laments are really due to the fact that no other person's impression of my sons – not even yours, not even Julca's, although I feel you as a part of myself – can possibly be a substitute for the impression I would get if I saw them face to face. Don't you think you'd see something new and different in the boys if you could see them together with me? But in that case, the boys would themselves be different, don't you agree? Truly and 'objectively' different.

My dear, I'd like you to give your mother a big kiss from me, and lots of love and an infinity of good wishes and greetings for her birthday. I think you've always known that I experience great difficulty, very great difficulty in exteriorising my feelings, and that fact may explain many disagreeable things. In Italian literature you'll find it written somewhere that Sardinia is an island, and that every Sardinian is an island within an island. I remember a very comical article by a journalist on the *Giornale d'Italia* who in 1920 attempted to explain away my intellectual and political tendencies in these terms. But perhaps there is a bit of truth in it,[3] enough to add emphasis anyway (though of course to 'add emphasis' is saying a fair amount. However I don't want to start analysing the thing. Let me say 'to add grammatical emphasis' and you can have a good laugh over it, and admire my whimsical modesty).

My dear, I embrace you with the greatest tenderness.

Antonio

1. *Il Manuale del Caporale*. See letter 13 and note.
2. Jules Valls (1832–85). French author and journalist. Became a Communard and founded *Le Cri du Peuple*. *Les Réfractaires*, published in 1866, is a collection of articles about the déclassés of Paris, written in a rather flamboyant and extravagant style.
3. 'Sardinia also left its mark on Gramsci's personality and values. What could be more suitable for a future master of dialectics than the petty-bourgeois poverty of his origins? For at a very early age Gramsci was faced with basic contradictions – between his aspirations, and the near impossibility of realising them; between his enquiring mind and the age-old immobility of his surroundings. In the end his learning and achievements were profoundly Italian, but the impulse that had led to them was Sardinian.' (John M. Cammett, *Antonio Gramsci and the Origins of Italian Communism*', Stanford, California, 1967, pp. 12–13). Gramsci was also very definitely and consciously a 'Southerner' as opposed to a Northern Italian. In his penetrating study of Pirandello, Oscar Büdel has a passage which is very much to the point in this context:

In the short story 'Il Professore Terremoto', Pirandello himself refers to the penchant of the southern mind for a dialectical approach to the vicissitudes of life and to human experience in general. It is interesting, for the significance Pirandello may have attached to his notion, that the passage in question did not appear in the first printing of the story, but was inserted subsequently: 'They are so tormentingly dialectical, these good Southern brethren of ours. They drive the point of their drill of reason deep into their sorrow to reach to the very bottom, and they go and go and go at it without ever stopping. They are not doing this for the sake of some cold mental exercise, but, on the contrary, in order to gain a deeper and more complete consciousness of their pain. (Oscar Büdel, *Pirandello*, Bowes and Bowes, London, 1966, pp. 14–15)

193

23 January 1937

Dear Julca,

You know that I've never been much used to receiving birthday greetings, nor to sending them either. To tell you the truth they all seem to me (or seemed to me) silly conventionalities, but in the case of the children it has certainly never been a convention (nor has it been in your own case, darling). But I think I've caught you all out this time. Unless I'm much mistaken you imagined you ought to wish me Happy Birthday on the 12th. Actually I was born on the 22nd, and I want the birthday to be celebrated in my own way: this time I want (I really do *want*) a good photograph of yourself and the boys. A good photograph, of course, taken by a photographer; not just an amateur effort. I can't understand why you don't send me photos more often. Because of the expense? I don't believe it. For what other reason? More than ten years have passed since we last saw each other; why shouldn't we see each other more often in this way? For me the question is certainly very different, and I'm sure you understand why: first, I'd have to go through all the police routine – and there's no second.

Darling Julca, please, send me some beautiful photos of all of you, group photos, and individual ones too.

I embrace you, my dear.

Antonio

194

23 January 1937

Dear Julik,

Draw just as you like, just for fun – there's no sense in drawing 'seriously', as if you were doing a job you didn't like. All the same, I'd like to see one or two of the drawings you turn out in school hours! How do you do them? Seriously, or like the ones you do for fun?

I'm sure that at school everything is going well, but are you keeping healthy too? Do you run and play outside as well as doodling funny faces on your drawing paper?

Many thanks for your message of good wishes. Today I have a bad headache and I can't write you a long letter.

Kisses.

Papa

Who is teaching you to play the violin?

195[1]

But this little son of mine called Julik, why does he never write to me?

You know you did promise to write me something every holiday – and to send it off as well, of course!

How is it that a boy who is ten years old doesn't keep his promises?

Dear Julik, I'd like to hear from you about how you're keeping, and how you're settling down to your new life.

I embrace you tenderly.

Papa

1. Letters 195 to 219 were evidently sent as enclosures with letters to Giulia, and are not dated.

196

Dear Julik,

So you're free of the hostel, and are going off to camp. Will you go back to school?

Why do you write at the very last moment, while waiting for the car to arrive?

Here's a big birthday hug for you – and a little watch, which I'm sending in the hope that it'll make you think about time, and therefore ... not leave writing till the last moment.

Kisses.

Papa

197

Dear Julik,

I've had news of you in letters from mamma and granny. But why don't you write something yourself? I am very happy when I get a letter from you, and what a lot of things there are which you could write about – the school, your comrades, your teachers, the trees you see, your games etc. And then, unless I'm wrong ... you promised to write me something every day of your holidays. You ought always to keep your promises, even if it means some kind of sacrifice – and I shouldn't think that writing something is as big a sacrifice for you as all that. You promised to give the letters to mamma on the days when she visits you at school. Dear Julik, here's a big hug.

Papa

198

Long live Julik! I've received a photograph of you, and I was very happy to be able to see my little son.

You look as if you've grown a lot since that other photograph was taken – you're bigger, and you've changed too. You're a real big boy now.

Why don't you write to me any longer? I'm looking forward to a long letter from you.

Kisses.

Your Papa

199

Darling Julik,

At last you've written me a few lines. I send you all the very best for your birthday. You're a big boy already, and growing up to be a real soldier. Did you like the watch? Will you write and tell me how you're getting on now you're back at school? I am feeling rather tired, so I'm not able to write much, either to Delio or to yourself.

I embrace you.

Papa

200

Dear Julik,

I've received your new drawings with great enthusiasm: I can see you're full of fun, so I'm sure you're healthy. But tell me: can you do drawings that are not just done for amusement's sake? Or rather, can you draw funny drawings 'seriously'? You haven't told me whether or not they give you drawing lessons at school, and whether you like doing 'serious' drawing as well. When I was a boy I was very fond of drawing, but my drawings were only laborious exercises; nobody had ever taught me how to draw. I used to copy the illustrations in a children's newspaper,[1] and try to enlarge them. I also tried to reproduce the basic colours by means of a system of my own which wasn't difficult but which demanded a lot of patience.

I still remember a picture which cost me at least three months' work: a little peasant boy had fallen, fully dressed, into a vat full of grapes ready for pressing, and a little peasant girl (a nice, plump, chubby-cheeked little thing) was looking at him half alarmed and half amused. The picture was one of a series illustrating the adventures of a great big billy-goat called Barbabucco, who was a terror if ever there was one: he used to steal up behind his enemies and butt them hard when they were least expecting it – he made them fly through the air in all directions. This usually happened to boys who had been teasing him. The end of each adventure was always very funny – as in the picture I copied.

What fun I had when I was enlarging the picture. I would take measurements with tape and compass, do a preliminary draft in pencil, make corrections etc. My brothers and sisters would come and watch me, and laugh – but they preferred to run around kicking up a racket, so they left me to my labours.

Dear Julik, I send you lots of kisses.

Papa

1. *Il Corriere dei Piccoli.*

201[1]

Dear Julik,

You've seen the sea for the first time. Write and tell me what you thought about it. Did you get a good mouthful of salt water when you went in for a bathe? Have you learnt to swim? Did you catch any little fish or any crabs alive?

I've seen little boys catching small fish in the sea, using a hollow brick to scoop them up. They caught enough to fill a bucket.

I embrace you.

Your Papa Antonio

1. Probably written at the clinic in Formia.

202

Dear Julik,

I liked your drawings a great deal, because they're yours. They're also very original; I don't imagine nature has ever invented such astounding things as you have. The fourth drawing is of a really extraordinary animal; it can't be a beetle, because it's too big – and, indeed, like most animals, it's only got four legs. Yet what long legs they are! It can't be a horse, because it hasn't got any ears that I can see (the first animal you drew hadn't got ears either; neither had one of the men). Maybe it's a tame lion ... and a transparent lion at that, because you can see both the feet of the man riding him.

Another thing that tickles me is that your men can walk on tiptoe in the most unlikely places – at the end of the branch of a tree, and on the heads of the animals (can that be why the animal's lost its ears?).

Dear Julik, are you annoyed because I'm making fun of your drawings? I really do like them just as they are; but I'd like to see, in addition, some of the drawings you do at school as well.

Kisses.

Papa

How are you getting on at school? Do you manage to get all your work done without getting tired and on edge? Do you like studying?

203

Dear Julik,

I've received the photograph and the note – but the two things don't seem to go together. In the letter you're mournful, you come very near grizzling like a little boy of five, whereas now you're a big strong boy, and ought to face up to whatever happens with calm, confidence and courage. You yourself told me some time ago that the reason you're going to this new school is in order not to lose a year's study. Don't you think that that's important?

In any case isn't it possible that you deserve the tellings-off you're getting? When you've got to do a thing, it's best to do it without grumbling, without whimpering like a little puppydog: otherwise you won't get any real profit out of it. I don't like the thought of a big boy like you grousing like that, because in the photograph you look determined, and calm as calm can be in your resolution to reach the goal you've chosen. That's how I would like to think of you, and I send you all my best wishes and loving kisses.[1]

Papa

It's Tania who makes me write when I'm not feeling well; that's why I write badly. Give me nought for everything.

1. 'I kiss you' is added in Russian.

204

Dear Giuliano,

You've only read a half of the story by Wells, and already you want to judge the writer's whole outlook (dozens and dozens of novels, collections of stories, essays on history, etc.). Isn't that 'a bit much'? Which story have you read? It could be the best or the worst or maybe the one which falls halfway between these extremes. The greatest poet of ancient Greece was Homer, and the Latin writer Horace says in one of his poems that Homer sometimes 'nods'. It's quite certain that in comparison with Homer H.G. Wells nods at least 360 days in the year; however, it's not impossible that in the other five days (or six days if it's a leap year) he may be wide awake, and may easily write something pleasing which would stand up to criticism.

Now and again you're a bit scatterbrained too; your letter is written in a hurry, and there are a lot of words left half finished. And yet I'm sure that you can actually write much better, with greater care and attention. So I won't judge you by this letter alone; I won't say 'Just look what a silly little son I've got.'

Dear Julik, don't get annoyed; always write everything you think, even if you do it in a hurry. You can always rethink it later on, and correct your mistakes; that's the way to get your thoughts in order. How sorry I am not to be able to discuss it all with you face to face. Don't think that I'm too much of a schoolmaster: I'd love to laugh and joke with you and Delio, and talk about all sorts of things that used to interest me a lot too when I was your age.

I embrace you tenderly.

Your Papa

205

Dear Julik,

This time I've received no letter from you. I'm sorry for that. It's true I didn't reply to your last one, but I wasn't feeling at all well. It would give me great pleasure if you wrote to me a lot. Indeed, if I'm not wrong, you promised that you would write something every day of the holidays, and then send me what you'd written, enclosed with Delio's letter, or Mamma's or Genia's. I'm afraid you're a bit disorganised; you've forgotten a thing that was your duty. You can write about anything you like; be sure I'll reply seriously.

After all you're getting on for being a big boy now, so you ought to have a certain sense of responsibility. Don't you agree? Tell me what you're doing at school, and whether you learn easily or not – tell me everything that interests you. If you're not interested in a certain thing and nevertheless have to learn it, how do you get on? And what games do you like best?

Dear Julik, every moment of your life is of interest to me.

I embrace you.

Papa

206

Darling Giuliano,

You want me to write to you about serious things. All right. But what are these 'serious things' that you'd like me to talk about in my letters? You're a boy, and for a boy it's not only 'grown-up' things that are serious but 'boyish' things too. That's only natural because they suit his age and the life he's living. Thinking them over, he equips himself to handle new experiences. Anyway, promise to write me something every five days; it'll make me very glad if you do that and show me what strength of will you have. I'll always answer (if I can) and very seriously too!

Dear Julik, I know you only from your letters and from the news which grown-ups send me about you: I know, all the same, that you're a fine little chap. But why haven't you written to tell me about your trip to the seaside? Wasn't that serious enough to talk about? Everything about you is a serious thing in my eyes, and interests me a great deal – games and all!

Kisses.

Your Papa Antonio

207

Dear Julik,

How goes it? Are you giving your little brain plenty to do? I was very pleased with your letter. Your way of writing is firmer than it used to be, and that shows you'll soon be a big boy.

You ask me what interests me most. The only answer I can give is that nothing interests me 'most', but that many things interest me a great deal at the same time. For example, as far as you are concerned, it's of interest to me that you should study well and profitably at school, but also that you should be strong and healthy and full of courage and determination. And, bound up with that, it's of interest to me that you sleep well, and eat with a good appetite etc. These things are all so tightly interwoven that if any single element is missing or defective, the whole bag of tricks falls to pieces.

That's why I didn't like to hear you say that you weren't able to answer one of my questions, namely, whether you go forward resolutely to reach your objective, which in this case just means to study well, to get strong and healthy, etc. There's no reason why you shouldn't answer that one, seeing it depends on you whether or not you discipline yourself, and resist impulses to do things that are just a waste of time etc. I'm writing seriously to you, because I see that you're not just a wee boy any longer, and also because you yourself once told me that you wanted to be treated seriously.

Actually I'm sure that you've got a lot of strength hidden away in that little mind; the fact that you tell me outright that you can't answer the question means that you think about things, and that you're responsible for what you do and write. What's more, it's clear from the photograph I've received that there's plenty of energy in you!

Evviva Julik! I love you very much. I kiss you.[1]

1. The last sentence is in Russian.

208

Dear Julik,

How are things going in your new school? Which do you like best – being at the seaside, or being near the forests, among the great trees? If you'd like to do something nice for me, why not describe one of your days, from the time you get up in the morning to when you go to bed at night. Then I'd be able to get a better picture of your life, and see you doing all the things you have to do in the course of the day. And give me a description of your surroundings, your companions, the schoolmasters, the animals, everything: tell me a little every time you write – that way you won't tire yourself. Write as if you were wanting to make me laugh, and then you'll get some fun out of it too.

Dear Julik, I embrace you.

Your Papa

209

Dear Delio,

This time you haven't said anything more about your theory that elephants might be the standard-bearers of a new civilisation. The elephants you've got just now are made out of soap, and therefore they might be said to be upholding civilisation (or one aspect of it, anyway!) in the bathroom. Poor elephants! It's true you talk about lots of other things as well, and I ought to start a whole heap of arguments with you. But I can't because I've got a headache and I don't always manage to concentrate, even on quite easy things.

I'm sure mamma and Genia and everyone else at home have long discussions with you about all sorts of things. I like the idea very much.

But what are the things that interest you most? Once upon a time you told me that you were interested in history, but then you didn't seem able to carry on with that subject, and went off at a tangent about elephants. Now it seems you're interested in monkeys as the ancestors of man.

However, I've a shrewd suspicion that you'd rather use your vivid imagination than get to know the real facts. Wouldn't it be a lot better to study real history, the history that can be written on the basis of actual documents that exist? It was quite natural for the men who lived fifty or sixty years ago to use scientific hypotheses as the basis for all sorts of wonderful imaginings; they lived at a time when the battle of ideas was at a very different stage of development. Today many problems have vanished into thin air, because life itself has overcome both protagonist and antagonist, and has created the builder.

Unfortunately, it's difficult to free ourselves from dead things. Yet the job can be done: just give them a good kick out of the road, and study nothing but things that are real and living.

Kisses.

Papa

210

Darling Delio,

I hope that when you get this letter you'll be well again, and that you'll have put on at least . . . ten pounds. Best wishes for a quick recovery: be sure that you eat lots and lots of food. I'm looking forward to a letter from you with plenty of good news of yourself, mamma Julca, grannie and grandad.

Kisses.

Papa

211

Darling Delio,

I don't know whether the elephant can (or could) evolve further and become an animal capable, like man, of dominating the forces of nature upon the earth and using them for his own ends – in the abstract it's hard to say. In point of fact the elephant hasn't had the same development that man has, and he certainly won't now, because man makes use of the elephant, whereas the elephant can't make use of man – even as foodstuff! What you say about the elephant using his feet to do the work of hands doesn't correspond to reality; the elephant has already got a 'technical' instrument, and that's its trunk. From an 'elephanty' point of view it's a marvellous instrument too. He can use it to pull trees up by the roots, defend himself in certain circumstances and so on.

You told me you liked history, and this is where we've landed ... on an elephant's trunk! My own view is that when we study history we shouldn't indulge in too many flights of fancy about what would have happened 'if' ... (if the elephant had started walking on his hind legs and given his brain a better chance of development, if ... if ... if the elephant had been born with wheels? Why then he'd have been a natural tram-car! And if he'd had wings? Just imagine a plague of elephants like a plague of locusts!)

It's very difficult as it is to study the history that really took place, because in the case of much of it all the relevant documents have been lost. So why waste time on suppositions that have no basis in fact? Another thing is that you tend to look at the world rather too much from the human point of view. Why should an elephant evolve in the same way as a man anyhow? Who knows whether some wise old elephant or some whimsical little Jumbo of a speculative turn of mind mayn't have asked himself (from his own point of view) why man has been so slow in developing a trunk?

I'll look forward to a long letter from you on the subject!

It hasn't been very cold here, and I haven't suffered from the cold this year so much as in the years gone by. There are always some flowers in bloom. I haven't a little bird to keep me company as you have, but off and on I see two pairs of blackbirds in the courtyard ... and one or two cats who try and stalk them. However this doesn't seem to worry the blackbirds in the least; they're invariably in high spirits, and very elegant and graceful into the bargain.

Kisses.

Papa

212

Dear Delio,

You've written me four lines which look as if they're out of a phrase-book for foreigners: 'The parrot is well.' (Give him my heartfelt congratulations!) 'What's the weather like?' 'We're having good weather here' etc.

But how are you getting on yourself? And what do you think of Pickwick? And how do you feel about your exams? Are you a wee bit nervous, or do you feel sure of yourself?

Your letters are getting terribly short these days, and short letters aren't very interesting. What's the reason? Do write longer letters.

Kisses.

Papa

213

Dear Delio,

I see that nowadays you're interested in monkeys. The photograph you send has come out very well: that monkey certainly looks as if he's a thinker! Perhaps he's thinking of the carobs he's going to eat, and about all the other food that the people in charge at the Zoo are going to give him.

And how about your parrot? I mentioned green salad, but I was thinking of some sparrows I used to have. What does your Polly eat? Things like lettuce, or fruit and vegetables such as beans and walnuts, chick-peas and almonds?

When I was a boy, our family had a parakeet that came from Abyssinia. All day long it pecked away at beans and chick-peas (we kept the almonds and walnuts to eat ourselves), and it was rather an off-putting creature because that was the only thing it could do and, as far as its appearance was concerned, one could hardly call it good-looking; it had an enormous head as big as the rest of its body, and it was yellowy-grey in colour. I'm sure your parrot is more beautiful, and nicer altogether. Congratulations on your studies, and on the badge you received.

I embrace you tenderly.

Your Papa

214

Dear Delio,

I've heard from mamma Julca that my last letter (and maybe others too?) caused you a bit of annoyance. Why didn't you tell me about it? If ever in any of my letters there's something you don't like, it's better that you should let me know, and explain your reasons. I love you very much, and I don't want to hurt you at all; I'm so very far away, and I can't take you in my arms and kiss you, or help you (as I should like) to solve the questions that come bobbing up in your little head.

I'm afraid you'll have to repeat that question you once asked me about Chekhov (the one I didn't reply to). I've racked my brains, but I can't remember for the life of me what it was. If you were making out that Chekhov was a 'social' writer, you were quite right – though before you pat yourself on the back too hard, remember that Aristotle said that man is a social animal. However, I imagine you meant more than that; for example, you may have meant that Chekhov gave expression to a particular social situation, that he expressed certain aspects of the life of his time and expressed them in such a way as to earn the title of 'progressive' writer. Personally I think that is true. In his own manner, in the ways which the culture of his day permitted, he helped to put paid to the middle classes, the intellectuals and the petite bourgeoisie as standard bearers of Russian history and of the future of the Russian people. They had the cheek to imagine that they were the pathfinders for all sorts of miraculous innovations, and Chekhov showed them up as they really were – poor things, bladders swollen out with putrid gases, eminently suitable targets for satire and ridicule.

Is that what you were getting at? Write and tell me. Of course I understand that you can't say everything about Chekhov in just a few words.

You mention that in the past the young Pioneers' newspaper has given a lot of space to Tolstoy and very little – almost none – to Gorky. Now Gorky is dead, and everyone is feeling sorrow at his loss,[1] this may appear unjust. But now, as always, we must judge things in a critical spirit, and therefore we mustn't forget that Tolstoy was a 'world' writer, one of the very few writers from any country to attain the highest perfection in his art. He is the fount from which torrents of emotion have sprung all over the world – torrents which spring to this day, even in men and women who have been blunted and coarsened by daily toil, and whose culture is rudimentary. The effect was the same even when his works appeared in wretched translations. Tolstoy really was a champion of civilisation and beauty, and in the world of today there is no-one who can equal him: to find company for him we must go back to Homer, Aeschylus, Dante, Shakespeare, Goethe, Cervantes ... and you can count the rest on the fingers of one hand.

I am pleased with your letter, and even more pleased to know that you are feeling better, and that you climbed up on to the wall to see the eclipse; also that you are going to go bathing, and go for walks in the woods. And, last but not least, that you mean to learn Italian. Actually, keeping strong and healthy is a worthwhile job in itself.

Dear Delio, here's a tight hug and a kiss for you.

Papa

1. Gorky died on 18 June 1936.

215

Dear Delio,

Why don't you give me news of your parrot? Is he still alive? Perhaps the reason you don't mention him is that I said once upon a time that you were always talking about him?

Lucky Delio! Tatianishka wants me to tell you that when I was your age

I had a little dog and that I'd gone half daft from the sheer joy of owning it. Imagine that! I'd say a dog (even a tiny little dog) is much more fun than a parrot – though maybe you think that should be the other way round – because he plays with his master, and gets very fond of him ... As for mine, it's plain he was always a wee puppy at heart and never grew up, because when he wanted to show how much he loved me, he would roll over on his back and pee all over himself ... He got himself well soaped, I can tell you!

He was very small – so small that for a long time he couldn't climb the stairs; his coat was long and black, so that he looked like a miniature poodle. I had clipped him to look like a toy lion, with mane and all, but he wasn't really a nice-looking animal. No, he was ugly – properly ugly, now I come to think of it. But what fun I had with him, and how I loved him!

My favourite game with him was this. When we went for walks in the country I'd deposit him on top of some overhanging rock, and then he would look at me and whimper, but he wouldn't dare to jump down. I would go off on a zigzag course, dodging from left to right; then I'd play possum in a hollow or in a ditch. The wee dog would yelp for a while; then he'd find his way down and rush off in pursuit. It was this part that was most fun, because the poor little chap (who was still a tiny puppy) would rush round in all directions, barking, and looking for me everywhere. He'd take a look into all the little ditches (big ones for him) and go nearly frantic, because I'd call him, and then dodge away into a new hide-out. What a scene of rejoicing when I finally let him find me! He would pee all over himself in streams!

Dear Delio, now will you write and tell me about your Polly?

Kisses.

Papa

216

Dear Delio,

I received the parrot's feather and the flowers, and I was delighted with them. But the feather has started me guessing: I can't picture to myself what the bird looks like, and I can't think why he should lose feathers as big as this one. Maybe the artificial heat in the house has affected his plumage in some way? I shouldn't imagine it's anything serious; when the good weather comes any itchy trouble he may have got will pass off. Perhaps the thing to do would be to give him something fresh to eat to make up for the sort of thing birds like that eat in the country they come from. I've read that birds kept in cages may start to suffer from malnutrition if they're not given the proper food. They lose their feathers and get a kind of mange (which, by the by, isn't contagious). A sparrow I once had began to suffer badly from this same complaint because his diet consisted of crumbs of poor-quality bread, but he picked up at once when I added a little green salad to the menu.

I don't remember now in what sense I was referring to 'imagination'; maybe I was talking about the tendency some people have to build castles in the air ... or skyscrapers on the point of a pin!

Dear Delio, here's a tight, tight hug.

Papa

217

Dear Delio,

This time you haven't written to me at all. In the photo of Giuliano I could see a corner of your room, including the parrot's cage. What a shame Polly wasn't in the photograph too!

I hope he'll soon recover completely with the help of the green salad (which ought, incidentally, to be cut up into very thin pieces) and the millet-paste, and that his feathers will grow again, long and bright and vivid.

Kisses.

Papa

218

Dear Delio,

I haven't read much of H.G. Wells, because I don't really care much for his books. I doubt if it would be an irreparable loss for your moral and intellectual development if you didn't read him either. Even his book on world history didn't impress me all that much, although he did try – and admittedly it's a novelty so far as the writing of history in Western Europe is concerned – to broaden the traditional horizon of our history, stressing the importance not merely of the Greeks, the Egyptians, the Romans etc., but also of the Chinese, the Mongols, the Indians etc. As a writer of tales of the imagination I think he's too stilted and mechanical; as an historian he lacks intellectual discipline, order and method.

Write and tell me whether you like my way of writing to you, and whether you understand everything.

I don't think I answered the letter you wrote before this one. I liked your idea of a world populated by elephants all walking upright on their hind-legs, and with very developed brains; certainly, if they were to live and multiply on the face of the globe, heaven alone knows the size of the skyscrapers they'd have to build! But what use would their brains be if they didn't have hands as well? Ostriches go around with their heads high in the air, and they stand upright on two legs, but that doesn't mean that their brains are highly developed. It's clear that in the case of man many favourable conditions had already combined to favour his evolution before he arrived at a point when a definite will to reach an end began to manifest itself, and he began to develop sufficient intelligence to organise the means necessary for reaching it. Quantity becomes quality in the case of man, and not in the case of other living creatures, or so it seems.

Write me a long letter.

Kisses.

Papa

219

Darling Delio,

I'm feeling a little tired, and I can't write much. But please write to me just the same, and tell me about everything at school that interests you.

I think you must like history, as I liked it when I was your age, because it deals with living people, and everything that concerns people, as many people as possible, all the people in the world in so far as they unite together in society, and work and struggle and make a bid for a better life, all that can't fail to please you more than anything else. Isn't that right?

I kiss you dearly.

Antonio

[Gramsci died on 27 April 1937.]